645+ Practice Questions for the
DIGITAL SAT®

2024 Edition

The Staff of The Princeton Review

PrincetonReview.com

Penguin
Random
House

The Princeton Review
110 East 42nd Street, 7th Floor
New York, NY 10017

Published in the United States by Penguin Random House LLC, New York.

ISBN: 978-0-593-51672-0
ISSN: 2837-9756

SAT is a trademark registered by the College Board, which is not affiliated with, and does not endorse, this product.

This book is the 2024 edition of Princeton Review SAT Prep. Some material in this book was previously published in Princeton Review PSAT Prep 2024, a trade paperback respectively published by Random House LLC in 2023.

The Princeton Review is not affiliated with Princeton University.

Editor: Aaron Riccio
Production Editors: Sarah Litt, Liz Dacey
Production Artist: Jason Ullmeyer
Content Developer: Amy Minster

Printed in the United States of America.

10 9 8 7 6 5 4 3 2 1

2024 Edition

The Princeton Review Publishing Team
Rob Franek, Editor-in-Chief
David Soto, Senior Director, Data Operations
Stephen Koch, Senior Manager, Data Operations
Deborah Weber, Director of Production
Jason Ullmeyer, Production Design Manager
Jennifer Chapman, Senior Production Artist
Selena Coppock, Director of Editorial
Orion McBean, Senior Editor
Aaron Riccio, Senior Editor
Meave Shelton, Senior Editor
Chris Chimera, Editor
Patricia Murphy, Editor
Laura Rose, Editor
Isabelle Appleton, Editorial Assistant

Penguin Random House Publishing Team
Tom Russell, VP, Publisher
Alison Stoltzfus, Publishing Director
Emily Hoffman, Assistant Managing Editor
Ellen Reed, Production Manager
Suzanne Lee, Designer
Eugenia Lo, Publishing Assistant

For customer service, please contact **editorialsupport@review.com**, and be sure to include:

- full title of the book
- ISBN
- page number

Acknowledgments

An SAT course is much more than clever techniques and powerful computer score reports. The reason our results are great is that our teachers care so much about their students. Many teachers have gone out of their way to improve the course, often going so far as to write their own materials, some of which we have incorporated into our course manuals as well as into this book. The list of these teachers could fill this page.

Special thanks to all those who contributed to this year's edition: Kenneth Brenner, Sara Kuperstein, Amy Minster, Scott O'Neal, Aleksei Alferiev, Brittany Budzon, Tania Capone, Remy Cosse, Stacey Cowap, Wazhma Daftanai, Harrison Foster, Beth Hollingsworth, Adam Keller, Kevin Keogh, Ali Landreau, Aaron Lindh, Jomil London, Sweena Mangal, Sionainn Marcoux, Valerie Meyers, Acacia Nawrocik-Madrid, Gabby Peterson, Kathy Ruppert, Jess Thomas, Jimmy Williams, and Suzanne Wint.

We are also, as always, very appreciative of the time and attention given to each page by Jason Ullmeyer, Sarah Litt, and Liz Dacey.

Finally, we would like to thank the people who truly have taught us everything we know about the SAT: our students.

Contents

Get More (Free) Content
at **PrincetonReview.com/prep**

As easy as 1·2·3

1 Go to PrincetonReview.com/prep or scan the **QR code** and enter the following ISBN for your book:
9780593516720

2 Answer a few simple questions to set up an exclusive Princeton Review account. *(If you already have one, you can just log in.)*

3 Enjoy access to your **FREE** content!

Once you've registered, you can...

- Take a full-length practice Digital SAT and/or ACT
- Get valuable advice about the college application process, including tips for writing a great essay and where to apply for financial aid
- Test yourself with an additional online Digital SAT practice test

- If you're still choosing between colleges, use our searchable rankings of *The Best 389 Colleges* to find out more information about your dream school
- Check to see if there have been any corrections or updates to this edition
- Get our take on any recent or pending updates to the Digital SAT

LET'S GO MOBILE! Access all of these free additional resources by downloading the new Princeton Review app at www.princetonreview.com/mobile/apps/highschool or scan the QR Code to the right.

Need to report a potential **content** issue?

Contact **EditorialSupport@review.com** and include:
- full title of the book
- ISBN
- page number

Need to report a **technical** issue?

Contact **TPRStudentTech@review.com** and provide:
- your full name
- email address used to register the book
- full book title and ISBN
- Operating system (Mac/PC) and browser (Chrome, Firefox, Safari, etc.)

Part I
Introduction

WHAT'S INSIDE

Welcome to *645+ Practice Questions for the Digital SAT.* As you've probably already guessed, this book contains practice questions for the Digital SAT, which we at The Princeton Review have created based on the information released by the College Board. We've rigorously analyzed available tests, and our content development teams have tirelessly worked to ensure that our material accurately reflects what you will see in terms of design, structure, style, and, most importantly, content on test day. We continually evaluate the data on each question to ensure validity and to refine the level of difficulty within each test to match that of the Digital SAT even more closely. Reach out to EditorialSupport@review.com if you feel something is amiss.

We are confident that if you work through these questions and evaluate your performance with our comprehensive explanations, you'll improve the skills that you need to score higher on the Digital SAT. Register your book at PrincetonReview.com to gain access to detailed, interactive score reports. Track your overall performance so that you get the most out of your test prep, and make sure to read the in-depth explanations that not only explain how to get the right answer but also why the other choices are incorrect. Through careful self-assessment, you can correct any recurring mistakes, as well as identify any weaknesses or gaps in knowledge that you can then focus your attention on studying.

But before we go any further, let's talk about the Digital SAT itself.

What's on the Digital SAT?

The Digital SAT is 2 hours and 14 minutes long.

The test consists of the following sections, in this order:

- Reading and Writing (2 modules, each 27 questions in 32 minutes)
    - All questions in the RW section are multiple-choice.
    - Two questions in each module are experimental and are not scored.
- A 10-minute break
- Math (2 modules, each 22 questions in 35 minutes)
    - Most questions in the Math section are multiple-choice.
    - The rest are "student-produced responses" (fill-ins).
    - Two questions in each module are experimental and are not scored.

Scoring on the Digital SAT

Scores from the Digital SAT will be reported in a matter of days, not weeks, as was the case with the paper-and-pencil test. Your score report for the Digital SAT will feature scores for each of the following:

- **Total Score:**
    The sum of the two section scores (Reading and Writing, Math), ranging from 400 to 1600
- **Section Scores:**
    1. Reading and Writing, ranging from 200 to 800
    2. Math, also ranging from 200 to 800

The following table summarizes the structure and scoring of the Digital SAT.

Category	Digital SAT
Time Overall	134 minutes plus 10-minute break
Components	• Reading and Writing section • Math section
Number of Questions	• Reading and Writing: 54, including 4 experimental questions • Math: 44, including 4 experimental questions
Answer Choices	• Reading and Writing: all multiple-choice with 4 answers per question • Math: 75% multiple-choice with 4 answers per question, 25% student-produced responses
Time by Section	• Reading and Writing: 64 minutes in two 32-minute modules • Math: 70 minutes in two 35-minute modules
Relationship Between Modules	• Module 1 has a broad mix of levels of difficulty. • Performance on Module 1 determines the difficulty of Module 2. • Students who do well on Module 1 will get a Module 2 that is harder, on average. • Students who do less well on Module 1 will get a Module 2 that is easier, on average.
Scoring	• The score is based on the number of questions correct and the difficulty of those questions. • There is no penalty for wrong answers or leaving questions blank, so it's in your best interest to guess rather than leave a question blank. • Students who do well on Module 1 are put into a higher bracket of possible scores. • Students who do less well on Module 1 are put into a lower bracket of possible scores. • Section scores range from 200 to 800. • Total score is the sum of the section scores and ranges from 400 to 1600.

HOW TO USE THIS BOOK

There are two ways that you can use the content in this book: you can take full-length practice tests or you can focus on honing your skills on specific concepts. You can even do a bit of both.

Most of the questions in this book are laid out as tests in the way that you'll encounter them on the Digital SAT. Each section (Reading and Writing or Math) begins with a module of mixed difficulty, and your performance on that module determines whether you will get the second module that is easier or harder on average. On the real Digital SAT, you'll automatically be given an easier or harder second module based on your performance on the first module of each subject. In this book, we've included both options for the second module, so if you'd like to take a full test, be sure to follow the guidelines provided at the start of each practice test so that you can mimic the length and difficulty level of the computer-based test as realistically as possible. (For Practice Test 4 in your online student tools, the test will automatically send you to the correct second module in each section.)

Use the paper tests in this book (Practice Tests 1–3) to work on your content knowledge and pace, and when you're ready to mimic the real digital testing experience, block off about 140 minutes to take Practice Test 4 in your online student tools. If you think you want to discover your areas of strength and weakness before tackling a full test, you can use the Diagnostic Drills that come before Test 1. These drills have a variety of concepts tested on the Digital SAT, and you can use them to warm up to the test or to see where you may need to focus your prep time. Given those insights, you may need to use some of the modules in this book as a source for more questions of those types, rather than as a complete practice test. You can also work on a test a single module at a time to perfect your pacing. The book also includes a bonus "harder" module for each section, and there is an additional practice test online. Don't forget to carefully review our detailed explanations! Whether you get a question right or not, its explanation is packed full of our powerful Digital SAT strategies and techniques and might help you to save time on future questions or to clarify where you might have gotten the right answer for the wrong reason.

Calculator use is allowed on all Math questions on the Digital SAT. The testing app includes a built-in Desmos calculator. For the paper tests in this book (Practice Tests 1–3), practice by using the calculator at Desmos.com. For the online-only test found in your student tools (Practice Test 4), use our testing app's built-in calculator.

WHEN YOU TAKE A TEST

Here are some suggestions for working through this book:

1. Keep track of your performance. Whether you're working through individual modules or taking each test as a whole, be sure to use the answer key to score yourself. For the paper tests, you'll want to do this after each Module 1 so that you can determine which of the two Module 2s to complete. It's also a good idea to log the time and date of each practice session so that you can track your progress on the in-book Practice Tests 1–3.

2. The Digital SAT is a timed test. You may be a star test-taker when you have all the time in the world to mull over the questions, but can you perform as well when the clock is ticking? Timing yourself will ensure you are prepared for the constraints of the actual test, just as our strategy-filled explanations can help you to discover faster methods for solving questions.

3. Don't cram it all in at once. It's hard enough to concentrate throughout one Digital SAT test—don't burn yourself out by taking multiple tests in a row. You wouldn't run two marathons back-to-back, so why treat your brain (which is like a muscle) in that way? Give yourself at least a couple of months before your anticipated "real" test date so that you can learn from any mistakes that were made on these practice tests.

4. Accordingly, take time to analyze your performance between tests or practice modules. As you actively review your work, your mind will be subtly taking notes and tweaking the way it handles future questions of a similar nature, shaving seconds off its processing time as it grows more accustomed to particular wordings or presentations.

GOOD LUCK!

We know that the Digital SAT may seem intimidating at first glance—but then again, after using this book, you'll be well beyond that first glance, so you're headed in the right direction. Also, as you prepare, whether you're stressed or relaxed, remember this key point: the Digital SAT doesn't measure the stuff that matters. It measures neither intelligence nor the depth and breadth of what you're learning in high school. It doesn't predict college grades as well as your high school grades do, and colleges know there is more to you as a student—and a person—than how you fare on a single test administered on a random day. This is a high-stakes test, and you should absolutely work hard and prepare. But don't treat it like it's some mythical monster or world-ending catastrophe. It's just a test, and we at The Princeton Review know tests. We're here for you every step of the way.

Part II
Diagnostic Drills

Diagnostic Drills

SAT Prep Test—Reading and Writing
Diagnostic Drills

Turn to Section 1 of your answer sheet to answer the questions in this section.

---

1 ☐ Mark for Review

Photo-based artist Deana Lawson can partially _____ her interest in the medium to her upbringing: her mother worked as an administrative assistant at Kodak, a well-known film and camera company, and her father was an employee of Xerox, a company known for its photocopier machines.

Which choice completes the text with the most logical and precise word or phrase?

(A) attribute

(B) adhere

(C) promote

(D) inherit

---

2 ☐ Mark for Review

Oral tradition is a type of communication method used by a variety of cultures to pass information, art, thoughts, and wisdom between generations. The intelligence can be shared through poetry, folktales, stories, and more and allows cultures to convey these traditions without, or along with, an established writing system. However, the transmission of ideas this way can present certain obstacles. It is difficult to verify whether the knowledge being transferred is correct and similar to its original version. As a result of this, many cultures use devices such as repetition, assonance, alliteration, and rhythmic timing. Through the use of devices like these, it is easier to recall the knowledge in order to correctly relay it to the next generation.

Which choice best states the main purpose of the text?

(A) To propose a solution to the obstacles faced by oral tradition

(B) To clarify that oral tradition can only be used in certain cultures

(C) To explain how cultures make it easier to remember knowledge from oral tradition

(D) To assert that oral tradition is more beneficial than a writing system is

CONTINUE ▶

3 ☐ Mark for Review

The following text is from Elizabeth von Arnim's 1922 novel *The Enchanted April*. Four women from England have rented an Italian castle for a month's vacation.

> The cook, who had been waiting in increasing agitation in the kitchen, watching the clock getting nearer to lunch-time while she still was without knowledge of what lunch was to consist of, had gone at last to Mrs. Fisher, who had immediately waved her away. She then wandered about the house seeking a mistress, any mistress, who would tell her what to cook, and finding none; and at last, directed by Francesca, who always knew where everybody was, came out to Lady Caroline.

According to the text, why does the cook go to see Lady Caroline?

(A) The cook wants to express her agitation regarding the condition of the kitchen.

(B) The cook wants to determine what she should prepare for lunch.

(C) The cook seeks approval for her planned menu.

(D) The cook has been sent by Francesca to deliver a message to Lady Caroline.

4 ☐ Mark for Review

Carbon dioxide emissions are known to have harmful environmental effects. Because the cement industry is one of the biggest producers of carbon dioxide emissions, developing more sustainable processes for manufacturing cement is of major concern. Researchers at Columbia University have developed a method that uses seawater to make cement by converting magnesium ions, which are highly abundant in the oceans, into magnesium hydroxides that can then be turned into magnesium-based cement. According to the researchers, not only does the resulting cement not produce carbon dioxide, but it can actually improve the environment.

Which finding, if true, would most directly support the researchers' claim?

(A) The magnesium-based cement is more energy-intensive than is traditionally made cement.

(B) Cement is traditionally produced from carbon rather than magnesium.

(C) The magnesium-based cement consumes carbon dioxide.

(D) Cement made from seawater is less costly to produce than is cement made from other methods.

CONTINUE ➡

5 ☐ Mark for Review

Themes Noted in Videos' Comments

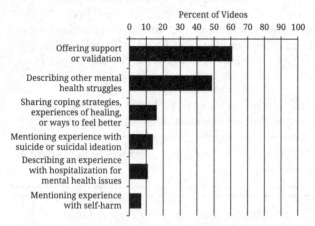

William Paterson University professor Corey H. Basch and her colleagues sought to determine how feedback on social media networks supports or harms users' mental health. They reviewed videos that were posted to the hashtag #mentalhealth and cataloged the comments to see how supportive they were. The researchers were encouraged by the positivity of the comments: specifically, _____.

Which choice most effectively uses data from the graph to complete the explanation?

(A) nearly 40% of the videos did not have comments with the theme of offering support or validation.

(B) the majority of the videos had comments offering support or validation, and nearly half had comments describing other mental health struggles.

(C) only 16% of the videos had comments focusing on sharing coping strategies, experiences of healing, or ways to feel better.

(D) there were more videos that had comments related to describing other mental health struggles than there were with comments focusing on describing an experience with hospitalization for mental health issues.

6 ☐ Mark for Review

The hippocampus is one of the major components of the human brain. When people suffer from Alzheimer's disease and other forms of dementia, the hippocampus is often the first area of the brain to display damage. The most common symptoms of early-stage Alzheimer's disease are short-term memory loss, difficulty learning new information, and disorientation, suggesting that _____.

Which choice most logically completes the text?

(A) the hippocampus plays a role in forming short-term memories and retaining new information.

(B) Alzheimer's disease is primarily diagnosed by examining a patient's hippocampus.

(C) people whose hippocampi are not damaged will not experience short-term memory loss.

(D) many parts of the brain are affected by Alzheimer's disease.

7 ☐ Mark for Review

University of Washington biologist Kate Stafford has recorded sounds in the deep waters of the Bering Strait to track whale migration. For Stafford, sound provides an advantage that sight cannot: one can continue to record sound at night or underneath ice _____ the challenges of deep-sea sound recording are not nearly as problematic as those of deep-sea diving.

Which choice completes the text so that it conforms to the conventions of Standard English?

(A) cover and

(B) cover,

(C) cover; and

(D) cover, and

CONTINUE ➤

8 ☐ Mark for Review

Researchers at the Intermountain Bird Observatory in Idaho wanted to study the effects of highway volume on local bird populations, so they created a fake road with 15 pairs of speakers playing the sounds of traffic noise. According to the study, the mere sounds of traffic _____ avian populations by a third and cut species diversity by a significant amount.

Which choice completes the text so that it conforms to the conventions of Standard English?

- (A) reduced
- (B) reducing
- (C) having reduced
- (D) to reduce

9 ☐ Mark for Review

Civil engineering as a profession is centuries old and has long been necessary for the functioning of modern government, as it includes designing and building roads and bridges. As long as people need to get to school or work, civil engineers _____ to be cornerstones of modern societies.

Which choice completes the text so that it conforms to the conventions of Standard English?

- (A) will continue
- (B) continued
- (C) have continued
- (D) are continuing

10 ☐ Mark for Review

The Nobel Prizes in specific fields, such as Physics, Chemistry, Literature, and Medicine, are typically awarded with little contention. The Nobel Peace Prize, on the other hand, tends to generate more debate. When given to first-year President Barack Obama in 2009, _____ because some believed that the choice was too politically motivated.

Which choice completes the text so that it conforms to the conventions of Standard English?

- (A) there was a good deal of controversy surrounding the award
- (B) the award's controversy received significant attention
- (C) the award caused a good deal of controversy
- (D) a controversy surrounded the award

11 ☐ Mark for Review

Although all states hold elections, there are many major differences in how they do so. _____ some states hold primaries, while others use caucuses, both meant to accomplish the goal of nominating major-party candidates for office.

Which choice completes the text with the most logical transition?

- (A) In addition,
- (B) In other words,
- (C) Consequently,
- (D) For example,

CONTINUE ➡

---

12 ☐ Mark for Review

While researching a topic, a student has taken the following notes:

- A polar vortex can have a significant effect on other areas of the globe when it breaks into two or more vortices.

- A break occurs when a shift in the jet stream causes a piece of the vortex to be broken off from the main cyclone and diverted along the path of the polar jet stream.

- In 1985, the United States suffered one of its worst weather events due to a break in the Arctic polar vortex.

- A wave of extreme cold swept through the United States, primarily in the East Coast and Midwest regions.

- In all, 129 deaths were attributed to the storm, over $2.3 billion in agricultural losses were reported, and hundreds of homes were lost to wind damage.

The student wants to explain the cause of a destructive weather event. Which choice most effectively uses relevant information from the notes to accomplish this goal?

(A) When a polar vortex breaks into two or more vortices, it can cause a wave of extreme cold.

(B) A weather event in 1985 caused 129 deaths, over $2.3 billion in agricultural losses, and hundreds of home losses, primarily in the East Coast and Midwest regions.

(C) In 1985, a piece of the Arctic polar vortex broke off from the main cyclone, causing a wave of extreme cold that led to deaths, agricultural losses, and wind damage to homes.

(D) A polar vortex can have a significant effect on other areas of the globe, like the Arctic polar vortex in 1985 for the East Coast and Midwest regions.

STOP
**If you finish before time is called, you may check your work on this section only.
Do not turn to any other section in the test.**

SAT Prep Test—Math
Diagnostic Drills

The questions in this section address a number of important math skills.
Use of a calculator is permitted for all questions.

NOTES

Unless otherwise indicated:

- All variables and expressions represent real numbers.
- Figures provided are drawn to scale.
- All figures lie in a plane.
- The domain of a given function f is the set of all real numbers x for which $f(x)$ is a real number.

REFERENCE

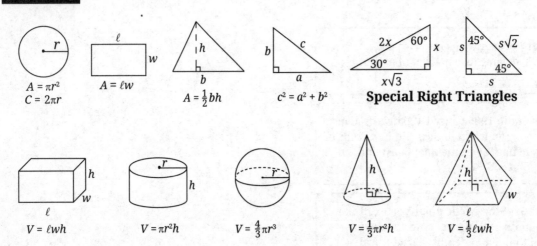

$A = \pi r^2$
$C = 2\pi r$

$A = \ell w$

$A = \frac{1}{2}bh$

$c^2 = a^2 + b^2$

Special Right Triangles

$V = \ell wh$

$V = \pi r^2 h$

$V = \frac{4}{3}\pi r^3$

$V = \frac{1}{3}\pi r^2 h$

$V = \frac{1}{3}\ell wh$

The number of degrees of arc in a circle is 360.
The number of radians of arc in a circle is 2π.
The sum of the measures in degrees of the angles of a triangle is 180.

CONTINUE

- -

For multiple-choice questions, solve each problem, choose the correct answer from the choices provided, and then fill in the circle with the answer letter. Enter only one answer for each question. You will not get credit for questions with more than one answer entered, or for questions with no answers entered.

For student-produced response questions, solve each problem and write your answer in the test book as described below.

- Enter your answer into the box provided.
- If you find **more than one correct answer**, enter only one answer.
- Your answer can be up to 5 characters for a **positive** answer and up to 6 characters (including the negative sign) for a **negative** answer.
- If your answer is a **fraction** that is too long (over 5 characters for positive, 6 characters for negative), write the decimal equivalent.
- If your answer is a **decimal** that is too long (over 5 characters for positive, 6 characters for negative), truncate it or round at the fourth digit.
- If your answer is a **mixed number** (such as $3\frac{1}{2}$), write it as an improper fraction (7/2) or its decimal equivalent (3.5).
- Don't enter **symbols** such as a percent sign, comma, or dollar sign in your answer.

1 🔖 Mark for Review

A climate scientist estimates that a certain state's average snowfall is decreasing by 0.4 inches per year. If the scientist's estimate is accurate, how many years will it take for the average annual snowfall to be 6 inches less than it is now?

2 🔖 Mark for Review

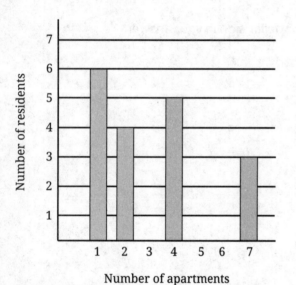

Number of apartments

The histogram shows the number of residents in each of 14 apartments. According to the data, which of the following is closest to the mean (average) number of residents per apartment?

Ⓐ 3

Ⓑ 3.25

Ⓒ 3.5

Ⓓ 4

3 🔖 Mark for Review

If $12x + 4 = 20$, what is the value of $6x + 5$?

Ⓐ 4

Ⓑ 6

Ⓒ 10

Ⓓ 13

4 🔖 Mark for Review

$$2y + x = -17$$
$$5x - 4y = -15$$

What is the solution (x, y) to the given system of equations?

Ⓐ $(-7, -5)$

Ⓑ $(-4, -1)$

Ⓒ $(-3, 0)$

Ⓓ $(5, -11)$

CONTINUE ➜

5 Mark for Review

$$f(x) = cx^2 + 30$$

For the given function f, c is a constant and $f(3) = 12$. What is the value of $f(-3)$?

(A) −12

(B) −2

(C) 0

(D) 12

6 Mark for Review

In the xy-plane, a parabola defined by the equation $y = (x - 8)^2$ intersects a line defined by the equation $y = 36$ at two points, P and Q. The x-coordinate of Q is greater than the x-coordinate of P. Which of the following ordered pairs represents the coordinates of P?

(A) (2, 36)

(B) (8, 36)

(C) (14, 36)

(D) (36, 2)

7 Mark for Review

x	$g(x)$
−1	−23
0	−19
1	−15
2	−11

The given table shows four values of x and the corresponding values of $g(x)$ for linear function g. Which equation defines $g(x)$?

(A) $g(x) = -23x + 8$

(B) $g(x) = -19x - 15$

(C) $g(x) = 4x - 19$

(D) $g(x) = 11x - 19$

8 Mark for Review

The estimated value of a truck declines at an annual rate of 7 percent. If the original value of the truck was $35,000, which of the functions of v best models the value of the truck, in dollars, t years later?

(A) $v(t) = 0.07(35,000)^t$

(B) $v(t) = 0.93(35,000)^t$

(C) $v(t) = 35,000(0.07)^t$

(D) $v(t) = 35,000(0.93)^t$

CONTINUE

---

9 ☐ Mark for Review

The equation $\left(\dfrac{a}{b}\right)^2 + 13 = 2c$ gives the relationship for distinct positive real numbers a, b, and c. Which of the following correctly expresses b in terms of a and c?

Ⓐ $\quad b = \dfrac{a}{\sqrt{2c-13}}$

Ⓑ $\quad b = \dfrac{2a}{\sqrt{c-13}}$

Ⓒ $\quad b = \left(\dfrac{a}{2c-13}\right)^2$

Ⓓ $\quad b = \left(\dfrac{2a}{2c-13}\right)^2$

10 ☐ Mark for Review

A train ticket costs 15 percent less during off-peak hours than during peak hours, and an 11 percent surcharge is added if the ticket is purchased from the conductor. If a ticket purchased from the conductor during off-peak hours costs t dollars, which of the following represents the price of a ticket purchased in the train station during peak hours, in terms of t?

Ⓐ $\quad \dfrac{t}{0.96}$

Ⓑ $\quad 0.96t$

Ⓒ $\quad \dfrac{t}{(0.85)(1.11)}$

Ⓓ $\quad (0.85)(1.11)t$

11 ☐ Mark for Review

The equation $3x^2 - bx + 12 = 0$, in which b is a positive constant, has exactly one real solution. What is the value of b?

☐

12 ☐ Mark for Review

Matthew constructs a fence around a patch of grass in his backyard. The patch has a width that is 8 feet more than 4 times the length. What is the perimeter of the fence if Matthew's patch of grass has an area of 5,472 square feet?

Ⓐ 364 feet

Ⓑ 376 feet

Ⓒ 396 feet

Ⓓ 400 feet

Diagnostic Drills: Answers and Explanations

DIAGNOSTIC DRILLS: MULTIPLE-CHOICE ANSWER KEY

Reading and Writing	
1.	A
2.	C
3.	B
4.	C
5.	B
6.	A
7.	D
8.	A
9.	A
10.	C
11.	D
12.	C

Math	
1.	15
2.	D
3.	D
4.	A
5.	D
6.	A
7.	C
8.	D
9.	A
10.	C
11.	12
12.	B

DIAGNOSTIC DRILLS—READING AND WRITING EXPLANATIONS

2. **A** This is a Vocabulary question, as it's asking for *the most logical and precise word or phrase*. Read the text and highlight what can help to fill in the blank, which describes the relationship between Lawson's *interest* and her *upbringing*. The first part of the sentence mentions that Lawson is a *Photo-based artist*, and the part after the colon mentions that both of her parents worked around film and photos. This suggests that there is a connection between her photography interest and her upbringing, so write "connect" in the annotation box.

    - (A) is correct because *attribute* means "give credit to," and she can partially credit her interest to her upbringing.

    - (B) is wrong because *adhere* means "stick."

    - (C) is wrong because the sentence doesn't indicate that Lawson is promoting her interest.

    - (D) is wrong because while her interest might be inherited, the sentence would say that she can "inherit" *her interest…to her upbringing*, which doesn't provide a clear meaning.

2. **C** This is a Purpose question, as it's asking for the *main purpose*. Read the text and highlight what can help to understand the overall purpose. The text introduces *Oral tradition* and then describes *obstacles* with this tradition. Then the author states what *many cultures use* as a result of the obstacle in order to facilitate *recall* of the *knowledge*, so write "introduce, tell about problem, tell about solution" in the annotation box.

    - (A) is wrong because the author isn't proposing a solution; the author is explaining what cultures already do.

    - (B) is wrong because the author doesn't state that it can *only* be used by certain cultures.

    - (C) is correct because the author describes a solution that makes it *easier to recall the knowledge* through *Oral tradition*.

    - (D) is wrong because the author mentions that oral tradition can be used *without, or along with, an established writing system* and never says one is *more beneficial*.

3. **B** This is a Retrieval question, as it says *According to the text*. Read the text and aim to highlight the reason given for why the cook goes *to see Lady Caroline*. The first sentence states that the cook was agitated and *was without knowledge of what lunch was to consist of*. The second sentence indicates that she was *seeking a mistress…who would tell her what to cook* and that she was then told to see Lady Caroline.

    - (A) is wrong because the cook's agitation isn't about *the condition of the kitchen*, which isn't mentioned.

    - (B) is correct because this is the reason stated in the text.

- (C) is wrong because the cook hasn't *planned* a *menu*; she wants to know what to cook.

- (D) is wrong because no *message* from *Francesca* is mentioned.

4. **C** This is a Claims question, as it asks to *support the researchers' claim*. Read the text and highlight the claim, which is that the magnesium-based cement *can actually improve the environment*. Eliminate answers that don't *support* this idea.

- (A) is wrong because this would be a downside, rather than a benefit, of the cement.

- (B) and (D) are wrong because they don't relate to *the environment*.

- (C) is correct because the text states that *Carbon dioxide emissions are known to have harmful environmental effects*, so if the cement *consumes carbon dioxide*, then it would reduce carbon dioxide and therefore *improve the environment*.

5. **B** This is a Charts question, as it asks for *data from the graph*. The table charts the percent of videos that had comments from certain categories. Read the text and highlight the claim, which is about the *positivity of the comments*. Eliminate any answer that doesn't provide an *explanation* of this statement or is inconsistent with the data on the graph.

- (A) is wrong because focusing on the videos that *did not have comments with the theme of offering support or validation* wouldn't explain the *positivity* of the comments.

- (B) is correct because it focuses on the positive comments (*support, validation, describing other mental health struggles*) that many of the videos had, which supports *positivity*.

- (C) and (D) are wrong because they don't relate to the *positivity of the comments*.

6. **A** This is a Conclusions question, as it asks for what *most logically completes the text*. Read the text and highlight the main ideas. The text states that *the hippocampus is often the first area of the brain to display damage* from Alzheimer's disease, and describes common symptoms of *early-stage Alzheimer's disease*. This suggests that the symptoms are related to damage to the hippocampus. Eliminate any answer that states a conclusion that isn't supported by the text.

- (A) is correct because if damage to *short-term memory* and *learning new information* are associated with *damage* to *the hippocampus*, then the hippocampus must play a role related to these functions.

- (B) is wrong because there is no information about how the disease is *diagnosed*.

- (C) is wrong because the text does not say that short-term memory loss could only be caused by damage to the hippocampus.

- (D) is wrong because while it could be true, the text never mentions any other *parts of the brain* besides the hippocampus.

7. **D** In this Rules question, punctuation is changing in the answer choices. Look for independent clauses. The part of the sentence after the colon says *one can continue to record sound at night or underneath ice cover*, which is an independent clause. The second part says *the challenges of deep-sea sound recording are not nearly as problematic as those of deep-sea diving*, which is also an independent clause. Eliminate any answer that can't correctly connect two independent clauses.

- (A) is wrong because a coordinating conjunction (*and*) without a comma can't connect two independent clauses.

- (B) is wrong because a comma without a coordinating conjunction can't connect two independent clauses.

- (C) is wrong because a semicolon can connect two independent clauses, but adding *and* to the second part makes it not an independent clause.

- (D) is correct because a comma + a coordinating conjunction (*and*) can connect two independent clauses.

8. **A** In this Rules question, verb forms are changing in the answer choices, so it's testing sentence structure. The subject of the sentence is *sounds*, and there is no main verb, so the answer must provide the main verb. Eliminate any answer that isn't in the correct form to be the main verb.

- (A) is correct because it's in the right form to be the main verb.

- (B) and (C) are wrong because an *-ing* verb can't be the main verb in a sentence.

- (D) is wrong because a "to" verb can't be the main verb in a sentence.

9. **A** In this Rules question, verbs are changing in the answer choices, so it's testing consistency with verbs. Find and highlight the subject, *civil engineers*, which is plural, so a plural verb is needed. All of the answers work with a plural subject, so look for a clue regarding tense. The previous sentence is in present tense (*is*), and this sentence begins with *As long as people need to get to school or work*, which is a shift to future tense. Highlight those words and write an annotation that says "future." Eliminate any answer not in future tense.

- (A) is correct because it's future tense.

- (B) is wrong because it's past tense.

- (C) is wrong because it's not future tense.

- (D) is wrong because it's present tense.

10. **C**   In this Rules question, the subjects of the answers are changing, which suggests it may be testing modifiers. Look for and highlight a modifying phrase: *When given to first-year President Barack Obama in 2009.* Whatever was *given* to Obama needs to come immediately after the comma. Eliminate any answer that doesn't start with something that could have been given to him.

- (A) is wrong because *there was* doesn't explain what was given to Obama.

- (B) and (D) are wrong because *controversy* wasn't *given* to Obama.

- (C) is correct because *the award* could have been given to Obama.

11. **D**   This is a transition question, so highlight ideas that relate to each other. The preceding sentence says *there are many major differences* in how states hold elections, and this sentence mentions one such difference. These ideas agree, so a same-direction transition is needed. Make an annotation that says "agree." Eliminate any answer that doesn't match.

- (A) is wrong because the second sentence isn't an additional point; it expands on the idea from the sentence before.

- (B) is wrong because the second sentence isn't a restatement of the first.

- (C) is wrong because the second sentence isn't a result of the first.

- (D) is correct because the second sentence gives an example of the differences.

12. **C**   This is a Rhetorical Synthesis question, so highlight the goal(s) stated in the question: *explain the cause of a destructive weather event.* Eliminate any answer that doesn't fulfill this purpose.

- (A) and (D) are wrong because no specific *destructive weather event* is mentioned.

- (B) is wrong because it doesn't mention the *cause* of the event.

- (C) is correct because it mentions the *destructive weather event* as well as what caused it.

DIAGNOSTIC DRILLS—MATH EXPLANATIONS

1. **15**   The question asks for the number of years it will take for the decrease in snowfall to equal 6 inches. The rate of decrease is 0.4 inches per year. Set up a proportion: $\frac{0.4 \text{ inches}}{1 \text{ year}} = \frac{6 \text{ inches}}{x \text{ years}}$. Cross-multiply to get $6 = 0.4x$, then divide by 0.4 to get $x = 15$ years. Therefore, it will take 15 years for the average annual snowfall to be 6 inches less than it is now. The correct answer is 15.

2. **D**   The question asks for the average number of residents per apartment based on the graph. There are 14 apartments: 1 apartment with 6 residents, 2 with 4 residents, 4 with 5 residents, and 7 with 3 residents. Add up all the residents: $6 + 4 + 4 + 5 + 5 + 5 + 5 + 3 + 3 + 3 + 3 + 3 + 3 + 3 = 55$. Divide by the number of apartments: $\frac{55}{14} = 3.929$. This is closest to 4. The correct answer is (D).

3. **D**   The question asks for the value of an expression. Manipulate the given equation to match the expression. Subtract 4 from both sides of the equation to get $12x = 16$. Divide the entire equation by 2 to get $6x = 8$. Add 5 to both sides of the equation to get $6x + 5 = 8 + 5 = 13$. The correct answer is (D).

4. **A**   The question asks for the solution to a system of equations. Test the values in the answer choices by plugging them into the two equations. In order to be the solution to the system of equations, the pair of values must satisfy both equations. Start with (A): $(-7, -5)$. Plug these values into the first equation to get $2(-5) + (-7) = -17$. This is true, so plug the values into the second equation to get $5(-7) - 4(-5) = -15$. Since this is also true, the correct answer is (A).

5. **D**   The question asks for the value of *a function*. Begin by finding the value of constant c. Since $f(3) = 12$, plug this into the function to get $f(3) = c(3)^2 + 30 = 12$. Therefore, $9c + 30 = 12$. Subtract 30 from both sides to get $9c = -18$. Divide both sides by 9 to get $c = -2$. Plug this into the original equation to get $f(x) = -2x^2 + 30$. The question asks for $f(-3)$, so plug in $x = -3$ to get $f(-3) = -2(-3)^2 + 30 = -2(9) + 30 = -18 + 30 = 12$. The correct answer is (D).

6. **A**   The question asks for the coordinates of point P. Points of intersection are solutions to both equations. Since $y = (x - 8)^2$ and $y = 36$, set $(x - 8)^2 = 36$. To solve, take the square root of both sides of the equation to get $x - 8 = \pm 6$. Always remember to use $\pm$ when taking the square root of both sides of an equation. Consider both possible equations. If $x - 8 = 6$, add 8 to both sides of the equation to get $x = 14$. If $x - 8 = -6$, add 8 to both sides of the equation to get $x = 2$. Therefore, points P and Q are at coordinates $(2, 36)$ and $(14, 36)$. Both ordered pairs appear in the answer choices, so make sure to determine which point is which. The question states that the x-coordinate of Q is greater than that of P, so P must be at $(2, 36)$. Another option is to use the built-in graphing calculator. Enter both equations, then scroll and zoom as needed to see the two points of intersection. Click on the gray dots to see the coordinates of the points: $(2, 36)$ and $(14, 36)$, Using either method, the correct answer is (A).

7. **C**   The question asks for the function that represents values given in a table. In function notation, the number inside the parentheses is the x-value that goes into the function, or the input, and the value that comes out of the function is the y-value, or the output. Together, they represent points on the graph of the function. The table shows pairs of values for x and $g(x)$, and the correct function must work for every pair of values. Test pairs of values from the table in the answer choices and eliminate functions that don't work. Avoid $x = 1$ because it is likely to make more than one answer work, which would require trying a second pair of values. Instead, make $x = 2$ and $g(x) =$ -11. Choice (A) becomes $-11 = -23(2) + 8$, or $-11 = -38$. This is not true, so eliminate (A). Choice (B) becomes $-11 = -19(2) - 15$, or $-11 = -53$; eliminate (B). Choice (C) becomes $-11 = 4(2) - 19$, or $-11 = -11$. Keep (C) but check (D) just in case. Choice (D) becomes $-11 = 11(2) - 19$, or $-11 = 3$; eliminate (D). The correct answer is (C).

8. **D**   The question asks for the equation that best models the decreasing value of the truck over time. Knowing the parts of the growth and decay formula can help with this question. That formula is *final amount* = (*original amount*)$(1 \pm rate)^{number\ of\ changes}$. In this case, the *original amount* is \$35,000, the *rate* is 7%, and the *number of changes* is t. Therefore, the value of the truck after t years is given by $v(t) = 35{,}000(1 - 0.07)^t$, or $v(t) = 35{,}000(0.93)^t$. It is also possible to solve this without knowing the formula by trying out some numbers. Say $t = 2$ years. In the first year, the truck loses 7% of its original value of \$35,000, so it loses \$2,450 of value to have a new value of \$32,550. In the second year, it loses 7% of the new value, or another \$2,278.50, for a final value of \$30,271.50 after 2 years. Now check the answers on a calculator, plugging in 2 for t, to see which one matches this value. Only (D) works. Either way, the correct answer is (D).

9. **A**   The question asks for an equation in terms of a specific variable. All the answers have b by itself, so isolate b in the equation and remember that anything done to one side of an equation also needs to be done to the other side. Subtract 13 from both sides of the equation to get $\left(\dfrac{a}{b}\right)^2 = 2c - 13$. Take the square root of both sides of the equation to get $\dfrac{a}{b} = \sqrt{2c - 13}$. Multiply both sides of the equation by b to get $a = b\sqrt{2c - 13}$, then divide both sides of the equation by $\sqrt{2c - 13}$ to get $\dfrac{a}{\sqrt{2c - 13}} = b$. Flip the two sides of the equation to get b on the left. The correct answer is (A).

10. **C**   The question asks for an expression to represent the price of a ticket bought in the train station during peak hours. There is a lot of abstract information in this question, so make up some numbers. Start from the simplest price, which is a peak ticket bought in the station. Make that price \$100 to make working with percentages easier. In that case, an off-peak ticket purchased in the station will be 15% off, or \$85. For an off-peak ticket purchased from the conductor, there is an 11% surcharge, so $\dfrac{11}{100} \times 85 = 9.35$, and \$85 + \$9.35 = \$94.35. This is the value of t, and the question is asking for the value of a peak ticket bought in the station, which is \$100. Now plug $t = \$94.35$ into the answer choices, and choose the one that equals \$100. The correct answer is (C).

11. **12** The question asks for the value of a constant when a quadratic has exactly one real solution. To determine the number of solutions to a quadratic, use the discriminant. The discriminant is the part of the quadratic formula under the square root sign, and it can be written as $D = b^2 - 4ac$. When the discriminant is positive, the quadratic has exactly two real solutions; when the discriminant is 0, the quadratic has exactly one real solution; and when the discriminant is negative, the quadratic has no real solutions. Since this quadratic has exactly one real solution, the discriminant must equal 0. The quadratic is in standard form, $ax^2 + bx + c = 0$, so $a = 3$, $b = -b$, and $c = 12$. Plug these into the discriminant formula, along with $D = 0$, to get $0 = (-b)^2 - 4(3)(12)$, which becomes $0 = b^2 - 144$. Add 144 to both sides of the equation to get $144 = b^2$, then take the square root of both sides of the equation to get $\pm 12 = b$. The question states that b is positive, so the correct answer is 12.

12. **B** The question asks for the perimeter of the fence Matthew will need around his patch of grass. The question says that the width is 8 feet more than 4 times the length. Take this statement and translate it into an equation. Translate *the width* to w. Translate *is* to =. Translate *8 feet more than* to _ + 8, leaving room on the left for what follows. Translate *4 times the length* to $4l$. Therefore, the statement translates to $w = 4l + 8$. The question also says that the area is 5,472. The area of a rectangle can be found using the formula $A = lw$. Substitute $A = 5,472$ and $w = 4l + 8$ to get $5,472 = l(4l + 8)$. Distribute the l to get $5,472 = 4l^2 + 8l$. Enter the equation into the built-in graphing calculator, but use x instead of l so the calculator will show a graph. The graph shows two solutions at (36, 0) and (−38, 0). The length must be positive, so $l = 36$. If $l = 36$, then $w = 4l + 8 = 4(36) + 8 = 152$. To find the perimeter, use $P = 2l + 2w = 2(36) + 2(152) = 376$. The correct answer is (B).

Part III
Practice Tests

Chapter 1
Practice Test 1

HOW TO EMULATE THE DIGITAL SAT ON PAPER

Practice Test 4 is available in your online student tools in a digital, adaptive environment. The three tests in this physical book are printed on paper, but otherwise emulate the digital test in every way: test style, difficulty, and content. Please use the checklist below to ensure that you are able to emulate the adaptive nature of the test and get the preparation that you need for test day. Feel free to use the versions of Module 2 that you do not take during your test as additional practice.

- ☐ Take Reading and Writing (RW) Module 1, allowing yourself 32 minutes to complete it.

- ☐ Go to the answer key starting on page 92 and determine the number of questions you got correct in RW Module 1.

- ☐ If you get fewer than 15 questions correct, take RW Module 2 – Easier, which starts on page 46. If you get 15 or more questions correct, take RW Module 2 – Harder, which starts on page 56.

- ☐ Whichever RW Module 2 you take, start immediately and allow yourself 32 minutes to complete it.

- ☐ Take a 10-minute break between RW Module 2 and Math Module 1.

- ☐ Take Math Module 1, allowing yourself 35 minutes to complete it.

- ☐ Go to the answer key starting on page 92 and determine the number of questions you got correct in Math Module 1.

- ☐ If you get fewer than 14 questions correct, take Math Module 2 – Easier, which starts on page 76. If you get 14 or more questions correct, take Math Module 2 – Harder, which starts on page 84.

- ☐ Whichever Math Module you take, start it immediately and allow yourself 35 minutes to complete it.

- ☐ After you finish the test, check your answers to RW Module 2 and Math Module 2.

- ☐ Only after you complete the entire test should you read the explanations for the questions, which start on page 93.

SAT Prep Test 1—Reading and Writing
Module 1

Turn to Section 1 of your answer sheet to answer the questions in this section.

The questions in this section address a number of important reading and writing skills. Each question includes one or more passages, which may include a table or graph. Read each passage and question carefully, and then choose the best answer to the question based on the passage(s).

All questions in the section are multiple-choice with four answer choices. Each question has a single best answer. Fill in the circle with the answer letter for the answer you think is best.

---

1 🔖 Mark for Review

Ghost Dance, written by playwright and Otoe-Missouria Tribe member Annette Arkeketa, gets its title from a ceremony performed in the late 1800s by Native American peoples as an act of resistance against the US government. The play tells of a corporate lawyer who returns home, reconnects with her family, and uses her legal _____ to help her tribe.

Which choice completes the text with the most logical and precise word or phrase?

(A) proceedings

(B) incentives

(C) monopoly

(D) prowess

2 🔖 Mark for Review

Hieroglyphs, the Ancient Egyptian writing system, utilized both letters and symbols and contained an estimated 1,000 characters. Before the discovery of the Rosetta Stone, an ancient stone slab containing a royal decree translated into three languages, these hieroglyphs had been largely _____: once the stone was analyzed, linguists could finally begin to understand the meaning of the mysterious symbols.

Which choice completes the text with the most logical and precise word or phrase?

(A) completed

(B) incomprehensible

(C) significant

(D) responsible

CONTINUE ➡

3 ☐ Mark for Review

Publicly accessible satellite imagery such as Google Earth has enabled scientists to document over 300 previously unknown desert kites, giant stone walls that can be up to several miles long and are often in the shape of a kite. Most archaeologists theorize that desert kites were used to trap wild animals, while some others propose that these structures were used to contain livestock; unfortunately, there is little evidence to _____ either claim.

Which choice completes the text with the most logical and precise word or phrase?

(A) invoke

(B) necessitate

(C) corroborate

(D) withdraw

4 ☐ Mark for Review

The following text is adapted from George Bernard Shaw's 1913 play *Pygmalion*.

MRS. PEARCE: Well, sir, whatever you choose to call it, I beg you not to let the girl hear you repeat it.

HIGGINS: Oh, very well, very well. Is that all?

MRS. PEARCE: No, sir. We shall have to be very particular with this girl as to personal cleanliness.

HIGGINS: Certainly. Quite right. Most important.

MRS. PEARCE: I mean not be slovenly about her dress or untidy in leaving things about.

As used in the text, what does the word "slovenly" most nearly mean?

(A) Tasteful

(B) Sympathetic

(C) Informal

(D) Unkempt

5 ☐ Mark for Review

The following text is adapted from Anton Chekhov's 1887 short story *The Lottery Ticket*. Ivan Dmitritch has a lottery ticket for which the first numbers match the winning number, but it is still uncertain whether his ticket is a winning ticket.

And pictures came crowding on Ivan's imagination, each more gracious and poetical than the last. And in all these pictures he saw himself well-fed, serene, healthy, felt warm, even hot! Here, after eating a summer soup, cold as ice, he lay on his back on the burning sand close to a stream or in the garden under a lime-tree. . . . It is hot. . . . His little boy and girl are crawling about near him, digging in the sand or catching ladybirds in the grass. He dozes sweetly, thinking of nothing, and feeling all over that he need not go to the office today, tomorrow, or the day after. Or, tired of lying still, he goes to the hayfield or to the forest for mushrooms.

Which choice best characterizes the overall structure of the text?

(A) It portrays a character falling asleep after eating well and then describes this character waking up to go to work.

(B) It depicts a character considering how his life might change and then details specific fantasies about this character's future lifestyle.

(C) It explains a character's thoughts about winning the lottery and then describes this character's somber mood after not winning.

(D) It explains a character's inspiration for purchasing a lottery ticket and then highlights his family's excitement about potentially winning the lottery.

CONTINUE →

6 ☐ Mark for Review

The following text is an excerpt from the 1799 poem "Pleasures of Hope" by Thomas Campbell.

> At summer eve, when heaven's aerial bow
> Spans with bright arch the glittering hills below,
> Why to yon mountain turns the musing eye,
> Whose sunbright summit mingles with the sky?
> Why do those cliffs of shadowy tint appear
> More sweet than all the landscape smiling near?
> 'Tis distance lends enchantment to the view,
> And robes the mountain in its azure hue.

Which choice best states the main purpose of the text?

(A) To question whether bright or dim lighting is more likely to make an individual commit a specific scene to memory

(B) To challenge the idea that people looking at natural scenes are more likely to experience depression than elation

(C) To describe how a measure of separation can enhance the allure of something

(D) To show how private experiences with inanimate objects affect the way individuals present themselves in public settings

7 ☐ Mark for Review

The following text is from Emily Pauline Johnson's 1903 poem "Fire-Flowers."

> And only where the forest fires have sped,
> Scorching relentlessly the cool north lands,
> <u>A sweet wild flower lifts its purple head,</u>
> <u>And, like some gentle spirit sorrow-fed,</u>
> <u>It hides the scars with almost human hands.</u>
>
> And only to the heart that knows of grief,
> Of desolating fire, of human pain,
> There comes some purifying sweet belief,
> Some fellow-feeling beautiful, if brief.
> And life revives, and blossoms once again.

Which choice best describes the function of the underlined portion in the text as a whole?

(A) It draws a distinction between the flower's precariousness and the author's convictions.

(B) It describes the forest as foreboding and inhospitable.

(C) It reveals the author's detachment from the overwhelming forces of nature.

(D) It portrays the flower as having overcome adversity.

CONTINUE →

8 ☐ Mark for Review

The following text is from Samuel Griswold Goodrich's 1836 poem "Song: The Robin."

> At misty dawn,
> At rosy morn,
> The Redbreast sings alone:
> At twilight dim,
> Still, still, his hymn
> Hath a sad, and sorrowing tone.
>
> Another day, his song is gay,
> For a listening bird is near—
> O ye who sorrow, come borrow, borrow,
> A lesson of robin here!

Which choice best states the main purpose of the text?

Ⓐ To demonstrate that the songs of birds vary extensively in tone and quality

Ⓑ To highlight a bird's similar rituals even at different times of the day

Ⓒ To convey that one may experience melancholy while alone but cheerfulness around others

Ⓓ To present endearing reminiscences of a morning spent watching birds carefully

9 ☐ Mark for Review

The end goal for many substance use disorder recovery programs is complete abstinence from alcohol and drugs. However, there is a growing trend toward multiple paths to recovery. Some experts argue that abstinence-only recovery programs should also consider harm reduction, which focuses on reducing substance use, as a viable stepping stone to addiction recovery. According to these experts, rigid abstinence-only programs fail to recognize that the best recovery plan is the one that works best for the specific individual in recovery.

Which choice best states the main idea of the text?

Ⓐ Individuals who have been in recovery for many years typically use several different recovery programs.

Ⓑ Harm reduction strategies that encourage individuals to limit their use of substances have proven more effective than abstinence-based recovery strategies.

Ⓒ Although harm reduction programs are controversial, some experts contend that focus on reducing substance use can help people recover from substance use disorders.

Ⓓ Some experts argue that the end goal of many substance use disorder recovery programs is suspect and problematic.

CONTINUE ➡

10 🔖 Mark for Review

The following text is adapted from W. T. Nichols's 1916 novel *The Safety First Club*. Sam is a teenager.

Sam Parker stepped out upon the side porch of his father's house, closing the door behind him with a slam. He was, as a matter of fact, in a fit of temper, which did not lessen as he surveyed the dull, gray sky, and saw its promise of a dismal day.

Which choice best states the main idea of the text?

Ⓐ Sam's bad mood worsens because of the prospect of poor weather.

Ⓑ Sam slams the door because his father has upset him.

Ⓒ Sam usually seeks fresh air as a means to improve his current mood.

Ⓓ Sam responds to dreary weather in a matter-of-fact manner.

11 🔖 Mark for Review

Number of Words Recalled out of 30 in Novel Versus Familiar Environments

Age group	Novel environment	Familiar environment
18–27	23	25
28–38	21	26
39–49	20	23
50–60	18	20
over 60	15	20

A group of researchers investigated the effects of a novel environment compared with a familiar environment on memory recall across different age groups. They found that, although word recall varied greatly across age groups under novel environments, word recall was similar across age groups under familiar environments. Therefore, they concluded that while age groups may differ in memory recall, people perform better under familiar environments than novel environments.

Which choice best describes data from the table that support the researchers' claim?

Ⓐ All five groups of participants had higher recall in the familiar environment, though the number of words recalled ranged from 20 to 26.

Ⓑ Among the age groups in the table, the group that had the highest word recall in novel environments also had the highest word recall in familiar environments.

Ⓒ Age groups 28–38 and 39–49 had approximately the same word recall in novel environments, but ages 39–49 had a higher word recall in familiar environments than did ages 28–38.

Ⓓ Among the age groups in the table, those ages 39–49 and those over 60 had the lowest word recall in novel and familiar environments.

CONTINUE ➡

12 ▢ Mark for Review

Height of Rose Bushes over Time

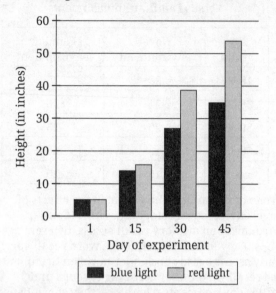

To investigate the effect of different filtered lights on the growth rate of rose bushes, a student in a chemistry class placed seedling rose bushes in either a blue filtered light enclosure or a red filtered light enclosure and tracked the growth process over 45 days. The student concluded that the increased height of rose bushes was influenced solely by red light and that blue light was not responsible for any growth.

Which choice best describes data from the graph that weaken the student's conclusion?

Ⓐ The height of rose bushes under blue filtered light also substantially grew by day 45.

Ⓑ The height of rose bushes was lower under blue filtered light than red filtered light on day 45.

Ⓒ The largest increase in height of rose bushes under red filtered light occurred from day 15 to day 30.

Ⓓ The height of rose bushes was the same in both light enclosures on day 1.

13 ▢ Mark for Review

"The Rainy Day" is an 1842 poem by Henry Wadsworth Longfellow. In the poem, Longfellow uses natural imagery to suggest that despite his emotional struggle there is still cause for hope, writing _____

Which quotation from "The Rainy Day" most effectively illustrates the claim?

Ⓐ "The day is cold, and dark, and dreary."

Ⓑ "The vine still clings to the mouldering wall."

Ⓒ "But the hopes of youth fall thick in the blast."

Ⓓ "Behind the clouds is the sun still shining."

14 ▢ Mark for Review

Although a key tenet in a physician-patient relationship is honesty, a survey showed that 50% of physicians regularly prescribe placebos, substances that have no medicinal effect. One possible explanation is that when creating a treatment plan, a physician may prescribe two or more medications for the patient to try. The patient will be informed that one of those medications is a placebo but will remain unaware as to which one, thus _____

Which choice most logically completes the text?

Ⓐ encouraging more physicians to prescribe placebos as a standard form of treatment.

Ⓑ hindering other instances of honesty in the typical physician-patient relationship.

Ⓒ prompting patients to request placebo treatment in lieu of traditional treatment methods.

Ⓓ maintaining honest communication in the physician-patient relationship.

CONTINUE ➡

15 ▢ Mark for Review

Exploring abyssal plains on the deep ocean floor is difficult because of the vastness of the _____ vehicles capable of withstanding the water pressure to travel to depths of 3,000 to 6,000 meters.

Which choice completes the text so that it conforms to the conventions of Standard English?

(A) plains and the lack of

(B) plains, and, the lack of

(C) plains, and the lack of,

(D) plains and the lack of,

16 ▢ Mark for Review

The effects of the Industrial Revolution, which greatly increased the levels of air pollution in Great Britain, Europe, and the US, are not completely known due to the lack of exact data. Fortunately, since _____ painted during the Industrial Revolution, researchers can use changes in the artists' depictions of the atmosphere to track the effects of air pollution.

Which choice completes the text so that it conforms to the conventions of Standard English?

(A) artists Joseph Turner, and Claude Monet

(B) artists Joseph Turner and Claude Monet

(C) artists, Joseph Turner and Claude Monet

(D) artists, Joseph Turner and Claude Monet,

17 ▢ Mark for Review

A team of researchers at Yunnan University School of Agriculture in Kunming, China, assessed the performance of a hybrid of two rice _____ *Oryza sativa*, which is domesticated Asian rice, and *Oryza longistaminata*, which is undomesticated African rice.

Which choice completes the text so that it conforms to the conventions of Standard English?

(A) species:

(B) species

(C) species;

(D) species.

18 ▢ Mark for Review

Chemehuevi photographer Cara Romero's work uses staging and digital tools to explore Indigenous life. In 2015, Romero utilized underwater photography to portray a moment from her tribe's _____ in 2017, Romero photographed Puebloans juxtaposed with TVs displaying traditional media depictions of Native Americans.

Which choice completes the text so that it conforms to the conventions of Standard English?

(A) history, then,

(B) history,

(C) history;

(D) history then,

CONTINUE ➤

19 ☐ Mark for Review

When writing about Antiguan-American novelist Jamaica Kincaid's books, _____ have connected it to the colonial relationship between England and Antigua.

Which choice completes the text so that it conforms to the conventions of Standard English?

- Ⓐ the examination by literary critics has been of Kincaid's exploration of the mother-daughter bond; they

- Ⓑ there are literary critics who have examined Kincaid's exploration of the mother-daughter bond, and they

- Ⓒ Kincaid's exploration of the mother-daughter bond has been examined by literary critics, who

- Ⓓ literary critics have examined Kincaid's exploration of the mother-daughter bond and

20 ☐ Mark for Review

Terrol Dew Johnson, a Tohono O'odham sculptor, weaver, and advocate for Indigenous foods, helped create a nonprofit community development organization, Tohono O'odham Community _____ *Native Foodways Magazine,* in 2013; and an art installation, "Meeting the Clouds Halfway," in 2016.

Which choice completes the text so that it conforms to the conventions of Standard English?

- Ⓐ Action, in 1996, a national publication,

- Ⓑ Action, in 1996; a national publication,

- Ⓒ Action; in 1996, a national publication,

- Ⓓ Action; in 1996, a national publication;

21 ☐ Mark for Review

The films of Israeli cinematographer Yael Bartana often touch on historical themes, such as the intertwining elements of Jewish and Polish identities and the experiences of Ashkenazi Jews in Europe in the 19th and 20th centuries. _____ Bartana looks to the future; some of her more recent works represent fictional dystopian scenarios that allow audiences to analyze the role of women in politics.

Which choice completes the text with the most logical transition?

- Ⓐ Therefore,

- Ⓑ For this reason,

- Ⓒ In fact,

- Ⓓ Still,

CONTINUE ➡

22 ☐ Mark for Review

While researching a topic, a student has taken the following notes:

- The US National Park Service (NPS) was established in 1916.
- In 1956, the NPS set a goal, called Mission 66, to expand the numbers of visitors by its fiftieth anniversary.
- The expansion of the US highway system and increased car ownership made remote places, like national parks, more accessible.
- Mission 66 led to the building of more than 100 visitor centers in the parks.
- NPS estimated that 80 million people would visit national parks in 1966, but the actual number was 127 million.

The student wants to emphasize the role infrastructure played in the achievement of a goal. Which choice most effectively uses relevant information from the notes to accomplish this goal?

(A) Expanded highways, increased car ownership, and new visitor centers helped the National Park Service increase the number of visitors by 1966.

(B) In 1956, the National Park Service wanted to expand the number of visitors the parks would welcome in 1966.

(C) The National Park Service celebrated its fiftieth anniversary by expanding infrastructure during Mission 66.

(D) National parks in the US were visited by 127 million people in 1966, the fiftieth anniversary of the National Park Service.

23 ☐ Mark for Review

While researching a topic, a student has taken the following notes:

- Vogelsang Pass is a mountain pass in California.
- It is located in Yosemite National Park.
- Its maximum elevation is 10,680 feet.
- Stevens Pass is a mountain pass in Washington.
- It is located in the Cascade Mountains.
- Its maximum elevation is 4,061 feet.

The student wants to compare the elevations of the two mountain passes. Which choice most effectively uses relevant information from the notes to accomplish this goal?

(A) Two examples of mountain passes in the US are the Vogelsang Pass in California and the Stevens Pass in Washington.

(B) The mountain pass in Yosemite National Park that has a maximum elevation of 10,680 feet is the Vogelsang Pass.

(C) Vogelsang Pass reaches a maximum elevation of 10,680 feet, while Stevens Pass reaches a maximum elevation of 4,061 feet.

(D) Some of the mountain passes in the US, including one mountain pass in Yosemite National Park in California, reach elevations of over 10,000 feet.

CONTINUE ▶

24 ☐ Mark for Review

While researching a topic, a student has taken the following notes:

- In 1876, German composer Richard Wagner debuted his epic music drama *Der Ring des Nibelungen*.
- His lengthy opera, consisting of four parts and fifteen hours of music, is based on the epic poem *Nibelungenlied* and Norse legendary sagas.
- In 1976, American composer Philip Glass debuted his opera *Einstein on the Beach*.
- Glass's lengthy opera, lasting for five hours, has four parts and does not have a narrative arc.
- Instead, it relies on repeated imagery and allusions to Albert Einstein's life and work.

The student wants to emphasize a similarity between the two operas. Which choice most effectively uses relevant information from the notes to accomplish this goal?

- (A) Wagner's opera is based on an epic poem, while Glass's opera is based on a real person.

- (B) Wagner's and Glass's operas are both lengthy, lasting fifteen hours and five hours, respectively.

- (C) Although Wagner and Glass are both composers, their operas differ in their subject matter.

- (D) German composer Wagner debuted his opera in 1876; American composer Glass debuted his opera in 1976.

25 ☐ Mark for Review

While researching a topic, a student has taken the following notes:

- A marsquake is a shaking that takes place on Mars's surface or in its interior, similar to an earthquake.
- NASA sent Viking 2 to observe Mars's seismic activity in the 1970s.
- In 2018, NASA sent the InSight Mars lander to Mars's surface.
- It measured seismic activity and observed the first confirmed marsquake in 2019 in the canyon system Valles Marineris.

The student wants to specify the reason the InSight mission went to Mars. Which choice most effectively uses relevant information from the notes to accomplish this goal?

- (A) Marsquakes occur on Mars, but one wasn't observed until 2019 in Valles Marineris, by the InSight Mars lander.

- (B) In 2018, the InSight Mars lander was sent to measure seismic activity on Mars and observed a marsquake a year later.

- (C) Although NASA sent Viking 2 to Mars in the 1970s, a marsquake wasn't observed until 2019, by the InSight Mars lander.

- (D) Viking 2 was sent to Mars in the 1970s to observe possible marsquakes, and the InSight Mars lander was sent in 2018.

CONTINUE →

26 ☐ Mark for Review

While researching a topic, a student has taken the following notes:

- Cathy Park Hong is a writer and professor.
- She writes about the experiences of marginalized people.
- She also experiments with multiple languages.
- Hong wrote her novel *Dance Dance Revolution* in 2007.
- Her non-fiction book *Minor Feelings* was published in 2020.

The student wants to emphasize a difference between the two books. Which choice most effectively uses relevant information from the notes to accomplish this goal?

(A) *Dance Dance Revolution* and *Minor Feelings* contain experiences of marginalized people and experiment with multiple languages.

(B) While Hong wrote both books, her 2007 work *Dance Dance Revolution* is a novel, and her 2020 work *Minor Feelings* is a non-fiction book.

(C) Hong has focused on the experiences of marginalized people in her writing, including the books *Dance Dance Revolution* and *Minor Feelings*.

(D) In the 2000s, Hong wrote two books, *Dance Dance Revolution* and *Minor Feelings*.

27 ☐ Mark for Review

While researching a topic, a student has taken the following notes:

- Bowhead whales once numbered between 25,000 and 100,000 individuals in the Greenland Sea and North Atlantic.
- During the whaling era, they were hunted to near extinction, and now there are an estimated 300 individuals.
- Researchers from the Greenland Institute and the University of Copenhagen recently spotted two calves in the Greenland Sea.
- Only two other calves have been spotted over the past forty years.
- The observation suggests that the population of bowhead whales may be increasing.

The student wants to emphasize the recent sighting's significance. Which choice most effectively uses relevant information from the notes to accomplish this goal?

(A) Researchers observed two bowhead whale calves, bringing the number up to four calf observations.

(B) After bowhead whales were nearly hunted to extinction in the whaling era, researchers have reason to believe that they may be increasing in number due to the rare sighting of two calves.

(C) The population of bowhead whales was estimated to be 300 individuals; two calves were recently observed in the Greenland Sea.

(D) Researchers observed bowhead whale calves in the Greenland Sea, where thousands of bowhead whales used to live.

YIELD

Once you've finished (or run out of time for) this section, use the answer key to determine how many questions you got right. If you got fewer than 15 questions right, move on to Module 2—Easier, otherwise move on to Module 2—Harder.

SAT Prep Test 1—Reading and Writing
Module 2—Easier

Turn to Section 1 of your answer sheet to answer the questions in this section.

---

1 ☐ Mark for Review

In the 1850s, in order to combat the destruction that moths were causing to New York City's trees, the city imported *Passer domesticus*, or the house sparrow, which was believed to _____ insects: unfortunately, officials later realized that the bird's diet only includes insects during the first couple weeks of life, after which the sparrows subsist mostly on grain.

Which choice completes the text with the most logical and precise word or phrase?

(A) consume

(B) evolve

(C) evacuate

(D) rescue

---

2 ☐ Mark for Review

By the time he turned 20, Pablo Neruda had already published two poetry books, which made him _____ poet in Chile. Being this well-known gave him the opportunity to publish three more books in the following years. Neruda became most famous for his poetry about intense romantic relationships.

Which choice completes the text with the most logical and precise word or phrase?

(A) an unknown

(B) a reserved

(C) a disliked

(D) a popular

CONTINUE

3 ☐ Mark for Review

The question of how quickly the universe is expanding has been _____ by scientists for many years. Recently, astrophysicists Jose Ezquiaga and Daniel Holz have devised a method for measuring the gravitational waves that result from two black holes colliding that may settle this issue.

Which choice completes the text with the most logical and precise word or phrase?

Ⓐ resolved

Ⓑ deliberated

Ⓒ assimilated

Ⓓ criticized

4 ☐ Mark for Review

British Tibetan artist Gonkar Gyatso's unique work is _____ his interest in rejuvenating Buddhist symbolic representation while incorporating the styles of classic Tibetan thangka paintings.

Which choice completes the text with the most logical and precise word or phrase?

Ⓐ rejected by

Ⓑ included in

Ⓒ inspired by

Ⓓ detached from

5 ☐ Mark for Review

Thyreophora is a group of dinosaurs that had thick plates of body armor, walked on four legs, and would grow to the length of a bus. However, paleontologist Sebastían Apesteguía and colleagues have discovered a new species named *Jakapil kaniukura*, which, _____ other armored dinosaurs, walked on two legs and was the size of a dog.

Which choice completes the text with the most logical and precise word or phrase?

Ⓐ exceeded by

Ⓑ courtesy of

Ⓒ contrary to

Ⓓ associated with

6 ☐ Mark for Review

Though it was previously thought that Vikings did not travel with animals, a recent analysis of animal bones in a Viking burial site has yielded significant results that challenge this assumption. Archaeologists claim that this _____ finding, coupled with the fact that the animal bones were found alongside human bones, indicates that Vikings kept some animals for companionship, instead of simply for labor.

Which choice completes the text with the most logical and precise word or phrase?

Ⓐ representative

Ⓑ polarizing

Ⓒ eminent

Ⓓ notable

CONTINUE ➔

---

7 ⬚ Mark for Review

Unlike commercial farming, subsistence agriculture is a way of farming that aims to provide solely for the farmer's household. When planting crops, farmers evaluate how much will be necessary in the year to come. By not growing more than is needed, farmers are able to _____ their family units without any additional wastage.

Which choice completes the text with the most logical and precise word or phrase?

(A) expose

(B) sustain

(C) imagine

(D) deprive

8 ⬚ Mark for Review

Text 1

The origin of culture in the Americas is a contentious debate between pre-Clovis and Clovis theories. Identified as a Paleoindian culture in New Mexico, the Clovis people have long been credited with being the first culture to colonize the Americas approximately 13,000 years ago. Later discoveries such as Monte Verde in South America and Topper in North America yielded stone tools that may date as far back as 16,000 years. These findings confirm the presence of an earlier culture of pre-Clovis people as the first to colonize the Americas.

Text 2

Many researchers and archaeologists refute a pre-Clovis theory due to the problematic nature of dating stone tools and attributing them to a particular society. However, recently, a team of researchers uncovered ancient human footprint tracks covering the shore at the White Sands National Park in New Mexico. The researchers identified the footprints as being between 21,000 and 22,000 years old by carbon dating the seeds found within the footprints. Thus, this discovery places the existence of a pre-Clovis people years earlier than any other pre-Clovis site evidence.

Based on the texts, how would the author of Text 2 most likely respond to the underlined claim in Text 1?

(A) By stating that the claim has merit, but the recent archaeological discovery provides stronger evidence than do the previously known sites such as Monte Verde and Topper

(B) By disagreeing with the claim because there is a lack of substantial dating evidence and few pre-Clovis sites

(C) By questioning the claim for being too broad with little supporting evidence, while Clovis theory evidence has been largely substantiated

(D) By agreeing with the claim but arguing that stone tools offer substantial evidence for a pre-Clovis theory

CONTINUE ➡

9 ☐ Mark for Review

The following text is adapted from Victor Hugo's 1862 novel *Les Misérables*.

Jean Valjean felt himself exasperated. And besides, human society had done him nothing but harm; he had never seen anything of it save that angry face which it calls Justice, and which it shows to those whom it strikes. Men had only touched him to bruise him. Every contact with them had been a blow. Never, since his infancy, since the days of his mother, of his sister, had he ever encountered a friendly word and a kindly glance. From suffering to suffering, he had gradually arrived at the conviction that life is a war; and that in this war he was the conquered.

According to the text, what is true about Jean Valjean?

Ⓐ He believes in the good of human society.

Ⓑ He is a soldier fighting at the warfront.

Ⓒ His mother is his closest family member.

Ⓓ He has experienced suffering in his life.

10 ☐ Mark for Review

"Little Boy Blue" is an 1888 poem by Eugene Field about the loss of a child told from the perspective of the child's toys. In this poem, Field conveys a sense of lingering curiosity despite the passage of time: _____

Which quotation from "Little Boy Blue" most effectively illustrates the claim?

Ⓐ "The little toy dog is covered with dust, / But sturdy and staunch he stands; / And the little toy soldier is red with rust, / And his musket molds in his hands."

Ⓑ "And that was the time when our Little Boy Blue / Kissed them and put them there. / "Now, don't you go till I come," he said, / "And don't you make any noise!"

Ⓒ "So toddling off to his trundle-bed / He dreamed of the pretty toys. / And as he was dreaming, an angel song / Awakened our Little Boy Blue."

Ⓓ "And they wonder, as waiting these long years through / In the dust of that little chair / What has become of our Little Boy Blue, / Since he kissed them and put them there."

CONTINUE

---

11 ☐ Mark for Review

Bumblebees are important pollinators, but their numbers have been greatly affected by habitat reduction and pesticide usage. Another factor affecting the bumblebee population is the harmful transmission of a parasite, *C. bombi*. A team of researchers hypothesized that shorter flower petals could reduce the parasite transmission. To test the hypothesis, researchers set up two bumblebee tents, one with long petaled flowers and the other with shortened petaled flowers of the same species. Next, they placed an even distribution of bumblebees with and without the parasite in each tent.

Which finding, if true, would most directly support the researchers' hypothesis?

Ⓐ More bumblebees in the shortened petaled flower tent had the parasite than did those in the long petaled flower tent.

Ⓑ More bumblebees in the long petaled flower tent had the parasite than did those in the shortened petaled flower tent.

Ⓒ No bumblebees in either tent contracted the parasite.

Ⓓ All bumblebees in both tents contracted the parasite.

12 ☐ Mark for Review

Japanese writer Haruki Murakami commands the ability to create a mood in his works about loneliness and isolation. The characters of his work are intricately detailed and well-developed to feel real and alive to the reader while their environments are surreal and otherworldly. In an essay, a student claims that the surreal landscapes presented in Murakami's works create alternate realities that emphasize a sense of existentialism.

Which quotation from a scholarly review of Murakami's work best supports the student's claim?

Ⓐ "The endings in Murakami's work are often left without resolution, thus allowing the reader's imagination to finish the story."

Ⓑ "Murakami's work has gained international recognition and has been translated in over 50 languages."

Ⓒ "Murakami's blend of the real and imaginary allows for an exploration into the human condition."

Ⓓ "Before Murakami became a writer, he owned a jazz club in Tokyo and wrote his first novel for fun."

CONTINUE ➡

13 ☐ Mark for Review

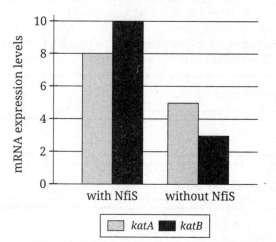

mRNA Expression Levels in *P. stutzeri*
With and Without NfiS Gene

Certain gene sequences in bacteria can increase mRNA expression of oxidative protective genes, such as *katA* and *katB*, thereby protecting their host plant from oxidative stress. A team of researchers hypothesized that a gene sequence called NfiS found in a mutant strain of the bacterium *P. stutzeri* coded for oxidative protective genes. To test this hypothesis, the team measured the mRNA expression levels of *katA* and *katB* in *P. stutzeri* with NfiS and *P. stutzeri* without NfiS after both were exposed to high levels of hydrogen peroxide.

Which choice best describes data in the graph that support the team's hypothesis?

Ⓐ The bacteria without NfiS had lower levels of *katA* and *katB* than did the bacteria with NfiS.

Ⓑ *katA* mRNA expression levels were around 8 in bacteria without NfiS, but closer to 5 in bacteria with NfiS.

Ⓒ Both bacteria had mRNA expression levels of at least 3 for *katA* and *katB*.

Ⓓ Bacteria with NfiS had a higher expression of *katB* than *katA*, while bacteria without NfiS had a higher expression of *katA* than *katB*.

14 ☐ Mark for Review

Recycling has a tremendous impact on preserving the environment by reducing pollution and greenhouse gases, but it also has a lasting effect on the social dynamics of communities in which it is practiced frequently. According to a recent survey of young adults in the United States, most young adults said that they knew the environmental benefits of recycling and listed examples. Meanwhile, only 8% of young adults said that recycling can improve communities overall. These results suggest that _____

Which choice most logically completes the text?

Ⓐ many young adults think they can only recycle in their households.

Ⓑ recycling can help individuals more than it can help communities.

Ⓒ recycling can be more beneficial than many young adults believe.

Ⓓ many young adults do not know where to find recycling bins.

CONTINUE

15 ☐ Mark for Review

Vaccines are important in helping prevent the spread of disease and illness, such as influenza. However, current vaccines that target influenza become less effective over time due to the mutations that occur in the hemagglutinin antigens which build resistance to treatment. A team of researchers at the University of Oklahoma designed a nano-peptide with influenza hemagglutinin proteins that increased IgG1 and IgG2 antibodies, proteins that target viruses, more than did vaccine administration alone. Additionally, due to its size, the nano-peptide did not generate mutations in the hemagglutinin antigens. Thus, the researchers believe that the nano-peptide can be useful in _____

Which choice most logically completes the text?

(A) curing other medical conditions, such as headaches and chronic pain.

(B) targeting other viruses without inducing resistance to treatment over time.

(C) determining whether IgG1 and IgG2 antibodies are necessary for immune response.

(D) developing mutated hemagglutinin antigens that slow the spread of influenza.

16 ☐ Mark for Review

During the Democratic National Convention in 1896, presidential hopeful William Jennings Bryan delivered the now-famous Cross of Gold speech, a speech that _____ the US's use of the gold standard.

Which choice completes the text so that it conforms to the conventions of Standard English?

(A) criticize

(B) criticizes

(C) were criticizing

(D) have criticized

17 ☐ Mark for Review

In Australia, epaulette sharks, a species of carpet shark, have a remarkable adaptation that helps them survive hostile environments. Although they spend most of their time in reefs, the sharks have the ability to walk on dry land and survive without oxygen for a few hours, _____ the sharks to find better oxygenated tidepools and more prey.

Which choice completes the text so that it conforms to the conventions of Standard English?

(A) allowed

(B) allowing

(C) to allow

(D) allows

CONTINUE ➤

18 ☐ Mark for Review

A sonic pulse of an anemometer, an instrument used to measure wind speed and direction, travels from one transducer to another, during which time it _____ to air speed, temperature, and pressure, providing valuable information to weather stations.

Which choice completes the text so that it conforms to the conventions of Standard English?

Ⓐ is reacting

Ⓑ had reacted

Ⓒ reacts

Ⓓ will react

19 ☐ Mark for Review

Researchers studying animals in extremely cold environments discovered that tiny snailfish are full of antifreeze proteins, a special type of protein that prevents the _____ from freezing in the icy waters.

Which choice completes the text so that it conforms to the conventions of Standard English?

Ⓐ fish's body's

Ⓑ fishes bodies

Ⓒ fishes body's

Ⓓ fish's bodies

20 ☐ Mark for Review

In *małni—towards the ocean, towards the shore* (2020), Native American filmmaker Sky Hopinka used chinuk wawa, an Indigenous language of the Pacific Northwest. The film is Hopinka's first feature-length film, but chinuk wawa and its speakers _____ included in his short films as well. In 2017, he made *Anti-Objects, or Space Without Path or Boundary*, which features one of the last speakers of chinuk wawa.

Which choice completes the text so that it conforms to the conventions of Standard English?

Ⓐ is

Ⓑ have been

Ⓒ has been

Ⓓ was

21 ☐ Mark for Review

In the portrait *Baba the Butcher and Gardener*, Spanish-Moroccan artist Anuar Khalifi paints a Moroccan man rather than a European man _____ people who are not traditionally seen in portraiture.

Which choice completes the text so that it conforms to the conventions of Standard English?

Ⓐ to spotlight

Ⓑ is spotlighting

Ⓒ spotlighted

Ⓓ spotlights

CONTINUE ➡

22 ☐ Mark for Review

In the 1940s, kite builder and flier Francis Rogallo was trying to find official support for his creation of a new self-inflating flexible wing when he decided to carry out experiments on his own time with his wife Gertrude Rogallo. Eventually, the Rogallos _____ a flexible wing that would become known as the Rogallo wing.

Which choice completes the text so that it conforms to the conventions of Standard English?

(A) were designing

(B) had designed

(C) design

(D) designed

23 ☐ Mark for Review

Created to reduce or eliminate barriers to trade, the North American Free Trade Agreement (NAFTA) established a trade bloc among three North American countries: Canada, Mexico, and the United States. By the time it was replaced in 2020, NAFTA _____ in effect for twenty-six years.

Which choice completes the text so that it conforms to the conventions of Standard English?

(A) will remain

(B) remains

(C) had remained

(D) has remained

24 ☐ Mark for Review

Ice drilling allows researchers to obtain samples from below the surface of ice and study different characteristics of the ice and its components. Many methods of ice drilling use motion or vibrations to break through the ice. However, some methods use heat energy. Thermal drills, _____ use hot steam or water to obtain the ice samples.

Which choice completes the text with the most logical transition?

(A) regardless,

(B) similarly,

(C) in comparison,

(D) for instance,

CONTINUE →

Bette Nesmith Graham, an American typist and secretary for W. W. Overton, Chairman of the Board of the Texas Bank and Trust, was introduced to a new invention, the electric typewriter. At first, the typewriter was useful, but Graham quickly became frustrated with the need to retype entire pages of notes to fix one minuscule error. Graham was determined to find a more efficient method and spent years testing and perfecting different ways to fix this issue. _____ Graham discovered the answer after observing the bank's windows being painted to celebrate the holiday season, and the first correction fluid was developed.

Which choice completes the text with the most logical transition?

(A) Moreover,

(B) Finally,

(C) Additionally,

(D) Alternately,

Zhou Tong was a Chinese archer and military tutor of the Song dynasty whose initial legacy developed from teaching children techniques with a bow and arrow. After his death, _____ his legacy shifted to his favorite pupil, Yue Fei, who taught the techniques to his soldiers and used them successfully in war.

Which choice completes the text with the most logical transition?

(A) hence,

(B) however,

(C) specifically,

(D) meanwhile,

Scientists at the University of Geneva were interested in how motivation affects decision-making. They trained mice to respond to a physical stimulus on the right sides of their bodies by providing a water source as a reward. _____ the mice began to ignore physical stimuli on the left sides of their bodies that didn't come with a reward.

Which choice completes the text with the most logical transition?

(A) As a result,

(B) Specifically,

(C) Nevertheless,

(D) Secondly,

STOP

**If you finish before time is called, you may check your work on this section only.
Do not turn to any other section in the test.**

SAT Prep Test 1—Reading and Writing
Module 2—Harder

Turn to Section 1 of your answer sheet to answer the questions in this section.

---

1 ☐ Mark for Review

After their first album was a hit, singer Ella Fitzgerald and trumpeter Louis Armstrong collaborated to perform in concert together at the Hollywood Bowl in 1956. Attendees regarded the performance as _____: even though the venue saw a record-breaking 20,000 audience members, many reported feeling a personal connection and a sense of closeness with the sensational artists on the stage.

Which choice completes the text with the most logical and precise word or phrase?

(A) intimate

(B) obscure

(C) insignificant

(D) unintelligible

---

2 ☐ Mark for Review

During her trip to Switzerland in 1868, established nurse Clara Barton met Dr. Louis Paul Amédée Appia, a Swiss surgeon who introduced her to the Red Cross. Appia assisted Barton in finding fiscal _____ for the American branch of the Red Cross. With his help and their funding, Barton founded the American Red Cross in May of 1881.

Which choice completes the text with the most logical and precise word or phrase?

(A) subsidiaries

(B) opponents

(C) companions

(D) benefactors

CONTINUE ➡

3 ☐ Mark for Review

The writing of Iraqi American poet Dunya Mikhail has been largely inspired by her _____ feelings about her home country: in many of her pieces, she expresses a deep love for her birthplace but laments the violence and war that eventually led her to flee.

Which choice completes the text with the most logical and precise word or phrase?

Ⓐ logical

Ⓑ ambivalent

Ⓒ celebratory

Ⓓ monotonous

4 ☐ Mark for Review

In the early-to-mid-1900s, negative pressure ventilators, or iron lungs, were widely used by doctors. However, with the invention of the modern ventilator, most medical professionals began to _____ the usefulness of the iron lung. A major drawback of the machine was that the patient was not able to be easily transported when attached to it.

Which choice completes the text with the most logical and precise word or phrase?

Ⓐ demonstrate

Ⓑ applaud

Ⓒ scrutinize

Ⓓ imitate

5 ☐ Mark for Review

Text 1

Traditional theories about the origin of human cooperation focused on the role of natural selection in the development of cooperative behaviors in all social animals, including humans. Over a period of many thousands of years, cooperation emerged as an adaptation in many animals because cooperation helped animals survive by allowing them to share resources and protect themselves from predators.

Text 2

In a recent book, anthropologist Richard Wrangham argues that humans, unlike other animals, evolved to be cooperative by purposefully restricting the breeding opportunities of the most aggressive males to create a species that was more docile and less violent. Wrangham cites physical changes in the human body, such as a decrease in size, a decrease in canine tooth size, and an increase in brain size, as evidence of a self-domestication process that helped humans to thrive.

Based on the texts, how would Wrangham (Text 2) most likely respond to the "traditional theories" presented in Text 1?

Ⓐ By contesting the idea that the evolution of cooperation shares striking commonalities among all cooperative species

Ⓑ By admitting the significance of natural selection but emphasizing the greater importance of physical changes in humans

Ⓒ By questioning the assumption that cooperation is an adaptation that promotes survival in animal species

Ⓓ By agreeing that natural selection played a similar role in the evolution of cooperation in both humans and other animals

CONTINUE ➡

6 ☐ Mark for Review

The following text was adapted from Elizabeth Sanxay Holding's 1921 novel *Rosaleen Among the Artists*.

Miss Julie dressed the little girl while she stood there like a doll. A beautiful child, too thin and altogether too small for her years, but very charmingly and gracefully built; the girl had deep-set clear grey eyes and a wistful small face, broad at the brow and tapering to a pointed chin, like a kitten's. And the girl had about her something that enslaved Miss Julie, some mystic and adorable quality that Miss Julie could not name, and that no one else saw.

According to the text, what is true about Miss Julie?

(A) She prefers kittens over other small animals.

(B) She would like to spend more time standing still.

(C) She likes nothing more than dressing little girls.

(D) She cannot describe why she finds a little girl enchanting.

7 ☐ Mark for Review

Among all species of hominins—a group that includes humans and relatives of humans—*Australopithecus* and *Homo floresiensis* have the smallest known brains, both about one-third the volume of modern human brains, a size always thought to imply a less complex brain structure. In a 2013 finding that revolutionized our conception of hominins, a team led by paleoanthropologist Lee Berger discovered the remains of *Homo naledi*, a species with a brain comparable in size to that of *Homo floresiensis* but with a complex structure similar to that of modern humans.

According to the text, why was Berger and his team's identification of *Homo naledi* significant?

(A) The discovery allows scientists to determine a precise chronology of brain size evolution among hominins.

(B) The discovery establishes the first evidence that hominin brain size may not be directly correlated with brain complexity.

(C) The discovery represents the first indication of a species with a brain shape similar to that of modern humans.

(D) The discovery provides evidence that the brains of hominin species can vary in size more than previously imagined.

CONTINUE

8 ☐ Mark for Review

Physicist Albert Einstein first proposed the existence of gravitational waves, ripples in space-time produced by violent events such as two black holes merging, in 1911. However, gravitational waves remained unproven until 2016, when Caltech and MIT scientists reported that they had directly measured these long-theorized waves using the Laser Interferometer Gravitational-Wave Observatory, a set of two identical detectors. When gravitational waves passed by, the detectors' arms were stretched and squeezed, slightly altering their lengths. This caused a tiny change in the laser light interference pattern that these detectors monitor—the first direct observation of gravitational waves.

Which choice best states the main idea of the text?

- (A) Scientists have invented a new way of measuring tiny changes in laser light interference patterns.

- (B) The most critical factor in allowing the detection of gravitational waves is having two identical detectors.

- (C) Gravitational waves are challenging to measure because of the violent nature of the events that create them.

- (D) Scientists have now managed to produce clear and convincing evidence confirming that gravitational waves exist.

9 ☐ Mark for Review

Electric vehicles are less harmful to the environment than their gas-powered counterparts because they release significantly fewer pollutants into the air. These pollutants are harmful to both the environment and individuals. For example, one such pollutant, nitrogen dioxide (NO_2), is highly correlated with asthma. It was theorized that electric vehicles might be correlated with better health outcomes. Researchers looked at California, a state with a relatively high adoption rate of electric vehicles, and compared the number of electric vehicles to the number of asthma-related hospital visits over time. They found that as the adoption of electric vehicles increased, the hospital visits decreased. The researchers concluded that electric vehicles have a positive effect on the health of individuals.

Which finding, if true, would most directly support the researchers' conclusion?

- (A) In industrialized nations, the rate of asthma-related hospital visits overall has declined over the last decade.

- (B) Cities that have constructed more bicycle lanes over the past decade have experienced decreased emission levels as well as decreased asthma-related hospital visits.

- (C) Though asthma has been linked to NO_2, several other pollutants created by gas-powered vehicles have also been shown to contribute to respiratory problems.

- (D) Communities that have not experienced widespread adoption of electric vehicles display static rates of asthma-related hospital visits.

CONTINUE ➡

10 ☐ Mark for Review

"The Necklace" is an 1884 short story by Guy de Maupassant. In the story, Madame Mathilde Loisel comes from humble beginnings, yet she yearns to be a part of the upper class. In describing Loisel, the narrator contrasts her background with her ambition, as when de Maupassant writes, _____

Which quotation from "The Necklace" most effectively illustrates the claim?

(A) "She was one of those pretty and charming girls who are sometimes, as if by a mistake of destiny, born in a family of clerks."

(B) "She came to know what heavy housework meant and the odious cares of the kitchen. She washed the dishes, using her rosy nails on the greasy pots and pans."

(C) "She had no dresses, no jewels, nothing. And she loved nothing but that; she felt made for that. She would so have liked to please, to be envied, to be charming, to be sought after."

(D) "She saw first of all some bracelets, then a pearl necklace, then a Venetian cross, gold and precious stones of admirable workmanship."

11 ☐ Mark for Review

Percentage of Materials that Compose
Tires of Passenger Cars and Trucks

Material	Passenger car	Truck
Natural rubber	21.2	37.1
Synthetic rubber	24.5	10.0
Process oil	4.4	0.8
Steel Wire	10.8	21.1

Tires are some of the most vital safety features of a passenger car or truck. Not only is a tire composed of various other materials besides rubber, but a tire also contains both natural and synthetic rubber. One of the functions of natural rubber is to increase tear resistance, and one of the purposes of synthetic rubber is to improve traction. Since trucks carry significantly heavier loads and drive longer distances than do passenger cars, their tires require higher tear resistance compared with those of passenger cars.

Which choice best describes data from the table that support the idea that truck tires require higher tear resistance than do those of passenger cars?

(A) The tires of a truck contain a lower percentage of synthetic rubber than do those of passenger cars.

(B) Though the tires of passenger cars and trucks, respectively, contain different percentages of process oil, they contain equivalent amounts of steel wire.

(C) The tires of a passenger car contain a lower percentage of steel wire compared with those of trucks.

(D) The tires of a truck contain a greater percentage of natural rubber compared with those of a passenger car.

CONTINUE →

12 ☐ Mark for Review

Miyake events are spikes in radiation that have occurred on Earth six times over the last 10,000 years, the most recent of which was in the first century CE. The dominant explanation for these radiation events has been solar flares. However, recent analysis of the rings inside trees has led to other ideas. The trees' rings can not only reveal how old a tree is, but also whether and when the tree was impacted by certain radioactive substances, so more can be learned about when Miyake spikes occurred and for how long. Some of the spikes in radiation seem to have lasted over a year, far longer than solar flares, which take place more on the order of hours. Scientists theorize that a series of many repeated solar flares is the cause of this anomaly.

Which finding, if true, would most directly undermine the scientists' theory?

(A) References to intense sky events that coincide with the timing of these radiation events are found in ancient writings.

(B) Carbon dating performed on the trees reveals them to be over 2,000 years old.

(C) Evidence is found showing that chlorine isotopes, which are produced in higher quantities during solar events, were present at the same time as these hypothesized radiation events.

(D) The rings of trees less than a thousand years old are analyzed and observed to have similar marks to those in the study.

13 ☐ Mark for Review

The Coinage Act of 1873 revised several policies relating to currency in the United States. Among the changes the act made were the omission of the coinage charge and the relocation of the Bureau of the Mint from Philadelphia to Washington, D.C. However, a provision of the bill that at the time was not as heavily discussed was the abolition of bimetallism, whereby the nation's currency had been based on both gold and silver. The government established a gold standard and so going forward would exchange only gold, and not silver, for currency, thus _____

Which choice most logically completes the text?

(A) ending all trade with nations that still used a silver standard.

(B) diminishing the value of gold in the eyes of both investors and citizens.

(C) encouraging citizens to spend their silver rather than hoard it.

(D) limiting the ability to repay debts for those who primarily had access to silver rather than gold.

CONTINUE →

---

14 ☐ Mark for Review

The evolutionary origin of the house cat has been puzzled over by palaeogeneticists and zooarchaeologists for many years. Traditionally, it was believed that cats were first domesticated in Ancient Egypt around 3,500 years ago. However, a recent analysis of the DNA of 979 individual cats (both wild and domestic) revealed five distinct lineages, four of which aligned perfectly with four subspecies of wildcats: *Felis silvestris silvestris* from Europe, *F. s. bieti* from China, *F. s. ornata* from Central Asia, and *F. s. cafra* from southern Africa. The fifth lineage contained *F. s. lybica*, a subspecies of wildcat from the Middle East, but it also included all of the individual domestic cats that were part of the sample studied, leading the team to conclude that _____

Which choice most logically completes the text?

(A) it is impossible to tell precisely where the modern domestic cat originates.

(B) there are five different geographic regions which are the birthplaces of five different species of domestic cat.

(C) cats were first domesticated in the Middle East and then later brought to Egypt.

(D) modern domestic cats can likely be traced back to the Middle East.

---

15 ☐ Mark for Review

The Devonian period, about 400 million years ago, was a time of many mass extinctions that eliminated an estimated 70% of the Earth's life forms, all of which lived in the ocean. Recently, geologists analyzed ancient lake deposits and observed that there were heightened nutrient levels at the same time that plant life was developing on land. As large-scale nutrient influxes yielded by plant roots have been observed in the modern world to result in algal blooms, which deplete an ocean's oxygen and prove harmful to the life forms living there, the researchers concluded that _____

Which choice most logically completes the text?

(A) all modern species of life in the ocean descend from the species that existed during the Devonian period.

(B) if the Devonian mass extinctions had never occurred, there would be significantly more species of plants on Earth today.

(C) the expansion of plant life on Earth was a direct cause of the Devonian mass extinctions.

(D) the Devonian mass extinctions never would have happened had trees not evolved in the way that they did.

CONTINUE ➡

16 ☐ Mark for Review

Oscar Abreu's paintings feature an abundance of colors, scratches, and shapes appearing almost random in nature. When considered as a whole, though, the paintings have a consistent _____ central figure made of layers of paint and scratches.

Which choice completes the text so that it conforms to the conventions of Standard English?

- (A) feature; a
- (B) feature, and a
- (C) feature. A
- (D) feature, a

17 ☐ Mark for Review

During flash floods, fire ants can form rafts, packing closely together to form a waterproof raft composed of their hydrophobic bodies. The _____ eggs from dangerous floods.

Which choice completes the text so that it conforms to the conventions of Standard English?

- (A) ants' raft protects the group's
- (B) ants raft protects the group's
- (C) ant's raft protects the group's
- (D) ants' raft protects the groups

18 ☐ Mark for Review

In the poem *If in America*, Asian American author Ed Bok Lee writes in the second person point of view _____ the perspective of a Hmong hunter accused of murder.

Which choice completes the text so that it conforms to the conventions of Standard English?

- (A) described
- (B) describes
- (C) to describe
- (D) is describing

19 ☐ Mark for Review

German visual artist Hans-Peter Feldmann's notable artistic works include *All the Clothes of a Woman*, a series of snapshots depicting women's _____ a book presenting images of 11 shoes borrowed from art gallery employees; and *100 Years*, an exhibition of 101 photos of individuals from 8 months to 100 years of age.

Which choice completes the text so that it conforms to the conventions of Standard English?

- (A) apparel; *11 Left Shoes,*
- (B) apparel, *11 Left Shoes,*
- (C) apparel; *11 Left Shoes*
- (D) apparel, *11 Left Shoes:*

CONTINUE ➡

20 ☐ Mark for Review

In 2010, scientist Abdool Karim led the clinical trial CAPRISA 004, a study investigating the effects of Tenefovir gel on the risk of contracting HIV. By interfering with the replication of HIV, _____

Which choice completes the text so that it conforms to the conventions of Standard English?

- (A) the spread of both HIV and other pathogens has been limited by Tenofovir.

- (B) limiting the spread of HIV and other pathogens has been achieved by Tenefovir.

- (C) Tenefovir's ability to limit the spread of HIV and other pathogens is impressive.

- (D) Tenefovir limits the spread of HIV and other pathogens.

21 ☐ Mark for Review

Santiago Ramón y Cajal is a Spanish neuroscientist who is most known for proposing the "neuron theory," which states that the brain consists of individual nerve cells which are separate and distinct. Cajal did not make this discovery _____ he worked closely with his student Rafael Lorente de Nó to perform crucial investigations on the nervous system.

Which choice completes the text so that it conforms to the conventions of Standard English?

- (A) alone; however,

- (B) alone, however;

- (C) alone however

- (D) alone, however,

22 ☐ Mark for Review

Compared to that of gray wolves, _____ the gene coding for black fur in these wolves is thought to be protective against the disease.

Which choice completes the text so that it conforms to the conventions of Standard English?

- (A) black wolves have a fur color that is associated with a greater amount of canine distemper virus (CDV) antibodies:

- (B) black wolves have a greater amount of canine distemper virus (CDV) antibodies, which is associated with the color of their fur:

- (C) black wolves' fur color is associated with a greater amount of canine distemper virus (CDV) antibodies:

- (D) a greater amount of canine distemper virus (CDV) antibodies is associated with the fur color of black wolves:

CONTINUE →

23 🔖 Mark for Review

Some linguists believe that people's spoken language can influence their perceptions of abstract concepts. _____ if a language does not have a word for an abstract concept, the people who exclusively speak the language may struggle to comprehend the abstract concept at all. For example, the Hopi language does not have a word that actually means "time"; therefore, some linguists once posited that people who speak this language may not understand the concept of time itself. However, this view of the Hopi language has been discredited.

Which choice completes the text with the most logical transition?

Ⓐ Specifically,

Ⓑ Thus,

Ⓒ Likewise,

Ⓓ Furthermore,

24 🔖 Mark for Review

Researchers at Curtin University found links between the creation of Earth's continents and when Earth moved through a debris-filled spiral arm of the galaxy. First, they discovered that the Earth's crust production spikes consistently approximately every 200 million years, which is consistent with the cycle of the Earth's motion through the galaxy. _____ they found that known asteroid impacts on Earth coincide with times when the planet would have been located in one of the arms.

Which choice completes the text with the most logical transition?

Ⓐ Second,

Ⓑ Nevertheless,

Ⓒ Therefore,

Ⓓ Similarly,

25 🔖 Mark for Review

Biosphere reserves are protected areas that are designated to provide opportunities to utilize or study certain species of animals and plants. _____ these areas typically contain a species with a unique characteristic or benefit to society. For example, the argan tree is protected in nature reserves in Morocco due to its significant role in the area as a fuel and food source.

Which choice completes the text with the most logical transition?

Ⓐ Thus,

Ⓑ Likewise,

Ⓒ Regardless,

Ⓓ Next,

CONTINUE ➡

---

26 ☐ Mark for Review

While researching a topic, a student has taken the following notes:

- Galicia is a region of Spain with a distinct culture.
- The region is autonomous and has its own government.
- In the 1920s, photographer Ruth Matilda Anderson visited Galicia several times and took black-and-white photographs.
- The photos highlight everyday life among rural residents of Galicia, prior to industrialization and urbanization.
- Anderson focused on documenting the cycle of life.

The student wants to introduce Anderson's photographs to an audience already familiar with Galicia. Which choice most effectively uses relevant information from the notes to accomplish this goal?

Ⓐ A region known as Galicia, which was photographed by Ruth Matilda Anderson, is autonomous with its own government.

Ⓑ Ruth Matilda Anderson's photographs demonstrate everyday life among rural residents of Galicia, prior to industrialization and urbanization.

Ⓒ An interest of Ruth Matilda Anderson's was the cycle of life, which she observed on her visits to Galicia in the 1920s.

Ⓓ Ruth Matilda Anderson's photographs highlight everyday life in Galicia, an autonomous region of Spain with a distinct culture.

---

27 ☐ Mark for Review

While researching a topic, a student has taken the following notes:

- In the mid-19th century, gold and silver prospectors brought burros to the deserts of the US Southwest.
- Burros are donkeys that were originally brought to North America from Europe in the late 15th century.
- Packs of burros were once used in mining, but many of them were left behind when prospectors abandoned the mines.
- Today, the burros' population has multiplied and grows by 20% each year.
- The burros are considered invasive because they consume large amounts of plants and water that are needed by native wildlife, and they have no natural predators.

The student wants to emphasize the increase in the burro population and specify why this increase occurred. Which choice most effectively uses relevant information from the notes to accomplish these goals?

Ⓐ Burros consume large amounts of plants and water that are needed by native wildlife, now that they have been left behind by gold and silver prospectors.

Ⓑ The population of burros in the US Southwest has multiplied and grows by 20% each year, and the burros are now considered invasive.

Ⓒ Burros, donkeys brought to North America from Europe, were once used in mining.

Ⓓ Since prospectors abandoned mines in the US Southwest, the population of burros has multiplied, as the burros have no natural predators.

STOP
If you finish before time is called, you may check your work on this section only.
Do not turn to any other section in the test.

THIS PAGE LEFT INTENTIONALLY BLANK.

SAT Prep Test 1—Math
Module 1

The questions in this section address a number of important math skills.
Use of a calculator is permitted for all questions.

Unless otherwise indicated:

- All variables and expressions represent real numbers.
- Figures provided are drawn to scale.
- All figures lie in a plane.
- The domain of a given function f is the set of all real numbers x for which $f(x)$ is a real number.

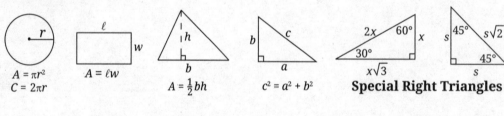

$A = \pi r^2$
$C = 2\pi r$

$A = \ell w$

$A = \frac{1}{2}bh$

$c^2 = a^2 + b^2$

Special Right Triangles

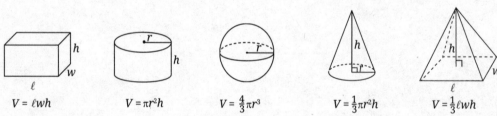

$V = \ell w h$

$V = \pi r^2 h$

$V = \frac{4}{3}\pi r^3$

$V = \frac{1}{3}\pi r^2 h$

$V = \frac{1}{3}\ell w h$

The number of degrees of arc in a circle is 360.
The number of radians of arc in a circle is 2π.
The sum of the measures in degrees of the angles of a triangle is 180.

CONTINUE ➡

_ _

For multiple-choice questions, solve each problem, choose the correct answer from the choices provided, and then fill in the circle with the answer letter. Enter only one answer for each question. You will not get credit for questions with more than one answer entered, or for questions with no answers entered.

For student-produced response questions, solve each problem and write your answer in the test book as described below.

- Enter your answer into the box provided.
- If you find **more than one correct answer**, enter only one answer.
- Your answer can be up to 5 characters for a **positive** answer and up to 6 characters (including the negative sign) for a **negative** answer.
- If your answer is a **fraction** that is too long (over 5 characters for positive, 6 characters for negative), write the decimal equivalent.
- If your answer is a **decimal** that is too long (over 5 characters for positive, 6 characters for negative), truncate it or round at the fourth digit.
- If your answer is a **mixed number** (such as $3\frac{1}{2}$), write it as an improper fraction (7/2) or its decimal equivalent (3.5).
- Don't enter **symbols** such as a percent sign, comma, or dollar sign in your answer.

CONTINUE ➡

---

1 ☐ Mark for Review

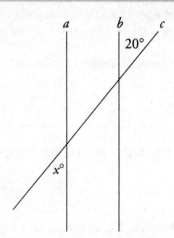

Note: Figure not drawn to scale.

In the figure shown, if line *a* is parallel to line *b*, what is the value of *x*?

(A) 20

(B) 70

(C) 120

(D) 160

2 ☐ Mark for Review

12, 12, 12, 17, 5, 8, 2, 10, 3, 11, 19, 9

The data set shown represents the masses, in grams, of different bacteria samples. What is the mean mass, in grams, of these bacteria samples?

3 ☐ Mark for Review

Which of the following equations has the same solution as $5a - 9 = 36$?

(A) $5a = -324$

(B) $5a = 4$

(C) $5a = 27$

(D) $5a = 45$

4 ☐ Mark for Review

What is the edge length, in inches, of a cube with a volume of 729 cubic inches?

(A) 9

(B) 27

(C) 121.5

(D) 182.25

5 ☐ Mark for Review

If $33\frac{1}{3}\%$ of *x* is 29, what is the value of *x*?

CONTINUE ➡

6 ☐ Mark for Review

The number of short songs, s, and long songs, l, that a singer practices in a day is given by the equation $3s + 4.5l = 108$. If the singer practices 15 short songs on a particular day, how many long songs does the singer practice that day?

(A) 4.5

(B) 14

(C) 67.5

(D) 108

7 ☐ Mark for Review

First Floor

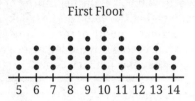

Second Floor

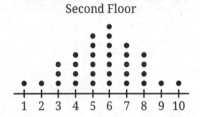

Each of the dot plots shown represents the number of books found on each bookshelf for two floors of a library. What statement best compares the standard deviations of the number of books on each bookshelf for these two floors?

(A) There is not enough information to compare these standard deviations.

(B) The standard deviation of the number of books found on each bookshelf for the first floor is equal to the standard deviation of the number of books found on each bookshelf for the second floor.

(C) The standard deviation of the number of books found on each bookshelf for the first floor is less than the standard deviation of the number of books found on each bookshelf for the second floor.

(D) The standard deviation of the number of books found on each bookshelf for the first floor is greater than the standard deviation of the number of books found on each bookshelf for the second floor.

CONTINUE

8 ☐ Mark for Review

A truck is worth $60,500 at the beginning of January. A model predicts that the value of the truck, v, will decrease by 12% each month of the coming year. Which equation best represents this model, where t is the number of months after January, for $t \leq 12$?

Ⓐ $v = 0.88(60,500)^t$

Ⓑ $v = 1.12(60,500)^t$

Ⓒ $v = 60,500(0.88)^t$

Ⓓ $v = 60,500(1.12)^t$

9 ☐ Mark for Review

If $9a^2 = 20a + 21$ and $a < 0$, what is the value of a?

Ⓐ -20

Ⓑ -3

Ⓒ $-\dfrac{20}{9}$

Ⓓ $-\dfrac{7}{9}$

10 ☐ Mark for Review

The function $h(x) = 12c^x$ is an exponential function, and c is a positive constant. If $h(5) = 12,288$, what is the value of $h(4)$?

11 ☐ Mark for Review

$$y = -7x - 21$$
$$y = (x + 3)(x - 4)$$

Which of the following is the solution to the given system of equations?

Ⓐ $(0, -3)$

Ⓑ $(-3, 0)$

Ⓒ $(-3, 4)$

Ⓓ $(4, -3)$

CONTINUE →

12 🔖 Mark for Review

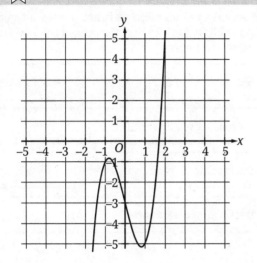

The graph of $y = f(x)$ for the function $f(x) = ax^3 + cx + d$ is shown. In the function, a, c, and d are constants. How many values of x satisfy $f(x) = 0$?

Ⓐ One

Ⓑ Two

Ⓒ Three

Ⓓ Four

13 🔖 Mark for Review

The amount of money in a bank account is represented by $g(m)$ in the equation $g(m) = 35{,}000(1.1)^{\frac{m}{12}}$. The variable m represents the number of months after the initial deposit. How long, in months, does it take for the amount of money in the account to increase by 10%?

⬚

14 🔖 Mark for Review

Triangles ABC and DEF are similar triangles. Angles A and D are right angles, and angle B corresponds to angle E. If $\cos(C) = \frac{23}{265}$, what is the value of $\cos(F)$?

Ⓐ $\frac{23}{265}$

Ⓑ $\frac{264}{265}$

Ⓒ $\frac{265}{264}$

Ⓓ $\frac{265}{23}$

15 🔖 Mark for Review

What is the slope of line a if line a is perpendicular to line b, defined as $9x = 3y - 6$?

⬚

CONTINUE ➡

16 🔖 Mark for Review

The measure of angle AOB in a circle with center O is 85°. What is the measure of the associated minor arc AB, in degrees?

17 🔖 Mark for Review

$$a = \frac{b+1}{c-1}$$

The given equation relates the variables a, b, and c, where a, b, and c are all greater than 0. Which equation expresses $c - 1$ in terms of a and b?

(A) $c - 1 = \frac{a}{b+1}$

(B) $c - 1 = a(b + 1)$

(C) $c - 1 = \frac{b+1}{a}$

(D) $c - 1 = (b + 1) - a$

18 🔖 Mark for Review

For all positive values of x, the function h is defined as $h(x)$ equals 33% of x. The function could be described as which of the following?

(A) Increasing linear

(B) Increasing exponential

(C) Decreasing linear

(D) Decreasing exponential

19 🔖 Mark for Review

Function a is defined by $a(x) = -2x^2 - 16x + 7.5$, and function b is defined by $b(x) = a(x - 7)$. What is the value of x when $b(x)$ is at its maximum?

(A) −11

(B) −4

(C) 3

(D) 7

CONTINUE ▶

20 ⬚ Mark for Review

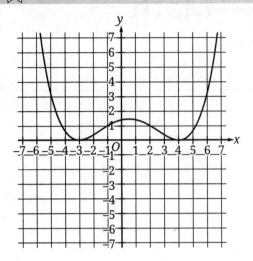

Which of the following equations could represent the graph shown in the xy-plane?

Ⓐ $y = \frac{1}{100}(x-3)(x+4)$

Ⓑ $y = \frac{1}{100}(x+3)(x-4)$

Ⓒ $y = \frac{1}{100}(x+3)^2(x-4)^2$

Ⓓ $y = \frac{1}{100}(x+3)(x-4)^2$

21 ⬚ Mark for Review

A parabola with the equation $y = x^2 - 2x + 16$ is graphed in the xy-plane. A line with the equation $y = -6x - k$, where k is a constant, intersects the parabola at exactly one point. What is the x-coordinate at the point of intersection?

Ⓐ −12

Ⓑ −2

Ⓒ 2

Ⓓ 12

22 ⬚ Mark for Review

Ounces of Flour per Industrial Batch

Cookies	240
Cupcakes	464

A baker has an order to make an equal number of industrial batches of cookies and cupcakes and requires 704 ounces of flour to make one batch each of cookies and cupcakes. The table displays the amounts of flour used, in ounces, for each batch. If the baker needs 4,928 ounces of flour for this order and plans to make equal batches of cupcakes and cookies, how much more flour, in ounces, will be used for cupcakes than for cookies?

Ⓐ 7

Ⓑ 224

Ⓒ 1,568

Ⓓ 4,224

YIELD

Once you've finished (or run out of time for) this section, use the answer key to determine how many questions you got right. If you got fewer than 14 questions right, move on to Module 2—Easier, otherwise move on to Module 2—Harder.

SAT Prep Test 1—Math
Module 2—Easier

DIRECTIONS

The questions in this section address a number of important math skills.
Use of a calculator is permitted for all questions.

NOTES

Unless otherwise indicated:

- All variables and expressions represent real numbers.
- Figures provided are drawn to scale.
- All figures lie in a plane.
- The domain of a given function f is the set of all real numbers x for which $f(x)$ is a real number.

REFERENCE

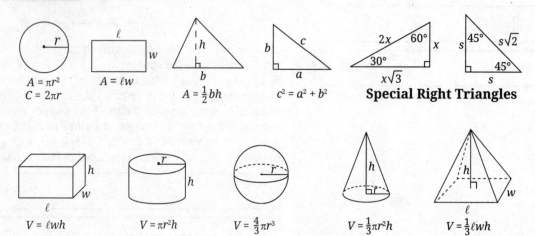

$A = \pi r^2$
$C = 2\pi r$

$A = \ell w$

$A = \frac{1}{2}bh$

$c^2 = a^2 + b^2$

Special Right Triangles

$V = \ell wh$

$V = \pi r^2 h$

$V = \frac{4}{3}\pi r^3$

$V = \frac{1}{3}\pi r^2 h$

$V = \frac{1}{3}\ell wh$

The number of degrees of arc in a circle is 360.
The number of radians of arc in a circle is 2π.
The sum of the measures in degrees of the angles of a triangle is 180.

CONTINUE

For multiple-choice questions, solve each problem, choose the correct answer from the choices provided, and then fill in the circle with the answer letter. Enter only one answer for each question. You will not get credit for questions with more than one answer entered, or for questions with no answers entered.

For student-produced response questions, solve each problem and write your answer in the test book as described below.

- Enter your answer into the box provided.
- If you find **more than one correct answer**, enter only one answer.
- Your answer can be up to 5 characters for a **positive** answer and up to 6 characters (including the negative sign) for a **negative** answer.
- If your answer is a **fraction** that is too long (over 5 characters for positive, 6 characters for negative), write the decimal equivalent.
- If your answer is a **decimal** that is too long (over 5 characters for positive, 6 characters for negative), truncate it or round at the fourth digit.
- If your answer is a **mixed number** (such as $3\frac{1}{2}$), write it as an improper fraction (7/2) or its decimal equivalent (3.5).
- Don't enter **symbols** such as a percent sign, comma, or dollar sign in your answer.

CONTINUE

1 ▢ Mark for Review

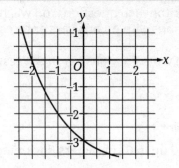

For the graph shown, what is the *x*-intercept?

Ⓐ (–2, 0)

Ⓑ (–3, 0)

Ⓒ (0, –2)

Ⓓ (0, –3)

2 ▢ Mark for Review

In the equation $a - 18 = 252$, what is the value of a?

Ⓐ 14

Ⓑ 234

Ⓒ 270

Ⓓ 4,536

3 ▢ Mark for Review

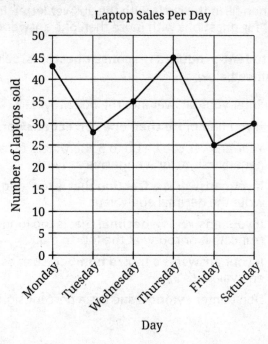

The chart shows laptop sales per day for the second week in October. Which day had the least number of laptops sold?

Ⓐ Monday

Ⓑ Tuesday

Ⓒ Thursday

Ⓓ Friday

4 ▢ Mark for Review

What is the measure of an angle, in <u>degrees</u>, if it measures $\frac{9\pi}{10}$ radians?

CONTINUE ➡

5 ☐ Mark for Review

If a stone weighs 350 centigrams, what is its weight in grams?
(1 gram = 100 centigrams)

(A) 0.35

(B) 3.5

(C) 35

(D) 3,500

6 ☐ Mark for Review

Each day, a certain computer completes 651 simulations of the same length. If the computer performs at a constant rate, which of the following equations represents the number of days, d, it will take the computer to perform s simulations?

(A) $d = \frac{s}{651}$

(B) $d = 651 - s$

(C) $d = 651 + s$

(D) $d = 651s$

7 ☐ Mark for Review

Wendy planted 6 rose bushes, each with the same number of flowers. After deer came into the yard and ate 12 of the flowers, there were 18 flowers remaining. How many flowers were originally on each rose bush?

8 ☐ Mark for Review

$$b = 2a - 17$$

If $a = 5$ in the given equation, what is the value of b?

9 ☐ Mark for Review

Which of the following equations represents the statement 27 is 7 less than 2 times the number y?

(A) $27 = 2y - 7$

(B) $27 = (2)(7)y$

(C) $27 - 7 = 2y$

(D) $27 = 7y - 2$

10 ☐ Mark for Review

For the equation $|30 - y| = 16$, what is one possible value of y?

CONTINUE

11 ☐ Mark for Review

Which of the following expressions is equivalent to $(y^2 - 5y + 10) + (3y^2 + 2y + 3)$?

- (A) $3y^2 - 3y + 13$
- (B) $3y^2 + 7y + 10$
- (C) $4y^2 - 3y + 13$
- (D) $4y^2 - 7y + 13$

12 ☐ Mark for Review

$$7y^2 - 14y$$

Which of the following expressions is equivalent to the given expression?

- (A) $y(7y - 2)$
- (B) $7y(y - 2)$
- (C) $14y(7y - 1)$
- (D) $y^2(7y - 14)$

13 ☐ Mark for Review

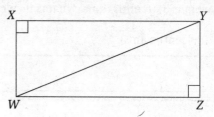

Note: Figure not drawn to scale.

In rectangle $WXYZ$, $WY = 25$ and $WX = 13$. Which expression represents the length of side XY?

- (A) $\sqrt{25 - 13}$
- (B) $25 - 13$
- (C) $\sqrt{(25)(13)}$
- (D) $\sqrt{25^2 - 13^2}$

14 ☐ Mark for Review

$$y = 3x$$
$$x - y = 14$$

For the given system of equations, what is the solution (x, y)?

- (A) $(-8, -24)$
- (B) $(-7, -21)$
- (C) $(-6, -18)$
- (D) $(-5, -15)$

CONTINUE

15 🔖 Mark for Review

x	−2	0	2	4
$g(x)$	27	17	7	−3

The table shows four values of x and their corresponding values of $g(x)$. If $g(x)$ is a linear function, which of the following equations defines $g(x)$?

Ⓐ $g(x) = -17x - 7$

Ⓑ $g(x) = -10x + 17$

Ⓒ $g(x) = -5x + 17$

Ⓓ $g(x) = -2x + 27$

16 🔖 Mark for Review

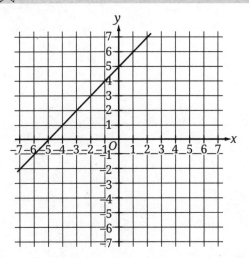

Which of the following could be the equation of the graph shown?

Ⓐ $y = -\dfrac{1}{2}x + 5$

Ⓑ $y = -x + 5$

Ⓒ $y = \dfrac{1}{2}x + 5$

Ⓓ $y = x + 5$

17 🔖 Mark for Review

$$q(x) = \frac{1}{9}x^4$$

The function q is defined by the given equation. For what value of x does $q(x) = 9$?

Ⓐ $\dfrac{1}{9}$

Ⓑ 3

Ⓒ $\dfrac{81}{4}$

Ⓓ 81

18 🔖 Mark for Review

What is the area, in square inches, of a square with a side length of 14 inches?

CONTINUE ➤

---

19 ☐ Mark for Review

In order to make enough french fries for one week at an amusement park, a fry cook needs to have at least 2,500 pounds of potatoes. He already has 260 pounds of potatoes in the kitchen and is expecting more sacks of potatoes to be delivered. If each sack of potatoes in the delivery contains 15 pounds of potatoes, which of the following is the minimum number of sacks of potatoes the fry cook needs in order to make enough french fries for the week?

Ⓐ 149

Ⓑ 150

Ⓒ 166

Ⓓ 167

20 ☐ Mark for Review

$$6x - 11y = 242$$

What is the y-intercept of the line when the given equation is graphed in the xy-plane?

Ⓐ (0, −22)

Ⓑ (0, −11)

Ⓒ (0, 11)

Ⓓ (0, 22)

CONTINUE

21 ☐ Mark for Review

In triangles PQR and STU, the measures of angles P and S are each $13°$, and the measures of angles Q and T are each $130°$. If sides PQ and ST have the same length, which additional piece of information is sufficient to prove that triangle PQR is congruent to triangle STU?

(A) No additional information is needed.

(B) The measure of angle R

(C) The length of side ST

(D) The lengths of sides QR and TU

22 ☐ Mark for Review

A book that is 280 pages long is divided into two sections, one with p pages and the other with q pages. If the number of pages in the section with p pages is 8 less than 3 times the number of pages in the section with q pages, how many pages are in the section with p pages?

(A) 91

(B) 96

(C) 182

(D) 208

STOP
If you finish before time is called, you may check your work on this section only.
Do not turn to any other section in the test.

SAT Prep Test 1—Math
Module 2—Harder

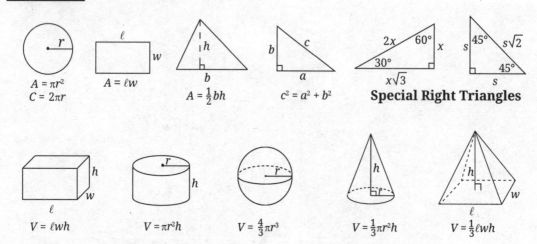

$A = \pi r^2$
$C = 2\pi r$

$A = \ell w$

$A = \frac{1}{2}bh$

$c^2 = a^2 + b^2$

Special Right Triangles

$V = \ell wh$

$V = \pi r^2 h$

$V = \frac{4}{3}\pi r^3$

$V = \frac{1}{3}\pi r^2 h$

$V = \frac{1}{3}\ell wh$

The number of degrees of arc in a circle is 360.
The number of radians of arc in a circle is 2π.
The sum of the measures in degrees of the angles of a triangle is 180.

CONTINUE

For **multiple-choice questions,** solve each problem, choose the correct answer from the choices provided, and then fill in the circle with the answer letter. Enter only one answer for each question. You will not get credit for questions with more than one answer entered, or for questions with no answers entered.

For **student-produced response questions,** solve each problem and write your answer in the test book as described below.

- Enter your answer into the box provided.
- If you find **more than one correct answer**, enter only one answer.
- Your answer can be up to 5 characters for a **positive** answer and up to 6 characters (including the negative sign) for a **negative** answer.
- If your answer is a **fraction** that is too long (over 5 characters for positive, 6 characters for negative), write the decimal equivalent.
- If your answer is a **decimal** that is too long (over 5 characters for positive, 6 characters for negative), truncate it or round at the fourth digit.
- If your answer is a **mixed number** (such as $3\frac{1}{2}$), write it as an improper fraction (7/2) or its decimal equivalent (3.5).
- Don't enter **symbols** such as a percent sign, comma, or dollar sign in your answer.

CONTINUE

---

1 ⬚ Mark for Review

How many solutions does the equation $2z + 8 = 2z - 4$ have?

Ⓐ Exactly one

Ⓑ Exactly two

Ⓒ Infinitely many

Ⓓ Zero

2 ⬚ Mark for Review

$$a + 5b = 30$$
$$-5b = 40$$

What is the value of a if (a, b) is the solution to the given system of equations?

Ⓐ 5

Ⓑ 10

Ⓒ 70

Ⓓ 170

3 ⬚ Mark for Review

Which of the following is equivalent to the expression $-8y^4 + 12y^4$?

Ⓐ $4y^4$

Ⓑ $20y^4$

Ⓒ $4y^8$

Ⓓ $20y^8$

4 ⬚ Mark for Review

Sophia was laying down mulch to fill garden beds of equal area. The amount of mulch, in cubic feet, Sophia had remaining after filling x garden beds can be estimated using the function $f(x) = -75x + 500$. In this context, which of the following statements is the best interpretation of the slope of the graph of $y = f(x)$ in the xy-plane?

Ⓐ Sophia had approximately 500 cubic feet of mulch when she started filling the garden beds.

Ⓑ Sophia used approximately 75 cubic feet of mulch for each garden bed.

Ⓒ Sophia had approximately 75 cubic feet of mulch when she started filling the garden beds.

Ⓓ Sophia used approximately 500 cubic feet of mulch for each garden bed.

5 ⬚ Mark for Review

An analysis of ticket sales for an opera showed that 6 times as many people attended the performance at night as attended the performance during the day. The analysis also showed that 2,500 more people attended the performance at night than attended the performance during the day. Based on the analysis, how many people attended the performance of the opera during the day if each person only attended one performance?

Ⓐ 500

Ⓑ 2,500

Ⓒ 3,000

Ⓓ 4,000

CONTINUE ▶

6 ☐ Mark for Review

$$y \geq x - 9$$
$$y \leq -3x - 5$$

In the *xy*-plane, which ordered pair (*x, y*) is a solution to the given system of inequalities?

(A) (−2, −4)

(B) (−2, 4)

(C) (2, −4)

(D) (2, 4)

7 ☐ Mark for Review

A right triangle has a hypotenuse with a length of 14 inches and a leg with a length of 8 inches. What is the value of integer *a* if the other leg of the triangle has a length of $2\sqrt{a}$ inches?

☐

8 ☐ Mark for Review

What is the measure of an angle, in <u>degrees</u>, if it measures $\frac{9\pi}{10}$ radians?

☐

9 ☐ Mark for Review

Triangles *ABC* and *DEF* are similar to each other, and *A*, *B*, and *C* correspond to *D*, *E*, and *F*, respectively. Angle *A* is a right angle, angle *E* measures 35°, and the length of $\overline{AB}$ is 15. What is the measure of angle *B*?

(A) 15°

(B) 35°

(C) 55°

(D) 90°

CONTINUE ➜

10 ⌷ Mark for Review

Value	Frequency in data set O	Frequency in data set P
15	11	1
18	9	3
21	7	7
24	3	9
27	1	11

Two data sets, O and P, are shown in the table. Each data set consists of 31 values, and the table shows the frequencies of the values for each data set. Which of the following best relates the medians of data set O and data set P?

(A) There is not enough information to compare the medians of data set O and data set P.

(B) The median of data set O is greater than the median of data set P.

(C) The median of data set O is less than the median of data set P.

(D) The median of data set O is equal to the median of data set P.

11 ⌷ Mark for Review

What is the product of the solutions to the equation $-4a(a - 3) = a(2a - 11) - 18$?

____

12 ⌷ Mark for Review

Zoe bought 46 jerseys for a youth soccer league. She packed the jerseys in a large boxes and b small boxes to store until the next season. This situation can be represented by the equation $7a + 6b = 46$. In this context, which of the following statements best describes the meaning of the number 7?

(A) The total number of jerseys packed in large boxes

(B) The total number of jerseys packed in small boxes

(C) The number of jerseys packed in each small box

(D) The number of jerseys packed in each large box

13 ⌷ Mark for Review

A line is graphed in the xy-plane that contains the points $(c, -14)$ and $(c + 9, -41)$, where c is a constant. If the y-intercept of the line is $(c + 2, k)$, what is the value of the constant k?

____

CONTINUE

14 ☐ Mark for Review

Max throws a Frisbee to his dog. When $0 \leq x \leq 10$, the Frisbee's height above the ground $g(x)$, in feet, x seconds after Max threw it, can be represented by the function $g(x) = -\frac{1}{2}(x - 4.9)^2 + 12$. In the xy-plane, which of the following statements is the best interpretation of the vertex of the graph of $g(x)$?

(A) The Frisbee was at a height of 4.9 feet above the ground when it was thrown.

(B) The Frisbee was at a height of 12 feet above the ground when it was thrown.

(C) The Frisbee was at a maximum height of 12 feet above the ground.

(D) The Frisbee was at a maximum height of 4.9 feet above the ground.

15 ☐ Mark for Review

The profit, in dollars, for selling a certain item can be represented by the function $P(x) = 50(x - 2.25) + 20$, where x is the number of items sold and $x \geq 3$. By what amount will the profit decrease if 3 fewer items are sold?

(A) $37.50

(B) $57.50

(C) $130.00

(D) $150.00

16 ☐ Mark for Review

$$6x - 11y = 242$$

What is the y-intercept of the line when the given equation is graphed in the xy-plane?

(A) (0, –22)

(B) (0, –11)

(C) (0, 11)

(D) (0, 22)

17 ☐ Mark for Review

A typical business suit requires 31.6 square feet of fabric. What is the area, in <u>square inches</u>, of this amount of fabric? (1 foot = 12 inches)

(A) 5.62

(B) 67.46

(C) 379.2

(D) 4,550.4

18 ☐ Mark for Review

$$3x^3 - 57x^2 + 252x$$

Two of the factors of the given expression are $(x + p)$ and $(x + q)$, where p and q are constants and $p < q$. What is the value of q?

CONTINUE

19 ☐ Mark for Review

$$27x = 39y + \frac{1}{4}$$
$$78y - 34x = 20x - b$$

When the given system of linear equations is graphed in the xy-plane, there are an infinite number of solutions. What is the value of the constant b?

---

20 ☐ Mark for Review

There are b backpackers on a trip, and one pallet of meals will provide the group with 57 meals. If each backpacker will eat 3 meals, which of the following represents the total number of pallets of meals, p, needed for the trip?

Ⓐ $p = \dfrac{b}{57}$

Ⓑ $p = \dfrac{b}{19}$

Ⓒ $p = 57b$

Ⓓ $p = 171b$

---

21 ☐ Mark for Review

In the function $f(x) = ax^2 - 6x + c$, a and c are constants. When graphed in the xy-plane, function f has a minimum value at (h, k) and a positive y-intercept. If $f(2) = f(18)$, which of the following must be true?

  I. $0 < a < 1$
  II. $c > 0$

Ⓐ I only

Ⓑ II only

Ⓒ I and II

Ⓓ Neither I nor II

---

22 ☐ Mark for Review

Which of the following represents a solution to the equation $\dfrac{k^2}{\sqrt{x^2 + k^2}} = 12 - \dfrac{x^2}{\sqrt{x^2 + k^2}}$, where x is a variable and k is a constant greater than 0?

Ⓐ $-k$

Ⓑ $\sqrt{12^2 - k^2}$

Ⓒ $\sqrt{k^2 + 12^2}$

Ⓓ $12^2 - k^2$

STOP
If you finish before time is called, you may check your work on this section only.
Do not turn to any other section in the test.

Chapter 2
Practice Test 1:
Answers and
Explanations

PRACTICE TEST 1: MULTIPLE-CHOICE ANSWER KEY

Reading and Writing				Math		
Module 1	Module 2 (Easier)	Module 2 (Harder)		Module 1	Module 2 (Easier)	Module 2 (Harder)
1. D	1. A	1. A		1. A	1. A	1. D
2. B	2. D	2. D		2. 10	2. C	2. C
3. C	3. B	3. B		3. D	3. D	3. A
4. D	4. C	4. C		4. A	4. 162	4. B
5. B	5. C	5. A		5. 87	5. B	5. A
6. C	6. D	6. D		6. B	6. A	6. A
7. D	7. B	7. B		7. D	7. 5	7. 33
8. C	8. A	8. D		8. C	8. −7	8. 162
9. C	9. D	9. D		9. D	9. A	9. B
10. A	10. D	10. C		10. 3072	10. 14 or 46	10. C
11. A	11. B	11. D		11. B	11. C	11. −3
12. A	12. C	12. D		12. A	12. B	12. D
13. D	13. A	13. D		13. 12	13. D	13. −20
14. D	14. C	14. D		14. A	14. B	14. C
15. A	15. B	15. C		15. $-\dfrac{1}{3}$	15. C	15. D
16. B	16. B	16. D		16. 85	16. D	16. A
17. A	17. B	17. A		17. C	17. B	17. D
18. C	18. C	18. C		18. A	18. 196	18. −7
19. D	19. D	19. A		19. C	19. B	19. $\dfrac{1}{2}$ or 0.5
20. B	20. B	20. D		20. D	20. A	20. B
21. D	21. A	21. B		21. B	21. A	21. C
22. A	22. D	22. C		22. C	22. D	22. B
23. C	23. C	23. A				
24. B	24. D	24. A				
25. B	25. B	25. A				
26. B	26. B	26. B				
27. B	27. A	27. D				

PRACTICE TEST 1—READING AND WRITING EXPLANATIONS

Module 1

1. **D** This is a Vocabulary question, as it asks for *the most logical and precise word or phrase*. Read the text and highlight what can help to fill in the blank, which describes what Arkeketa *uses* to *help her tribe*. Arkeketa is a *lawyer*, so she must have used her *legal* "skill" to help the tribe. Write "skill" in the annotation box and use Process of Elimination.

   - (A) is wrong because *proceedings* means "events."

   - (B) is wrong because *incentives* means "perks."

   - (C) is wrong because *monopoly* means "lack of competition."

   - (D) is correct because *prowess* matches with "skill."

2. **B** This is a Vocabulary question, as it asks for *the most logical and precise word or phrase*. Read the text and highlight what can help to fill in the blank, which describes the *hieroglyphs*. The blank is followed by a colon, which indicates that the second part of the sentence will elaborate on the first. It states that *linguists could finally…understand the meaning* and makes a time-change contrast with the first part of the sentence; therefore, prior to this analysis, the hieroglyphs were "not understood." Write "not understood" in the annotation box and use Process of Elimination.

   - (A) is wrong because *completed* doesn't match with "not understood."

   - (B) is correct because *incomprehensible* means "unable to be understood."

   - (C) and (D) are wrong because neither *significant* nor *responsible* matches with "not understood."

3. **C** This is a Vocabulary question, as it asks for *the most logical and precise word or phrase*. Read the text and highlight what can help to fill in the blank, which describes how *evidence* relates to the claim. Evidence can primarily support or disprove a claim, so look for the direction the text is going. The first part of the sentence describes two theories, and then the sentence says *unfortunately* and mentions *little evidence*. This suggests that the blank should be something like "support"—there's little evidence to support either theory. Write "support" in the annotation box and use Process of Elimination.

   - (A) is wrong because *invoke* means "call on."

   - (B) is wrong because *necessitate* is too strong to match "support."

   - (C) is correct because *corroborate* means "support."

   - (D) is wrong because *withdraw* is the opposite of "support."

4.   **D**   This is a Vocabulary question, as it asks what a word *most nearly means*. Read the text and highlight what can help to understand the underlined word. The previous line from Mrs. Pearce states that the girl's *personal cleanliness* is important. This line begins with *I mean*, so it elaborates on the previous point by stating that the girl should *not* be *slovenly*. If personal cleanliness is important, then the girl should not be "unclean." Write "unclean" in the annotation box and use Process of Elimination.

   • (A) and (B) are wrong because they are both positive words but "unclean" is negative.

   • (C) is wrong because *informal* does not necessarily imply being "unclean."

   • (D) is correct because *unkempt* matches with "unclean."

5.   **B**   This is a Purpose question, as it asks for the *overall structure*. Read the text and highlight what can help to understand the structure. The text describes the *pictures* in *Ivan's imagination* of what his life would be like if he won the lottery, so write "describe Ivan's fantasies" in the annotation box and use Process of Elimination.

   • (A) is wrong because *eating well* happens in Ivan's imagination, not in real life.

   • (B) is correct because it matches the annotation.

   • (C) is wrong because the text doesn't reveal whether Ivan has actually won or not.

   • (D) is wrong because the text is about Ivan's excitement, not that of his family.

6.   **C**   This is a Purpose question, as it asks for the *main purpose*. Read the text and highlight what can help to understand the overall purpose. The poem asks two questions about why the *mountains* and *cliffs* are more appealing to look at than the landscapes that are *near*. Then it answers the questions by stating that *distance lends enchantment to the view*, so write "explain that far things are more appealing to look at" in the annotation box and use Process of Elimination.

   • (A) is wrong because *bright or dim lighting* isn't the focus of the text.

   • (B) is wrong because the text doesn't describe *depression* or *elation*.

   • (C) is correct because it matches the annotation.

   • (D) is wrong because the text doesn't discuss *the way individuals present themselves*.

7.   **D**   This is a Purpose question, as it asks for the *function* of a part of the text. Read the text and highlight what can help to understand the function of the underlined text. The text describes a place *where the forest fires have sped* and states in the underlined portion that in this place a *flower* still lives and *hides the scars* from the fire. Then the author connects the nature scenario to human life by stating that *life revives* even after *grief* and *pain*. Write "flower survives after fires" in the annotation box and use Process of Elimination.

   • (A) is wrong because the flower is described as resilient rather than precarious.

   • (B) is wrong because the underlined portion describes the flower, not the forest.

- (C) is wrong because *detachment* and *overwhelming forces of nature* aren't supported by the text.

- (D) is correct because it matches the annotation, as *adversity* means suffering or challenges.

8. **C** This is a Purpose question, as it asks for the *main purpose*. Read the text and highlight what can help to understand the overall purpose. The text states that throughout the day *The Redbreast sings alone* and describes its song as *sad* and *sorrowing*. Then the author states that on another day the bird's *song is gay* because *a listening bird is near*, and the author states that those who *sorrow* should take a lesson from the bird. Write "sad alone, happy with others" in the annotation box and use Process of Elimination.

    - (A) is wrong because the poem only describes one bird's song.

    - (B) is wrong because the time of day is mentioned only to show that the sad song lasted all day.

    - (C) is correct because it matches the annotation.

    - (D) is wrong because the author doesn't mention *watching birds*.

9. **C** This is a Main Idea question, as it asks for the *main idea*. Read and highlight the main phrases or lines that the other sentences seem to support. The text begins with a contrast between programs that require *complete abstinence* and *harm reduction* and then criticizes the *abstinence-only programs* for not being adaptable to individuals' needs, so write "harm reduction programs good" in the annotation box and use Process of Elimination.

    - (A) is wrong because the text says that *multiple paths to recovery* could be considered depending on the individual, not that an individual typically uses multiple methods.

    - (B) is wrong because it's too strong; the text doesn't say that harm reduction is *proven more effective*.

    - (C) is correct because it matches the annotation.

    - (D) is wrong because the text doesn't say that experts disagree with *the end goal* of the programs.

10. **A** This is a Main Idea question, as it asks for the *main idea*. Read and highlight the main phrases or lines that the other sentences seem to support. The text states that Sam slams the door and that he was *in a fit of temper*. Then it mentions that the promise of *a dismal day* did not *lessen* his bad mood, so write "Sam in bad mood and weather bad" in the annotation box and use Process of Elimination.

    - (A) is correct because it matches the annotation.

    - (B) is wrong because the text never states why Sam is in a bad mood to begin with.

    - (C) is wrong because the text only describes the events of one part of one morning, not Sam's personality in general.

    - (D) is wrong because there is no evidence that Sam's response is *matter-of-fact*.

11.   **A**   This is a Charts question, as it asks for *data from the table*. The table charts the number of words recalled in novel and familiar environments for different age groups. Read the text and highlight the *claim*, which is that *people perform better under familiar environments than novel environments*. Eliminate any answer that doesn't *support* this conclusion or is inconsistent with the data on the graph.

   •   (A) is correct because it demonstrates the higher number of words recalled in the familiar rather than the novel environment.

   •   (B), (C), and (D) are wrong because they don't relate to the familiar environment resulting in more words recalled compared with the novel environment.

12.   **A**   This is a Charts question, as it asks for *data from the graph*. The graph charts the heights of the bushes exposed to different light colors over time. Read the text and highlight the *conclusion*, which is that *the increased height of rose bushes was influenced solely by red light and that blue light was not responsible for any growth*. Eliminate any answer that doesn't *weaken* this conclusion or is inconsistent with the data on the graph.

   •   (A) is correct because it weakens the conclusion by explaining that the plant with blue light *also substantially grew*, so the cause of the growth was not *solely* due to the red light.

   •   (B) is wrong because it supports, rather than weakens, the conclusion.

   •   (C) is wrong because it doesn't relate to whether blue or red light caused growth.

   •   (D) is wrong because it doesn't relate to growth at all.

13.   **D**   This is a Claims question, as it asks for a *quotation* to *illustrate the claim*. Read the text and highlight the claim, which is that *Longfellow uses natural imagery to suggest that despite his emotional struggle there is still cause for hope*. Eliminate answers that don't *illustrate* this idea.

   •   (A) is wrong because they relate to *emotional struggle* but not *hope*.

   •   (B) is wrong because it doesn't relate to *emotional struggle* or *hope*.

   •   (C) is wrong because it is negative toward *hopes*, rather than believing in hope.

   •   (D) is correct because the *clouds* could refer to the *emotional struggle* and the *sun still shining* could refer to *cause for hope*.

14.   **D**   This is a Conclusions question, as it asks for the choice that *most logically completes the text*. Read the text and highlight the main ideas. The text states that *a key tenet in a physician-patient relationship is honesty* but then states that *placebos*, which have *no medicinal effect* are commonly prescribed. Then, the text offers a potential explanation, so the answer should explain how honesty is maintained while placebos are prescribed. Eliminate any answer that states a conclusion that isn't supported by the text.

   •   (A) and (C) are wrong because they don't relate to honesty, which is part of what the example is explaining.

- (B) is wrong because it doesn't explain how honesty and prescribing placebos can coexist, as it states that the honest relationship is harmed.

- (D) is correct because it shows that the doctor is able to prescribe a placebo but the relationship is still honest.

15. **A** In this Rules question, punctuation is changing in the answer choices. The answers contain commas in several places, so use Process of Elimination to eliminate any answers that don't use commas correctly.

- (A) is correct because no punctuation is needed.

- (B) is wrong because there shouldn't be commas before and after *and*.

- (C) and (D) are wrong because a comma should never follow a preposition (*of*).

16. **B** In this Rules question, punctuation is changing in the answer choices. The word *artists* is a title for Turner and Monet, so no punctuation should be used. Eliminate answers that use punctuation.

- (A) is wrong because a comma isn't used with the word *and* to separate a list of only two items.

- (B) is correct because titles before names have no punctuation.

- (C) and (D) are wrong because a comma isn't used after a title.

17. **A** In this Rules question, punctuation is changing in the answer choices. Look for independent clauses. The first part of the sentence says *A team of researchers at Yunnan University School of Agriculture in Kunming, China, assessed the performance of a hybrid of two rice species*, which is an independent clause. The second part of the sentence says *Oryza sativa, which is domesticated Asian rice, and Oryza longistaminata, which is undomesticated African rice*, which is a list of the two rice species. Eliminate any option that doesn't correctly connect the independent clause to the list.

- (A) is correct because a colon is used when the second part explains the first, such as by providing a list of things.

- (B) is wrong because some punctuation is needed to separate the independent clause from the list.

- (C) is wrong because a semicolon can only connect two independent clauses, and the list isn't an independent clause.

- (D) is wrong because the period makes the list its own sentence, which doesn't work because it's not an independent clause.

18.   **C**   In this Rules question, punctuation with a transition is changing in the answer choices. Look for independent clauses. The first part of the sentence says *In 2015, Romero utilized underwater photography to portray a moment from her tribe's history*, which is an independent clause. The second part of the sentence says *in 2017, Romero photographed Puebloans juxtaposed with TVs displaying traditional media depictions of Native Americans*, which is also an independent clause. Eliminate any answer that can't correctly connect two independent clauses.

- (A), (B), and (D) are wrong because two independent clauses can only be connected with a comma if there is a coordinating conjunction after the comma, and *then* isn't a coordinating conjunction.

- (C) is correct because a semicolon can connect two independent clauses.

19.   **D**   In this Rules question, the subjects of the answers are changing, which suggests it may be testing modifiers. Look for and highlight a modifying phrase: *When writing about Antiguan-American novelist Jamaica Kincaid's books*. Whoever is *writing* needs to come immediately after the comma. Eliminate any answer that doesn't start with someone who can write.

- (A) is wrong because *the examination* can't be *writing*.

- (B) is wrong because someone who can write doesn't come at the beginning.

- (C) is wrong because *Kincaid's exploration* can't be *writing*.

- (D) is correct because *literary critics* can be *writing*.

20.   **B**   In this Rules question, commas and semicolons are changing in the answer choices. The sentence already contains a semicolon near the end, and the part after it is not an independent clause, which suggests that the sentence contains a list separated by semicolons. Use the third example to determine the structure of each item: Creation by Johnson, Comma, Name, Comma, Year. Make an annotation of this pattern and eliminate any answer that doesn't follow it.

- (A) is wrong because it doesn't have a semicolon to separate the first item from the second.

- (B) is correct because it follows the pattern of the third item.

- (C) and (D) are wrong because they don't have a comma before the year.

21.   **D**   This is a transition question, so highlight ideas that relate to each other. The first sentence says *The films of Israeli cinematographer Yael Bartana often touch on historical themes*, and this sentence says *Bartana looks to the future*. These ideas disagree, so an opposite-direction transition is needed. Make an annotation that says "disagree." Eliminate any answer that doesn't match.

- (A), (B), and (C) are wrong because they are same-direction transitions.

- (D) is correct because *still* is opposite-direction.

22. **A** This is a Rhetorical Synthesis question, so highlight the goal(s) stated in the question: *emphasize the role infrastructure played in the achievement of a goal*. Eliminate any answer that doesn't fulfill this purpose.

- (A) is correct because it shows how different types of *infrastructure* helped to *increase the number of visitors by 1966*, and the second bullet point states that expanding the number of visitors was the NPS's goal.

- (B) is wrong because it includes a *goal* but doesn't relate it to *infrastructure*.

- (C) is wrong because it mentions *infrastructure* but doesn't relate it to a *goal*.

- (D) is wrong because it doesn't mention *infrastructure* or a *goal*.

23. **C** This is a Rhetorical Synthesis question, so highlight the goal(s) stated in the question: *compare the elevations of the two mountain passes*. Eliminate any answer that doesn't fulfill this purpose.

- (A) is wrong because it mentions *two mountain passes* but doesn't compare their *elevations*.

- (B) and (D) are wrong because each mentions the elevation of only one mountain pass.

- (C) is correct because it includes the *elevations* of both *mountain passes*.

24. **B** This is a Rhetorical Synthesis question, so highlight the goal(s) stated in the question: *emphasize a similarity between the two operas*. Eliminate any answer that doesn't fulfill this purpose.

- (A) and (D) are wrong because each emphasizes a difference *between the two operas*.

- (B) is correct because it describes a *similarity between the two operas*.

- (C) is wrong because it says the *operas differ* instead of emphasizing a *similarity*.

25. **B** This is a Rhetorical Synthesis question, so highlight the goal(s) stated in the question: *specify the reason the InSight mission went to Mars*. Eliminate any answer that doesn't fulfill this purpose.

- (A) is wrong because it describes something that was observed by the *InSight mission* but doesn't specify that this was the purpose of the mission.

- (B) is correct because it specifies why the Mars lander was sent to Mars: *to measure seismic activity*.

- (C) is wrong because it doesn't say why the Mars lander was sent to Mars.

- (D) is wrong because it specifies why *Viking 2 was sent to Mars* but doesn't specify why the *InSight mission* was sent to Mars.

26. **B** This is a Rhetorical Synthesis question, so highlight the goal(s) stated in the question: *emphasize a difference between the two books*. Eliminate any answer that doesn't fulfill this purpose.

- (A) and (C) are wrong because each describes a similarity between *the two books*.

- (B) is correct because it describes the different genres of *the two books*.

- (D) is wrong because it mentions the two books but doesn't provide a *difference* between them.

27. **B** This is a Rhetorical Synthesis question, so highlight the goal(s) stated in the question: *emphasize the recent sighting's significance*. Eliminate any answer that doesn't fulfill this purpose.

- (A), (C), and (D) are wrong because they don't explain why the sighting is significant.

- (B) is correct because it explains why the sighting is significant, stating that it is *rare* and gives scientists *reason to believe* a change in the whale population.

Module 2 – Easier

1. **A** This is a Vocabulary question, as it asks for *the most logical and precise word or phrase*. Read the text and highlight what can help to fill in the blank, which describes what the sparrow was believed to do to *insects*. The second part of the sentence uses the word *unfortunately* and states that *the bird's diet only includes insects during the first couple weeks of life*. This suggests that the belief about the sparrow was incorrect, and given that it was being used against moths, it must have been believed to "eat" insects. Write "eat" in the annotation box and use Process of Elimination.

- (A) is correct because *consume* can mean "eat."

- (B) is wrong because *evolve* means "change."

- (C) is wrong because *evacuate* means "leave."

- (D) is wrong because *rescue* doesn't match with "eat."

2. **D** This is a Vocabulary question, as it asks for *the most logical and precise word or phrase*. Read the text and highlight what can help to fill in the blank, which describes what kind of *poet* Neruda was after the publication of two books. The second sentence says *Being this well-known*, and the word *this* refers back to something that was previously mentioned. Since being well-known wasn't previously mentioned, that must be the meaning of the blank. Write "well-known" in the annotation box and use Process of Elimination.

- (A) is wrong because it's the opposite.

- (B) is wrong because *reserved* means "quiet."

- (C) is wrong because the whole text is positive, not negative.

- (D) is correct because *popular* matches with "well-known."

3.   **B**   This is a Vocabulary question, as it asks for *the most logical and precise word or phrase*. Read the text and highlight what can help to fill in the blank, which describes how this *question* has been treated by scientists. The end of the second sentence says that the new method *may settle this issue*, which suggests that it has been "debated" by scientists. Write "debated" in the annotation box and use Process of Elimination.

   - (A) is wrong because it's the opposite of "debated."

   - (B) is correct because *deliberated* means "debated."

   - (C) is wrong because *assimilated* means "blended in."

   - (D) is wrong because *criticized* doesn't match with "debated."

4.   **C**   This is a Vocabulary question, as it asks for *the most logical and precise word or phrase*. Read the text and highlight what can help to fill in the blank, which describes the relationship between Gyatso's *work* and *his interest in rejuvenating Buddhist symbolic representation*. Since *symbolic representation* matches with art, his work must be "related to" his interest in some way. Write "related to" in the annotation box and use Process of Elimination.

   - (A) and (D) are wrong because they are both negative words, and the blank should be positive.

   - (B) is wrong because the idea that his work is *included in his interest* doesn't provide a clear meaning.

   - (C) is correct because *inspired by* matches with "related to."

5.   **C**   This is a Vocabulary question, as it asks for *the most logical and precise word or phrase*. Read the text and highlight what can help to fill in the blank, which describes the relationship between the *new species* and *other armored dinosaurs*. The sentence says that the new species *walked on two legs and was the size of a dog*, while the previous sentence says that other armored dinosaurs *walked on four legs* and *would grow to the length of a bus*. Thus, the new species is different from other ones. Write "different from" in the annotation box and use Process of Elimination.

   - (A), (B), and (D) are wrong because they are all positive words, and the answer should be a contrasting word.

   - (C) is correct because *contrary to* matches with "different from."

6.   **D**   This is a Vocabulary question, as it asks for *the most logical and precise word or phrase*. Read the text and highlight what can help to fill in the blank, which describes the *finding*. The first sentence, which describes the finding, states that it *has yielded significant results that challenge* a previous *assumption*. Write "significant" in the annotation box and use Process of Elimination.

   - (A) is wrong because *representative* means "similar to others."

   - (B) is wrong because *polarizing* means "controversial."

- (C) is wrong because *eminent* means "high-ranking."

- (D) is correct because *notable* matches with "significant."

7. **B** This is a Vocabulary question, as it asks for *the most logical and precise word or phrase*. Read the text and highlight what can help to fill in the blank, which describes what *farmers are able* to do by *not growing more than is needed*. The first sentence says that in this method the farming *aims to provide solely for the farmer's household*. Write "provide for" in the annotation box and use Process of Elimination.

    - (A) is wrong because *expose* means "reveal."

    - (B) is correct because *sustain* matches with "provide for."

    - (C) is wrong because *imagine* doesn't match with "provide for."

    - (D) is wrong because *deprive* means "take from" or "deny," which is the opposite.

8. **A** This is a Dual Texts question, as it has two texts. The question asks how *the author of Text 2* would respond to *the underlined claim in Text 1*. Start by understanding the claim in Text 1. Text 1 introduces a debate, mentions the old view (Clovis people were the first), then describes evidence for a new view (there were people before the Clovis people). The underlined claim states that the discoveries at two sites support the pre-Clovis theory. Next, look for a similar idea in Text 2 to see how its author feels about this claim. Text 2 begins by referencing the old view but then uses the word *However* and then explains how evidence from *White Sands National Park* supports the pre-Clovis theory, stating that this evidence for the theory is *earlier than any other pre-Clovis site evidence*. Therefore, Text 2's author would "support the claim based on different evidence." Write that in the annotation box and use Process of Elimination.

    - (A) is correct because it matches the annotation.

    - (B) and (C) are wrong because they state that the author wouldn't support the claim.

    - (D) is wrong because *stone tools* are not part of the evidence the author used.

9. **D** This is a Retrieval question, as it says *According to the text*. Read the text and highlight what it says about *Jean Valjean*. The text says *human society had done him nothing but harm* and states that he had never *encountered a friendly word and a kindly glance*. Then, the last sentence refers to his *suffering* and describes his view of life. Eliminate any answer that isn't supported by the text.

    - (A) is wrong because it's the opposite of Valjean's negative view of society.

    - (B) is wrong because *war* is used as a metaphor in the last sentence; the text doesn't say Valjean is a *soldier*.

    - (C) is wrong because his *mother* is mentioned but not stated to be his *closest family member*.

    - (D) is correct because it is supported by several phrases in the text.

10. **D** This is a Claims question, as it asks for a *quotation* to *illustrate the claim*. Read the text and highlight the claim, which is that *Field conveys a sense of lingering curiosity despite the passage of time*. Eliminate answers that don't *illustrate* this idea.

   - (A) and (B) are wrong because they relate to *the passage of time* but not *lingering curiosity*.

   - (C) is wrong because it doesn't relate to *the passage of time* or *lingering curiosity*.

   - (D) is correct because *these long years through* relates to *the passage of time*, and the idea of *waiting and wondering what became of the boy* supports *a sense of lingering curiosity*.

11. **B** This is a Claims question, as it asks for an answer that would *support the researchers' hypothesis*. Read the text and highlight the hypothesis, which is that *shorter flower petals could reduce the parasite transmission*. Eliminate answers that don't *support* this idea.

   - (A) is wrong because it contradicts the hypothesis; the hypothesis states that shorter petals correlate with less parasite transmission.

   - (B) is correct because it matches the hypothesis.

   - (C) and (D) are wrong because they don't mention the length of the petals.

12. **C** This is a Claims question, as it asks for an answer that would *support the student's claim*. Read the text and highlight the claim, which is that *the surreal landscapes presented in Murakami's works create alternate realities that emphasize a sense of existentialism*. Eliminate answers that don't *support* this idea.

   - (A), (B), and (D) are wrong because they don't relate to *alternate realities* or *existentialism*.

   - (C) is correct because *blend of real and imaginary* matches with *alternate realities* and *an exploration into the human condition* matches with *existentialism*.

13. **A** This is a Charts question, as it asks for *data in the graph*. The graph charts the mRNA expression levels of oxidative protective genes in a bacterium with and without a certain gene. Read the text and highlight the *hypothesis*, which is that *a gene sequence called NfiS found in a mutant strain of the bacterium P. stutzeri coded for oxidative protective genes*. Eliminate any answer that doesn't *support* this hypothesis or is inconsistent with the data on the graph.

   - (A) is correct because it's consistent with the hypothesis, as the *With NfiS* bars correlate with higher expression levels of the oxidative protective genes than those of the *Without NfiS* bars.

   - (B) is wrong because the numbers are not consistent with the figure.

   - (C) is wrong because it doesn't relate to the hypothesis in terms of the effect of NfiS.

   - (D) is wrong because the hypothesis is about the effect of NfiS; the text doesn't contrast katA and katB.

14. **C** This is a Conclusions question, as it asks for the choice that *most logically completes the text*. Read the text and highlight the main ideas. The text states that recycling *has a tremendous effect on preserving the environment* but *also has a lasting effect on the social dynamics of communities*. Then it describes survey results showing that young adults knew about the *environmental benefits* but not the community effect. Eliminate any answer that states a conclusion that isn't supported by the text.

  - (A) is wrong because *only* is too strong; nothing about recycling in a household versus another place is mentioned.

  - (B) is wrong because it draws a comparison that isn't supported by the text.

  - (C) is correct because the text emphasizes the *lasting effect on the social dynamics of communities* that young adults aren't aware of.

  - (D) is wrong because *bins* are never mentioned.

15. **B** This is a Conclusions question, as it asks for the choice that *most logically completes the text*. Read the text and highlight the main ideas. The text states that *current vaccines that target influenza become less effective over time due to the mutations…which build resistance to treatment*. Then it describes a new treatment that *did not generate mutations*, so perhaps it could solve this problem. Eliminate any answer that states a conclusion that isn't supported by the text.

  - (A) is wrong because there is no evidence that *other medical conditions* could be treated with this method.

  - (B) is correct because it focuses on the benefit of the new treatment, that it could target a virus without causing resistance.

  - (C) is wrong because no comparison between IgG1 and IgG2 was made.

  - (D) is wrong because the text states that the *mutations* are a bad thing and reduce the effectiveness of vaccines.

16. **B** In this Rules question, verbs are changing in the answer choices, so it's testing consistency with verbs. Find and highlight the subject, *speech*, which is singular, so a singular verb is needed. Write an annotation saying "singular." Eliminate any answer that is not singular.

  - (A), (C), and (D) are wrong because they are plural.

  - (B) is correct because it's singular.

17.   **B**   In this Rules question, verb forms are changing in the answer choices, so it's testing sentence structure. The sentence already contains an independent clause followed by a comma. Thus, the phrase after the comma must be a phrase that describes the *ability*. Eliminate any answer that does not correctly form this phrase.

- (A), (C), and (D) are wrong because the describing phrase should begin with an *-ing* verb.

- (B) is correct because it correctly describes the *ability* as *allowing* something to happen.

18.   **C**   In this Rules question, verbs are changing in the answer choices, so it's testing consistency with verbs. Find and highlight the subject, *is*, which is singular, so a singular verb is needed. All of the answers work with a singular subject, so look for a clue regarding tense. Earlier in the sentence, the present-tense verb *travels* appears, and this part of the sentence begins with *during which time*, so it's the same time as the traveling. Highlight those words and write an annotation that says "present." Eliminate any answer not in present tense.

- (A) is wrong because *is reacting* is in present tense but isn't consistent with *travels*.

- (B) is wrong because it's in past tense.

- (C) is correct because it's in present tense and is consistent with *travels*.

- (D) is wrong because it's in future tense.

19.   **D**   In this Rules question, apostrophes with nouns are changing in the answer choices. Determine whether each word possesses anything. The *fish* possess the *bodies*, but the *bodies* don't possess anything. Eliminate any answer that doesn't match this.

- (A) is wrong because *body* shouldn't be possessive.

- (B) and (C) are wrong because *fish* should have an apostrophe since the sentence describes "their" bodies.

- (D) is correct because *fish's* is possessive and *bodies* is not.

20.   **B**   In this Rules question, verbs are changing in the answer choices, so it's testing consistency with verbs. Find and highlight the subject, *chinuk wawa and its speakers*, which is plural, so a plural verb is needed. Write an annotation saying "plural." Eliminate any answer that isn't plural.

- (A), (C), and (D) are wrong because they are singular.

- (B) is correct because *have been* is plural.

21. **A**   In this Rules question, verb forms are changing in the answer choices, so it's testing sentence structure. The phrase describes how and why the artist painted a certain man. Eliminate any answer that does make the phrase clear and correct.

   • (A) is correct because it states that the artist painted a *Moroccan man…to spotlight people who are not traditionally seen,* which provides a clear and correct meaning.

   • (B), (C), and (D) are wrong because they are all in a "main verb" form, but the sentence already has a main verb, *paints.*

22. **D**   In this Rules question, verbs are changing in the answer choices, so it's testing consistency with verbs. Find and highlight the subject, *the Rogallos,* which is plural, so a plural verb is needed. All of the answers work with a plural subject, so look for a clue regarding tense. The previous sentence uses past tense verbs (*was trying* and *decided*). This sentence describes what *Eventually* happened, but the verb later in the sentence is *would become known,* which suggests that the invention of the flexible wing also happened in the past, so highlight these clues and write an annotation that says "past." Eliminate any answer not in past tense.

   • (A) is wrong because while it is in past tense, it doesn't make it clear that the design was completed, which conflicts with the information later in the sentence.

   • (B) is wrong because while it is in past tense, *had designed* conflicts with the previous sentence, as this is something that came after what happened in that sentence, whereas *had* suggests it came before.

   • (C) is wrong because it's in present tense.

   • (D) is correct because it's in past tense.

23. **C**   In this Rules question, verbs are changing in the answer choices, so it's testing consistency with verbs. Find and highlight the subject, *NAFTA,* which is singular, so a singular verb is needed. All of the answers work with a singular subject, so look for a clue regarding tense. The first part of the sentence says *in 2020,* which indicates past tense is required, so write an annotation that says "past." Eliminate any answer not in past tense.

   • (A) is wrong because it's in future tense.

   • (B) is wrong because it's in present tense.

   • (C) is correct because it's in past tense.

   • (D) is wrong because *has remained* suggests that the agreement continues to today, but the sentence states that it ended in 2020.

24. **D** This is a transition question, so highlight ideas that relate to each other. The preceding sentence says *some methods use heat energy,* and this sentence describes a method that uses heat. These ideas agree, so a same-direction transition is needed. Make an annotation that says "agree." Eliminate any answer that doesn't match.

- (A) and (C) are wrong because they are opposite-direction transitions.

- (B) is wrong because this sentence doesn't indicate something that is similar to something else.

- (D) is correct because this sentence is an example of a method that uses heat energy.

25. **B** This is a transition question, so highlight ideas that relate to each other. The preceding sentence says *Graham was determined to find a more efficient method and spent years testing and perfecting different ways to fix this issue,* and this sentence says *Graham discovered the answer.* These ideas agree, so a same-direction transition is needed. Make an annotation that says "agree." Eliminate any answer that doesn't match.

- (A) and (C) are wrong because this sentence doesn't indicate an additional point.

- (B) is correct because *finally* is same-direction and matches with *years testing and perfecting.*

- (D) is wrong because it is an opposite-direction transition.

26. **B** This is a transition question, so highlight ideas that relate to each other. The first sentence says that Tong's *initial legacy developed from teaching children techniques with a bow and arrow,* and this sentence says *his legacy shifted to his favorite pupil.* These ideas disagree, so an opposite-direction transition is needed. Make an annotation that says "disagree." Eliminate any answer that doesn't match.

- (A), (C), and (D) are wrong because they are same-direction transitions.

- (B) is correct because *however* is opposite-direction.

27. **A** This is a transition question, so highlight ideas that relate to each other. The preceding sentence says *They trained mice to respond to a physical stimulus on the right sides of their bodies by providing a water source as a reward,* and the second sentence says *the mice began to ignore physical stimuli on the left sides of their bodies that didn't come with a reward.* These ideas agree, so a same-direction transition is needed. Make an annotation that says "agree." Eliminate any answer that doesn't match.

- (A) is correct because *as a result* is same-direction and correctly indicates that the response of the mice was a result of the training.

- (B) is wrong because this sentence isn't more specific than the previous one.

- (C) is wrong because it is an opposite-direction transition.

- (D) is wrong because this sentence doesn't indicate a second point.

Module 2 – Harder

1. **A**   This is a Vocabulary question, as it asks for *the most logical and precise word or phrase*. Read the text and highlight what can help to fill in the blank, which describes how the *Attendees* viewed the *performance*. The blank is followed by a colon, which indicates that the second part of the sentence will elaborate on the first. It states that although the audience was large, *many reported feeling a personal connection and a sense of closeness* with the artists. Write "personal" in the annotation box and use Process of Elimination.

   - (A) is correct because *intimate* matches with "personal."

   - (B) is wrong because *obscure* means "not well known."

   - (C) is wrong because *insignificant* doesn't match with "personal."

   - (D) is wrong because *unintelligible* means "not able to be understood."

2. **D**   This is a Vocabulary question, as it asks for *the most logical and precise word or phrase*. Read the text and highlight what can help to fill in the blank, which describes who or what Barton found. The last sentence says *With his help* (referring to Appia) *and their funding*, so the blank refers to the people who funded the organization. Write "funders" in the annotation box and use Process of Elimination.

   - (A) is wrong because *subsidiaries* means "those at a lower level."

   - (B) is wrong because *opponents* compete rather than help.

   - (C) is wrong because *companions* doesn't indicate that they gave money.

   - (D) is correct because *benefactors* are those who give.

3. **B**   This is a Vocabulary question, as it asks for *the most logical and precise word or phrase*. Read the text and highlight what can help to fill in the blank, which describes Mikhail's *feelings about her home country*. The phrase with the blank is followed by a colon, which indicates that the second part of the sentence will elaborate on the first. It describes her *deep love for her birthplace* and then uses the contrast word *but* to state that she *laments the violence and war*. This suggests opposing feelings, so write "mixed" in the annotation box and use Process of Elimination.

   - (A) is wrong because *logical* doesn't match with "mixed."

   - (B) is correct because *ambivalent* means "feeling two different ways."

   - (C) is wrong because *celebratory* is very positive, but the text suggests that her feelings are mixed.

   - (D) are wrong because *monotonous* means "dull."

4. **C** This is a Vocabulary question, as it asks for *the most logical and precise word or phrase*. Read the text and highlight what can help to fill in the blank, which describes what *medical professionals began* to do. The second sentence uses the word *However* to draw a contrast with the first sentence. The first sentence states that iron lungs *were widely used*, so the contrast suggests that doctors stopped using them as much. Therefore, the doctors "questioned" *the usefulness* of the device. Write "question" in the annotation box and use Process of Elimination.

    - (A), (B), and (D) are wrong because they are all positive words, and the answer should be negative.

    - (C) is correct because *scrutinize* matches with "question."

5. **A** This is a Dual Texts question, as it has two texts. The question asks how *Wrangham (Text 2)* would respond to *the "traditional theories"* in Text 1. Start by finding and highlighting the "traditional theories" in Text 1: they *focused on the role of natural selection in the development of cooperative behaviors in all social animals, including humans*. The text goes on to explain that *cooperation emerged as an adaptation* because it *helped animals survive*. Next, look for a similar idea in Text 2 to see how Wrangham feels about these theories. The first sentence includes the phrase *humans, unlike other animals*, which already goes against the traditional theories, as they grouped humans with *all social animals*. Therefore, Wrangham would "disagree—humans developed cooperation differently from other animals." Write that in the annotation box and use Process of Elimination.

    - (A) is correct because it matches the annotation.

    - (B) and (D) are wrong because *natural selection* isn't mentioned in Text 2, so it's not clear how Wrangham feels about the concept.

    - (C) is wrong because Wrangham does agree that cooperation promotes survival: the last sentence says it *helped humans to thrive*.

6. **D** This is a Retrieval question, as it says *According to the text*. Read the text and highlight what it says about *Miss Julie*. The text says that Miss Julie *dressed the little girl*, who *had something about her that enslaved Miss Julie, some mystic and adorable quality that Miss Julie could not name*. Eliminate any answer that isn't supported by the text.

    - (A) is wrong because the text states that the girl's chin was like a kitten's; it doesn't state Miss Julie's preferences regarding kittens.

    - (B) is wrong because the text says that the girl *stood* but doesn't mention Miss Julie wanting to stand.

    - (C) is wrong because the text never states how much Miss Julie likes *dressing little girls*.

    - (D) is correct because it matches what the text says in the last sentence.

7. **B** This is a Retrieval question, as it says *According to the text*. Read the text and highlight what it says about *why* the discovery was *significant*. The text states that the finding *revolutionized our conception of hominins* in that small brains were *thought to imply a less complex brain structure*, but the discovery included a small brain with a complex structure. Eliminate any answer that isn't supported by the text.

    • (A) is wrong because no *precise chronology* is mentioned.

    • (B) is correct because it matches the highlighting.

    • (C) is wrong because the text doesn't say that this is the first similar brain to humans' brains; it's the first one that was so small.

    • (D) is wrong because the discovery relates to the complexity of the small brain, not its size alone.

8. **D** This is a Main Idea question, as it asks for the *main idea*. Read and highlight the main phrases or lines that the other sentences seem to support. The text states that Einstein *proposed the existence of gravitational waves…in 1911* but they *remained unproven until 2016*. Then the text explains how scientists found the proof and ends by saying that this was *the first direct observation of gravitational waves*. Write "Einstein's gravitational waves proven 100 years later" in the annotation box and use Process of Elimination.

    • (A) is wrong because the text doesn't state that the scientists' method was *new*.

    • (B) is wrong because the text doesn't say that *having two identical detectors* is *the most critical factor*.

    • (C) is wrong because the text doesn't say that the *violent nature of the events* is the reason that the waves are *challenging to measure*.

    • (D) is correct because it matches the annotation.

9. **D** This is a Claims question, as it asks for an answer that would *support the researchers' conclusion*. Read the text and highlight the claim, which is that *electric vehicles have a positive effect on the health of individuals* because researchers found that *as the adoption of electric vehicles increased, the hospital visits decreased*. Eliminate answers that don't *support* this idea.

    • (A), (B), and (C) are wrong because they don't mention *electric vehicles*.

    • (D) is correct because if hospital visit frequency didn't change in places without electric vehicles, it helps support the idea that the electric vehicles could be the cause of the decrease.

10. **C** This is a Claims question, as it asks for an answer that would *illustrate the claim*. Read the text and highlight the claim, which is that *the narrator contrasts her background with her ambition*. Eliminate answers that don't *illustrate* this idea.

    • (A), (B), and (D) are wrong because they don't mention Loisel's *ambition*, that is, what she desires.

- (C) is correct because *no dresses, no jewels, nothing* illustrates her impoverished background and *She would have so liked...* describes her *ambition*.

11. **D** This is a Charts question, as it asks for *data from the table*. The graph charts the percentages of certain materials in the tires of passenger cars and trucks. Read the text and highlight the *idea* mentioned in the question, which is that truck *tires require higher tear resistance compared with those of passenger cars*. Read more of the text to see how that connects to the table. The third sentence states that *natural rubber* can *increase tear resistance*, so if truck tires require higher tear resistance, they must include more natural rubber. Eliminate any answer that doesn't *support* this idea or is inconsistent with the data on the graph.

- (A) is wrong because having less synthetic rubber doesn't necessarily mean it has more natural rubber.

- (B) and (C) are wrong because they don't mention natural rubber.

- (D) is correct because having more natural rubber suggests the truck tires are meant to have higher tear resistance.

12. **D** This is a Claims question, as it asks for an answer that would *undermine the scientists' theory*. Read the text and highlight the theory, which is that *a series of many repeated solar flares is the cause* of Miyake events. The other information states that the events have occurred *six times over the last 10,000 years*, most recently *in the first century CE*, and *solar flares* have been the main explanation, but they're too brief to match with what tree rings show. Thus, *a series of many repeated solar flares* could have caused the spikes. Eliminate answers that don't *undermine*, or weaken, the theory.

- (A) is wrong because it doesn't relate to any of the support for the theory.

- (B) is wrong because it strengthens the theory, as it suggests that the trees were old enough to show evidence of Miyake events.

- (C) is wrong because it doesn't relate to the tree ring evidence or whether there were *many repeated solar flares*.

- (D) is correct because if trees *less than a thousand years old* had the same marks, then it suggests that the marks weren't from Miyake events, given that the last one was over 1,000 years ago. This weakens the theory by suggesting that the tree ring analysis may not be useful.

13. **D** This is a Conclusions question, as it asks for the choice that *most logically completes the text*. Read the text and highlight the main ideas. The text states that the Coinage Act bill abolished *bimetallism*, so instead of *both gold and silver* having value, only gold was used for currency. Eliminate any answer that states a conclusion that isn't supported by the text.

- (A) is wrong because *trade* with other *nations* isn't related to the text.

- (B) is wrong because gold would have had more value, not less.

- (C) is wrong because if silver had less value, people wouldn't necessarily be encouraged to spend it.

- (D) is correct because if silver was no longer used for currency, people who *primarily had access to silver rather than gold* might not be able to pay for things.

14. **D** This is a Conclusions question, as it asks for the choice that *most logically completes the text*. Read the text and highlight the main ideas. The text states that *The evolutionary origin of the house cat has been puzzled over* and says that the traditional view is that they were *first domesticated in Ancient Egypt.* Then, it describes a *DNA analysis* that showed that *all of the individual domestic cats* from the study were part of a group that came *from the Middle East.* So, that suggests the house cat may also have come from the Middle East. Eliminate any answer that states a conclusion that isn't supported by the text.

- (A) is wrong because the text does provide evidence for the origin of the house cat.

- (B) is wrong because the text states that all of the house cats were in the fifth group.

- (C) is wrong because there's not enough evidence in the text to say where house cats were *brought* later.

- (D) is correct because if all of the house cats were in the group from the Middle East, they likely came from there.

15. **C** This is a Conclusions question, as it asks for the choice that *most logically completes the text*. Read the text and highlight the main ideas. The text states that *The Devonian period…was a time of many mass extinctions* and that all of Earth's life forms *lived in the ocean* at that time. Then it states that *there were heightened nutrient levels* in ancient lakes *at the same time that plant life was developing on land.* Then it says that *nutrient influxes* can cause an ocean's oxygen to be depleted and *prove harmful to the life forms living there.* Eliminate any answer that states a conclusion that isn't supported by the text.

- (A) is wrong because *all* species is too extreme to be supported by the text.

- (B) is wrong because no conclusion can be drawn about what might have happened *if the Devonian mass extinctions had never occurred.*

- (C) is correct because it suggests that the plants caused nutrient influxes that harmed life in the water, which the text states was where *all of Earth's life forms* lived, so that could be the cause of the extinctions.

- (D) is wrong because no conclusion can be drawn about what *would have happened.*

16. **D** In this Rules question, punctuation is changing in the answer choices. Look for independent clauses. The first part of the sentence says *When considered as a whole, though, the paintings have a consistent feature*, which is an independent clause. The second part of the sentence says *a central figure made of layers of paint and scratches*, which is not an independent clause. Eliminate any option that isn't correctly punctuated.

    • (A) and (C) are wrong because the second part of the sentence isn't an independent clause, so it can't stand alone, nor can it be separated by a semicolon, which links independent clauses.

    • (B) is wrong because a comma + a coordinating conjunction (*and*) only links two independent clauses.

    • (D) is correct because a comma can connect the independent clause to the describing phrase in the second part.

17. **A** In this Rules question, apostrophes with nouns are changing in the answer choices. Determine whether each word possesses anything. The ants possess the raft, and the group possesses the eggs. Eliminate any answer that doesn't match this.

    • (A) is correct because *ants* and *group* are possessive.

    • (B) is wrong because *ants* should have an apostrophe, since the ants possess the raft.

    • (C) is wrong because *ants* should be plural; as written, it refers to only one ant.

    • (D) is wrong because *group* should have an apostrophe, as the group possesses the eggs.

18. **C** In this Rules question, verb forms are changing in the answer choices, so it's testing sentence structure. The phrase after the comma describes why the author *writes in the second person point of view*. Eliminate any answer that does not make the phrase clear and correct.

    • (A), (B), and (D) are wrong because they are all in the "main verb" form, but the sentence already contains a main verb (*writes*).

    • (C) is correct because it states that the author *writes in the second person point of view to describe the perspective*, which provides a clear and correct meaning.

19. **A** In this Rules question, commas and semicolons are changing in the answer choices. The sentence already contains a semicolon near the end, and the part after it is not an independent clause, which suggests that the sentence contains a list separated by semicolons. Use the third example to determine the structure of each item: Work, Comma, Description. Make an annotation of this pattern and eliminate any answer that doesn't follow it.

    • (A) is correct because it follows the pattern of the third item.

    • (B) and (D) are wrong because they don't have a semicolon after the first item.

    • (C) is wrong because a comma should follow the name of the work.

20. **D** In this Rules question, the subjects of the answers are changing, which suggests it may be testing modifiers. Look for and highlight a modifying phrase: *By interfering with the replication of HIV.* Whatever is *interfering with* the replication of the disease needs to come immediately after the comma. Eliminate any answer that doesn't start with something that could interfere.

    - (A) is wrong because *the spread of HIV* can't interfere with HIV's replication.

    - (B) is wrong because *limiting the spread of HIV* isn't a thing that could interfere with HIV's replication.

    - (C) is wrong because *Tenefovir's ability* can't interfere with HIV's replication.

    - (D) is correct because *Tenefovir*, a drug, can interfere with HIV replication.

21. **B** In this Rules question, punctuation with a transition is changing in the answer choices. Look for independent clauses. The first part of the sentence says *Cajal did not make this discovery alone.* There is an option to add *however* to this independent clause. This statement does contrast with the previous sentence, which states that Cajal proposed the *"neuron theory,"* so *however* belongs in the first part of the sentence. Eliminate options with *however* in the second part.

    - (A) is wrong because it puts *however* in the second part of the sentence.

    - (B) is correct because it puts *however* with the first independent clause and puts a semicolon between the two independent clauses.

    - (C) is wrong because two independent clauses must be separated with some type of punctuation.

    - (D) is wrong because the sentence contains two independent clauses, which cannot be connected with commas alone.

22. **C** In this Rules question, the subjects of the answers are changing, which suggests it may be testing modifiers. Look for and highlight a modifying phrase: *Compared to that of gray wolves.* Whatever is *Compared to that of gray wolves* needs to come immediately after the comma. Eliminate any answer that doesn't start with something that can be *compared* and state what *that* refers to.

    - (A) and (B) are wrong because *black wolves* themselves can't be compared to an attribute of *gray wolves*.

    - (C) is correct because *that* refers to the *fur color* and it refers to another type of wolf, making the comparison parallel.

    - (D) is wrong because it doesn't make a clear comparison to an attribute of gray wolves.

23. **A**   This is a transition question, so highlight ideas that relate to each other. The preceding sentence says *Some linguists believe that people's spoken language can influence their perceptions of abstract concepts,* and this sentence says *if a language does not have a word for an abstract concept, the people who exclusively speak the language may struggle to comprehend the abstract concept at all.* These ideas agree, so a same-direction transition is needed. Make an annotation that says "agree." Eliminate any answer that doesn't match.

- (A) is correct because *specifically* is a same-direction transition, and this sentence is a more specific piece of information related to the preceding sentence.

- (B) is wrong because *thus* suggests a conclusion that isn't stated in the text.

- (C) and (D) are wrong because they suggest an additional point rather than a specification.

24. **A**   This is a transition question, so highlight ideas that relate to each other. The preceding sentence says *First, they discovered that the Earth's crust production spikes consistently approximately every 200 million years,* and this sentence says *they found that known asteroid impacts on Earth coincide with times when the planet would have been located in one of the arms.* These ideas agree, so a same-direction transition is needed. Make an annotation that says "agree." Eliminate any answer that doesn't match.

- (A) is correct because it is a same-direction transition and is consistent with the use of *First* in the preceding sentence.

- (B) is incorrect because *Nevertheless* is opposite-direction.

- (C) and (D) are wrong because they're not consistent with *First* in the preceding sentence.

25. **A**   This is a transition question, so highlight ideas that relate to each other. The preceding sentence says *Biosphere reserves are protected areas that are designated to provide opportunities to utilize or study certain species of animals and plants,* and this sentence says *these areas typically contain a species with a unique characteristic or benefit to society.* These ideas agree, so a same-direction transition is needed. Make an annotation that says "agree." Eliminate any answer that doesn't match.

- (A) is correct because it is a same-direction transition, and this sentence is a conclusion based on the evidence in the previous sentence.

- (B) is wrong because there is no second thing that shares a similarity with what was previously discussed.

- (C) is wrong because *Regardless* is opposite-direction.

- (D) is wrong because the sentences don't describe a sequence of events.

26. **B** This is a Rhetorical Synthesis question, so highlight the goal(s) stated in the question: *introduce Anderson's photographs to an audience already familiar with Galicia*. Eliminate any answer that doesn't *introduce Anderson's photographs* in a way that assumes the audience is familiar with Galicia.

    • (A) and (C) are wrong because they don't provide an introduction to *Anderson's photographs*.

    • (B) is correct because it introduces *Anderson's photographs* and doesn't describe *Galicia* since the audience is familiar with it.

    • (D) is wrong because it describes *Galicia*, but the audience is already familiar with it.

27. **D** This is a Rhetorical Synthesis question, so highlight the goal(s) stated in the question: *emphasize the increase in the burro population and specify why this increase occurred*. Eliminate any answer that doesn't fulfill this purpose.

    • (A) and (C) are wrong because they don't *emphasize the increase in the burro population*.

    • (B) is wrong because it doesn't *specify why the increase occurred*.

    • (D) is correct because it emphasizes *the increase in the burro population* (it has *multiplied*) and includes a rationale for *why this increase occurred* (they have *no natural predators*).

PRACTICE TEST 1—MATH EXPLANATIONS

Module 1

1. **A**   The question asks for the value of an angle on a figure. The figure is already drawn and labeled, but redraw it on the scratch paper if that makes it easier to see what's going on. When a line intersects two parallel lines, two kinds of angles are created: big and small. All of the small angles are equal to each other, all of the big angles are equal to each other, and any small angle plus any big angle = 180°. Angle x and the angle labeled 20° are both small angles. Thus, angle x also measures 20°. The correct answer is (A).

2. **10**   The question asks for the mean, or average, of a data set. For averages, use the formula $T = AN$, in which T is the *Total*, A is the *Average*, and N is the *Number of things*. There are 12 values in the data set, so $N = 12$. Find the *Total* by adding the 12 integers to get $T = 12 + 12 + 12 + 17 + 5 + 8 + 2 + 10 + 3 + 11 + 19 + 9$, which becomes $T = 120$. The average formula becomes $120 = (A)(12)$. Divide both sides of the equation by 12 to get $10 = A$. The correct answer is 10.

3. **D**   The question asks for the equation that has the same solution as the given equation. The answer choices all have the term $5a$ on the left side, so isolate that term. Move everything else to the other side of the equation. Since the left side of the equation has -9, add 9 to both sides of the equation. The equation becomes $5a = 45$. The correct answer is (D).

4. **A**   The question asks for a measure on a geometric figure. Start by drawing a cube on the scratch paper, as best as possible, keeping in mind that a cube has three dimensions. Next, label the figure with the given information. The edge length is not given, so use the values in the answers. Try the easier of the middle numbers and start with (B), 27. Label the edge of the cube as 27. Next, write down the formula for the volume of a cube, either from memory or after looking it up on the reference sheet. The reference sheet doesn't give the formula for the volume of a cube, but it does give the volume of a rectangular solid: $V = lwh$. All three sides of a cube are the same length, so the formula becomes $V = s^3$. Plug in 27 for s to get $V = 27^3$, or $V = 19,683$. This is not the volume of 729 given in the question, so eliminate (B). The result was too large, so also eliminate (C) and (D). To check (A), plug $s = 9$ into the volume formula to get $V = 9^3$, or $V = 729$. This matches the value given in the question. The correct answer is (A).

5. **87**   The question asks for a value based on a percentage. Translate the English to math in bite-sized pieces. *Percent* means out of 100, so translate $33\frac{1}{3}\%$ as $\dfrac{33\frac{1}{3}}{100}$. Translate *of* as times, or ×. Translate *is* as equals. The equation becomes $\dfrac{33\frac{1}{3}}{100}(x) = 29$. Multiply both sides of the equation by 100 to

get $33\frac{1}{3}x = 2{,}900$. Multiply both sides of the equation by 3 to get $100x = 8{,}700$, then divide both

sides of the equation by 100 to get $x = 87$. The correct answer is 87.

6. **B** The question asks for a value based on an equation. The question states that the number of long songs is represented by l, and that the number of short songs, s, is 15. Plug $s = 15$ into the equation and solve for l. The equation becomes $3(15) + 4.5l = 108$, or $45 + 4.5l = 108$. Subtract 45 from both sides of the equation to get $4.5l = 63$. Divide both sides of the equation by 4.5 to get $l = 14$. The correct answer is (B).

7. **D** The question asks for a comparison of the standard deviations of two data sets. Standard deviation is a measure of the spread of a group of numbers. A group of numbers close together has a small standard deviation, whereas a group of numbers spread out has a large standard deviation. The distribution of books is more spread out on the first floor than it is on the second floor. This can be seen visually by looking at the shapes of the two graphs: the shape of the dot plot for the first floor is more flat, whereas the shape of the dot plot for the second floor is a steeper curve, with more values clustered around the middle. This means that the standard deviation for the first-floor data is greater than that for the second-floor data. The correct answer is (D).

8. **C** The question asks for an equation that represents a specific situation. The value is decreasing by a certain percentage over time, so this question is about exponential decay. Write down the growth and decay formula, which is *final amount* = (*original amount*)$(1 \pm rate)^{number\ of\ changes}$. In this case, v is the *final amount*, t is the *number of changes*, and the question states that the *original amount* is 60,500. Eliminate (A) and (B) because they do not have 60,500 as the original amount in front of the parentheses. Since this situation involves a decrease, the original amount must be multiplied by $(1 - rate)$. The rate given in the question is 12% or 0.12, so the value in parentheses should be $1 - 0.12$, or 0.88. Eliminate (D), which does not have this rate because it adds 0.12 rather than subtracting it. The only remaining answer is (C), and it matches the exponential decay formula. The correct answer is (C).

9. **D** The question asks for the negative solution to a quadratic equation. To begin solving for a, move everything to the left side of the equation and set it equal to 0 to get $9a^2 - 20a - 21 = 0$. The equation is now a quadratic in standard form, which is $ax^2 + bx + c$. However, this quadratic is difficult to factor, so look for a different approach. One approach is to use the built-in calculator. Enter the expression without "= 0" into the built-in calculator, then scroll and zoom as needed to see the negative x-intercept, which is at approximately $(-0.778, 0)$. Eliminate (A) and (B) because they are integers. Check the other two fractions using a calculator: $-\frac{20}{9} \approx -2.22$, and $-\frac{7}{9} \approx -0.778$, so (D) is correct. Another approach is to use the values the answers: plug in the value for x from each answer choice one at a time until one of them makes the equation true. Yet another approach is to use the quadratic formula to find both solutions. Using any method, the correct answer is (D).

10. **3072**   The question asks for the value of a function. In function notation, the number inside the parentheses is the x-value that goes into the function, or the input, and the value that comes out of the function is the y-value, or the output. According to the question, $h(5) = 12,288$, so when the input is 5, the output is 12,288. Plug in $h(x) = 12,288$ and $x = 5$, and solve for c. The function becomes $12,288 = 12c^5$. Divide both sides of the equation by 12 to get $1,024 = c^5$. Take the fifth root of both sides of the equation to get $4 = c$. The question asks for the value of $h(4)$, so plug $x = 4$ and $c = 4$ into the function, and solve for $h(4)$. The function becomes $h(4) = (12)(4)^4$, or $h(4) = (12)(256)$, and finally $h(4) = 3,072$. Leave out the comma when entering the answer in the fill-in box. The correct answer is 3072.

11. **B**   The question asks for the solution to a system of equations. The most efficient method is to enter both equations into the built-in calculator, then scroll and zoom as needed to find the point of intersection. Click on the gray dot to see that the coordinates of the point are $(-3, 0)$. Another approach is to use the values in the answers. Rewrite the answer choices on the scratch paper and label them "(x, y)." Start with one of the answers in the middle and try (B). Plug $x = -3$ and $y = 0$ into the first equation to get $0 = -7(-3) - 21$, or $y = 21 - 21$, and finally $0 = 0$. This is true, but the pair of values must work in both equations. Plug the same values into the second equation to get $0 = (-3 + 3)(-3 - 4)$, or $0 = 0(-7)$, and finally $0 = 0$. The point $(-3, 0)$ makes both equations true, so it is the solution to the system of equations. Using either method, the correct answer is (B).

12. **A**   The question asks about the graph of a function. In function notation, the number inside the parentheses is the x-value that goes into the function, or the input, and the value that comes out of the function is the y-value, or the output. Together, they represent points on the graph of the function. The question asks for the number of values of x that make $f(x) = 0$. Since $f(x) = y$, $y = 0$, and the question is asking for the x-intercepts. Look at the graph and count how many times the graph of the function crosses the x-axis. There is one x-intercept, between $(1, 0)$ and $(2, 0)$. The correct answer is (A).

13. **12**   The question asks for the value of a variable based on an equation. The amount of money is increasing by a certain percentage over time, so this question is about exponential growth. Write down the growth and decay formula, which is *final amount* = (*original amount*)(1 ± *rate*)$^{number\ of\ changes}$. In this case, the *final amount* is $g(m)$, the *original amount* is 35,000, and the *number of changes* is $\dfrac{m}{12}$. The amount is increasing, so set 1.1 equal to (1 + *rate*) to get a *rate* of 0.1, or 10%. Since the amount of money will increase by 10% with a single change, the *number of changes* can also be expressed as 1. Write the equation $\dfrac{m}{12} = 1$, then multiply both sides of the equation by 12 to get $m = 12$. The correct answer is 12.

14.   **A**   The question asks for the value of a trigonometric function. Start by drawing two right triangles that are similar to each other, meaning they have the same proportions but are different sizes. Be certain to match up the corresponding angles that are given in the question, and put the longest side opposite the right angle. The drawing should look something like this:

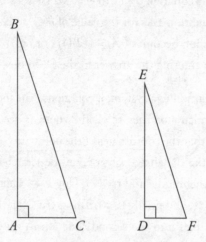

Next, label the figures with the information given. Use SOHCAHTOA to remember the trig functions, and label the sides. The CAH part of the acronym defines the cosine as $\frac{adjacent}{hypotenuse}$. The question states that $\cos(C) = \frac{23}{265}$, so label the side adjacent to angle C as 23 and label the hypotenuse as 265. The drawing now looks like this:

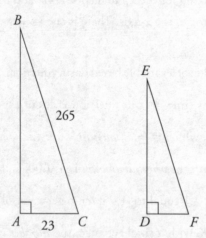

The question states that the triangles are similar, and that angle B corresponds to angle E. Because two pairs of angles have the same measure, the third pair will as well, so angle C corresponds to angle F. Trig functions are proportional, so $\cos(C) = \cos(F)$. Since $\cos(C) = \frac{23}{265}$, $\cos(F)$ is also $\frac{23}{265}$. The correct answer is (A).

15. $-\dfrac{1}{3}$ The question asks for the slope of a line. The question states that *line a is perpendicular to line b*, which means they have slopes that are negative reciprocals of each other. The question gives the equation of line *b*, so find the slope of that line. First, convert the equation of line *b* into slope-intercept form, $y = mx + b$, in which *m* is the slope and *b* is the *y*-intercept. Add 6 to both sides of the equation to get $9x + 6 = 3y$, and then flip the two sides of the equation to get $3y = 9x + 6$. Divide both sides of the equation by 3 to get $y = 3x + 2$. The slope of line *b* is thus 3. The negative reciprocal of 3 is $-\dfrac{1}{3}$, so the slope of line *a* is $-\dfrac{1}{3}$. It is also possible to convert the equation of line *b* into standard form by subtracting $3y$ from both sides of the equation to get $9x - 3y = -6$. In standard form, $Ax + By = C$, the slope is $-\dfrac{A}{B}$. In this case, $A = 9$ and $B = -3$, so the slope of line *b* is $-\dfrac{9}{-3} = 3$. The negative reciprocal of 3 is $-\dfrac{1}{3}$, so the slope of line *a* is $-\dfrac{1}{3}$. Using either form of a linear equation, the correct answer is $-\dfrac{1}{3}$.

16. **85** The question asks for the measure of an angle on a geometric figure. Start by drawing the figure on the scratch paper, then label it with the information given. Draw a circle, and label the center as *O*. Label points *A* and *B* on the circle, and label angle *AOB* as 85°. The drawing should look something like this:

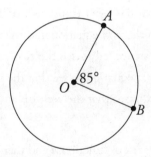

When an arc measure is in degrees, the arc length is the same number of degrees as the central angle that defines it. The correct answer is 85.

17. **C** The question asks for an equation in terms of specific variables. The question asks about the relationship among variables and there are variables in the answer choices, so plugging in is an option. However, that might get messy when working with equations with three variables, and all of the answer choices have $c - 1$ on the left side of the equation, so the other option is to solve for $c - 1$. To begin to isolate $c - 1$, multiply both sides of the equation by $c - 1$ to get $a(c - 1) = b + 1$. Divide both sides of the equation by *a* to get $c - 1 = \dfrac{b + 1}{a}$. The correct answer is (C).

18. **A** The question asks for a description of a function based on a percent. Compare the answer choices. Two choices say that the function is increasing, and two say it is decreasing. To determine whether the function is increasing or decreasing, one method is to graph it using the built-in calculator. The calculator automatically adds "of" after the percent sign, so translate "equals" as "=" and enter $f(x) = 33\% \ x$. The graph of this function is a line going upward to the right, so it is increasing. Eliminate (C) and (D) because they describe a decreasing function. Also eliminate (B) because the graph is a straight line, not a curve like the graph of an exponential function would be. Another option is to plug in increasing values for x and compare the corresponding values of $f(x)$. Plug in $x = 1$ to get $f(1) = \dfrac{33}{100}(1) = 0.33$. Plug in $x = 2$ to get $f(2) = \dfrac{33}{100}(2) = 0.66$. Plug in $x = 3$ to get $f(3) = \dfrac{33}{100}(3) = 0.99$. The difference between $f(2)$ and $f(1)$ is $0.66 - 0.33 = 0.33$, and the difference between $f(3)$ and $f(2)$ is $0.99 - 0.66 = 0.33$. The values of $f(x)$ increase by the same amount each time, so the function represents a linear increase. Using either method, the correct answer is (A).

19. **C** The question asks for a value of x for which a function reaches its maximum. A parabola reaches its minimum or maximum value at its vertex, so find the x-coordinate of the vertex. The question asks about the graph of a function that has been translated, or shifted, from the graph of the function given in the question. Enter both the $a(x)$ equation and the $b(x)$ equation into the built-in graphing calculator, then scroll and zoom as needed to see the two parabolas. Either use the color-coding or click on the entry field with the $b(x)$ equation to see that the parabola on the right is the graph of $b(x)$. Click on the gray dot at the vertex to see that the vertex is at $(3, 39.5)$. The question asks for the value of x, which is 3, so (C) is correct.

Another approach is to find the vertex of function a and then apply the shift. Either use the graphing calculator or know that, when a quadratic is in standard form, which is $ax^2 + bx + c$, the x-coordinate of the vertex can be found using the formula $h = -\dfrac{b}{2a}$. In this quadratic, $a = -2$ and $b = -16$, so the x-coordinate of the vertex is $-\dfrac{-16}{2(-2)} = -\dfrac{16}{4} = -4$. When graphs are transformed, or translated, subtracting inside the parentheses shifts the graph to the right. Thus, $x - 7$ shifts the graph seven units to the right, which shifts the x-coordinate of the vertex from -4 to $-4 + 7 = 3$. Using either method, the correct answer is (C).

20. **D** The question asks for an equation that represents a graph. One approach is to enter the equation from each answer choice into the built-in graphing calculator and see which graph looks like the graph in the question. Since the answers are all in factored form, another approach is to use the factors. If

$(x - a)$ is a factor of a polynomial, a is a solution. This graph intersects the x-axis at $(-3, 0)$ and $(4, 0)$, so the factors must include $(x + 3)$ and $(x - 4)$. Eliminate (A), which does not contain these factors. At both points on the x-axis, the graph touches the x-axis and then curves away. These are called double roots, and double roots have even exponents. Thus, both solutions should be squared, which is true in (D). Without knowing about double roots, it is possible to answer the question by plugging in a point that is on the graph but is not on the x-axis. When $x = 2$, $y = 1$, so plug those values into the remaining answer choices. Choice (B) becomes $1 = \dfrac{1}{100}(2 + 3)(2 - 4)$, or $1 = \dfrac{1}{100}(5)(-2)$, and then $1 = -\dfrac{10}{100}$. This is not true, so eliminate (B). Choice (C) becomes $1 = \dfrac{1}{100}(2 + 3)(2 - 4)^2$, or $1 = \dfrac{1}{100}(5)(4)$, and then $1 = \dfrac{20}{100}$. Eliminate (C). Choice (D) becomes $1 = \dfrac{1}{100}(2 + 3)^2(2 - 4)^2$, or $1 = \dfrac{1}{100}(25)(4)$, and then $1 = 1$. This is true, so (D) is the correct equation. The built-in calculator, knowledge of double roots, and plugging in points are all viable options. Using any method, the correct answer is (D).

21. **B** The question asks for a value in a system of equations. One method is to enter both equations into the built-in calculator. Then plug in each possible value for k from the answer choices, either by entering the numbers one at a time or by using the slider tool, and then scroll and zoom as needed to see where, if at all, the two graphs intersect. When k = –12, there is a single point of intersection indicated by a gray dot. Click on the dot to see that the coordinates of the point of intersection are (–2, 24). The question asks for the x-value, which is –2, so the answer is (B).

To solve algebraically, start by finding the value of k. The equations are both equal to y, so set them equal to each other. The new equation becomes $x^2 - 2x + 16 = -6x - k$. Put the quadratic in standard form by setting one side equal to 0. Add $6x$ to both sides of the equation to get $x^2 + 4x + 16 = -k$, then add k to both sides of the equation to get $x^2 + 4x + 16 + k = 0$.

The question states that the line *intersects the parabola at exactly one point*, so use the discriminant. The discriminant is the part of the quadratic formula under the square root sign, and it can be written as $D = b^2 - 4ac$. When the discriminant is positive, the quadratic has exactly two real solutions; when the discriminant is 0, the quadratic has exactly one real solution; when the discriminant is negative, the quadratic has no real solutions. In this case, the quadratic has exactly one real solution, so the discriminant must equal 0.

In this equation, the constant k is part of the c term in the discriminant. With the equation in standard form, which is $ax^2 + bx + c = 0$, $a = 1$, $b = 4$, and $c = 16 + k$. Plug these values into the discriminant formula and set it equal to 0 to get $(4)^2 - 4(1)(16 + k) = 0$. Simplify the left side of the equation to get $16 - 4(16 + k) = 0$. Distribute the -4 to get $16 - 64 - 4k = 0$. Simplify further to get

−48 − 4*k* = 0, then add 48 to both sides of the equation to get −4*k* = 48. Finally, divide both sides of the equation by −4 to get *k* = −12.

Read carefully: the question asks for the value of *x*, not the value of *k*. Plug −12 into the standard form quadratic for constant *k* to get $x^2 + 4x + 16 + (-12) = 0$. Simplify the left side of the equation to get $x^2 + 4x + 4 = 0$. Factor the quadratic to get $(x + 2)(x + 2) = 0$. If *x* + 2 = 0, then *x* = −2. It is also possible to enter both of the original equations into the built-in graphing calculator, substituting −12 for *k*, and then scroll and zoom to find the *x*-coordinate of the point of intersection, which is −2. Using either method, the correct answer is (B).

22. **C** The question asks for a value based on data. To find the difference between the numbers of ounces of flour used for cookies and for cupcakes, first subtract the numbers of ounces to get 464 − 240 = 224. This is not the final answer because it only represents the difference between the numbers of ounces of flour used per batch, not all the flour in the scenario. Eliminate (B) because it does not answer the final question. Next, set up a proportion representing the difference between the numbers of ounces of flour out of the total ounces of flour used. The proportion is $\frac{224}{704} = \frac{x}{4,928}$. Cross-multiply to get 704*x* = 1,103,872, then divide both sides of the equation by 704 to get *x* = 1,568. The correct answer is (C).

Module 2 – Easier

1. **A** The question asks for the *x*-intercept of a graph. The *x*-intercept of a graph is defined as the point where the graph crosses the *x*-axis. This happens when *y* = 0. Find *y* = 0 on the graph and trace left—using the mouse pointer or the edge of the scratch paper as needed—to see that the graph crosses the *x*-axis at *x* = −2. Points on a graph are represented as ordered pairs in the form (*x*, *y*), with the *x*-value first and the *y*-value second, so the point at the *x*-intercept is (−2, 0). The correct answer is (A).

2. **C** The question asks for the solution to an equation. To solve for *a*, add 18 to both sides of the equation. The equation becomes *a* = 270. The correct answer is (C).

3. **D** The question asks for a value based on a graph. To find the day on which the number of laptops sold was the least, first check the units on each axis of the line graph. The *x*-axis shows the days of the week in order from left to right, and the *y*-axis shows number of laptops sold in ascending order from low to high. Thus, the least number of laptop sales will be represented by the lowest point on the line graph. Find the lowest point on the graph, then look at the *x*-axis at that point. The graph reaches its lowest point on Friday. The correct answer is (D).

4. **162**   The question asks for the measure of an angle and gives conflicting units. Either write down a conversion between radians and degrees from memory or open the reference sheet, which states that the *number of degrees of arc in a circle is 360* and that the *number of radians of arc in a circle is 2π*. Thus, 360 degrees = 2π radians. This reduces to the other conversion, which is 180 degrees = π radians. Set up a proportion, being sure to match up units. The proportion is $\frac{180 \text{ degrees}}{\pi \text{ radians}} = \frac{x \text{ degrees}}{\frac{9\pi}{10} \text{ radians}}$. Cross-multiply to get $(\pi)(x) = (180)\left(\frac{9\pi}{10}\right)$. Simplify to get $\pi x = 162\pi$, then divide both sides of the equation by π to get $x = 162$. The correct answer is 162.

5. **B**   The question asks for a measurement and gives conflicting units. To convert centigrams to grams, set up a proportion. Be sure to match up units. The question states that *1 gram = 100 centigrams*, so the proportion is $\frac{1 \text{ gram}}{100 \text{ centigrams}} = \frac{x \text{ grams}}{350 \text{ centigrams}}$. To solve for *x*, cross-multiply to get $(100)(x) = (1)(350)$, which becomes $100x = 350$. Divide both sides of the equation by 100 to get $x = 3.5$. The correct answer is (B).

6. **A**   The question asks for a function that models a specific situation. There are variables in the answer choices, and the question asks about the relationship between values, so plug in. Make $d = 2$ to keep the math easy. If the computer completes 651 simulations in 1 day, it will complete 651(2) = 1,302 simulations in 2 days. Plug $d = 2$ and $s = 1,302$ into the answer choices, and eliminate any that don't work. Choice (A) becomes $2 = \frac{1,302}{651}$, or 2 = 2. Keep (A), but check the remaining answers just in case. Choice (B) becomes 2 = 651 – 1,302, or 2 = –651. This is not true, so eliminate (B). Choice (C) becomes 2 = 651 + 1,302, or 2 = 1,953; eliminate (C). Choice (D) becomes 2 = 651(1,302), or 2 = 847,602; eliminate (D). The correct answer is (A).

7. **5**   The question asks for a value given a specific situation. Translate the information in bite-sized pieces. The question states that *after deer came into the yard and ate 12 flowers, there were 18 flowers remaining*. To find the original number of flowers, add 18 and 12 to get 18 + 12 = 30 flowers. The question also states that Wendy *planted 6 rose bushes*. Divide the 30 flowers by the 6 rose bushes to find the original number of flowers per rose bush: $\frac{30}{6} = 5$. The correct answer is 5.

8. **-7**   The question asks for a value based on an equation. Plug $a = 5$ into the equation, and solve for b. The equation becomes $b = 2(5) - 17$. Follow the order of operations and multiply first to get $b = 10 - 17$. Next, subtract to get $b = -7$. The correct answer is -7.

9. **A**   The question asks for an equation that represents a given situation. Translate the information into bite-sized pieces and eliminate after each piece. Translate *is* as equals, so the correct equation should include "27 =". Eliminate (C) because it does not include this piece. Translate *7 less than* as -7. Eliminate (B) and (D) because they do not include this piece. Only (A) remains, and it correctly translates *7 less than 2 times the number y* as $2y - 7$. The correct answer is (A).

10. **14 or 46**   The question asks for a value given an equation with an absolute value. With an absolute value, the value inside the absolute value bars can be either positive or negative, so this equation has two possible solutions. To find one solution, either set $30 - y$ equal to 16 or set $30 - y$ equal to -16, and solve for y. When $30 - y = 16$, add y to both sides of the equation to get $30 = 16 + y$, then subtract 16 from both sides of the equation to get $14 = y$. When $30 - y = -16$, add y to both sides of the equation to get $30 = y - 16$, then add 16 to both sides of the equation to get $46 = y$. The correct answer is 14 or 46.

11. **C**   The question asks for an equivalent form of an expression. Use bite-sized pieces and process of elimination to tackle this question. Start by combining the terms that have y^2. Add y^2 to $3y^2$ to get $4y^2$. Eliminate (A) and (B) because they do not include $4y^2$. Compare the remaining answer choices: (C) and (D) have different terms that include y, so combine the terms that have y. Add $-5y$ to $2y$ to get $-3y$. Eliminate (D) because it does not include $-3y$. The correct answer is (C).

12. **B**   The question asks for an equivalent form of an expression. Both terms contain a multiple of 7 and y, so one approach is to factor out $7y$ to get $7y(y - 2)$. Check that (B) is correct by distributing the $7y$: $7y(y) = 7y^2$, and $7y(-2) = -14y$, so $7y(y - 2)$ is an equivalent form of $7y^2 - 14y$. There are variables in the answer choices, so another option is to plug in. Plug in a simple number for y, such as $y = 3$. The expression becomes $7(3)^2 - 14(3)$. Simplify the expression to get $7(9) - 42$, then $63 - 42$, and finally 21. This is the target value; write it down and circle it. Now plug $y = 3$ into each answer choice and eliminate any that do not match the target value of 21. Choice (A) becomes $3[7(3) - 2)] = 3(21 - 2) = 3(19) = 57$. This does not match the target value, so eliminate (A). Choice (B) becomes $7(3)(3 - 2) = 21(1) = 21$. This matches the target value, so keep (B), but check the remaining answers just in case. Choice (C) becomes $14(3)[7(3) - 1] = 42(21 - 1) = 42(20) = 840$. Eliminate (C). Choice (D) becomes $3^2[7(3) - 14] = 9(21 - 14) = 9(7) = 63$. Eliminate (D). Using either method, the correct answer is (B).

13. **D**   The question asks for a measurement on a geometric figure. Start by redrawing the figure, then label it with information from the question. Label diagonal WY as 25, and label side WX as 13. Side XY is the other leg of triangle WXY. To find the length of XY, use the Pythagorean Theorem: $a^2 + b^2 = c^2$. Plug in the known values to get $13^2 + b^2 = 25^2$. Let the answers help: the answers all have 13 and 25

instead of the result you would get by squaring and subtracting, so keep the equation in this form. To find the value of b, subtract 13^2 from both sides of the equation to get $b^2 = 25^2 - 13^2$, and then take the square root of both sides of the equation to get $b = \sqrt{25^2 - 13^2}$. The correct answer is (D).

14. **B** The question asks for the solution to a system of equations. One method is to enter both equations into a graphing calculator, then scroll and zoom as needed to find the point of intersection. The graph shows one point of intersection at $(-7, -21)$, which is (B). Another approach is to use the values in the answers. Rewrite the answer choices on the scratch paper and label them "(x, y)." Start with one of the middle x-values and try (B). Plug $x = -7$ and $y = -21$ into the first equation to get $-21 = 3(-7)$, or $-21 = -21$. This is true, but the solution must work in both equations. Plug the point in (B) into the second equation to get $-7 - (-21) = 14$, or $14 = 14$. This is also true, so $(-7, -21)$ is a solution to the system of equations. Using either method, the correct answer is (B).

15. **C** The question asks for the function that represents values given in a table. In function notation, the number inside the parentheses is the x-value that goes into the function, or the input, and the value that comes out of the function is the y-value, or the output. The table includes four input and output values, and the correct equation must work for every pair of values. Plug in values from the table and eliminate functions that don't work. Because positive numbers are generally easier to work with, and 0 is likely to make more than one answer work, try the third column of the table and plug $x = 2$ and $g(x) = 7$ into the answer choices. Choice (A) becomes $7 = -17(2) - 7$, or $7 = -34 - 7$, and then $7 = -41$. This is not true, so eliminate (A). Choice (B) becomes $7 = -10(2) + 17$, or $7 = -20 + 17$, and then $7 = -3$. Eliminate (B). Choice (C) becomes $7 = -5(2) + 17$, or $7 = -10 + 17$, and then $7 = 7$. Keep (C), but check the remaining answer just in case. Choice (D) becomes $7 = -2(2) + 27$, or $7 = -4 + 27$, and then $7 = 23$. Eliminate (D). The correct answer is (C).

16. **D** The question asks for an equation that represents a graph. To find the best equation, compare features of the graph to the answer choices. The equations in the answer choices are all in the form $y = mx + b$, in which m is the slope and b is the y-intercept. All of the answer choices have the same y-intercept, 5, so focus on the slope. The line is ascending from left to right, so it has a positive slope. Eliminate (A) and (B) because they have negative slopes. Find the slope by using the formula $slope = \frac{y_2 - y_1}{x_2 - x_1}$. The graph has points at $(-5, 0)$ and $(0, 5)$, so plug those values into the slope formula to get $slope = \frac{5 - 0}{0 - (-5)}$, which becomes $slope = \frac{5}{5}$, or $slope = 1$. Eliminate (C) because it has a slope of $\frac{1}{2}$ instead of 1. Another option is to enter all four of the equations in the answer choices into the built-in calculator and see which one looks like the graph in the question. Using either method, the correct answer is (D).

17. **B** The question asks for a value given a function. In function notation, the number inside the parentheses is the x-value that goes into the function, or the input, and the value that comes out of the function is the y-value, or the output. The question provides an output value of 9, so set $q(x)$ equal to 9 and solve for x. The equation becomes $9 = \frac{1}{9}x^4$. Multiply both sides of the equation by 9 to get $81 = x^4$, then take the fourth root of both sides of the equation to get $\pm 3 = x$. Only 3 is in an answer choice, so (B) is correct. Since the answers are numbers that could represent the x-value, another option is to use the values in the answers. Start with a number in the middle that's easy to work with, so try (B), 3. Plug 3 into the function for x to get $q(3) = \frac{1}{9}(3)^4$, which becomes $q(3) = \frac{1}{9}(81)$, and then $q(3) = 9$. This matches the output value given in the question, so stop here. Using either method, the correct answer is (B).

18. **196** The question asks for the area of a square. Write out the formula for the area of a square, which is $Area = side^2$, or $A = s^2$. Plug in the side length given in the question to get $A = 14^2$, or $A = 196$. The correct answer is 196.

19. **B** The question asks for the minimum value given a specific situation. Since the question asks for a specific value and the answers contain numbers in increasing order, use the values in the answers. Rewrite the answer choices on the scratch paper and label them "number of sacks." Next, pick a value to start with. Since the question asks for the minimum, start with the smallest number, 149. If there are 149 sacks and each sack weighs 15 pounds, the total weight is $(15)(149) = 2,235$ pounds. Add the weight of the potatoes the cook already has in the kitchen for a combined weight of $2,235 + 260 = 2,495$ pounds. The question states that the *fry cook needs to have at least 2,500 pounds of potatoes*, so this result is too small. The result was close, so try the next largest number, which is (B), 150. If there are 150 sacks with a weight of 15 pounds each, the total weight is $(15)(150) = 2,250$ pounds. Add the weight of the potatoes the cook already has for a combined weight of $2,250 + 260 = 2,510$ pounds. The combined weight is greater than 2,500 pounds, so stop here. The correct answer is (B).

20. **A** The question asks for the y-intercept of a line. A y-intercept is a point where $x = 0$. One approach is to enter the equation into the built-in graphing calculator, then scroll and zoom as needed to find the point where the graph intersects the y-axis. The graph shows the y-intercept at $(0, -22)$, which is (A). Because the answers are points that could be the y-intercept, another approach is to use the values in the answers. Using (A), for example, plug $y = -22$ and $x = 0$ into the equation to get $6(0) - 11(-22) = 242$, which becomes $0 + 242 = 242$, and then $242 = 242$. This is true, so $(0, -22)$ is the y-intercept. Using either method, the correct answer is (A).

21. **A**   The question asks for information that will provide proof of congruent triangles. Start by drawing a figure. Triangles are congruent when they have the same three angle measures and the same three side lengths, so draw two identical triangles on the scratch paper. Next, label the figures with information from the question: label angles *P* and *S* as 13° and angles *Q* and *T* as 130°. Use hash marks to indicate that sides *PQ* and *ST* are the same length. The drawing should look something like this:

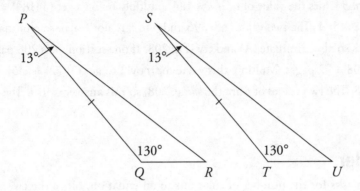

Since two pairs of corresponding angles are the same size, the third pair of corresponding angles will also be the same size. All triangles contain 180°, so the third angle in each triangle is 180° − 13° − 130° = 37°. Label this on the figure, which now looks like this:

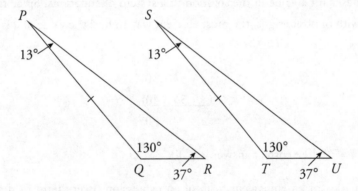

Look at the answer choices and use Process of Elimination. Eliminate (B) because the measure of angle *R* could already be determined from the information in the question, so it is not additional information. The two triangles are similar because they have the same three angle measurements. However, this only means that the lengths of corresponding sides are proportional, not necessarily that the lengths of corresponding sides are the same, so the angle measures alone are not enough to determine whether the triangles are congruent. Move on to the information about side lengths, and evaluate the remaining answer choices.

The question states that *sides PQ and ST have the same length.* When two pairs of angles and the side between them are equal, the triangles are congruent and the angle-side-angle rule (ASA for short) applies. Because sides *PQ* and *ST* are the same length and are between two pairs of angles that have the same measure, this proves that the triangles are congruent. Eliminate (C) because knowing the specific length of side *ST* is not necessary. Eliminate (D) because only one set of equivalent side lengths was needed to prove that the triangles are congruent. The correct answer is (A).

22. **D**   The question asks for a value given a specific situation. Since the question asks for a specific value and the answers contain numbers in increasing order, use the values in the answers. Rewrite the answer choices on the scratch paper and label them as "*p*." Next, start with a number in the middle and try (B), 96. The question states that *a book that is 280 pages long is divided into two sections.* If one section, *p*, is 96 pages, the other section, *q*, is 280 – 96 = 184 pages. The question also states that the value of *p* is *8 less than 3* times the value of *q*. If *q* = 184, multiply by 3 to get (3)(184) = 552, then subtract 8 to get 552 – 8 = 544. The two values of *p*, 96 and 544, are not equal, so eliminate (B). A larger value of *p* is needed, so also eliminate (A) and try (D), 208. If one section, *p*, is 208 pages, the other section, *q*, is 280 – 208 = 72 pages. Multiply this value for *q* by 3 to get (3)(72) = 216, then subtract 8 to get 216 – 8 = 208. The two values of *p* are the same, 208, so this answer works. The correct answer is (D).

Module 2 – Harder

1. **D**   The question asks for the number of solutions to an equation. Since the two sides of the equation have the same variable term, 2*z*, but a different constant, no value of *z* will make the equation true. To check this, subtract 2*z* from both sides of the equation to get 8 = –4. This is not true, so the equation has zero solutions. The correct answer is (D).

2. **C**   The question asks for a value in the solution to a system of equations. Since the equations contain the term 5*b* with opposite signs, the most efficient way to find the value of *a* is to stack and add the two equations.

$$a + 5b = 30$$
$$+ (\quad -5b = 40)$$
$$a \quad\quad = 70$$

The result is *a* = 70. The correct answer is (C).

3. **A**   The question asks for an equivalent form of an expression. Every term in the expression includes y^4 multiplied by a number. Since the two terms are like terms, they can simply be added together. Add the coefficients to get –8 + 12 = 4. Thus, $-8y^4 + 12y^4 = 4y^4$. The correct answer is (A).

4. **B**   The question asks for the interpretation of a feature of the graph of a function. Start by reading the final question, which asks for the best interpretation of the slope. In a linear graph that represents an amount over time, the slope represents the rate of change. Eliminate (A) and (C) because they refer to the volume of mulch at a single point in time, not to the change over time. Since the slope is the change after each bed is filled, plug 0 and 1 into the function for *x*. When *x* = 0, the function becomes *f*(0) = –75(0) + 500, or *f*(0) = 500. When *x* = 1, the function becomes *f*(1) = –75(1) + 500, or *f*(1) = 425. Since 500 – 425 = 75, 75 is the amount of mulch used for each garden bed. The correct answer is (B).

5.   **A**   The question asks for a value given a specific situation. Since the question asks for a specific value and the answers contain numbers in increasing order, use the values in the answers. Rewrite the answer choices on the scratch paper and label them "# attended day." Next, pick one of the middle numbers and try (B), 2,500. The question states that *6 times as many people attended the performance at night as attended the performance during the day.* If 2,500 people attended during the day, (6)(2,500) = 15,000 people attended at night. The question also states that *2,500 more people attended the performance at night than attended the performance during the day.* If 2,500 people attended the performance during the day, 2,500 + 2,500 = 5,000 people attended the performance during the night. The two numbers of people who attended the performance during the night, 15,000 and 5,000, are not equal, so eliminate (B). It may be difficult to determine whether a larger or smaller number is needed, so pick a direction and try (A), 500. If 500 people attended during the day, (6)(500) = 3,000 people attended at night. Using the other piece of information, if 500 people attended the performance during the day, 500 + 2,500 = 3,000 people attended at night. In both cases, the number of people who attended the performance at night is 3,000, and the number of people who attended the performance during the day is 500, so stop here. The correct answer is (A).

6.   **A**   The question asks for the point that satisfies a system of inequalities. The answers contain specific points, so use the values in the answers. Rewrite the answer choices on the scratch paper and label them "(x, y)." Test the ordered pairs in both inequalities, and look for an ordered pair that makes both inequalities true. Start with one of the answers in the middle, so try (C). Plug $x = 2$ and $y = -4$ into the first inequality to get $-4 \geq 2 - 9$, which becomes $-4 \geq -7$. This is true, so plug the same values into the second inequality to get $-4 \leq -3(2) - 5$, which becomes $-4 \leq -6 - 5$, and then $-4 \leq -11$. This is not true, so eliminate (C). The right side of the second inequality needs to be larger, so use a negative value for x and try (A). Plug $x = -2$ and $y = -4$ into the first inequality to get $-4 \geq -2 - 9$, which becomes $-4 \geq -11$. This is true, so plug the same values into the second inequality to get $-4 \leq -3(-2) - 5$, which becomes $-4 \leq 6 - 5$, and then $-4 \leq 1$. This is also true, which means the point in (A) makes both inequalities true, so (A) is correct. Another approach is to enter both inequalities into the built-in calculator and see which of the four points in the answer choices is in the area of the intersection of the two graphs in the graphing area. Using either method, the correct answer is (A).

7.   **33**   The question asks for a value based on a geometric figure. Begin by drawing a right triangle and labeling the hypotenuse (the side opposite the right angle) as 14 and the legs (which are the two sides that are not the hypotenuse) as 8 and $2\sqrt{a}$. The drawing should look something like this:

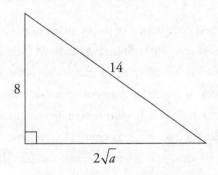

To solve for a, use the Pythagorean Theorem: $a^2 + b^2 = c^2$. Plug in the given values to get $8^2 + \left(2\sqrt{a}\right)^2 = 14^2$. This becomes $64 + 4a = 196$. Subtract 64 from both sides of the equation to get $4a = 132$. Divide both sides of the equation by 4 to get $a = 33$. The correct answer is 33.

8. **162** The question asks for the measure of an angle and gives conflicting units. Either write down a conversion between radians and degrees from memory or open the reference sheet, which states that the *number of degrees of arc in a circle is 360* and that the *number of radians of arc in a circle is 2π*. Thus, 360 degrees = 2π radians. This reduces to the other conversion, which is 180 degrees = π radians. Set up a proportion, being sure to match up units. The proportion is $\dfrac{180 \text{ degrees}}{\pi \text{ radians}} = \dfrac{x \text{ degrees}}{\dfrac{9\pi}{10} \text{ radians}}$. Cross-multiply to get $(\pi)(x) = (180)\left(\dfrac{9\pi}{10}\right)$. Simplify to get $\pi x = 162\pi$, then divide both sides of the equation by π to get $x = 162$. The correct answer is 162.

9. **B** The question asks for the measure of an angle on a geometric figure. Start by drawing two triangles that are similar to each other, meaning they have the same proportions but are different sizes. Be sure to match up the corresponding angles that are given in the question and label all information given. The drawing should look something like this:

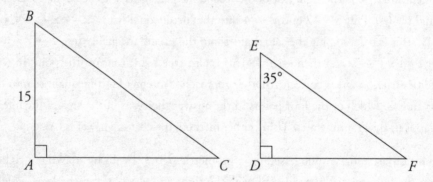

Since angle E corresponds to angle B, angle B also has a measure of 35°. The correct answer is (B).

10. **C** The question asks for the best comparison of the medians of two data sets shown in a frequency table. The median is the middle value of a list of numbers ordered from least to greatest. The question states that each data set consists of 31 values, so the middle value is the 16th, with $16 - 1 = 15$ values to the left and $31 - 16 = 15$ values to the right. A frequency table has two columns: the left-hand column contains the values, and the right-hand column contains the number of times each value occurs, or its frequency. In data set O, for example, 15 occurs 11 times and 18 occurs 9 times. In data set P, on the other hand, 15 occurs 1 time and 18 occurs 3 times. Use the frequency table to find the 16th

value of each data set. In data set O, the first 11 numbers are 15, then the next 9 are 18, so the 16th value is 18. In data set P, the first number is 15, then the next 3 are 18, then the next 7 are 21. This accounts for the first $1 + 3 + 7 = 11$ numbers, and the next 9 are 24, so the 16th value is 24. The median of data set O, 18, is less than the median of data set P, 24. The correct answer is (C).

11. **−3** The question asks for the product of the solutions to an equation. To solve algebraically, isolate the variable. Distribute on each side of the equation to get $-4a^2 + 12a = 2a^2 - 11a - 18$. Add $4a^2$ to both sides of the equation to get $12a = 6a^2 - 11a - 18$, and then subtract $12a$ from both sides of the equation to get $0 = 6a^2 - 23a - 18$. When a quadratic is in standard form, which is $ax^2 + bx + c$, the shortcut to find the product of the solutions is $\frac{c}{a}$. In this quadratic, $a = 6$ and $c = -18$. Plug in these values for a and c to get $\frac{-18}{6}$, which becomes −3. Without knowing this shortcut, it is still possible to find the answer by using the quadratic formula to find the two solutions and then multiplying them. Using either method, the correct answer is −3.

12. **D** The question asks for the interpretation of a term in context. Start by reading the final question, which asks for the meaning of the number 7. Rewrite the equation on the scratch paper. Then label the parts of the equation with the information given, and eliminate answers that do not match the labels. The question states that a represents large boxes, b represents small boxes, and 46 is the number of jerseys. Thus, the number 7 has something to do with large boxes. Eliminate (B) and (C) because they refer to small boxes, not large boxes. Compare the remaining answers: the difference is whether 7 is the total number of jerseys packed in large boxes or the number of jerseys packed in each large box. Eliminate (A) because the total number of jerseys packed in large boxes is represented by $7a$, not by 7. The correct answer is (D).

13. **−20** The question asks for the value of a constant in the coordinates of a point on a line. The constant k represents the y-coordinate of the y-intercept of the line. First, determine the values of the points on the line. The question gives the y-intercept of the line as $(c + 2, k)$. The y-intercept is the point at which the line crosses the y-axis; at that point, the value of the x-coordinate is 0. Thus, $c + 2 = 0$, so $c = -2$. Write down that the y-intercept is $(0, k)$, and then plug in −2 for c in the points given in the question to get $(-2, -14)$ and $(-2 + 9, -41)$, which becomes $(7, -41)$. Use those two points to calculate the slope of the line using the formula $slope = \frac{y_2 - y_1}{x_2 - x_1}$. The formula becomes $slope = \frac{-41 - (-14)}{7 - (-2)}$. Simplify to get $slope = -\frac{27}{9}$, or $slope = -3$. Since the y-intercept of the same line is $(0, k)$, use the slope formula again: plug in −3 for the slope, the y-intercept $(0, k)$, and one of the points, such as $(-2, -14)$.

The slope formula becomes $-3 = \dfrac{k - (-14)}{0 - (-2)}$. Simplify to get $-3 = \dfrac{k + 14}{2}$. Multiply both sides of the equation by 2 to get $-6 = k + 14$, and then subtract 14 from both sides of the equation to get $-20 = k$.

The correct answer is −20.

14. **C** The question asks for the interpretation of a feature of a graph in context. Start by reading the final question, which asks for the best interpretation of the vertex of the graph. Enter the function into the built-in calculator, then scroll and zoom as needed to find the vertex. The point is (4.9, 12). (The other way to find the vertex is to recognize that the equation is in vertex form, $a(x - h)^2 + k$, in which (h, k) is the vertex.) The question states that $g(x)$ represents the distance above the ground, and, in function notation, $g(x) = y$. Therefore, the y-value of the vertex, 12, represents the distance above the ground. Eliminate (A) and (D) because they state that the Frisbee was 4.9 feet above the ground, which is the x-value of the vertex, not the y-value.

Compare the remaining answer choices. The difference between (B) and (C) is whether the vertex represents the height when the Frisbee was thrown or the maximum height of the Frisbee. When the Frisbee was thrown, 0 seconds had elapsed. Time is on the x-axis, so $x = 0$ when the Frisbee was thrown. However, the vertex has an x-coordinate of 4.9, not 0, so eliminate (B). The correct answer is (C).

15. **D** The question asks for a change in value based on a function. In function notation, the number inside the parentheses is the x-value that goes into the function, and the value that comes out of the function is the y-value. Since the question is about the relationship between variables, plug in two different values for the number of items sold, x, to determine the decrease in profit. Start by plugging $x = 10$ into the function to get $P(10) = 50(10 - 2.25) + 20$. Either enter the equation into the built-in calculator or start solving to get $P(10) = 50(7.75) + 20$. Continue solving to get $P(10) = 387.50 + 20$, and then $P(10) = 407.50$. Next, decrease the x-value by 3, and plug $x = 7$ into the function to get $P(7) = 50(7 - 2.25) + 20$. Again, either use the built-in calculator or start solving to get $P(7) = 50(4.75) + 20$. Continue solving to get $P(7) = 237.50 + 20$, and then $P(7) = 257.50$. The difference between the two values is $407.50 - 257.50 = 150$. The correct answer is (D).

16. **A** The question asks for the y-intercept of a line. A y-intercept is a point where $x = 0$. One approach is to enter the equation into the built-in graphing calculator, then scroll and zoom as needed to find the point where the graph intersects the y-axis. The graph shows the y-intercept at (0, −22), which is (A). Because the answers are points that could be the y-intercept, another approach is to use the values in the answers. Using (A), for example, plug $y = -22$ and $x = 0$ into the equation to get $6(0) - 11(-22) = 242$, which becomes $0 + 242 = 242$, and then $242 = 242$. This is true, so (0, −22) is the y-intercept. Using either method, the correct answer is (A).

17. **D** The question asks for a measurement and gives conflicting units. The question provides the conversion that 1 foot = 12 inches but gives the area of fabric in square feet. Because the conversion equation is in linear units, not square units, it is necessary to convert to square feet and square inches. Square both parts of the conversion equation to get 1^2 foot = 12^2 inches, or 1 square foot = 144 square inches. Next, set up a proportion, being sure to match up units. The proportion is $\dfrac{1 \text{ square foot}}{144 \text{ square inches}} = \dfrac{31.6 \text{ square feet}}{x \text{ square inches}}$. Cross-multiply to get $4{,}550.4 = x$. Therefore, the fabric measures 4,550.4 square inches. The correct answer is (D).

18. **–7** The question asks for a constant in a factor of a polynomial. To begin factoring the expression, factor $3x$ out of the entire expression to get $3x(x^2 - 19x + 84)$. Now factor the quadratic part of the expression. Find two numbers that multiply to 84 and add to –19. These are –12 and –7. Thus, the full expression factors into $3x(x - 12)(x - 7)$. The two possible values for q in the binomial $(x + q)$ are –12 and –7. Since $p < q$, the value of q is –7. The correct answer is –7.

19. **$\dfrac{1}{2}$ or** The question asks for a value in a system of equations. A system of linear equations in two variables **0.5** has an infinite number of solutions if the two equations are equivalent. Start by rearranging the two equations so they are in the same form. Subtract $20x$ from both sides of the second equation to get $78y - 54x = -b$. Then add $78y$ to both sides of the second equation to get $-54x = -78y - b$. Finally, divide both sides of the second equation by –2 to get $27x = 39y + \dfrac{1}{2}b$. The equations are now in the same form. In order for the system of equations to have an infinite number of solutions, all of the terms must be the same. The x-terms are both $27x$, and the y-terms are both $39y$, so the constants must also be the same. Thus, $\dfrac{1}{2}b = \dfrac{1}{4}$. Multiply both sides of the equation by 2 to get $b = \dfrac{2}{4}$. This can be entered in the fill-in box, reduced to $\dfrac{1}{2}$, or entered in decimal form as .5 or 0.5. The correct answer is $\dfrac{1}{2}$, 0.5, or another equivalent form.

20. **B** The question asks for an equation that models a specific situation. There are variables in the answer choices, so plug in. Choose a number that works well with the conditions of the question: since 57 divided by 3 is 19, make $b = 19$ backpackers. The question states that each backpacker needs 3 meals, so $3(19) = 57$ meals are needed in total. To find p, the number of pallets of meals needed, divide the number on each pallet, 57, by the number of meals needed, 57, to get 1. This is the target value; write it down and circle it.

Now plug $b = 19$ into the answer choices and eliminate any that do not match the target value. Choice (A) becomes $p = \dfrac{19}{57}$, or $p = \dfrac{1}{3}$. This does not match the target value of 1, so eliminate (A).

Choice (B) becomes $p = \dfrac{19}{19}$, or $p = 1$. This matches the target value, so keep (B), but check the remaining answers just in case. Choice (C) becomes $p = 57(19)$, or $p = 1{,}083$; eliminate (C). Choice (D) becomes $p = 171(19)$, or $p = 3{,}249$; eliminate (D). The correct answer is (B).

21. **C** The question asks for a true statement about a function. The question states that the graph of function f has a minimum value at (h, k). This means the parabola opens upward and has a vertex at (h, k). When a quadratic is in standard form, $ax^2 + bx + c$, the sign of a indicates which way the parabola opens. When a is positive, the parabola opens upward, and when a is negative, the parabola opens downward. Since this parabola opens upward, a must be positive. However, a could be greater than 1 or a fraction between 0 and 1, so this is not enough information to determine whether statement (I) must be true.

The question also states that $f(2) = f(18)$, which means that, on the graph of the parabola, the point where $x = 2$ and the point where $x = 18$ have the same y-coordinate. The axis of symmetry of a parabola is midway between any two points with the same y-coordinate. Find the midpoint of the two x-coordinates given to find the axis of symmetry: $\dfrac{2 + 18}{2} = \dfrac{20}{2} = 10$. The axis of symmetry goes through the vertex, so the x-coordinate of the vertex, or h, is 10.

When a quadratic is in standard form, which is $ax^2 + bx + c$, the x-coordinate of the vertex can be found using the formula $h = -\dfrac{b}{2a}$. In this quadratic, $a = a$ and $b = -6$. Since $h = 10$, the formula becomes $10 = -\dfrac{-6}{2a}$. Multiply both sides of the equation by $2a$ to get $20a = 6$, then divide both sides of the equation by 20 to get $a = \dfrac{6}{20}$, or $a = \dfrac{3}{10}$. This is greater than 0 and less than 1, so statement (I) is true. Eliminate (B) and (D) because they do not include (I) as a true statement.

To check statement (II), plug in a value to determine whether that condition must be true. To evaluate whether c must be greater than 0, see what happens when c equals 0. Plug $c = 0$ and $a = \dfrac{3}{10}$ into the quadratic to get $\dfrac{3}{10}x^2 - 6x = 0$. Enter this into the built-in calculator to see the graph of the function. The question states that the graph of the function has a positive y-intercept, so scroll and zoom as needed to find the gray dot that represents the y-intercept. The point is at $(0, 0)$, which is not positive. Test a negative value: make $c = -1$ by changing the quadratic in the graphing calculator to $\dfrac{3}{10}x^2 - 6x - 1$. The y-intercept is now at $(0, -1)$, which is also not positive. Test a positive value: make $c = 1$ by changing the quadratic in the graphing calculator to $\dfrac{3}{10}x^2 - 6x + 1$. The y-intercept is now at $(0, 1)$, which is positive. Thus, c must be greater than 0, and statement (II) is true. Eliminate (A) because it does not contain statement (II). The correct answer is (C).

22. **B**   The question asks for a solution to a given equation. The constant k is in the answer choices, so plug in a value for k. Make $k = 2$. The equation becomes $\dfrac{2^2}{\sqrt{x^2 + 2^2}} = 12 - \dfrac{x^2}{\sqrt{x^2 + 2^2}}$. Enter this equation into the built-in calculator to get a graph of the solutions for x. Scroll and zoom as needed to see that the graph shows two solutions at slightly greater than −12 and slightly less than 12. These are the approximate target values; write them down and circle them.

Now plug $k = 2$ into the answer choices and eliminate any that do not match either of the target values. Choice (A) becomes −2. This is not close to −12 or 12, so eliminate (A). Choice (B) becomes $\sqrt{12^2 - 2^2}$. Use a calculator to get a result of ≈ 11.83. This is slightly less than 12, so keep (B), but check the remaining answers just in case. Choice (C) becomes $\sqrt{2^2 + 12^2}$. Use a calculator to get a result of ≈ 12.16. This is close to one of the solutions, but it is greater than 12 rather than less than 12; eliminate (C). Choice (D) becomes $12^2 - 2^2 = 144 - 4 = 140$. This is too large; eliminate (D). The correct answer is (B).

Chapter 3
Practice Test 2

HOW TO EMULATE THE DIGITAL SAT ON PAPER

Practice Test 4 is available in your online student tools in a digital, adaptive environment. The three tests in this physical book are printed on paper, but otherwise emulate the digital test in every way: test style, difficulty, and content. Please use the checklist below to ensure that you are able to emulate the adaptive nature of the test and get the preparation that you need for test day. Feel free to use the versions of Module 2 that you do not take during your test as additional practice.

- ☐ Take Reading and Writing (RW) Module 1, allowing yourself 32 minutes to complete it.

- ☐ Go to the answer key starting on page 202 and determine the number of questions you got correct in RW Module 1.

- ☐ If you get fewer than 15 questions correct, take RW Module 2 – Easier, which starts on page 152. If you get 15 or more questions correct, take RW Module 2 – Harder, which starts on page 163.

- ☐ Whichever RW Module 2 you take, start immediately and allow yourself 32 minutes to complete it.

- ☐ Take a 10-minute break between RW Module 2 and Math Module 1.

- ☐ Take Math Module 1, allowing yourself 35 minutes to complete it.

- ☐ Go to the answer key starting on page 202 and determine the number of questions you got correct in Math Module 1.

- ☐ If you get fewer than 14 questions correct, take Math Module 2 – Easier, which starts on page 184. If you get 14 or more questions correct, take Math Module 2 – Harder, which starts on page 192.

- ☐ Whichever Math Module you take, start it immediately and allow yourself 35 minutes to complete it.

- ☐ After you finish the test, check your answers to RW Module 2 and Math Module 2.

- ☐ Only after you complete the entire test should you read the explanations for the questions, which start on page 203.

SAT Prep Test 2—Reading and Writing
Module 1

Turn to Section 1 of your answer sheet to answer the questions in this section.

DIRECTIONS

The questions in this section address a number of important reading and writing skills. Each question includes one or more passages, which may include a table or graph. Read each passage and question carefully, and then choose the best answer to the question based on the passage(s).

All questions in the section are multiple-choice with four answer choices. Each question has a single best answer. Fill in the circle with the answer letter for the answer you think is best.

---

1 ▢ Mark for Review

Even though no woman pilot had ever successfully crossed the Atlantic Ocean while flying solo when she made her attempt, female aviator Amelia Earhart did not consider this feat _____. Piloting a Lockheed Vega 5B in 1932 completely by herself, Earhart successfully navigated a nonstop transatlantic flight, and she was later presented with the United States Distinguished Flying Cross for this accomplishment.

Which choice completes the text with the most logical and precise word or phrase?

(A) definitive

(B) enigmatic

(C) impracticable

(D) appropriate

---

2 ▢ Mark for Review

Contemporary composer Max Richter's experimental electronic music is _____ looping and phrasing techniques featuring spoken word pieces and elements of electronica. Drawing from his studies with Luciano Berio, Richter artfully revisualizes traditional classical music by weaving synthesizer sounds with samples, resulting in unique compositions that go beyond either source.

Which choice completes the text with the most logical and precise word or phrase?

(A) portrayed by

(B) coupled with

(C) denoted through

(D) constructed from

CONTINUE ➡

---

3 ☐ Mark for Review

Certain scientists theorize that at least some of the hydrocarbons found in oil that is drilled from deep wells rose up from the mantle that sits below the Earth's crust, suggesting that these hydrocarbons may be _____ in origin: chemically created without having any association with living organisms.

Which choice completes the text with the most logical and precise word or phrase?

(A) flexible

(B) genuine

(C) inorganic

(D) alterable

4 ☐ Mark for Review

While Ludwig van Beethoven, a renowned composer, grew increasingly deaf from 1801 until his death in 1827, his musical output was seemingly not substantially _____ his deteriorating hearing: 8 of his 9 symphonies and 15 of his 17 choral works were composed during this period.

Which choice completes the text with the most logical and precise word or phrase?

(A) limited to

(B) inhibited by

(C) developed from

(D) understood in

5 ☐ Mark for Review

The following text is adapted from James Fenimore Cooper's 1846 novel *Jack Tier, or the Florida Reef*. Mrs. Budd is traveling by boat with her niece, who has never been on a boat before.

Mrs. Budd had made one voyage previously, and she <u>fancied</u> that she knew all about a vessel. Never did she feel her great superiority over her niece as when discussing boats, about which she did know something.

As used in the text, what does the word "fancied" most nearly mean?

(A) Formulated

(B) Imagined

(C) Conceded

(D) Characterized

CONTINUE ➡

6 ☐ Mark for Review

The following text is from James Elroy Flecker's 1916 poem "No Coward's Tale."

> I am afraid to think about my death,
> When it shall be, and whether in great pain
> I shall rise up and fight the air for breath
> Or calmly wait the bursting of my brain.
>
> I am no coward who could seek in fear
> A folklore solace or sweet Indian tales:
> I know dead men are deaf and cannot hear
> The singing of a thousand nightingales.
>
> I know dead men are blind and cannot see
> The friend that shuts in horror their big eyes,
> And they are witless—O I'd rather be
> A living mouse than dead as a man dies.

Which choice best describes the overall structure of the text?

- (A) The speaker confesses his anxiety about a subject, then explains why his beliefs lead him to a certain preference.

- (B) The speaker explains why his fears are intensifying, then outlines his philosophy of life.

- (C) The speaker laments his cowardice, then forecasts a deep transformation in his beliefs.

- (D) The speaker denies his personal failings, then criticizes the failings of others.

7 ☐ Mark for Review

Dogs can discriminate between the smell of their own urine and that of the urine of another dog, and they act especially interested in their own urine when its scent has been altered by the addition of an odorous chemical. Psychologist Alexandra Horowitz made this determination by assessing dogs' level of interest in an odorous stimulus based on the amount of time dogs spent sniffing their own urine compared to the time spent sniffing their own urine mixed with aniseed oil. Dogs demonstrated some interest when presented with their unadulterated urine, but they demonstrated far more interest when presented with their urine adulterated with another scent.

According to the text, how did Horowitz determine the level of interest shown by dogs in the study?

- (A) She noted the way each dog approached its own urine.

- (B) She measured the time each dog spent sniffing the scents.

- (C) She investigated how each dog responded to the urine of other dogs.

- (D) She tested each dog's facial reactions to aniseed oil.

CONTINUE ⟶

---

8 ☐ Mark for Review

The Great Barrier Reef is composed of over 2,900 individual reefs that span more than 1,400 miles. Although the Great Barrier Reef is the world's largest structure made of living entities, marine biologists are concerned that reef coverage has declined significantly since 1950, in part due to land-based chemicals polluting the ocean. These biologists believe that strictly controlling the use of fertilizers, herbicides, and pesticides will allow the Great Barrier Reef to regenerate.

According to the text, why are biologists concerned about the Great Barrier Reef?

Ⓐ Its already huge structure cannot accommodate many more new reefs.

Ⓑ It can't expand into new areas because it requires fertilizer to grow.

Ⓒ It is no longer generating new reefs.

Ⓓ It once spread over a much larger area than it does today.

---

9 ☐ Mark for Review

Culinary master George Auguste Escoffier may have invented the bouillon cube and designed the operational system of the modern professional kitchen, but it is his first cookbook *Le Guide Culinaire* that makes Escoffier a legend. This 1903 masterpiece was pivotal to the evolution of fine cooking. In this collection of over 5,000 international and French recipes, Escoffier popularized and modernized traditional French cooking methods, embracing seasonal ingredients while rejecting fussy garnishes. Revered by many as the ultimate culinary reference book, *Le Guide Culinaire* is considered one of the leading texts on cuisine to this day.

Which choice best describes the main idea of the text?

Ⓐ Escoffier was an accomplished author whose writings encouraged many readers to create their own recipes.

Ⓑ Escoffier's innovative and influential cookbook *Le Guide Culinaire* wasn't recognized as essential by many until long after it was first released in 1903.

Ⓒ Escoffier is renowned for his many culinary inventions, including the bouillon cube.

Ⓓ Escoffier's extensive cookbook *Le Guide Culinaire* is a highly influential collection of recipes.

CONTINUE ➡

10 ☐ Mark for Review

The Y. M. C. A. Boys of Cliffwood is a 1916 novel by Brooks Henderley. In the novel, Henderley portrays Dick Horner as a good-hearted boy whose adventurous nature can cause him trouble: _____

Which quotation from *The Y. M. C. A. Boys of Cliffwood* most effectively illustrates the claim?

Ⓐ "Dick sighed many times. He somehow was thinking of that golden prize which Mr. Holwell had offered for the best farce, and which would be awarded a few nights after Christmas. If only he had won that, there were so many things he had planned to buy with the twenty-five dollars that would have made the Great Day seem so much more joyful."

Ⓑ "As the evening set in Dick felt his gloomy fears increase rather than diminish. It was strange, too, because as a general thing the boy had always been of a cheery disposition, and able to stand up under all manner of ordinary troubles."

Ⓒ "Dick did not have so bad a reputation in the town as the big bully, Nat Silmore, but all the same the stories that drifted to the ears of his anxious mother often caused her gentle heart pain. Dick, upon being appealed to, always promised to turn over a new leaf, and then in the end his natural overflow of wild spirits led him into some new mischief, for which in turn he would be sorry."

Ⓓ "Dick took the letter and looked hard at it. When he saw it was addressed on a typewriter, and that in the upper left-hand corner there was printed the name of a law firm in New York, somehow he was seized with a sense of coming trouble."

11 ☐ Mark for Review

Hula dancing has been an important Hawaiian tradition for hundreds of years. Deeply spiritual and meaningful, hula dances originally honored gods and chiefs and were used to pass down stories that explained all manners of natural phenomena. Over the last 100 years, commercialized hula dancers have been applauded by millions of tourists. However, to recognize the full significance of hula dancing, audience members must have a strong familiarity with the history and stories behind it. Therefore, _____

Which choice most logically completes the text?

Ⓐ hula dancing is more meaningful to those who understand its traditions than are other forms of dance.

Ⓑ hula dancing is among the most popular of all commercialized traditional dance forms.

Ⓒ those with extensive knowledge of hula dancing generally prefer hula to other forms of artistic expression.

Ⓓ tourists are less likely to appreciate hula dancing as fully as are natives who are well-versed in its traditions.

CONTINUE →

12 ▢ Mark for Review

The Riace bronzes are two statues of warriors found buried off the coast of southern Italy in 1972. Many art historians claim that the heightened attention to certain anatomical details in these figures proves that they were cast in the 5th century BCE Greece during the Early Classical period. However, Greek sculpture expert B. S. Ridgway argues that these statues were produced centuries later during a period when artists consciously imitated Early Classical style. The fact that these statues were cast in an Early Classical style, thus, _____

Which choice most logically completes the text?

(A) would be challenging to explain if these statues were not cast in the 5th century BCE.

(B) does not definitively prove that these statues originated in the 5th century BCE.

(C) indicates that later statues typically heightened anatomical detail.

(D) proves that these statues did not originate in the 5th century BCE.

13 ▢ Mark for Review

Most psychology PhD programs require students to complete a dissertation, a research-based paper that asserts theories about a psychology topic. To demonstrate their thorough knowledge of their subjects, students must include an extensive review of related literature and research. Education expert Mark Baron contends that although citations are necessary in any literature review, too many direct quotes can result in a stilted dissertation that is difficult to read; paraphrasing the views of other scientists could consequently _____

Which choice most logically completes the text?

(A) allow students to create dissertations that are linguistically clearer and more comprehensible.

(B) result in psychology dissertations that are more popular among non-scientists.

(C) help students' theories better match the consensus views of most renowned psychologists.

(D) enable students to present their theories without having to include numerous scientific citations.

14 ▢ Mark for Review

An American tennis player considered one of the greatest _____ Althea Gibson was the first African American player to win a Grand Slam title, the French Championship, in 1956.

Which choice completes the text so that it conforms to the conventions of Standard English?

(A) ever:

(B) ever;

(C) ever,

(D) ever

CONTINUE ➤

15 Mark for Review

A photographer and member of the Swinomish and Tulalip tribes, Matika Wilbur started traveling throughout all 50 US states in 2012 to complete Project _____ a multi-year photography project dedicated to documenting contemporary Indigenous life in the more than 562 federally recognized tribes in the US.

Which choice completes the text so that it conforms to the conventions of Standard English?

(A) 562

(B) 562,

(C) 562 and

(D) 562; and

16 Mark for Review

Paul Baran's invention of packet switching allowed for a more efficient and cost-effective way to transmit data and forms the basis of the modern _____ packet switching's invention, networks transmitted data by relying on circuit switching, a method that depends on a single physical connection between two points.

Which choice completes the text so that it conforms to the conventions of Standard English?

(A) internet and before

(B) internet. Before

(C) internet, before

(D) internet before

17 Mark for Review

According to local legend, the wild Chincoteague ponies on Assateague Island in the US are descendants of Spanish horses. Recently, while studying bones at a 16th-century historical site, _____ reveals a genetic link between the ponies and early Spanish horses.

Which choice completes the text so that it conforms to the conventions of Standard English?

(A) the discovery archaeologist Nicolas Delsol made is that a horse tooth

(B) a horse tooth, which archaeologist Nicolas Delsol discovered,

(C) archaeologist Nicolas Delsol's discovery of a horse tooth

(D) archaeologist Nicolas Delsol discovered a horse tooth that

18 Mark for Review

American Anthony Atala is a doctor and bioengineer whose research is helping people with diseased or damaged organs. Listed as one of *Time* magazine's top ten medical breakthroughs in 2011, _____ has the potential to help the many people waiting for organ donors.

Which choice completes the text so that it conforms to the conventions of Standard English?

(A) the organ developed by Atala was fully lab-grown and

(B) Atala's development of fully lab-grown organs

(C) Atala's team developed fully lab-grown organs, which

(D) Atala developed fully lab-grown organs; this

CONTINUE

19 ☐ Mark for Review

When NASA needed tools that were safe for astronauts to use during the Apollo space missions, American company Black & Decker was tasked with developing those tools. In 1979, the company introduced the DustBuster, which _____ of the larger and bulkier traditional vacuum cleaner.

Which choice completes the text so that it conforms to the conventions of Standard English?

Ⓐ is a cordless, lightweight variation

Ⓑ were cordless, lightweight variations

Ⓒ are cordless, lightweight variations

Ⓓ were a cordless, lightweight variation

20 ☐ Mark for Review

Thomas Herbert Elliot Jackson earned his living as a soldier and a coffee farmer, but he was also keenly interested in lepidopterology, the study of moths and _____ the largest collection of native African butterflies and donating his specimens to museums around the world.

Which choice completes the text so that it conforms to the conventions of Standard English?

Ⓐ butterflies, amassing

Ⓑ butterflies amassing

Ⓒ butterflies. Amassing

Ⓓ butterflies; amassing

21 ☐ Mark for Review

The tidal flats, or mudflats, in Korea provide safe habitats for many different species and are listed as Wetland Protected Areas under the Wetlands Conservation Act. _____ these sites still face a wide variety of threats from humans: construction of bridges, mining, wind farms, and fishing all decrease the biodiversity of the flats.

Which choice completes the text with the most logical transition?

Ⓐ However,

Ⓑ Likewise,

Ⓒ Therefore,

Ⓓ Furthermore,

22 ☐ Mark for Review

James Soong was initially predicted to win the 2000 Taiwanese presidential election until news broke of his potential involvement in corrupt financial practices. _____ Shui-bian Chen was elected president of Taiwan alongside Annette Lu as vice president, ending over 50 years of control by the Chinese Nationalist Party.

Which choice completes the text with the most logical transition?

Ⓐ Specifically,

Ⓑ Likewise,

Ⓒ Moreover,

Ⓓ Afterward,

CONTINUE ➡

23 ☐ Mark for Review

American artist Simone Leigh has stated that her works are intended to put Black women in the forefront and highlight their complex relationships with various societal structures. For her sculpture *Brick House*, Simone created an enormous bronze bust of a Black woman with a torso that resembles a clay house; the sculpture was originally placed in New York City among old and new high-rise buildings. _____ Leigh's exhibition *The Waiting Room* explores an alternative vision of healthcare that is shaped by the African-American female experience.

Which choice completes the text with the most logical transition?

- (A) Similarly,
- (B) For instance,
- (C) Nevertheless,
- (D) Therefore,

24 ☐ Mark for Review

While researching a topic, a student has taken the following notes:

- In 1980, video game designers and programmers Roberta and Ken Williams released an adventure game that combined text with images.
- Their game, *Mystery House*, was inspired by author Agatha Christie's mysteries.
- Players of the game find themselves locked in a house that they have to explore.
- As they explore, they meet other characters and learn that they have to find and stop a murderer.
- Images of each location in the house accompanied the text of the game.
- The game was successful because all of the other adventure games at the time only had text.

The student wants to explain an advantage of the format of *Mystery House*. Which choice most effectively uses relevant information from the notes to accomplish this goal?

- (A) Using images and text, programmers Roberta and Ken Williams created *Mystery House*, a video game murder mystery.
- (B) The format of *Mystery House* was successful because it combined text and images, unlike other video games at the time.
- (C) To find and stop the murderer, players explored a house and met other characters.
- (D) *Mystery House* contained images of each location of a house that players could explore.

CONTINUE ➡

25 ☐ Mark for Review

While researching a topic, a student has taken the following notes:

- Alice Catherine Evans discovered that the bacteria *Bacillus abortus* causes brucellosis in 1917.

- Brucellosis is a disease that can affect cows and humans.

- Evans found that consuming raw, unpasteurized cow milk could lead to infection in humans.

- She recommended pasteurization, treating food with mild heat, for dairy milk.

- Her vital work led to wider acceptance of pasteurization and a reduction in the occurrence of brucellosis.

The student wants to emphasize the significance of Evans's research. Which choice most effectively uses relevant information from the notes to accomplish this goal?

(A) Evans discovered that humans could become infected with the bacteria *Bacillus abortus* from drinking raw, unpasteurized cow milk.

(B) Based on her research into brucellosis, Evans recommended pasteurization, treating food with mild heat, for dairy milk.

(C) Evans made the connection between the bacteria *Bacillus abortus* and the disease brucellosis in 1917.

(D) Evans's 1917 discovery of the connection between *Bacillus abortus* and brucellosis was vital to the public's wider acceptance of pasteurization and reduction in brucellosis infections.

26 ☐ Mark for Review

While researching a topic, a student has taken the following notes:

- Physicists K. Alex Müller and Georg Bednorz were researching cuprates, a type of material, at IBM.

- In 1986, they observed that the cuprates could superconduct at a temperature of 30 kelvins.

- Superconductive materials carry an electric current without any resistance.

- The first observation of superconductivity was of a mercury wire at 4 kelvins, in 1911.

- Cuprates were labeled "high-temperature superconductors."

The student wants to contrast the superconductivity of mercury wire with that of cuprates. Which choice most effectively uses relevant information from the notes to accomplish this goal?

(A) While mercury wire becomes superconductive at 4 kelvins, cuprates are high-temperature superconductors, becoming superconductive at 30 kelvins.

(B) Cuprates are "high-temperature superconductors," unlike mercury wire, because they superconduct at a temperature of 30 kelvins.

(C) Materials can become superconductive and carry an electric current without any resistance at different temperatures.

(D) Although mercury wire's superconductivity was observed in 1911, cuprates' superconductivity was not observed until over seventy years later.

CONTINUE →

27 🔖 Mark for Review

While researching a topic, a student has taken the following notes:

- In the 1950s and '60s, the drug thalidomide was used in Europe to treat multiple conditions, including morning sickness experienced in pregnancy.

- The drug, however, was not safe for developing fetuses and led to many negative consequences.

- This situation prompted many countries to adopt better drug regulation and monitoring.

- In the US, the 1962 Kefauver-Harris Amendment added a requirement for a drug to be approved for sale.

- The Amendment required drug manufacturers to provide proof of the effectiveness of the drugs.

The student wants to present the significance of the Kefauver-Harris Amendment to an audience unfamiliar with the medication thalidomide. Which choice most effectively uses relevant information from the notes to accomplish this goal?

(A) Before the Kefauver-Harris Amendment, drug manufacturers were not required to prove a drug's effectiveness.

(B) The negative effects of the use of thalidomide in Europe in the 1950s and '60s led to the 1962 Kefauver-Harris Amendment.

(C) The 1962 Kefauver-Harris Amendment, which requires proof of a drug's effectiveness, was a result of the negative consequences of the morning sickness medication thalidomide.

(D) The medication thalidomide was used to treat morning sickness when the Kefauver-Harris Amendment went into effect.

YIELD

Once you've finished (or run out of time for) this section, use the answer key to determine how many questions you got right. If you got fewer than 15 questions right, move on to Module 2—Easier, otherwise move on to Module 2—Harder.

SAT Prep Test 2—Reading and Writing
Module 2—Easier

Turn to Section 1 of your answer sheet to answer the questions in this section.

1 ☐ Mark for Review

Environmental analysts are tasked with _____ the complete ecological evaluation of goods through the use of life-cycle assessments: by looking at the manufacture, distribution, and use of a commercial product, they can find out the environmental impact of a product.

Which choice completes the text with the most logical and precise word or phrase?

(A) separating

(B) convincing

(C) operating

(D) determining

2 ☐ Mark for Review

For Ghanaian coffin artist Paa Joe, remaining _____ is key to his art form. Customers approach him in a time of grief, hoping to get a custom piece designed to embody meaningful characteristics of their deceased loved ones. After carefully drawing up a design, Joe honors their requests through his work and creates a unique coffin to memorialize the life of the individual who will be placed in it; he believes his designs are a way to carry a piece of life in this world to the afterlife.

Which choice completes the text with the most logical and precise word or phrase?

(A) compassionate

(B) hesitant

(C) assertive

(D) insensitive

CONTINUE

3 ☐ Mark for Review

In the early 2000s, due to a lack of _____ ways to prevent the disease, the threat of being infected by HIV grew exponentially in South Africa. However, in 2007, South African epidemiologist Quarraisha Abdool Karim was the lead investigator in a study that tested the efficacy of Tenefovir, a gel that was found to lower the risk of contracting HIV by 39%.

Which choice completes the text with the most logical and precise word or phrase?

(A) inefficient

(B) unreasonable

(C) effective

(D) charismatic

4 ☐ Mark for Review

The Birmingham campaign was created in the early 1960s to draw attention to the injustice in the lives of African Americans in Alabama with nonviolent sit-ins, boycotts, and marches. These _____ attempts for change resulted in mass arrests of protestors and physical attacks from police and their dogs.

Which choice completes the text with the most logical and precise word or phrase?

(A) indifferent

(B) peaceful

(C) essential

(D) bland

5 ☐ Mark for Review

Months before the 1998 bombing of the US Embassy in Nairobi, Prudence Bushnell, the US ambassador to Kenya, unsuccessfully requested increased security for her mission several times. When Washington was not able to _____ her appeal, she wrote to US Secretary of State Madeleine Albright pleading for support but was ignored.

Which choice completes the text with the most logical and precise word or phrase

(A) certify

(B) mistake

(C) approve

(D) demonstrate

6 ☐ Mark for Review

Despite being a best-selling writer, Georgette Heyer continuously _____ to engage in all forms of publicity for her publications after the success of her novel *These Old Shades*. She so believed that her private life was irrelevant to the success of her novels that her fans didn't learn of her married name until after her death.

Which choice completes the text with the most logical and precise word or phrase?

(A) refused

(B) aspired

(C) needed

(D) proceeded

CONTINUE ▶

7 ☐ Mark for Review

In the late 1960s, Dr. Donald Hopkins was hired by the Centers for Disease Control to help implement a program to eradicate smallpox in Sierra Leone. The country had had a major outbreak of the disease one year before Hopkins' arrival and had the highest number of recorded cases in the world. Upon their arrival, Hopkins and his team immediately began mass distribution of the smallpox vaccine, using any means of transportation necessary. Through the use of jet injectors, they were able to vaccinate 1,000 people every 60 minutes.

Which choice best states the main purpose of the text?

(A) To present the effects of smallpox on Sierra Leone

(B) To describe Hopkins' career with the Centers for Disease Control

(C) To highlight the availability of the smallpox vaccine

(D) To explain how Hopkins addressed smallpox in Sierra Leone

8 ☐ Mark for Review

The following text is from James E. McGirt's 1906 poem "A Sailor's Departure."

My dearest child, I have no wealth to give you,
No ring of gold to you can I impart;
Going, yet why should going grieve you?
You have my heart.

In calm, in storm, no matter how the weather,
My one great thought shall ever be of thee;
Tell me, I pray thee, tell me whether
You'll think of me?

Which choice best states the main purpose of the text?

(A) To assure a loved one that she will not be forgotten

(B) To explain why the speaker loves an individual so dearly

(C) To justify to a loved one why the speaker is leaving and when he will be back

(D) To instruct a loved one on what to do while the speaker is gone

CONTINUE ➡

9 ☐ Mark for Review

Text 1

The Great Famine of Ireland was an era in Irish history that resulted in hunger and sickness throughout the country. The Irish Lumper potato crop was exposed to the bacteria *Phytophthora infestans* in the 1840s, creating devastating effects. Upon studying the physical impacts of the infestation of the potatoes, scientists originally believed the disease was caused by the US-1 strain of the bacteria. This variety of the bacteria is a very common source of damage to crops and is still responsible for the destruction of crops today.

Text 2

An interested group of researchers tested dried leaves from small, shriveled, inedible potato plants preserved from the Great Famine of Ireland. After collecting the leaves, the researchers were able to analyze them alongside the DNA of modern US-1 strains of the bacteria and found that US-1 was not the cause of the catastrophe. It was concluded that, although the US-1 strain is a common cause of crop loss, a formerly undiscovered strain of the bacteria, HERB-1, was actually at fault for the famine.

Based on the texts, what would the researchers in Text 2 most likely say about the scientists' initial belief in Text 1?

(A) It is mistaken because the scientists made the assumption that HERB-1 was the strain that caused the famine.

(B) It is logical because the US-1 strain is similar to the HERB-1 strain but only affects potato crops.

(C) It is sensible because of how common the US-1 strain is, but the DNA analysis suggests that HERB-1 was to blame.

(D) It is puzzling because it is unclear why the scientists would think that US-1 caused the famine.

10 ☐ Mark for Review

The following text is from Amy Lowell's 1912 poem "Diya," originally "Delta-iota-psi-alpha."

> Ah, Dearest, you are good to love me so,
> And yet I would not have it goodness, rather
> Excess of selfishness in you to need
> Me through and through, as flowers need the sun.
> I wonder can it really be that you
> And I are here alone, and that the night
> Is full of hours, and all the world asleep,
> And none can call to you to come away.

Based on the text, in what way is the speaker like the sun?

(A) She shines brightly on others.

(B) She provides something that is needed.

(C) She is completely alone.

(D) She is asleep at night with the rest of the world.

11 ☐ Mark for Review

The Haunted Orchard is a 1912 short story by Richard Le Gallienne. In the story, the main character suspects that his orchard is haunted by the spirit of a young girl. As a result, he is eager to help bring peace to the restless spirit, stating _____

Which quotation from *The Haunted Orchard* most effectively illustrates the claim?

(A) "I had lived in the old house for about a month, when one afternoon a strange thing happened to me."

(B) "And the next day I had a curious confirmation of my theory."

(C) "Poor child! tell me of your grief – that I may help your sorrowing heart to rest."

(D) "But, of course, there was no answer; yet that night I dreamed a strange dream."

CONTINUE ➔

12 | Mark for Review

Characteristics of Biomes

Type of biome	Maximum temperature (°F)	Annual precipitation
Temperate forest	86	30–59
Desert	100	0–10
Boreal forest	68	12–35
Tropical forest	77	79–394
Grassland	86	20–35

An ecologist is interested in studying the habitats of animals living within a biome that has a range of annual precipitation that includes 30 inches but does not exceed a maximum temperature of 80°F. Based on the characteristics of biomes, he decided to study the animals living within a _____

Which choice most effectively uses data from the table to complete the text?

(A) temperate forest.

(B) tropical forest.

(C) grassland.

(D) boreal forest.

13 | Mark for Review

Properties of Five Unknown Elements

Element	Boiling point (K)	Heat Capacity (J/g*k)	Electron affinity (kJ/mol)	First ionization energy (eV)
A	2,835	0.38	118.4	7.726
B	2,435	0.235	125.6	7.576
C	3,003	0.44	112	7.639
D	2,022	0.13	35.1	7.417
E	717.8	0.71	200	10.36

Unknown elements can be identified as metals or nonmetals based on a variety of characteristics. Metals are generally considered to have high boiling points (over 1,500 K) and low electron affinities (less than 150 kJ/mol), while nonmetals have low boiling points (less than 1,000 K) and very high electron affinities. A science student collected information about five unknown elements in the table above and stated that four of the elements are metals and one element is a nonmetal.

Which choice best describes data from the table that support the student's assertion?

(A) Four of the five elements have boiling points above 1,500 K, and all except for element E have electron affinities of less than 150 kJ/mol.

(B) Element E has a low boiling point of 717.8 K and a high first ionization energy of 10.36 eV.

(C) Four of the five elements have a first ionization energy around 7 eV, and all except element D have a heat capacity above 0.2 J/g*K.

(D) All of the elements have a heat capacity from 0.13 and 0.44 J/g*K, and only element E has an electron affinity greater than 150 kJ/mol.

CONTINUE ➤

14 ☐ Mark for Review

An art student is studying *chiaroscuro*, one of the specific painting styles used in the Renaissance period that features contrasting light and dark artistic elements within an art piece. While attending a local art museum to view its exhibit of Renaissance chiaroscuro paintings, the student notices the inclusion of a modern art portrait depicting Leonardo da Vinci, a famous Renaissance artist and inventor. However, the portrait does not contain elements of chiaroscuro and, thus, the student believes that the work was included as a way to attract new visitors.

Which statement, if true, would most directly support the student's claim?

Ⓐ New museum visitors rarely visit the second floor of the museum, which contains exhibits from the Renaissance, Baroque, and Neoclassical art periods.

Ⓑ The Renaissance exhibit also included other modern art portraits of Impressionist and Expressionist artists.

Ⓒ The portrait of Leonardo da Vinci was placed at the entrance to the Renaissance exhibit.

Ⓓ The exhibit's curators displayed the modern portrait of Leonardo da Vinci because of its appeal to people who don't normally visit art museums.

15 ☐ Mark for Review

Studies on the effects of bilingualism on cognitive development have shown an array of benefits, such as improved memory recall, cognitive processing, and executive function. A team of researchers decided to compare the task-switching abilities of different bilinguals (Spanish-English, Chinese-English, and French-English speakers) to English monolinguals. All bilingual groups demonstrated a significantly shorter time spent on task-switching tests than did the English monolinguals. Thus, the researchers claim that bilinguals can switch between tasks at a faster rate due to their routine use of language-switching.

Which finding, if true, would most strongly support the researchers' claim?

Ⓐ Bilinguals who speak both languages every day are faster at task-switching than are bilinguals who speak one of the languages less frequently.

Ⓑ Both bilinguals and English monolinguals take a long time to complete cognitive processing tasks.

Ⓒ English monolinguals have better memory recall than bilinguals do.

Ⓓ Bilingual students tend to be academic achievers, and academic achievers are known to be faster at task-switching than the general population is.

CONTINUE ➡

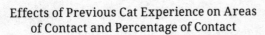

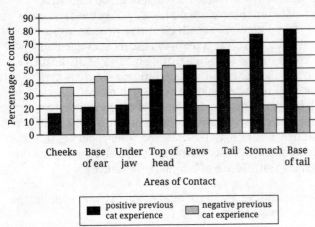

Effects of Previous Cat Experience on Areas of Contact and Percentage of Contact

16 ☐ Mark for Review

Which choice best describes data in the graph that support the researchers' claim?

Ⓐ Participants with previous positive cat experiences had lower percentages of contact in areas disliked by cats than did participants with previous negative cat experiences.

Ⓑ Participants with previous negative cat experiences had greater percentages of contact in areas preferred by cats than did participants with previous positive cat experiences.

Ⓒ Participants with previous positive cat experiences had similar percentages of contact for the cats' cheeks, base of ear, and under jaw areas.

Ⓓ Participants with previous negative cat experiences had more contact with cats' top of head than paws.

Cats are generally known to be sensitive to human interactions and prefer certain contact areas, such as the cheeks, base of ear, and under the jaw, while disliking contact on the stomach or the base of the tail. A team of researchers investigated the effect of previous cat experience, either in the form of pet ownership or random interactions with cats, and whether this made participants more likely to exhibit good cat handling techniques according to the cats' preferred contact areas. Participants were asked to spend five minutes in a pen with a cat on three different occasions. The percentage of contact and areas contacted during this time were observed and plotted in the graph above. The researchers claimed that previous positive cat experience was not predictive of good cat handling techniques; in fact, participants with previous negative cat experience demonstrated better cat handling techniques.

CONTINUE ➡

17 ☐ Mark for Review

Japanese producer and writer Hayao Miyazaki is renowned for the movie products of Studio Ghibli. Although the studio's films are presented through animation, the stories remain relevant to both children and adults. Drawing from Japanese elements, Miyazaki crafts poignant stories about humans and the environment as told through the eyes of children. For example, in *Princess Mononoke,* the nature spirits, referred to as *shishigami,* fight to preserve their forest against human industrialization. Miyazaki showcases the importance of protecting the environment for civilization to thrive, not through destruction but through communing with nature.

Which choice best describes Miyazaki's approach to film, as presented in the text?

Ⓐ He is inspired by nature spirits when writing his films.

Ⓑ He incorporates Japanese elements into his animated films.

Ⓒ He showcases Japanese and Western influences equally in his films.

Ⓓ He believes that films about environmental preservation will encourage people to commune with nature.

18 ☐ Mark for Review

In response to attacks by herbivorous insects, thale cress plants _____ with their neighbors by releasing volatile compounds called jasmonates. When nearby plants detect jasmonates in contact with their leaves, they bolster their defenses against herbivory by increasing the production of chemical insect repellents.

Which choice completes the text so that it conforms to the conventions of Standard English?

Ⓐ communicating

Ⓑ communicate

Ⓒ to communicate

Ⓓ having communicated

19 ☐ Mark for Review

Farmers throughout the islands of Polynesia _____ sweet potato as a staple crop since before the arrival of European explorers. Surprisingly, the plant is now known to have been domesticated in the Americas, leading some scientists to propose theories of pre-Columbian voyages from Polynesia to the west coast of South America; other researchers suggest travel by Indigenous Americans in the opposite direction.

Which choice completes the text so that it conforms to the conventions of Standard English?

Ⓐ having grown

Ⓑ to grow

Ⓒ growing

Ⓓ have grown

CONTINUE ➡

20 ◻ Mark for Review

In 1972, Jamaican American musician Clive Campbell, performing as DJ Kool Herc, first mixed extended percussion sections, or "breaks," into samples of older records. After this, breaks _____ one of the defining elements of the musical structure of hip hop.

Which choice completes the text so that it conforms to the conventions of Standard English?

Ⓐ became

Ⓑ become

Ⓒ had become

Ⓓ will become

21 ◻ Mark for Review

When German climatologist Alfred Wegener first published his hypothesis of continental drift in 1912, he was unable to come up with a plausible mechanism to explain how the continents could _____ it was not until the discovery of seafloor spreading at mid-ocean ridges that his idea became widely accepted.

Which choice completes the text so that it conforms to the conventions of Standard English?

Ⓐ move,

Ⓑ move

Ⓒ move and

Ⓓ move, and

22 ◻ Mark for Review

Since the European robin (*Erithacus rubecula*), like many other species of birds, is required to migrate seasonally to survive, it _____ between its summer and winter ranges by using a protein called cryptochrome in its eyes to sense the planet's magnetic field.

Which choice completes the text so that it conforms to the conventions of Standard English?

Ⓐ would navigate

Ⓑ navigates

Ⓒ navigated

Ⓓ had navigated

23 ◻ Mark for Review

Science commentator Anjana Ahuja wrote that a total solar eclipse is "the greatest show on Earth." This spectacular sight happens relatively rarely because of the eccentricity of the Moon's orbit. A total solar eclipse (visible only from a narrow strip of the Earth's surface during each event) is _____ the Moon appears large enough to completely obscure the solar disc.

Which choice completes the text so that it conforms to the conventions of Standard English?

Ⓐ observed wherever

Ⓑ observed, wherever

Ⓒ observed; wherever

Ⓓ observed. Wherever

CONTINUE ➡

24 ☐ Mark for Review

Canadian Cree/Métis poet and artist Gregory Scofield initially was ashamed of his Métis background and longed to be purely Cree. _____ Scofield learned to appreciate the Métis aspects of his identity after participating in a yearly Métis festival celebrating the culture.

Which choice completes the text with the most logical transition?

Ⓐ Additionally,

Ⓑ In fact,

Ⓒ Nevertheless,

Ⓓ Besides,

25 ☐ Mark for Review

The dulcimer is a three- or four-stringed instrument with diatonic fretting. While ancient versions have been found dating back to the early 1800s within Scotch and Irish communities in the Appalachian Mountains, there is very little archaeological or written evidence linking this instrument to the actual countries of Scotland or Ireland. _____ the history of the instrument is largely up for debate.

Which choice completes the text with the most logical transition?

Ⓐ Still,

Ⓑ However,

Ⓒ Furthermore,

Ⓓ Therefore,

26 ☐ Mark for Review

While researching a topic, a student has taken the following notes:

- Eric Gansworth is a Haudenosaunee author who writes about contemporary Native American life and culture.

- He published his young adult poetic memoir *Apple: Skin to the Core* in 2020.

- *Apple: Skin to the Core* discusses Gansworth's childhood on a Tuscarora reservation.

- Gansworth was an enrolled citizen of the Onondaga Nation but was raised within the Tuscarora Nation.

The student wants to describe *Apple: Skin to the Core* to an audience unfamiliar with Eric Gansworth. Which choice most effectively uses relevant information from the notes to accomplish this goal?

Ⓐ Eric Gansworth's *Apple: Skin to the Core* discusses being raised within the Tuscarora Nation.

Ⓑ Gansworth's 2020 book *Apple: Skin to the Core*, which discusses growing up on a Tuscarora reservation, focuses on contemporary Native American life and culture.

Ⓒ *Apple: Skin to the Core*, a 2020 book by Haudenosaunee author Eric Gansworth, discusses Gansworth's childhood as an enrolled citizen of the Onondaga Nation being raised on a Tuscarora reservation.

Ⓓ Haudenosaunee author Eric Gansworth published *Apple: Skin to the Core* in 2020.

CONTINUE →

---

27 ☐ Mark for Review

While researching a topic, a student has taken the following notes:

- When clothes develop holes or rips, they can be repaired with hand sewing.

- The running stitch is the most basic stitch and can be used to join two pieces of fabric.

- For areas of garments that are subject to greater pulling, the running stitch is not always ideal because it is relatively weak.

- Backstitch, which is a variation of the running stitch that has no gaps because it goes back over previous stitches, can be used to repair clothes.

- This stitch is strong and flexible.

The student wants to explain an advantage of backstitch. Which choice most effectively uses relevant information from the notes to accomplish this goal?

- Ⓐ Two methods for repairing clothes, the running stitch and backstitch, differ in their strength.

- Ⓑ To repair clothes that have holes or rips, both the basic running stitch and backstitch, a variation with no gaps, can be used.

- Ⓒ Going back over previous stitches produces stronger and more flexible repairs than does the running stitch, which is relatively weak.

- Ⓓ In repairing clothing that has holes or rips, the running stitch is not always ideal.

STOP

**If you finish before time is called, you may check your work on this section only.
Do not turn to any other section in the test.**

SAT Prep Test 2—Reading and Writing
Module 2—Harder

Turn to Section 1 of your answer sheet to answer the questions in this section.

DIRECTIONS

The questions in this section address a number of important reading and writing skills. Each question includes one or more passages, which may include a table or graph. Read each passage and question carefully, and then choose the best answer to the question based on the passage(s).

All questions in the section are multiple-choice with four answer choices. Each question has a single best answer. Fill in the circle with the answer letter for the answer you think is best.

---

1 ☐ Mark for Review

According to ecologists, bumblebees are particularly _____ the effects of climate change. When bumblebees are under stress during the early developmental stages of their life cycle, their wings grow to be asymmetrical, and scientists have observed that there has been an increase in imbalanced wings which coincided with the escalated temperatures caused by climate change.

Which choice completes the text with the most logical and precise word or phrase?

(A) unaffected by

(B) incongruent with

(C) independent of

(D) susceptible to

2 ☐ Mark for Review

Recent measurements of the mass of a certain subatomic particle, the W boson, were higher than would ordinarily be predicted by the Standard Model of particle physics. While these findings won't necessarily require that scientists _____ the Standard Model, the new data might indicate that some modifications to our understanding of the nature of these particles are warranted.

Which choice completes the text with the most logical and precise word or phrase?

(A) overhaul

(B) withhold

(C) embrace

(D) misapprehend

CONTINUE

3. Practice Test 2 | **163**

---

3 ☐ Mark for Review

Archimedes of Syracuse, an ancient Greek scientist active in the third century BCE, is predominantly renowned for a method for measuring volume using water displacement. However, in 1906, a parchment containing Archimedes's writings was discovered which revealed that he was also a pioneering mathematician who had _____ calculus, describing concepts thought to have been first developed in the 1500s.

Which choice completes the text with the most logical and precise word or phrase?

A exemplified

B verified

C anticipated

D translated

4 ☐ Mark for Review

The Permian-Triassic extinction eliminated 90 percent of Earth's life and so was thought to have had a devastating effect on the remaining ecosystems. However, some scientists posit that the plants left over weren't as _____ as assumed; analysis of the reptile Palacrodon's fossilized teeth reveals that it had a diet of vegetation, indicating that plants at this time period were surprisingly resilient.

Which choice completes the text with the most logical and precise word or phrase?

A assailable

B determinate

C objectionable

D liminal

5 ☐ Mark for Review

John Ball, a revolutionary priest active in the years following the Black Death during the late 14th century, quickly gained notoriety for _____ both religious and secular authorities: this condemnation was aimed at tearing down the class system in place at the time and establishing a new, egalitarian society.

Which choice completes the text with the most logical and precise word or phrase?

A proselytizing

B censuring

C envisaging

D declaring

CONTINUE →

6 ☐ Mark for Review

The following text is adapted from Hubert Crackanthorpe's 1896 short story "Anthony Garstin's Courtship."

A stampede of huddled sheep, wildly scampering over the slaty shingle, emerged from the leaden mist that muffled the fell-top, and a shrill shepherd's whistle broke the damp stillness of the air. And presently a man's figure appeared, following the sheep down the hillside. He halted a moment to whistle curtly to his two dogs, who, laying back their ears, chased the sheep at top speed beyond the brow; then, his hands deep in his pockets, he strode vigorously forward. A streak of white smoke from a toiling train was creeping silently across the distance: the great, grey, desolate undulations of treeless country showed no other sign of life.

Which choice best describes the function of the underlined sentence in the text as a whole?

Ⓐ It emphasizes the man's solitude and the stillness of his environment.

Ⓑ It suggests that the man longs to travel away from his dull home.

Ⓒ It provides a description of what the man sees on his daily walk.

Ⓓ It illustrates the vastness of the surroundings compared to the train's destination.

7 ☐ Mark for Review

The following text is adapted from Mary Johnston's 1915 novel *The Fortunes of Garin*. Garin, a young man bound to serve Lord Raimbaut, has been given an opportunity to leave and assist a church leader.

Garin sought his inn and his horse. He was in Roche-de-Frêne upon Raimbaut's business, but that over, he had leave to ride to Castel-Noir and spend three days with his brother. The merry-making in the town tempted, but the way was long and he must go. A chain of five girls crossed his path, laughing, making dancing steps, their robes kilted high, red and yellow flowers in their hair. "What a beautiful young man!" said their eyes. "Stay—stay!" Garin wanted to stay—but he was not without judgment and he went.

Which choice best describes the function of the underlined sentence in the text as a whole?

Ⓐ It exemplifies a circumstance that is established in the previous sentence.

Ⓑ It foreshadows an emotion that a character experiences in the following sentence.

Ⓒ It provides a visual description of several characters in the scene.

Ⓓ It hints at the urgency a character feels about the task before him.

CONTINUE ➤

8 ⬚ Mark for Review

The following text is adapted from Charles Dickens's 1859 historical novel *A Tale of Two Cities*.

There were a king with a large jaw and a queen with a plain face, on the throne of England; there were a king with a large jaw and a queen with a fair face, on the throne of France. In both countries it was clearer than crystal to the lords of the State preserves of loaves and fishes, that things in general were settled for ever.

Which choice best states the main purpose of the text?

(A) To compare and contrast the conditions of two competing nations

(B) To establish that the ruling classes enjoyed an apparent stability in their respective nations

(C) To assert that the kings of each nation were similar to each other but the queens were strikingly distinct

(D) To criticize the upper classes for hoarding food and withholding resources from the lower classes

9 ⬚ Mark for Review

Text 1

While both normal cells and cancer cells use the sugar glucose as an energy source, normal cells use mitochondria to process the glucose, whereas cancer cells, in need of a larger amount of energy, utilize a different, faster process. Thus, cancer cells process a sizable amount of glucose, which is unsurprising, but the mystery that has puzzled oncologists concerns the large amount of glucose that is excreted as waste—if cancer cells have such a high need for glucose, why are they processing the sugar so inefficiently?

Text 2

Dr. Gary Patti and colleagues have studied the mechanisms by which glucose is absorbed by cancer cells and compared them to the processes utilized by normal cells. Patti discovered that cancer cells have an upper limit for the amount of glucose that can be processed efficiently, as has long been observed in normal cells.

Based on the texts, how would Patti and colleagues (Text 2) most likely respond to the "mystery" discussed in Text 1?

(A) By proposing that further research into mitochondria is necessary in order to understand this issue

(B) By asserting that though normal cells and cancer cells process glucose differently, they both have a maximum threshold for the amount of glucose that can be efficiently converted into energy

(C) By arguing that not nearly as much glucose is required by cancer cells as was previously assumed

(D) By suggesting that, contrary to what was originally presumed, cancer cells are actually using the same mitochondrial processes that normal cells are

CONTINUE ➡

10 ☐ Mark for Review

Personality is typically measured by five traits: extraversion, emotional stability, agreeableness, conscientiousness, and openness to experience. Psychologist Jean M. Twenge and colleagues have hypothesized that sociocultural environment—the evolving attitudes, behavior, and values in society—affects an individual's personality in addition to genetics and family environment, two factors that are more studied and thus better understood. Twenge purports to have found support for this relationship between sociocultural environment and personality. She looked at high school students and compared their birth cohorts (all people born the same year as a given individual) with their scores on the Eysenck Personality Inventory and Eysenck Personality Questionnaire, two scales by which an individual's level of extraversion can be measured.

Which finding from the researchers' study, if true, would most strongly support Twenge's hypothesis?

Ⓐ Female participants scored significantly higher than did their male counterparts in both emotional stability and openness to experience.

Ⓑ High school students from 1990 scored higher in extraversion than did high school students from 1970.

Ⓒ Those who grew up in households above a certain income level scored significantly higher in agreeableness than those from a lower socioeconomic bracket.

Ⓓ Participants from the older birth cohort used a greater number of words when describing their personalities than did those from the younger birth cohort.

11 ☐ Mark for Review

Mexican Maya author Marisol Ceh Moo writes in both Spanish and Yucatec (one of the 33 Mayan languages). She gained notoriety upon publication of her debut novel *Teya, the Heart of a Woman*, the first novel written by a woman in the Yucatec language. Traditionally, Maya authors primarily write short stories, songs, and poems. They typically focus on retelling myths or writing about subjects such as Mayan culture and Indigenous peoples. Instead, Ceh Moo sets her story in contemporary times and depicts the life, career, and assassination of a young leader of a group of communist revolutionaries.

Which choice best describes Ceh Moo's approach to literature, as presented in the text?

Ⓐ She is influenced by the myths of Maya culture but gives them a modern spin by setting her stories in the present day.

Ⓑ She pays tribute to her Maya heritage while simultaneously defying the expectations that come from working in a Mayan language

Ⓒ She takes inspiration from both her Maya and Mexican heritages equally.

Ⓓ She uses her work to criticize both colonialist powers and the traditionalists of her own culture.

CONTINUE →

12 ☐ Mark for Review

Effects of Enhancement Measures on Flowers and Wild Bees

Enhancement measure	Mean flower abundance (number of individuals per species)	Mean flower species richness (number of different species)	Mean wild bee abundance (number of individuals per species)	Mean wild bee species richness (number of different species)
Control	82.4	2.6	0.6	0.5
Flower strip	302.1	6.2	6.7	3.1
Hedge	177.5	2.4	2.1	1.3
Improved hedge	249.7	4.2	3.1	1.6

Knowing that wild bees play an essential role in the cultivation of crops via pollination while noting that such bees are often scarce because of insufficient pollen, ecologists Vivien von Königslöw, Felix Fornoff, and Alexandra-Maria Klein studied the impact of three different additions to a landscape: perennial flower strips, hedges, and improved hedges that included a layer of sown herb. While all of the attempted methods for attracting more bees were successful to varying degrees when compared with a control group of regular ground vegetation, the researchers concluded that flower strips were most effective, observing that _____

Which choice most effectively uses data from the table to support the research team's conclusion?

(A) when hedges were enhanced with a layer of sown herb, the number of flower species was greater than that yielded by regular hedges.

(B) flower strips attracted significantly more wild bees than did the control group, suggesting that bees are more attracted to flowers than to the ground vegetation.

(C) for each metric of abundance and species richness that was measured, the flower strip yielded the greatest numbers.

(D) the control group actually had a more diverse array of flower species than did the improved hedges.

CONTINUE

Effect of Physically Active Lessons on Academic Success

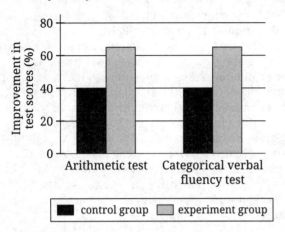

It has been suggested that the inclusion of physically active lessons with the regular mathematical curriculum can aid in academic success. To investigate this hypothesis, psychologist Daniele Magistro and colleagues looked at two groups of students: an experimental group that received physically active mathematics lessons and a control group that received the usual mathematics curriculum. At the end of a two-year period, both groups of students were subjected to a battery of tests of their cognitive function, including an arithmetic test and a categorical verbal fluency test (which tested their ability to describe mathematical calculations in words). Magistro and his colleagues recommended that physically active lessons be henceforth included in the mathematics curriculum.

13 ☐ Mark for Review

Which choice best describes data from the graph that support Magistro and colleagues' recommendation?

Ⓐ The students in the control group performed worse in verbal fluency at the end of the study than they did at the start.

Ⓑ The experimental group improved to a higher degree on the categorical verbal fluency test than on the arithmetic test.

Ⓒ While both groups increased their arithmetic and verbal fluency skills, the experimental group's increases were significantly greater than those of the control group.

Ⓓ Both the control group and the experimental group showed an improvement on the arithmetic test of at least 40%.

CONTINUE

14 ☐ Mark for Review

The Seagull is an 1895 play by Anton Chekhov. In the play, the character of Konstantin Treplev is an ambitious playwright and the son of a famous actress. Yearning to create an innovative style of theater, Treplev is heavily critical of the art form's established tropes, as is evident when he _____

Which choice most effectively uses a quotation from *The Seagull* to illustrate the claim?

(A) says of the stage, "Just like a real theater! See, there we have the curtain, the foreground, the background, and all."

(B) says of his craft, "Writing is a pleasure to me, and so is reading the proofs, but no sooner does a book leave the press than it becomes odious to me; it is not what I meant it to be; I made a mistake to write it at all; I am provoked and discouraged."

(C) introduces his play to the audience, "O, ye time-honored, ancient mists that drive at night across the surface of this lake, blind you our eyes with sleep, and show us in our dreams that which will be in twice ten thousand years!"

(D) says of other productions, "when playwrights give us under a thousand different guises the same, same, same old stuff, then I must needs run from it, as Maupassant ran from the Eiffel Tower that was about to crush him by its vulgarity."

15 ☐ Mark for Review

According to conventional wisdom, positive visualization—the act of developing a mental picture of one's future success—can enhance people's ability to achieve their goals. Psychologists Heather Barry Kappes and Gabriele Oettingen tested this notion with a study that looked at the effect that such fantasies had on participants' actual accomplishments. Participants were divided into two groups: the members of the experimental group were told to actively visualize attaining their goals for the week ahead, while the members of the control group were given no specific strategy for accomplishing their goals. At the end of the week, Kappes and Oettingen compared the relative successes of each group.

Which finding from Kappes and Oettingen's study, if true, would most directly weaken the claim made by people who favor the conventional view of positive visualization?

(A) The members of the control group accomplished fewer goals than did those in the experimental group, but the members of the control group reported greater feelings of pride in their accomplishments.

(B) Participants who were practicing positive visualization accomplished a slightly higher number of their goals than did those who utilized a different technique.

(C) Even though the participants in the control group were told they could select any strategy they wanted for achieving their goals, the vast majority of them elected to use positive visualization.

(D) Compared to the participants who were engaged in the practice of positive visualization, those who were not told to visualize attaining goals reported higher numbers of goals accomplished by the end of the week.

CONTINUE ➤

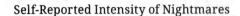
Self-Reported Intensity of Nightmares

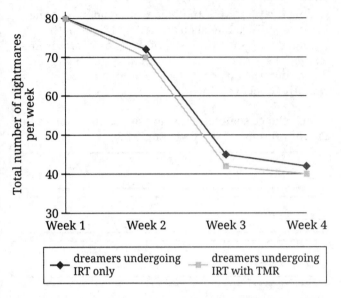

dreamers undergoing IRT only — dreamers undergoing IRT with TMR

The primary treatment for chronic nightmares is Imagery Rehearsal Therapy (IRT), by which the dreamer, after waking from a nightmare, talks through a reimagining of the dream to give it a positive ending. A supplemental intervention, Targeted Memory Reactivation (TMR), recruits the use of musical notes. With TMR, a dreamer already undergoing IRT is made to hear a certain piano chord when discussing the new positive ending of the dream. Then, that same piano chord is played during the person's next sleep. It is claimed that IRT is made even more effective when utilizing TMR. A graduate student tested this claim by observing the effects of each treatment on 50 participants over a four-week period and was surprised to observe that _____

16 Mark for Review

Which choice most effectively uses data from the graph to complete the statement?

(A) the maximum number of nightmares for participants of both groups occurred during the first week of the study.

(B) participants who underwent IRT along with TMR experienced only a slightly greater decrease in nightmares than did those undergoing IRT without TMR.

(C) at week 2, participants who underwent IRT with TMR reported having fewer nightmares than those who underwent IRT without TMR.

(D) although the participants of both forms of treatment experienced reduced nightmare intensity throughout the course of the study, the rate at which their nightmares decreased tapered off toward the end of the study.

17 ▢ Mark for Review

A team of psychologists led by Stefan Stieger, Hannah M. Graf, and Stella P. Riegler investigated the hypothesis that social media use is positively correlated with a lower body self-image, termed appearance satisfaction. The researchers recorded the participants' social media engagement and utilized a physical analogue scale (PAS) to measure appearance satisfaction. Participants angled their forearms to signify their sense of appearance satisfaction. A horizontal forearm at 0° indicated the lowest scale value, whereas 90° indicated the highest. Participants used social media to engage with a variety of accounts: some accounts belonged to known people such as friends and family, while other accounts belonged to users unknown to the participants. Social media engagement with known targets resulted in a reduction of appearance satisfaction of 12.4°, while for unknown targets there was a 5.9° reduction, which suggests that _____

Which choice most logically completes the text?

- (A) people experience lower appearance satisfaction when they engage with content from strangers compared with that from friends.

- (B) the physical analogue scale is more effective when measuring social media engagement with known targets than with unknown targets.

- (C) there is some evidence for a correlation between social media use and lower appearance satisfaction, but it is not significant.

- (D) social media engagement with content by people whom one knows personally is correlated with lower appearance satisfaction.

18 ▢ Mark for Review

During the West African Ebola virus epidemic in the 2010s, Yoshihiro Kawaoka and Alhaji N'jai—both affiliated with the University of Wisconsin–Madison—studied the virus and then eliminated the VP30 gene that allows the virus to attach to human cells _____ a potential Ebola vaccine.

Which choice completes the text so that it conforms to the conventions of Standard English?

- (A) and creating

- (B) created

- (C) creating

- (D) to create

19 ▢ Mark for Review

The watering of cultivated crops is sometimes based on a system known as irrigation scheduling, in which farmers use certain factors about the land and weather—specifically, the soil quality and projected _____ determine when and how much water is needed.

Which choice completes the text so that it conforms to the conventions of Standard English?

- (A) rainfall, to

- (B) rainfall—to

- (C) rainfall: to

- (D) rainfall to

CONTINUE ➡

20 ⬚ Mark for Review

On February 4, 1961, comedian Lenny Bruce was unsure whether anyone would show up for his performance at Carnegie Hall because of a massive blizzard. The audience was _____ flocking to the theater despite two feet of snow and a ban on driving to see the show that would become the well-known recording *The Carnegie Hall Concert.*

Which choice completes the text so that it conforms to the conventions of Standard English?

- Ⓐ determined; however,
- Ⓑ determined, however,
- Ⓒ determined, however;
- Ⓓ determined, however

21 ⬚ Mark for Review

A recent study by a team of researchers at the University of Washington discovered a surprising source of atmosphere- and climate-changing _____ passive degassing, a process that occurs when volcanoes are not active but are leaking sulfur into the atmosphere to the extent that, according to the new research, it is a greater amount of sulfur than the amounts released during eruptions or by another common source of sulfur, marine phytoplankton.

Which choice completes the text so that it conforms to the conventions of Standard English?

- Ⓐ gases. Volcanoes'
- Ⓑ gases; volcanoes'
- Ⓒ gases: volcanoes'
- Ⓓ gases volcanoes'

22 ⬚ Mark for Review

In 1995, animal behaviorist Temple Grandin wrote *Thinking in Pictures* about her life with autism and her pattern of visual thinking. A 2006 edition of the book added two more patterns of _____ some autistic people may be music and math thinkers, others verbal logic thinkers. Grandin continued to write about patterns of thinking in her 2013 book *The Autistic Brain: Thinking Across the Spectrum.*

Which choice completes the text so that it conforms to the conventions of Standard English?

- Ⓐ thinking though
- Ⓑ thinking, though
- Ⓒ thinking,
- Ⓓ thinking:

23 ⬚ Mark for Review

Although it has become much dimmer than it was originally, the Centennial Light in California, known as the world's longest-lasting light bulb, began operating in the late 1890s. There were a few time periods when it briefly went out due to power failures and other technological challenges. _____ the bulb was connected to an uninterruptible power supply to determine how long it could actually burn.

Which choice completes the text with the most logical transition?

- Ⓐ Similarly,
- Ⓑ Consequently,
- Ⓒ Additionally,
- Ⓓ By contrast,

CONTINUE ➡

24 ☐ Mark for Review

While researching a topic, a student has taken the following notes:

- One of the world's oldest law schools was the law school of Berytus in Beirut, Lebanon.
- The exact date of its founding is unknown, but it was active during the time of the Roman Empire.
- Students at the law school went through four or five years of study focused on Roman law to become jurists, or legal scholars.
- Time in class included lectures, analyses of cases, reading and revision of classical legal texts, and discussions.
- Famous instructors included a group of seven revered law scholars known as the "ecumenical masters."

The student wants to explain how the law school of Berytus prepared jurists. Which choice most effectively uses relevant information from the notes to accomplish this goal?

(A) The law school of Berytus taught students Roman law for multiple years in classes that included lectures and analyses.

(B) A group of seven revered law scholars known as the "ecumenical masters" taught at the law school of Berytus.

(C) Active during the time of the Roman Empire, the law school of Berytus prepared students to become jurists.

(D) The law school of Berytus trained students to become jurists, or legal scholars, of Roman law.

25 ☐ Mark for Review

While researching a topic, a student has taken the following notes:

- In 1929, astronautics theorist Herman Potočnik described a geosynchronous orbit, or an Earth-centered orbit with an orbital period that is the same length of time as the Earth's rotation.
- Satellites with a geosynchronous orbit have an altitude of 35,786 km.
- Currently, there are 5,465 satellites in orbit around Earth, with 565 in geosynchronous orbit.
- 4,700 satellites are at low orbit with an altitude below 2,000 km and an orbital period less than 128 minutes.
- 140 satellites are at medium orbit with an altitude between 2,000 and 35,786 km and an orbital period greater than 2 hours but less than 24 hours.

The student wants to emphasize how high satellites in geosynchronous orbit are relative to those in low and medium orbits. Which choice most effectively uses the relevant information from the notes to accomplish this goal?

(A) While most satellites are at low orbit, satellites at geosynchronous orbit have an altitude of 35,786 km.

(B) Of the 5,465 satellites in orbit around the Earth, 4,700 of them are at low orbit with an altitude below 2,000 km and 565 are at a geosynchronous orbit.

(C) Herman Potočnik described a geosynchronous orbit, which has a period the same length as Earth's rotation, while other orbits used by satellites have shorter periods.

(D) Satellites in geosynchronous orbit have an altitude of 35,786 km, which is a higher altitude than that of satellites in both low and medium orbits.

CONTINUE →

26 ☐ Mark for Review

While researching a topic, a student has taken the following notes:

- Some animals use bright colors, such as red or yellow, to attract mates, while other animals use the same colors to warn predators.
- Researchers were curious whether there was an explanation for why animals evolved colors for one goal or the other.
- The researchers found that animals whose ancestors were active during the day use colors to attract mates.
- They also found that animals whose ancestors were active during the night use colors to warn predators.
- Warning predators with colors is known as aposematism.

The student wants to emphasize a similarity between the two ways animals use colors. Which choice most effectively uses relevant information from the notes to accomplish this goal?

(A) As well as using bright colors to attract mates, animals use colors such as red or yellow to warn predators.

(B) Animals can use bright colors for two different goals, one of which is known as aposematism.

(C) The two different goals of animals' bright colors are determined by the time of day the animals' ancestors were active.

(D) Animals evolved to use bright colors in two different ways: to attract mates or to warn predators.

27 ☐ Mark for Review

While researching a topic, a student has taken the following notes:

- Some species of fireflies, such as *Photinus carolinus*, seem to synchronize their flashes, even in large groups.
- A team of researchers from the University of Pittsburgh wanted to mimic the flashes by utilizing a model from neuroscience which describes brain cells' behavior.
- The model, called an elliptic burster, was used to simulate the flashes of firefly groups, ranging from one individual to a large swarm.
- The model was able to mimic flashes consistent with real-life observations of firefly swarms.
- The model could be used to make predictions about how the pattern of firefly flashes may be altered due to environmental changes or human impacts.

The student wants to present the study and its methodology. Which choice most effectively uses relevant information from the notes to accomplish this goal?

(A) Researchers at the University of Pittsburgh found that the elliptic burster model could simulate firefly flashes consistent with real-life observations.

(B) University of Pittsburgh researchers studied the synchronicity of the flashes of *Photinus carolinus*, a species of fireflies.

(C) Hoping to mimic the synchronous flashes of fireflies, researchers at the University of Pittsburgh used an elliptic burster to mimic real-life observations of fireflies' flashes.

(D) A study found that the pattern of fireflies flashing could be simulated using a model from neuroscience that describes brain cells' behavior.

STOP
**If you finish before time is called, you may check your work on this section only.
Do not turn to any other section in the test.**

SAT Prep Test 2—Math
Module 1

The questions in this section address a number of important math skills.
Use of a calculator is permitted for all questions.

NOTES

Unless otherwise indicated:

- All variables and expressions represent real numbers.
- Figures provided are drawn to scale.
- All figures lie in a plane.
- The domain of a given function f is the set of all real numbers x for which $f(x)$ is a real number.

REFERENCE

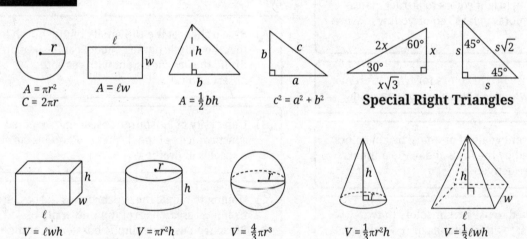

$A = \pi r^2$
$C = 2\pi r$

$A = \ell w$

$A = \frac{1}{2}bh$

$c^2 = a^2 + b^2$

Special Right Triangles

$V = \ell w h$

$V = \pi r^2 h$

$V = \frac{4}{3}\pi r^3$

$V = \frac{1}{3}\pi r^2 h$

$V = \frac{1}{3}\ell w h$

The number of degrees of arc in a circle is 360.
The number of radians of arc in a circle is 2π.
The sum of the measures in degrees of the angles of a triangle is 180.

CONTINUE

For multiple-choice questions, solve each problem, choose the correct answer from the choices provided, and then fill in the circle with the answer letter. Enter only one answer for each question. You will not get credit for questions with more than one answer entered, or for questions with no answers entered.

For student-produced response questions, solve each problem and write your answer in the test book as described below.

- Enter your answer into the box provided.
- If you find more than one correct answer, enter only one answer.
- Your answer can be up to 5 characters for a positive answer and up to 6 characters (including the negative sign) for a negative answer.
- If your answer is a fraction that is too long (over 5 characters for positive, 6 characters for negative), write the decimal equivalent.
- If your answer is a decimal that is too long (over 5 characters for positive, 6 characters for negative), truncate it or round at the fourth digit.
- If your answer is a mixed number (such as $3\frac{1}{2}$), write it as an improper fraction (7/2) or its decimal equivalent (3.5).
- Don't enter symbols such as a percent sign, comma, or dollar sign in your answer.

CONTINUE

1 ⬚ Mark for Review

A social media account posts at a constant rate. The relationship between the number of posts, p, and the number of days, d, is given by the equation $p = 45d$. How many posts does the account make during a 3-day period?

Ⓐ 45

Ⓑ 48

Ⓒ 90

Ⓓ 135

2 ⬚ Mark for Review

Which of the following equations represents a line in the xy-plane if the line passes through the point (0, 10) and has a slope of -3?

Ⓐ $y = -3x - 10$

Ⓑ $y = -3x + 10$

Ⓒ $y = 3x - 10$

Ⓓ $y = 3x + 10$

3 ⬚ Mark for Review

What is the value of $\frac{x}{12}$ if $\frac{12}{x} = \frac{1}{7}$?

4 ⬚ Mark for Review

Triangles MNO and XYZ are similar right triangles. Angles N and Y each have a measure of $90°$, and angle O corresponds to angle Z. If angle X has a measure of $23°$, what is the measure of angle M?

Ⓐ $23°$

Ⓑ $67°$

Ⓒ $90°$

Ⓓ $157°$

5 ⬚ Mark for Review

If a, g, and n are positive numbers, which of the following expressions is equivalent to $(a^2g^{-4}n)(a^3g^{-2}n)$?

Ⓐ $a^{-1}g^{-2}n^2$

Ⓑ $a^5g^{-12}n$

Ⓒ $a^5g^{-6}n^2$

Ⓓ a^6g^8n

CONTINUE ➡

6 ☐ Mark for Review

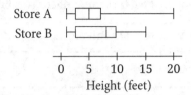

Store A

Store B

0   5   10   15   20
Height (feet)

The box plots represent the height, in feet, of ladders available at two hardware stores. Which of the following is a true statement based on the box plots?

(A) The mean height of the ladders at store A is greater than the mean height of the ladders at store B.

(B) The mean height of the ladders at store B is greater than the mean height of the ladders at store A.

(C) The median height of the ladders at store A is greater than the median height of the ladders at B.

(D) The median height of the ladders at store B is greater than the median height of the ladders at store A.

7 ☐ Mark for Review

$$y = x^2 + 6$$
$$y = 150$$

When the given equations are graphed in the xy-plane, they intersect at the point (x, y). Which of the following is a possible value of x?

(A) 5

(B) 6

(C) 12

(D) 25

8 ☐ Mark for Review

Based on a random sample of adults, it is estimated that the proportion of adults who have insomnia is 0.35. The margin of error associated with the sample is 0.07. Which of the following is the most appropriate conclusion about the proportion of adults with insomnia in the population based on this estimate and margin of error?

(A) It is likely that the proportion is less than 0.28.

(B) It is likely that the proportion is greater than 0.42.

(C) It is likely that the proportion is between 0.28 and 0.42

(D) It is likely that the proportion is exactly 0.35.

9 ☐ Mark for Review

$$y = 10x - 20$$
$$2y = 10x - 20$$

Two equations are given. At how many points do their graphs intersect in the xy-plane?

(A) Zero

(B) Exactly one

(C) Exactly two

(D) Infinitely many

CONTINUE

10 ☐ Mark for Review

The graph of the linear function g in the xy-plane passes through the points $(-3, 39)$ and $(0, 3)$. If $y = g(x)$, which of the following equations defines g?

(A) $g(x) = -12x + 3$

(B) $g(x) = -6x + 3$

(C) $g(x) = 3x + 36$

(D) $g(x) = 39x + 42$

11 ☐ Mark for Review

What is the value of k if $ab = 27$ and $2abk = 27$?

12 ☐ Mark for Review

The amount of money d, in dollars, that Sarah has saved from babysitting is modeled by the function $d(w) = 150 + 50w$, where w is the number of weeks since she started babysitting. What is the predicted amount of money, in dollars, that Sarah saved every week?

(A) 3

(B) 50

(C) 150

(D) 200

13 ☐ Mark for Review

The population of a certain town decreases by 150 people every 5 years. The population of the town is best described by what kind of function?

(A) Decreasing linear

(B) Decreasing exponential

(C) Increasing linear

(D) Increasing exponential

14 ☐ Mark for Review

$$x - 9y = -30$$
$$x - 27y = -12$$

If (x, y) is the solution to the given system of equations, what is the value of x?

15 ☐ Mark for Review

The equation $y = x^2 + 16x - 39$ relates the variables x and y. If (a, b) is the minimum value of this equation, what is the value of a?

CONTINUE ➜

16 Mark for Review

The function g is defined by $g(x) = 12 - 2x$. In the xy-plane, the x-intercept of the graph of $y = g(x)$ is at $(m, 0)$, and the y-intercept is at $(0, n)$. What is the value of $m - n$?

(A) −18

(B) −6

(C) 12

(D) 18

17 Mark for Review

A scale model of a square park has an area that is $\frac{1}{4,096}$ of the area of the actual park. If the side length of the actual park is x times the side length of the scale model, what is the value of x?

18 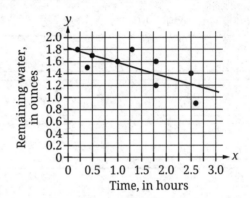 Mark for Review

The scatterplot shows the water remaining in a series of cups that initially held the same volume of water and were left sitting in the sun for several hours. A line of best fit is also shown.

Which of the following is closest to the water remaining in a cup, in ounces, predicted by the line of best fit when 1.25 hours have elapsed?

(A) 1.2

(B) 1.5

(C) 1.7

(D) 1.8

CONTINUE

19 ☐ Mark for Review

An angle is made of two smaller angles, A and B. If Angle A measures 150 degrees, and the measure of Angle B is $\frac{1}{3}$ the measure of Angle A, what is the combined measure of both angles, in <u>radians</u>?

 (A) $\frac{5\pi}{18}$

 (B) $\frac{5\pi}{6}$

 (C) $\frac{9\pi}{10}$

(D) $\frac{10\pi}{9}$

20 ☐ Mark for Review

A sample of a certain radioactive element is tested and found to have 16,000 radioactive units. Two hours later, it is tested again and found to have 4,000 radioactive units. The formula $R = S(0.25)^{pt}$, where R is the number of radioactive units remaining t hours after the first test, and p and S are constants, models this situation. What is the value of p?

(A) $\frac{1}{4,000}$

(B) $\frac{1}{120}$

(C) $\frac{1}{2}$

(D) 2

CONTINUE ▶

21 ☐ Mark for Review

$$1 = \frac{\sqrt{7x + 65}}{\sqrt{(x+3)^2}}$$

What is the greatest solution to the given equation?

[_____]

22 ☐ Mark for Review

If c is a constant less than 26, which of the following are solutions to the equation $(x + 3c)(80 + x) = 80 + x$?

   I. -80
   II. $-3c$
   III. $1 - 3c$

(A) I only

(B) III only

(C) I and II only

(D) I and III only

YIELD
Once you've finished (or run out of time for) this section, use the answer key to determine how many questions you got right. If you got fewer than 15 questions right, move on to Module 2—Easier, otherwise move on to Module 2—Harder.

SAT Prep Test 2—Math
Module 2—Easier

The questions in this section address a number of important math skills.
Use of a calculator is permitted for all questions.

Unless otherwise indicated:

- All variables and expressions represent real numbers.
- Figures provided are drawn to scale.
- All figures lie in a plane.
- The domain of a given function f is the set of all real numbers x for which $f(x)$ is a real number.

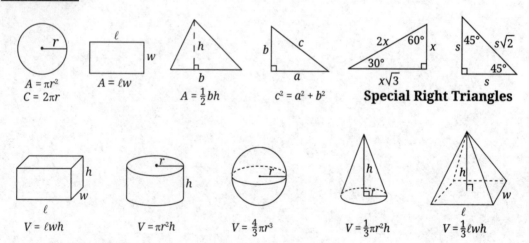

$A = \pi r^2$
$C = 2\pi r$

$A = \ell w$

$A = \frac{1}{2}bh$

$c^2 = a^2 + b^2$

Special Right Triangles

$V = \ell wh$

$V = \pi r^2 h$

$V = \frac{4}{3}\pi r^3$

$V = \frac{1}{3}\pi r^2 h$

$V = \frac{1}{3}\ell wh$

The number of degrees of arc in a circle is 360.
The number of radians of arc in a circle is 2π.
The sum of the measures in degrees of the angles of a triangle is 180.

CONTINUE

_____

For multiple-choice questions, solve each problem, choose the correct answer from the choices provided, and then fill in the circle with the answer letter. Enter only one answer for each question. You will not get credit for questions with more than one answer entered, or for questions with no answers entered.

For student-produced response questions, solve each problem and write your answer in the test book as described below.

- Enter your answer into the box provided.
- If you find **more than one correct answer**, enter only one answer.
- Your answer can be up to 5 characters for a **positive** answer and up to 6 characters (including the negative sign) for a **negative** answer.
- If your answer is a **fraction** that is too long (over 5 characters for positive, 6 characters for negative), write the decimal equivalent.
- If your answer is a **decimal** that is too long (over 5 characters for positive, 6 characters for negative), truncate it or round at the fourth digit.
- If your answer is a **mixed number** (such as $3\frac{1}{2}$), write it as an improper fraction (7/2) or its decimal equivalent (3.5).
- Don't enter **symbols** such as a percent sign, comma, or dollar sign in your answer.

1 Mark for Review

What is 60% of 300?

- (A) 30
- (B) 120
- (C) 180
- (D) 240

2 Mark for Review

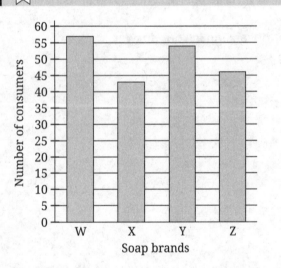

The bar graph shows the results of a market research survey that asked consumers to choose their favorite brand of soap. How many consumers chose Brand Y?

- (A) 43
- (B) 46
- (C) 54
- (D) 57

3 Mark for Review

If $2b - 12 = 144$, what is the value of b?

[_____]

4 Mark for Review

A street artist takes 5 minutes to draw one portrait. At this rate, how many portraits would the artist draw in 35 minutes?

[_____]

5 Mark for Review

$$h(x) = 3x - 2$$

The function h is defined by the equation given. If $h(x) = 10$, what is the value of x?

[_____]

CONTINUE

---

6 ☐ Mark for Review

The function f is defined by $f(x) = x^2 - 15$. If $f(x) = 49$, what is the value of x?

(A) 7

(B) 8

(C) 15

(D) 32

---

7 ☐ Mark for Review

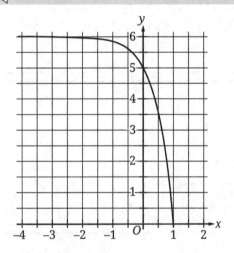

What is the y-intercept of the graph shown?

(A) $(0, 5)$

(B) $(0, 6)$

(C) $(5, 0)$

(D) $(6, 0)$

---

8 ☐ Mark for Review

Dalisha is given a stipend of $3,600 to pay her student housing rent of $450 per month. If $m \leq 8$, which equation represents the amount remaining in the stipend, s, in dollars, after m months?

(A) $s = 450m - 3{,}600$

(B) $s = 450 - 3{,}600m$

(C) $s = 3{,}600m - 450$

(D) $s = 3{,}600 - 450m$

---

9 ☐ Mark for Review

$$\frac{3}{6 - 3y} + \frac{1}{y - 4}$$

Which of the following expressions is equivalent to the given expression?

(A) $-\dfrac{6}{(y-4)(6-3y)}$

(B) $\dfrac{6}{(y-4)(6-3y)}$

(C) $\dfrac{4}{2y+2}$

(D) $\dfrac{18}{(y-4)(6-3y)}$

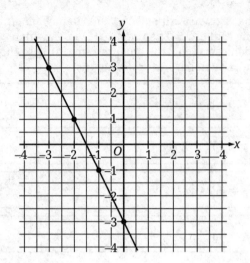

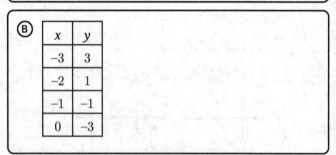

A linear relationship between x and y is shown in the graph. Which of the following tables contains values of x and their corresponding values of y?

Ⓐ
x	y
−3	−3
−2	−2
−1	−1
0	0

Ⓑ
x	y
−3	3
−2	1
−1	−1
0	−3

Ⓒ
x	y
−3	−3
−2	−1
−1	−1
0	3

Ⓓ
x	y
−3	3
−2	2
−1	1
0	−3

CONTINUE

11 ⌸ Mark for Review

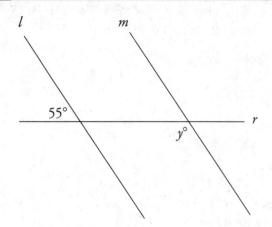

Note: Figure not drawn to scale.

In the figure shown, if line *l* is parallel to line *m*, what is the value of *y*?

12 ⌸ Mark for Review

If a circle has a radius of 4 meters, what is the circumference, in meters, of the circle?

Ⓐ 2π

Ⓑ 4π

Ⓒ 8π

Ⓓ 16π

13 ⌸ Mark for Review

Distinct positive numbers *a*, *b*, and *c* are related by the equation $9a - 2b = c$. Which of the following equations correctly expresses *a* in terms of *b* and *c*?

Ⓐ $a = \dfrac{2b + c}{9}$

Ⓑ $a = \dfrac{2b}{9} + c$

Ⓒ $a = 2b + \dfrac{c}{9}$

Ⓓ $a = 9(2b + c)$

14 ⌸ Mark for Review

Which of the following systems of inequalities, when graphed in the *xy*-plane, includes the point (2, –5) as a solution?

Ⓐ $x \le 0$
    $y \le 0$

Ⓑ $x \le 0$
    $y \ge 0$

Ⓒ $x \ge 0$
    $y \le 0$

Ⓓ $x \ge 0$
    $y \ge 0$

CONTINUE

15 ▢ Mark for Review

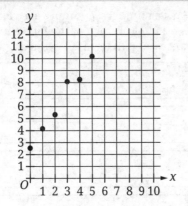

Which of the following linear equations best models the relationship between x and y shown in the scatterplot?

Ⓐ $y = -1.5x - 2.6$

Ⓑ $y = -1.5x + 2.6$

Ⓒ $y = 1.5x - 2.6$

Ⓓ $y = 1.5x + 2.6$

16 ▢ Mark for Review

The population of a certain species of fish is decreasing at a rate of 4 percent each year. Assuming the decline continues at the same rate, there will be approximately 804,944 fish of this species remaining 5 years from now. Which of the following equations could be used to find p, the current population of this species of fish?

Ⓐ $p = 804{,}944(0.96)^5$

Ⓑ $804{,}944 = p(0.96)^5$

Ⓒ $p = 804{,}944(1.04)^5$

Ⓓ $804{,}944 = p(1.04)^5$

17 ▢ Mark for Review

If $3|a + 2| - 5|a + 2| = -24$, what is the negative value of a?

18 ▢ Mark for Review

If $ax^7(8x + 7) = 56x^8 + 49x^7$, and a is a constant, what is the value of a?

19 ▢ Mark for Review

The expression $\pi(3r)(r)^2$ can represent the volume, in cubic feet, of a cylindrical barrel. If r is the radius, in feet, of the barrel, which term represents the height, in feet, of the barrel?

Ⓐ r

Ⓑ 3

Ⓒ $3r$

Ⓓ r^2

CONTINUE ➡

20 ☐ Mark for Review

p	q
-2	-10
1	8
4	20

The table shows values of p and their corresponding values of q. Which of the following inequalities could represent the relationship between p and q?

Ⓐ $q < 6p + 3$

Ⓑ $q > 6p + 3$

Ⓒ $q < 3p + 6$

Ⓓ $q > 3p + 6$

21 ☐ Mark for Review

$$g(x) = (x - 2)(x - 4)(x + 3)$$
$$h(x) = g(x + 3)$$

Functions g and h are defined by the given equations. The graph of $y = h(x)$ has x-intercepts at $(m, 0)$, $(n, 0)$, and $(p, 0)$. If m, n, and p are distinct constants, what is the value of mnp?

Ⓐ -21

Ⓑ -8

Ⓒ 0

Ⓓ 6

22 ☐ Mark for Review

A square with a diagonal length of 8 centimeters (cm) has a circle inscribed in it. What is the area, in cm^2, of the circle?

Ⓐ 4π

Ⓑ 8π

Ⓒ 16π

Ⓓ 32π

STOP
**If you finish before time is called, you may check your work on this section only.
Do not turn to any other section.**

SAT Prep Test 2—Math
Module 2—Harder

The questions in this section address a number of important math skills.
Use of a calculator is permitted for all questions.

NOTES

Unless otherwise indicated:

- All variables and expressions represent real numbers.
- Figures provided are drawn to scale.
- All figures lie in a plane.
- The domain of a given function f is the set of all real numbers x for which $f(x)$ is a real number.

REFERENCE

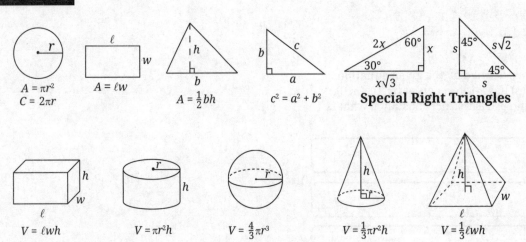

$A = \pi r^2$
$C = 2\pi r$

$A = \ell w$

$A = \frac{1}{2}bh$

$c^2 = a^2 + b^2$

Special Right Triangles

$V = \ell wh$

$V = \pi r^2 h$

$V = \frac{4}{3}\pi r^3$

$V = \frac{1}{3}\pi r^2 h$

$V = \frac{1}{3}\ell wh$

The number of degrees of arc in a circle is 360.
The number of radians of arc in a circle is 2π.
The sum of the measures in degrees of the angles of a triangle is 180.

CONTINUE

For multiple-choice questions, solve each problem, choose the correct answer from the choices provided, and then fill in the circle with the answer letter. Enter only one answer for each question. You will not get credit for questions with more than one answer entered, or for questions with no answers entered.

For student-produced response questions, solve each problem and write your answer in the test book as described below.

- Enter your answer into the box provided.
- If you find **more than one correct answer**, enter only one answer.
- Your answer can be up to 5 characters for a **positive** answer and up to 6 characters (including the negative sign) for a **negative** answer.
- If your answer is a **fraction** that is too long (over 5 characters for positive, 6 characters for negative), write the decimal equivalent.
- If your answer is a **decimal** that is too long (over 5 characters for positive, 6 characters for negative), truncate it or round at the fourth digit.
- If your answer is a **mixed number** (such as $3\frac{1}{2}$), write it as an improper fraction (7/2) or its decimal equivalent (3.5).
- Don't enter **symbols** such as a percent sign, comma, or dollar sign in your answer.

CONTINUE ➔

1 🔖 Mark for Review

If $y - 7 = x$, which table gives three values of x and their corresponding values of y?

Ⓐ
x	y
4	3
5	2
6	1

Ⓑ
x	y
4	11
5	12
6	13

Ⓒ
x	y
4	11
5	2
6	13

Ⓓ
x	y
4	13
5	12
6	11

2 🔖 Mark for Review

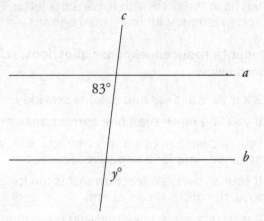

Note: Figure not drawn to scale.

In the figure shown, line c intersects parallel lines a and b. What is the value of y?

Ⓐ 7

Ⓑ 83

Ⓒ 97

Ⓓ 173

3 🔖 Mark for Review

The number 24 is what percentage of 80?

Ⓐ 24%

Ⓑ 30%

Ⓒ 56%

Ⓓ 70%

CONTINUE ➡

4 ◻ Mark for Review

The function f is defined by $f(x) = 3x + 12$. For what value of x is $f(x) = 27$?

5 ◻ Mark for Review

The function g is defined by $g(x) = 120(x)^0$, when $x \neq 0$.

What is the value of $g\left(\dfrac{1}{3}\right)$?

(A) 0

(B) 40

(C) 120

(D) 360

6 ◻ Mark for Review

In right triangle LMN, angle N is a right angle, and the value of $\tan(L)$ is $\dfrac{\sqrt{7}}{3}$. What is the value of $\sin(M)$?

(A) $\dfrac{\sqrt{7}}{7}$

(B) $\dfrac{\sqrt{7}}{4}$

(C) $\dfrac{3}{4}$

(D) $\dfrac{3\sqrt{7}}{7}$

7 ◻ Mark for Review

$$g(x) = (-11)(5)^x - 17$$

The function g is defined by the given equation. Which of the following is the y-intercept when $y = g(x)$ is graphed in the xy-plane?

(A) $(0, -11)$

(B) $(0, 5)$

(C) $(0, -17)$

(D) $(0, -28)$

8 ◻ Mark for Review

$$\frac{3}{6 - 3y} + \frac{1}{y - 4}$$

Which of the following expressions is equivalent to the given expression?

(A) $-\dfrac{6}{(y - 4)(6 - 3y)}$

(B) $\dfrac{6}{(y - 4)(6 - 3y)}$

(C) $\dfrac{4}{2y + 2}$

(D) $\dfrac{18}{(y - 4)(6 - 3y)}$

CONTINUE ➡

9 ☐ Mark for Review

The function q is defined by $q(x) = (x - 9)(x + 2)(x + 9)$. When the graph of $y = q(x)$ is translated down 10 units in the xy-plane, the graph of $y = r(x)$ is the result. What is the value of $r(0)$?

10 ☐ Mark for Review

If a rectangular prism has a height of 10 feet, a length of 12 feet, and a volume of 6,000 cubic feet, what is the surface area, in square feet, of the prism?

11 ☐ Mark for Review

For the function f, when the value of x increases by 1, the value of $f(x)$ increases by 28%. Which of the following equations defines f if $f(0) = 11$?

Ⓐ $f(x) = 0.72(11)^x$

Ⓑ $f(x) = 1.28(11)^x$

Ⓒ $f(x) = 11(0.72)^x$

Ⓓ $f(x) = 11(1.28)^x$

12 ☐ Mark for Review

Which of the following tables gives three values of x and their corresponding values of y that are all solutions to the inequality $y > 4x - 5$?

Ⓐ

x	y
2	0
4	8
6	16

Ⓑ

x	y
2	6
4	14
6	22

Ⓒ

x	y
2	6
4	14
6	19

Ⓓ

x	y
2	3
4	11
6	19

CONTINUE

13 ☐ Mark for Review

Which of the following expressions is (are) a factor of $5x^2 - 61x + 66$?

   I. $x - 11$
  II. $5x - 6$

(A) I only

(B) II only

(C) I and II

(D) Neither I nor II

14 ☐ Mark for Review

$$4 - 5y = 7x + 5y$$
$$7x - 4 = ky$$

The given system of equations has infinitely many solutions. What is the value of the constant k?

(A) -10

(B) -5

(C) 5

(D) 10

15 ☐ Mark for Review

If $3|a + 2| - 5|a + 2| = -24$, what is the negative value of a?

16 ☐ Mark for Review

A vendor sells vases for \$6.50 and bowls for \$12.30. The maximum combined number of vases and bowls she can sell during one weekend is 750. If during that weekend she sells only vases and bowls and earns at least \$7,780, what is the maximum number of vases she could sell?

17 ☐ Mark for Review

For a certain chemistry experiment, the number of moles of product increases each minute by $r\%$ of the number of moles the preceding minute. The function $g(x) = 78,500(1.52)^{\frac{x}{60}}$ models the number of moles of product created x seconds after the start of the experiment. What is the value of r?

(A) 48

(B) 52

(C) 60

(D) 554

CONTINUE ➜

18 ☐ Mark for Review

The function g is defined by the equation $g(x) = -3(5)^x$. Which of the following equations defines the function h if $h(x) = g(x + 3)$?

- (A) $h(x) = -27(125)^x$

- (B) $h(x) = -9(15)^x$

- (C) $h(x) = -9(5)^x$

- (D) $h(x) = -375(5)^x$

19 ☐ Mark for Review

One solution to the equation $x^2 + 4x - 14 = 0$ can be written as $-2 - \sqrt{c}$. What is the value of the constant c?

- (A) 18

- (B) 23

- (C) 36

- (D) 72

CONTINUE

20 Mark for Review

The equation $7x(7x + 6) = -c$ has exactly two real solutions. If c is an integer constant, what is the greatest possible value of c?

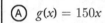

21 Mark for Review

A band member earns \$500 for the first four concerts performed during a given month plus a flat rate for each additional concert that month. The band member earned a total of \$900 for playing 6 concerts in a month. Which function g gives the total earnings, in dollars, for x concerts, where $x \geq 4$?

(A) $g(x) = 150x$

(B) $g(x) = 150x + 500$

(C) $g(x) = 200x - 300$

(D) $g(x) = 200x + 500$

22 Mark for Review

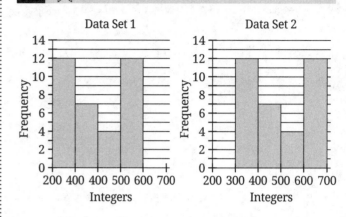

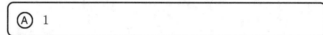

The histograms summarize two data sets, each with 35 integers. For each histogram, the intervals each represent the frequency of integers greater than or equal to the number at the left of the bar and less than the number at the right of the bar. For example, the first interval represents the frequency of integers greater than or equal to 200 and less than 300. What is the greatest possible difference between the means of the two data sets?

(A) 1

(B) 35

(C) 100

(D) 199

STOP
If you finish before time is called, you may check your work on this section only.
Do not turn to any other section.

Chapter 4
Practice Test 2:
Answers and
Explanations

PRACTICE TEST 2: MULTIPLE-CHOICE ANSWER KEY

Reading and Writing				Math		
Module 1	Module 2 (Easier)	Module 2 (Harder)		Module 1	Module 2 (Easier)	Module 2 (Harder)
1. C	1. D	1. D		1. D	1. C	1. B
2. D	2. A	2. A		2. B	2. C	2. C
3. C	3. C	3. C		3. 7	3. 78	3. B
4. B	4. B	4. A		4. A	4. 7	4. 5
5. B	5. C	5. B		5. C	5. 4	5. C
6. A	6. A	6. A		6. D	6. B	6. C
7. B	7. D	7. A		7. C	7. A	7. D
8. D	8. A	8. B		8. C	8. D	8. A
9. D	9. C	9. B		9. B	9. A	9. −172
10. C	10. B	10. B		10. A	10. B	10. 2440
11. D	11. C	11. B		11. $\frac{1}{2}$ or .5	11. 125	11. D
12. B	12. D	12. C		12. B	12. C	12. B
13. A	13. A	13. C		13. A	13. A	13. C
14. C	14. D	14. D		14. −39	14. C	14. A
15. B	15. A	15. D		15. −8	15. D	15. −14
16. B	16. B	16. B		16. B	16. B	16. 249
17. D	17. B	17. D		17. 64	17. −14	17. B
18. B	18. B	18. D		18. B	18. 7	18. D
19. A	19. D	19. B		19. D	19. C	19. A
20. A	20. A	20. B		20. C	20. A	20. 8
21. A	21. D	21. C		21. 8	21. D	21. C
22. D	22. B	22. D		22. D	22. B	22. D
23. A	23. A	23. B				
24. B	24. C	24. A				
25. D	25. D	25. D				
26. A	26. C	26. C				
27. C	27. C	27. C				

PRACTICE TEST 2—READING AND WRITING EXPLANATIONS

Module 1

1. **C** This is a Vocabulary question, as it asks for *the most logical and precise word or phrase*. Read the text and highlight what can help to fill in the blank, which describes how Earhart didn't *consider* her *feat*. The beginning of the sentence draws a contrast by saying *Even though no woman pilot had accomplished this*, so Earhart must not have considered it "impossible." Write "impossible" in the annotation box and use Process of Elimination.

    - (A) is wrong because *definitive* means "certain."

    - (B) is wrong because *enigmatic* means "mysterious."

    - (C) is correct because *impracticable* means "impossible."

    - (D) is wrong because *appropriate* doesn't match with "impossible."

2. **D** This is a Vocabulary question, as it asks for *the most logical and precise word or phrase*. Read the text and highlight what can help to fill in the blank, which describes how the *music* relates to *looping and phrasing techniques* with certain elements. The second sentence states that Richter weaves *synthesizer sounds with samples*, which elaborates on the aspects of his compositions mentioned in the previous sentence. Therefore, the blank should be something like "made of." Write "made of" in the annotation box and use Process of Elimination.

    - (A) is wrong because *portrayed by* means "modeled by."

    - (B) is wrong because the music isn't *coupled with* those elements; it's made from them.

    - (C) is wrong because *denoted* means "named."

    - (D) is correct because *constructed from* matches with "made of."

3. **C** This is a Vocabulary question, as it asks for *the most logical and precise word or phrase*. Read the text and highlight what can help to fill in the blank, which describes the *hydrocarbons*. The part with the blank is followed by a colon, which indicates that the second part of the sentence will elaborate on the first. It defines the blank as *chemically created without having any association with living organisms*, so write "not associated with living things" in the annotation box and use Process of Elimination.

    - (A) and (D) are wrong because *flexible* and *alterable* mean "able to change."

    - (B) is wrong because *genuine* means "sincere."

    - (C) is correct because *inorganic* matches with "not associated with living things."

4.　**B**　This is a Vocabulary question, as it asks for *the most logical and precise word or phrase*. Read the text and highlight what can help to fill in the blank, which describes how Beethoven's *musical output* related to *his deteriorating hearing*. The part with the blank is followed by a colon, which indicates that the second part of the sentence will elaborate on the first. It states that almost all of his symphonies and choral works were written after he started losing his hearing. Therefore, it would seem that his output was *not substantially* "harmed by" his hearing loss. Write "harmed by" in the annotation box and use Process of Elimination.

- (A) is wrong because while "limited by" could work, *limited to* means "excluding others."

- (B) is correct because *inhibited by* matches with "harmed by."

- (C) and (D) are wrong because they are both positive, and a negative word is needed here.

5.　**B**　This is a Vocabulary question, as it asks what a word *most nearly means*. Read the text and highlight what can help to understand the underlined word. The blank is followed by *knew all about a vessel*. The second sentence says that Mrs. Budd *knew something* about *boats*, which is what *a vessel* refers to. Therefore, she "believed" she knew about boats. Write "believed" in the annotation box and use Process of Elimination.

- (A) is wrong because *formulated* means "created."

- (B) is correct because *imagined* matches with "believed."

- (C) is wrong because *conceded* means "gave in."

- (D) is wrong because *characterized* means "described."

6.　**A**　This is a Purpose question, as it asks for the *overall structure*. Read the text and highlight what can help to understand the structure. The narrator describes fear of thinking about his death and concludes by stating that he would rather be *A living mouse than dead as a man dies*, so write "fear of death, would rather be alive" in the annotation box and use Process of Elimination.

- (A) is correct because it matches the annotation.

- (B) is wrong because the text never says that the fears *are intensifying*.

- (C) is wrong because there is no *transformation* of beliefs.

- (D) is wrong because the speaker doesn't criticize anyone else.

7.　**B**　This is a Retrieval question, as it says *According to the text*. Read the text and highlight what it says about how Horowitz determined the dogs' *level of interest*. The second sentence states that her determination of interest was *based on the amount of time dogs spent sniffing* certain odors. Eliminate any answer that isn't supported by the text.

- (A) is wrong because the study included another substance besides the dogs' *own urine*.

- (B) is correct because it matches the reason given in the text.

- (C) is wrong because *the urine of other dogs* wasn't included in the study.

- (D) is wrong because *facial reactions* weren't mentioned.

8. **D** This is a Retrieval question, as it says *According to the text.* Read the text and highlight what it says about *why* biologists are *concerned about the Great Barrier Reef.* The second sentence says *marine biologists are concerned that reef coverage has declined significantly.* Eliminate any answer that isn't supported by the text.

- (A) is wrong because accommodating *new reefs* isn't mentioned.

- (B) is wrong because the text says that *fertilizers* are harmful, not beneficial, to reefs.

- (C) is wrong because *generating new reefs* isn't mentioned.

- (D) is correct because if the reef coverage has declined, then its size was once larger.

9. **D** This is a Main Idea question, as it asks for the *main idea.* Read and highlight the main phrases or lines that the other sentences seem to support. The text introduces Escoffier and states that *his first cookbook* made him *a legend.* The text goes on to explain the aspects of the book that made it influential, so write "Escoffier's cookbook was important" in the annotation box and use Process of Elimination.

- (A) is wrong because the text doesn't mention readers creating *their own recipes.*

- (B) is wrong because the text doesn't say that the cookbook wasn't considered to be influential until later.

- (C) is wrong because it only refers to information in the first sentence, not the *main idea.*

- (D) is correct because it matches the annotation.

10. **C** This is a Claims question, as it asks for a *quotation* that *illustrates the claim.* Read the text and highlight the claim, which is that *Dick Horner* is *a good-hearted boy whose adventurous nature can cause him trouble.* Eliminate answers that don't *illustrate* this idea.

- (A), (B), and (D) are wrong because they don't state that Horner's *adventurous nature* is the source of his trouble.

- (C) is correct because it mentions his *wild spirits* and *some new mischief,* and the idea that he *promised to turn over a new leaf* and *would be sorry* matches with *good-hearted.*

11. **D** This is a Conclusions question, as it asks for the choice that *most logically completes the text*. Read the text and highlight the main ideas. The text describes hula's *spiritual and meaningful* background and states that *commercialized hula dancers have been applauded by millions of tourists*. Then the text provides a contrast, stating that *audience members must have a strong familiarity with the history* in order to *recognize the full significance*. Eliminate any answer that states a conclusion that isn't supported by the text.

• (A) is wrong because *other forms of dance* aren't mentioned.

• (B) is wrong because the author doesn't compare hula to other *dance forms*.

• (C) is wrong because *other forms of artistic expression* aren't mentioned.

• (D) is correct because the text suggests that *tourists* may not *recognize the full significance* of hula, whereas *natives*, who may be aware of the *spiritual and meaningful* history of the dance, may understand it more.

12. **B** This is a Conclusions question, as it asks for the choice that *most logically completes the text*. Read the text and highlight the main ideas. The text states that *Many art historians* think that an aspect of two statues *proves that they were cast* in *the Early Classical Period*. Then the text offers a contrast, stating that someone else thinks the statues could have been made later, when *artists consciously imitated Early Classical style*. Eliminate any answer that states a conclusion that isn't supported by the text.

• (A) is wrong because the text does explain how the statues could have been made in a different time period.

• (B) is correct because it's consistent with the alternative view provided in the text, which questions the first time period proposed.

• (C) is wrong because the text doesn't provide enough information to know what was true about *later statues* in general.

• (D) is wrong because *proves* is too strong; the alternate theory calls into question the previous viewpoint but doesn't necessarily prove it wrong.

13. **A** This is a Conclusions question, as it asks for the choice that *most logically completes the text*. Read the text and highlight the main ideas. The text introduces *dissertations* and identifies a problem with them, which is that *citations are necessary* but *too many direct quotes* can make the dissertation *difficult to read*. Therefore, *paraphrasing* instead of using *direct quotes* could make a dissertation easier to read. Eliminate any answer that states a conclusion that isn't supported by the text.

• (A) is correct because it shows how *paraphrasing* could solve the problem stated in the text.

• (B) is wrong because popularity *among non-scientists* isn't related to the text.

- (C) is wrong because *the consensus views of most renowned psychologists* aren't related to the text.

- (D) is wrong because the text states that *citations are necessary*; it's *too many direct quotes* that are the problem.

14. **C** In this Rules question, punctuation is changing in the answer choices. The first part of the sentence says *An American tennis player considered one of the greatest ever*, which is an introductory phrase that is not essential to the sentence's meaning. It should therefore be followed by a comma to separate it from the rest of the sentence. Eliminate answers that do not have a comma.

- (A), (B), and (D) are wrong because they don't use a comma.

- (C) is correct because it uses a comma after the introductory phrase.

15. **B** In this Rules question, punctuation is changing in the answer choices. Look for independent clauses. The first part of the sentence says *A photographer and member of the Swinomish and Tulalip tribes, Matika Wilbur started traveling throughout all 50 US states in 2012 to complete Project 562*, which is an independent clause. The second part of the sentence says *a multi-year photography project dedicated to documenting contemporary Indigenous life in the more than 562 federally recognized tribes in the US*, which is not an independent clause. Eliminate any option that doesn't correctly connect the independent clause to the describing phrase that follows.

- (A) is wrong because the sentence needs a comma to separate the independent clause and the describing phrase.

- (B) is correct because it correctly connects the independent clause and the describing phrase.

- (C) and (D) are wrong because the word *and* suggests two things, but the last part is a description of *Project 562*, not a separate thing.

16. **B** In this Rules question, punctuation is changing in the answer choices. Look for independent clauses. The first part of the sentence says *Paul Baran's invention of packet switching allowed for a more efficient and cost-effective way to transmit data and forms the basis of the modern internet*, which is an independent clause. The second part says *before packet switching's invention, networks transmitted data by relying on circuit switching*, which is also an independent clause. Eliminate any answer that can't correctly connect two independent clauses.

- (A) is wrong because a coordinating conjunction (*and*) without a comma can't connect two independent clauses.

- (B) is correct because the period makes each independent clause its own sentence, which is fine.

- (C) is wrong because a comma without a coordinating conjunction can't connect two independent clauses.

- (D) is wrong because some type of punctuation is needed in order to connect two independent clauses.

17. **D** In this Rules question, the subjects of the answers are changing, which suggests it may be testing modifiers. Look for and highlight a modifying phrase: *while studying bones at a 16th-century historical site*. Whoever is *studying bones* needs to come immediately after the comma. Eliminate any answer that doesn't start with someone who can study something.

- (A) and (C) are wrong because a *discovery* can't study something.

- (B) is wrong because a *horse tooth* can't study something.

- (D) is correct because an *archaeologist* can study something.

18. **B** In this Rules question, the subjects of the answers are changing, which suggests it may be testing modifiers. Look for and highlight a modifying phrase: *Listed as one of Time magazine's top ten medical breakthroughs in 2011*. Whatever is *Listed as* a *breakthrough* needs to come immediately after the comma. Eliminate any answer that doesn't start with something that is a *medical breakthrough*.

- (A) is wrong because an *organ* itself isn't a *medical breakthrough*.

- (B) is correct because the *development* of *organs* is a *medical breakthrough*.

- (C) is wrong because a *team* isn't a *medical breakthrough*.

- (D) is wrong because a doctor isn't a *medical breakthrough*.

19. **A** In this Rules question, verbs are changing in the answer choices, so it's testing consistency with verbs. Find and highlight the subject, *DustBuster*, which is singular, so a singular verb is needed. Write an annotation saying "singular." Eliminate any answer that is not singular.

- (A) is correct because it's singular.

- (B), (C), and (D) are wrong because they are plural.

20. **A** In this Rules question, punctuation is changing in the answer choices. Look for independent clauses. The first part of the sentence says *Thomas Herbert Elliot Jackson earned his living as a soldier and a coffee farmer, but he was also keenly interested in lepidopterology, the study of moths and butterflies*, which is an independent clause. The second part of the sentence says *amassing the largest collection of native African butterflies and donating his specimens to museums around the world*, which is not an independent clause. Eliminate any option that doesn't correctly connect an independent to a describing phrase.

- (A) is correct because a comma can be used between the independent clause and the describing phrase.

- (B) is wrong because there should be a comma between the independent clause and the describing phrase, as there is a shift in ideas.

- (C) and (D) are wrong because both a period and a semicolon connect two independent clauses, and the second part of the sentence isn't an independent clause.

21.   **A**   This is a transition question, so highlight ideas that relate to each other. The preceding sentence says *The tidal flats...are listed as Wetland Protected Areas under the Wetlands Conservation Act*, and this sentence says *these sites still face a wide variety of threats from humans*. These ideas disagree, so an opposite-direction transition is needed. Make an annotation that says "disagree." Eliminate any answer that doesn't match.

   • (A) is correct because *However* is an opposite-direction transition.

   • (B), (C), and (D) are wrong because they are same-direction transitions.

22.   **D**   This is a transition question, so highlight ideas that relate to each other. The preceding sentence describes what happened with *James Soong*, and this sentence states that *Shui-bian Chen* won the election instead of Soong. These ideas disagree, so an opposite-direction transition is needed. Make an annotation that says "disagree." Eliminate any answer that doesn't match.

   • (A), (B), and (C) are wrong because they are all same-direction transitions.

   • (D) is correct because *Afterward* suggests a change in time, which can function as an opposite-direction transition.

23.   **A**   This is a transition question, so highlight ideas that relate to each other. The first sentence describes Leigh's intentions behind her art. The second sentence gives an example of Leigh's art, and this sentence provides a second example. These ideas agree, so a same-direction transition is needed. Make an annotation that says "agree." Eliminate any answer that doesn't match.

   • (A) is correct because *Similarly* is same-direction and shows that this sentence is a second example of Leigh's work.

   • (B) is wrong because this sentence isn't an example of a claim from the sentence right before it.

   • (C) is wrong because it is an opposite-direction transition.

   • (D) is wrong because this sentence isn't a conclusion based on previously stated evidence.

24.   **B**   This is a Rhetorical Synthesis question, so highlight the goal(s) stated in the question: *explain an advantage of the format of Mystery House*. Eliminate any answer that doesn't fulfill this purpose.

   • (A) and (D) are wrong because the *format* is mentioned but no *advantage* of it is stated.

   • (B) is correct because it shows how the game's *format* was different from *other games at the time*, giving it an advantage.

   • (C) is wrong because it doesn't mention the *format*.

25.   **D**   This is a Rhetorical Synthesis question, so highlight the goal(s) stated in the question: *emphasize the significance of Evans's research*. Eliminate any answer that doesn't fulfill this purpose.

   • (A), (B), and (C) are wrong because they don't say why the discovery is significant.

- (D) is correct because *vital to the public's wider acceptance of pasteurization and reduction in brucellosis infections* shows how the discovery is significant.

26. **A** This is a Rhetorical Synthesis question, so highlight the goal(s) stated in the question: *contrast the superconductivity of mercury wire with that of cuprates.* Eliminate any answer that doesn't fulfill this purpose.

- (A) is correct because it contrasts the different temperatures at which each material becomes a superconductor.

- (B) is wrong because it doesn't specifically say at what temperature *mercury wire* becomes a superconductor, so it doesn't *contrast* their *superconductivity*.

- (C) is wrong because it doesn't mention *mercury wire*.

- (D) is wrong because it doesn't contrast the two materials' *superconductivity*.

27. **C** This is a Rhetorical Synthesis question, so highlight the goal(s) stated in the question: *present the significance of the Kefauver-Harris Amendment to an audience unfamiliar with the medication thalidomide.* Eliminate any answer that doesn't *present the significance* in a way that assumes the audience is *unfamiliar with the medication thalidomide.*

- (A) and (B) are wrong because they don't describe *thalidomide* but the audience is *unfamiliar* with it.

- (C) is correct because it describes the *significance of the Kefauver-Harris Amendment* and describes *thalidomide* since the audience is *unfamiliar* with it.

- (D) is wrong because it doesn't describe the *significance of the Kefauver-Harris Amendment.*

Module 2 – Easier

1. **D** This is a Vocabulary question, as it asks for *the most logical and precise word or phrase.* Read the text and highlight what can help to fill in the blank, which describes what *Environmental analysts* need to do *through the use of life-cycle assessments.* The part after the colon describes how *life-cycle assessments* are used to *find out the environmental impact of a product,* so write "finding out" in the annotation box and use Process of Elimination.

- (A), (B), and (C) are wrong because they don't match with "finding out."

- (D) is correct because *determining* matches with "finding out."

2.   **A**   This is a Vocabulary question, as it asks for *the most logical and precise word or phrase*. Read the text and highlight what can help to fill in the blank, which describes how *Paa Joe* remains as he produces his art. The text describes Joe as *carefully drawing up* designs, honoring people's requests, memorializing *the life of the individual*, and believing that *his designs* will *carry a piece of life in this world to the afterlife*. All of these details suggest that Joe is "considerate," so write that in the annotation box and use Process of Elimination.

- (A) is correct because *compassionate* matches with "considerate."

- (B) and (D) are wrong because they are negative words, and the text describes Joe using positive language.

- (C) is wrong because *assertive* means "confident."

3.   **C**   This is a Vocabulary question, as it asks for *the most logical and precise word or phrase*. Read the text and highlight what can help to fill in the blank, which refers to *ways to prevent the disease* that were lacking *In the early 2000s*. The second sentence provides a contrast with *However* and states that in 2007 a gel was invented that could *lower the risk*. This contrast suggests that "successful" ways *to prevent the disease* were lacking prior to 2007, so write "successful" in the annotation box and use Process of Elimination.

- (A) and (B) are wrong because they are both negative words, but "successful" is positive.

- (C) is correct because *effective* matches with "successful."

- (D) is wrong because *charismatic* means "charming and likeable."

4.   **B**   This is a Vocabulary question, as it asks for *the most logical and precise word or phrase*. Read the text and highlight what can help to fill in the blank, which describes the *attempts for change*. The text states that the actions included *nonviolent sit-ins, boycotts, and marches*, so write "nonviolent" in the annotation box and use Process of Elimination.

- (A) is wrong because *indifferent* means "not having an opinion."

- (B) is correct because *peaceful* matches with "nonviolent."

- (C) is wrong because *essential* doesn't match with "nonviolent."

- (D) is wrong because *bland* means "dull."

5. **C** This is a Vocabulary question, as it asks for *the most logical and precise word or phrase*. Read the text and highlight what can help to fill in the blank, which describes how *Washington* did *not* respond to Bushnell's *appeal*. The first sentence states that Bushnell *unsuccessfully requested increased security for her mission several times*, and the last part of the text says that after *Washington was not able* to do something, she pleaded to a specific person *for support but was ignored*. All of this suggests that Washington was not able to "fulfill" *her appeal* for *increased security*, so write "fulfill" in the annotation box and use Process of Elimination.

- (A) is wrong because *certify* means "confirm," but Bushnell was looking for *increased security*, so certifying the request would only suggest confirming that she had made it, not responding to it.

- (B) is wrong because *mistake* is a negative word, and a positive word is needed here.

- (C) is correct because approving her appeal would suggest providing the requested security.

- (D) is wrong because *demonstrate* doesn't match with "fulfill."

6. **A** This is a Vocabulary question, as it asks for *the most logical and precise word or phrase*. Read the text and highlight what can help to fill in the blank, which describes how Heyer did or did not *engage in all forms of publicity for her publications*. There is a contrast with *Despite being a best-selling writer*, which suggests that Heyer may not have engaged in publicity. Furthermore, the second sentence says *She so believed that her private life was irrelevant to the success of her novels*, which also indicates that she didn't like publicity, so write "didn't want" in the annotation box and use Process of Elimination.

- (A) is correct because *refused* matches with "didn't want."

- (B), (C), and (D) are wrong because they are all positive words, but "didn't want" is negative.

7. **D** This is a Purpose question, as it asks for the *main purpose*. Read the text and highlight what can help to understand the overall purpose. The text introduces *Dr. Donald Hopkins* and states that he was hired *to help implement a program to eradicate smallpox in Sierra Leone*. Then it explains how he used *mass distribution of the smallpox vaccine* to reduce the incidence of disease, so write "tell how Hopkins helped with smallpox" in the annotation box and use Process of Elimination.

- (A) and (C) are wrong because they don't mention *Hopkins*.

- (B) is wrong because the text doesn't state that this encapsulates Hopkins' whole *career*.

- (D) is correct because it matches the annotation.

8.   **A**   This is a Purpose question, as it asks for the *main purpose*. Read the text and highlight what can help to understand the overall purpose. The poem states that the speaker has *no wealth to give* to someone but states, *You have my heart*. Then the speaker vows to always think of this person and asks whether this thought is mutual, so write "leaving but will always think of the person" in the annotation box and use Process of Elimination.

   - (A) is correct because it matches the annotation.

   - (B) is wrong because the text never says *why* the speaker loves the other person.

   - (C) is wrong because the text never says *when he will be back*.

   - (D) is wrong because no instructions are given.

9.   **C**   This is a Dual Texts question, as it has two texts. The question asks what *the researchers in Text 2* would say about *the scientists' initial belief in Text 1*. Start by understanding the *initial belief* in Text 1. Text 1 describes the famine resulting from damage to the potato crop and states that *scientists originally believed the disease was caused by the US-1 strain of the bacteria*. Next, look for a similar idea in Text 2 to see how its author feels about this view. Text 2 describes research on potato plants from the famine and states that the researchers *found that US-1 was not the cause of the catastrophe*. The text goes on to state that *although the US-1 strain is a common cause of crop loss, a formerly undiscovered strain* caused the famine. Therefore, the researchers in Text 2 would "say the claim makes sense but is wrong." Write that in the annotation box and use Process of Elimination.

   - (A) is wrong because the mistaken viewpoint is about *US-1*, not *HERB-1*.

   - (B) is wrong because *only affects potato crops* is never stated.

   - (C) is correct because it matches the annotation.

   - (D) is wrong because Text 2 acknowledges that *US-1* is *a common cause of crop loss*, so the researchers do understand *why the scientists would think that US-1 caused the famine*.

10.   **B**   This is a Retrieval question, as it says *Based on the text*. Read the text and highlight what it says about *the speaker* being *like the sun*. The text mentions the other person needing the speaker *through and through, as flowers need the sun*. Eliminate any answer that isn't supported by the text.

   - (A) is wrong because the speaker is not described as shining.

   - (B) is correct because it matches the highlighted text.

   - (C) is wrong because the sun is not described as being *completely alone*.

   - (D) is wrong because *the world* is described as *asleep*, but neither the speaker nor the sun is.

11. **C** This is a Claims question, as it asks for a *quotation* to *illustrate the claim*. Read the text and highlight the claim, which is that *the main character* is *eager to help bring peace to the restless spirit*, a *young girl* whom he *suspects* is haunting his orchard. Eliminate answers that don't *illustrate* this idea.

   • (A) and (B) are wrong because they mention the character's suspicion but not his desire to *help bring peace* to the spirit.

   • (C) is correct because *that I may help your sorrowing heart to rest* supports *eager to help bring peace* from the claim.

   • (D) is wrong because it doesn't clearly mention anything about the *spirit* or helping it.

12. **D** This is a Charts question, as it asks for *data from the table*. The graph charts several biomes, their maximum temperatures, and their annual precipitation ranges. Read the text and highlight the specifications mentioned, which are *a range of annual precipitation that includes 30 inches* and *does not exceed a maximum temperature of 80°F*. Start with the temperature maximum, which leaves only boreal forest and tropical forest. Then, of those two, boreal forest is the one that includes 30 inches in its precipitation range.

   • (A), (B), and (C) are wrong because they don't meet both specifications from the text.

   • (D) is correct because it meets both specifications.

13. **A** This is a Charts question, as it asks for *data from the table*. The graph charts several elements, their boiling points, heat capacities, electron affinities, and first ionization energies. Highlight the *assertion* in the text, which is that *four of the elements are metals and one element is a nonmetal*. The text associates *boiling points* and *electron affinities* with being a metal or a nonmetal, so eliminate any answers that refer to other characteristics, are inconsistent with the table, or don't support the assertion.

   • (A) is correct because *boiling points above 1,500 K* would mean that four are metals, and the same four having *electron affinities of less than 150 kJ/mol* further matches with the description of metals, which is consistent with the student's assertion.

   • (B) is wrong because it only mentions one element, but the claim relates to all five.

   • (C) is wrong because *first ionization energy* and *heat capacity* aren't stated in relation to whether elements are metals or nonmetals.

   • (D) is wrong because *heat capacity* isn't stated in relation to determining whether an element is a metal or a nonmetal.

14. **D** This is a Claims question, as it asks for an answer that would *support the student's claim*. Read the text and highlight the claim, which is that *the work was included as a way to attract new visitors*. Eliminate answers that don't *support* this idea.

   • (A) is wrong because it contradicts the claim by suggesting that *new visitors* wouldn't be interested in this type of exhibit.

- (B) and (C) are wrong because they don't relate to *new visitors*.

- (D) is correct because *appeal to people who don't normally visit art museums* matches with *attract new visitors*.

15. **A** This is a Claims question, as it asks for an answer that would *support the researchers' claim*. Read the text and highlight the claim, which is that *bilinguals can switch between tasks at a faster rate due to their routine use of language-switching*. Eliminate answers that don't *support* this idea.

- (A) is correct because it supports the idea that there is a link between speaking two languages and task-switching.

- (B) is wrong because it's not consistent with the *faster rate* for bilinguals in the claim.

- (C) is wrong because it doesn't relate to the claim about task-switching.

- (D) is wrong because it weakens the claim by providing an alternate cause for bilinguals' faster rate of task-switching.

16. **B** This is a Charts question, as it asks for *data in the graph*. The graph charts the percentage of cat contact in different spots for people with previous positive cat experience and those with previous negative cat experience. Highlight the *claim* in the text, which is that *previous positive cat experience was not predictive of good cat handling techniques; in fact, participants with previous negative cat experience demonstrated better cat handling techniques*. Read more of the text to identify the link between good and bad cat handling techniques and the contact areas: cats *prefer certain contact areas, such as the cheeks, base of ear, and under the jaw, while disliking contact on the stomach or the base of the tail*. Eliminate any answer that doesn't *support* the claim or is inconsistent with the data on the graph.

- (A) is wrong because it contradicts the claim, as *lower percentages of contact in areas disliked by cats* would be in line with good cat handling techniques, which the claim said was associated with those who had *previous negative cat experience*.

- (B) is correct because it is consistent with the claim and supported by the graph.

- (C) is wrong because *similar percentages of contact* isn't consistent with the contrast stated in the claim.

- (D) is wrong because it doesn't relate to a difference between those with positive experience and those with negative experience.

17.   **B**   This is a Conclusions question, as it asks for something *presented in the text*. Highlight what the text says about *Miyazaki's approach to film*: the films use *animation* but *remain relevant to both children and adults*, they draw from *Japanese elements*, and they include *poignant stories about humans and the environment as told through the eyes of children*. The text also states that Miyazaki *showcases the importance of protecting the environment* through *communing with nature*. Eliminate any answer that states a conclusion that isn't supported by the text.

   •   (A) is wrong because *nature spirits* are mentioned in relation to one movie, not his approach as a whole.

   •   (B) is correct because it's fully supported by the text.

   •   (C) is wrong because *Western influences* aren't mentioned as playing an equal role to *Japanese elements*.

   •   (D) is wrong because the text never states what Miyazaki believes his films *will encourage* people to do.

18.   **B**   In this Rules question, verb forms are changing in the answer choices, so it's testing sentence structure. The subject of the sentence is *thale cress plants*, and there is no main verb, so the answer must provide the main verb. Eliminate any answer that isn't in the correct form to be the main verb.

   •   (A) and (D) are wrong because an *-ing* verb can't be the main verb in a sentence.

   •   (B) is correct because it's in the right form to be the main verb.

   •   (C) is wrong because a "to" verb can't be the main verb in a sentence.

19.   **D**   In this Rules question, verb forms are changing in the answer choices, so it's testing sentence structure. The subject of the sentence is *Farmers*, and there is no main verb, so the answer must provide the main verb. Eliminate any answer that isn't in the correct form to be the main verb.

   •   (A) and (C) are wrong because an *-ing* verb can't be the main verb in a sentence.

   •   (B) is wrong because a "to" verb can't be the main verb in a sentence.

   •   (D) is correct because it's in the right form to be the main verb.

20.   **A**   In this Rules question, verbs are changing in the answer choices, so it's testing consistency with verbs. Find and highlight the subject, *breaks*, which is plural, so a plural verb is needed. All of the answers work with a plural subject, so look for a clue regarding tense. The previous sentence describes something that happened in the past, *In 1972*, and this sentence describes what happened *After this*, but still in the past, as the sentence is explaining a *defining element* of hip hop today. Highlight these phrases and write an annotation that says "past." Eliminate any answer not in past tense.

   •   (A) is correct because it's in past tense.

   •   (B) is wrong because it's in present tense.

- (C) is wrong because *had become* suggests that this event happened prior to another event, but it happened after the events of the previous sentence.

- (D) is wrong because it's in future tense.

21. **D** In this Rules question, punctuation is changing in the answer choices. Look for independent clauses. The first part of the sentence says *he was unable to come up with a plausible mechanism to explain how the continents could move*, which is an independent clause. The second part says *it was not until the discovery of the seafloor spreading at mid-ocean ridges that his idea became widely accepted*, which is also an independent clause. Eliminate any answer that can't correctly connect two independent clauses.

- (A) is wrong because a comma without a coordinating conjunction can't connect two independent clauses.

- (B) is wrong because some type of punctuation is needed in order to connect two independent clauses.

- (C) is wrong because a coordinating conjunction (*and*) without a comma can't connect two independent clauses.

- (D) is correct because it connects the independent clauses with a comma + a coordinating conjunction (*and*), which is acceptable.

22. **B** In this Rules question, verbs are changing in the answer choices, so it's testing consistency with verbs. Find and highlight the subject, *it*, which is singular, so a singular verb is needed. All of the answers work with a singular subject, so look for a clue regarding tense. The sentence uses a present tense verb: *is*. Highlight this verb, which is in present tense, so write an annotation that says "present." Eliminate any answer not in present tense.

- (A) is wrong because it's not in present tense.

- (B) is correct because it's in present tense.

- (C) and (D) are wrong because they're in past tense.

23. **A** In this Rules question, punctuation is changing in the answer choices. The first part of the sentence says *A total solar eclipse…is observed*, which is an independent clause. The second part says *wherever the Moon appears large enough to completely obscure the solar disc*, which is a describing phrase that is not an independent clause. Eliminate any answer that doesn't correctly connect the independent clause to the describing phrase that follows.

- (A) is correct because no punctuation should be used here.

- (B) is wrong because the comma suggests that the second part of the sentence is not essential to the sentence's meaning, but the phrase is essential in order to specify where the eclipse is observed.

- (C) is wrong because a semicolon links two independent clauses, and the second part isn't independent.

- (D) is wrong because the second part is not an independent clause, so it can't stand on its own.

24.   C   This is a transition question, so highlight ideas that relate to each other. The preceding sentence says *Canadian Cree/Métis poet and artist Gregory Scofield initially was ashamed*, and this sentence says *Scofield learned to appreciate the Métis aspects of his identity*. These ideas disagree, so an opposite-direction transition is needed. Make an annotation that says "disagree." Eliminate any answer that doesn't match.

- (A), (B), and (D) are wrong because they are same-direction transitions.

- (C) is correct because *Nevertheless* is an opposite-direction transition.

25.   D   This is a transition question, so highlight ideas that relate to each other. The preceding sentence says *there is very little archaeological or written evidence linking this instrument to the actual countries of Scotland or Ireland*, and this sentence says *the history of the instrument is largely up for debate*. These ideas agree, so a same-direction transition is needed. Make an annotation that says "agree." Eliminate any answer that doesn't match.

- (A) and (B) are wrong because they are opposite-direction transitions.

- (C) is wrong because this sentence isn't an additional point.

- (D) is correct because this sentence offers a conclusion based on the evidence in the previous sentence.

26.   C   This is a Rhetorical Synthesis question, so highlight the goal(s) stated in the question: *describe Apple: Skin to the Core to an audience unfamiliar with Eric Gansworth*. Eliminate any answer that doesn't describe the book in a way that assumes the audience is *unfamiliar with Eric Gansworth*.

- (A) and (B) are wrong because they don't provide information about Gansworth, and the audience is unfamiliar, so he should be described.

- (C) is correct because it describes the book and introduces Gansworth since the audience is unfamiliar with him.

- (D) is wrong because it doesn't *describe* the book.

27.   C   This is a Rhetorical Synthesis question, so highlight the goal(s) stated in the question: *explain an advantage of backstitch*. Eliminate any answer that doesn't fulfill this purpose.

- (A) and (B) are wrong because they don't describe *an advantage of backstitch*.

- (C) is correct because it describes *an advantage of backstitch*.

- (D) is wrong because it doesn't mention the technique of *backstitch*.

Module 2 – Harder

1. **D** This is a Vocabulary question, as it asks for *the most logical and precise word or phrase*. Read the text and highlight what can help to fill in the blank, which describes the relationship between *bumble-bees* and *the effects of climate change*. The following sentence explains how the bees' *imbalanced wings* have *coincided with the escalated temperatures caused by climate change*, so the bees must be affected by it. Write "affected by" in the annotation box and use Process of Elimination.

   - (A) and (C) are wrong because they're the opposite of the annotation.

   - (B) is wrong because *incongruent with* means "not matching up with."

   - (D) is correct because *susceptible to* matches with "affected by."

2. **A** This is a Vocabulary question, as it asks for *the most logical and precise word or phrase*. Read the text and highlight what can help to fill in the blank, which refers to what scientists *won't necessarily* have to do to *the Standard Model* as a result of the *findings*. The previous sentence states that *Recent measurements* were different from what *would ordinarily be predicted by the Standard Model*. Then there is a contrast word (*While*), and after the blank the text says that *the new data might indicate that some modifications…are warranted*. So, scientists won't necessarily have to "get rid of" the Standard Model, but some changes might be needed. Write "get rid of" in the annotation box and use Process of Elimination.

   - (A) is correct because *overhaul* matches with "get rid of."

   - (B) is wrong because *withhold* means "not provide."

   - (C) is wrong because it's the opposite of the annotation.

   - (D) is wrong because *misapprehend* means "misunderstand."

3. **C** This is a Vocabulary question, as it asks for *the most logical and precise word or phrase*. Read the text and highlight what can help to fill in the blank, which refers to the link between Archimedes and *calculus*. The text states that Archimedes, who was *active in the third century BCE* and is also described as *pioneering*, had described *concepts thought to have been first developed in the 1500s*. This is referring to *calculus*, so Archimedes worked with calculus before it was thought to have been developed. Write "invented" or "worked with before" in the annotation box and use Process of Elimination.

   - (A) is wrong because *exemplified* means "was an example of."

   - (B) is wrong because *verified* means "confirmed to be true," but the text suggests that Archimedes might have originated the ideas, not confirmed them.

   - (C) is correct because *anticipated* means "saw before it happened," which matches the annotation.

   - (D) is wrong because *translated* doesn't match the annotation.

4. **A** This is a Vocabulary question, as it asks for *the most logical and precise word or phrase*. Read the text and highlight what can help to fill in the blank, which refers to an aspect of the *plants left over* that was *assumed*. The previous sentence says that the extinction *was thought to have had a devastating effect on the remaining ecosystems*. This sentence begins with a contrast (*However*), and the second part of the sentence suggests that the plants were still surviving. Therefore, they weren't as "destroyed" as it was assumed. Write "destroyed" in the annotation box and use Process of Elimination.

    - (A) is correct because *assailable* means "vulnerable" or "able to be destroyed," and the idea that the plants weren't as vulnerable as they were assumed to be is consistent with the text.

    - (B) is wrong because *determinate* means "having defined limits."

    - (C) is wrong because *objectionable* means "controversial."

    - (D) is wrong because *liminal* means "in an intermediate stage."

5. **B** This is a Vocabulary question, as it asks for *the most logical and precise word or phrase*. Read the text and highlight what can help to fill in the blank, which describes what Ball *gained notoriety* for doing to *religious and secular authorities*. The part with the blank is followed by a colon, indicating that the second part of the sentence will explain the first. It begins with *this condemnation*, so the blank must mean "condemning." Write "condemning" in the annotation box and use Process of Elimination.

    - (A) is wrong because *proselytizing* means "trying to convert."

    - (B) is correct because *censuring* means "condemning."

    - (C) is wrong because *envisaging* means "visualizing."

    - (D) is wrong because *declaring* isn't a negative word like "condemning."

6. **A** This is a Purpose question, as it asks for the *function* of a sentence. Read the text and highlight what can help to understand the function of the underlined sentence. The text describes how the *man* instructs his *two dogs* to herd the sheep. The setting is described in terms of *the damp stillness of the air* and *the hillside*. Then the underlined sentence expands on the description of the setting and uses the phrases *creeping silently across the distance*, *desolate, treeless country*, and *no other sign of life*. Write "show how isolated the man's environment is" in the annotation box and use Process of Elimination.

    - (A) is correct because it matches the annotation.

    - (B) is wrong because no information is given on what the man *longs* to do.

    - (C) is wrong because the text does not state that the man makes a *daily walk*.

    - (D) is wrong because no comparison is made to *the train's destination*.

7. **A** This is a Purpose question, as it asks for the *function* of a sentence. Read the text and highlight what can help to understand the function of the underlined sentence. The text details Garin's actions on his *business* and then states that *The merry-making in the town tempted, but the way was long and he must go*. Then the underlined sentence gives an example of the *merry-making* that Garin had to refuse to join, as the text goes on to say that he *wanted to stay* but decided to leave. Write "example of merry-making" in the annotation box and use Process of Elimination.

    •   (A) is correct because it matches the annotation.

    •   (B) is wrong because no *emotion* of Garin's is foreshadowed in this sentence.

    •   (C) is wrong because, while it does visually describe the girls, they are not really part of the text's *scene* (they only cross his path), and this statement does not match with the *function* of the sentence; it's used to give an example of the merrymaking, not to describe characters.

    •   (D) is wrong because the underlined sentence doesn't give any information about Garin or his *urgency*.

8. **B** This is a Purpose question, as it asks for the *main purpose*. Read the text and highlight what can help to understand the overall purpose. The text describes the king and queen of *England* and the king and queen of *France* and then says that *In both countries* it was clear *that things in general were settled for ever*, so write "describe settled ruling situation in England and France" in the annotation box and use Process of Elimination.

    •   (A) is wrong because there is no *contrast* between the *conditions* of the two countries.

    •   (B) is correct because it matches the annotation.

    •   (C) is wrong because the similarity and difference stated are not part of the *main purpose* of the text.

    •   (D) is wrong because the text doesn't mention *hoarding food* or *withholding resources*.

9. **B** This is a Dual Texts question, as it has two texts. The question asks how *Patti and colleagues* in Text 2 would respond to *the "mystery" discussed in Text 1*. Start by understanding the *"mystery"* in Text 1. Text 1 states that the *mystery…concerns the large amount of glucose that is excreted as waste* from cancer cells. Next, look for a similar idea in Text 2 to see how *Patti and colleagues* feel about this mystery. Text 2 states that *Patti discovered that cancer cells have an upper limit for the amount of glucose that can be processed efficiently, as has long been observed in normal cells*. Therefore, Patti and colleagues in Text 2 would say exactly that, so use Process of Elimination with this highlighted portion.

    •   (A) is wrong because *further research* is not mentioned in Text 2.

    •   (B) is correct because it matches the highlighting in Text 2.

- (C) is wrong because the amount of glucose that *is required by cancer cells* isn't mentioned in Text 2; it's the amount that is absorbed and processed.

- (D) is wrong because Text 2 doesn't mention *mitochondrial processes*.

10. **B** This is a Claims question, as it asks for the choice that would *support Twenge's hypothesis*. Read the text and highlight the hypothesis, which is that *sociocultural environment…affects an individual's personality in addition to genetics and family environment*. Eliminate answers that don't *support* this idea.

- (A) is wrong because gender isn't related to *sociocultural environment*, as defined by the text.

- (B) is correct because students in the 1970s versus those in the 1990s would have grown up within different sociocultural environments and, according to the hypothesis, would therefore have different personality traits.

- (C) is wrong because *income level* isn't related to *sociocultural environment*, as defined by the text.

- (D) is wrong because the *number of words* people used to describe their personalities doesn't have a clear link to anything in the text.

11. **B** This is a Conclusions question, as it asks for something *presented in the text*. Highlight what the text says about *Ceh Moo's approach to literature*: she wrote *the first novel written by a woman in the Yucatec language*, which is untraditional because *Maya authors primarily write* works other than novels. The text goes on to describe another way Ceh Moo's story is different from traditional ones. Eliminate any answer that states a conclusion that isn't supported by the text.

- (A) is wrong because the text doesn't say that Ceh Moo takes the *myths* and sets them in the present day.

- (B) is correct because it's fully supported by the text.

- (C) is wrong because the text doesn't say that these influences are equal.

- (D) is wrong because the text never states that Ceh Moo's work criticizes anything.

12. **C** This is a Charts question, as it asks for *data from the table*. The table charts the mean flower abundance and species richness as well as mean wild bee abundance and species richness for four environments. Highlight the *conclusion* in the text, which is that *flower strips were most effective*. The text defines success in terms of *attracting more bees*, so higher values in the table correlate with effectiveness. Eliminate any answers that are inconsistent with the table or don't support the conclusion.

- (A) and (D) are wrong because they don't mention *flower strips*, which were the enhancement measure in the conclusion.

- (B) is wrong because it only compares flower strips to the *control group*, which doesn't support the conclusion that the flower strips were *most effective* among the interventions.

- (C) is correct because it compares the flower strips to everything else in the table, supporting the fact that they were *most effective*.

13. **C** This is a Charts question, as it asks for *data from the graph*. The graph charts the percentage improvement in test scores for two test types for a control group and an experimental group. Highlight the *recommendation* in the text, which is that *physically active lessons* should be *included in the mathematics curriculum*. The text states that the experimental group *received physically active mathematics lessons*, so to support the recommendation, the experimental group would need to have more improvements than the control group. Eliminate any answers that are inconsistent with the graph or don't support the recommendation.

- (A) is wrong because both groups improved their scores.

- (B) is wrong because it doesn't compare the experimental group to the control group, so the effect of the lessons isn't evident.

- (C) is correct because it suggests that the physically active lessons had benefits.

- (D) is wrong because it doesn't show the benefit of the physically active lessons.

14. **D** This is a Claims question, as it asks for a *quotation* that *illustrates the claim*. Read the text and highlight the claim, which is that *Treplev is heavily critical of the art form's* (theater's) *established tropes*. Eliminate answers that don't *illustrate* this idea.

- (A) and (C) are wrong because they don't contain anything critical.

- (B) is wrong because it doesn't mention the theater.

- (D) is correct because *other productions* and *playwrights* refer to the theater, and *the same, same, same old stuff* and *must needs run from it* suggest the speaker's disdain for the *established tropes*.

15. **D** This is a Claims question, as it asks for something that would *weaken the claim*. Highlight the *claim made by people who favor the conventional view of positive visualization*, which is that positive visualization *can enhance people's ability to achieve their goals*. Eliminate answers that don't *weaken* this idea.

- (A) is wrong because if *members of the control group accomplished fewer goals*, this would support, not weaken, the claim that positive visualization helps people achieve their goals.

- (B) is wrong because accomplishing even *a slightly higher number of their goals* would support the claim that positive visualization is effective, and the task here is to *weaken* the claim.

- (C) is wrong because no result is given for the effect of positive visualization on accomplishing goals.

- (D) is correct because it contradicts the claim by stating that those who were not told to use positive visualization actually accomplished more goals.

16. **B** This is a Charts question, as it asks for *data from the graph*. The graph charts the number of nightmares over four weeks for dreamers undergoing two types of interventions. Highlight the *claim* in the text, which is that *IRT is made even more effective when utilizing TMR*. Then, the sentence states that the graduate student *was surprised to observe* something, so the blank must refer to something that goes against the claim. Eliminate any answers that are inconsistent with the graph or don't go against the claim.

- (A) and (D) are wrong because they don't relate to whether TMR is effective.

- (B) is correct because if the decrease was only *slightly greater* for the group with TMR, this would somewhat weaken the idea that TMR makes the treatment *more effective* and could therefore be a surprising result.

- (C) is wrong because this result is consistent with the claim, so it wouldn't be surprising.

17. **D** This is a Conclusions question, as it asks for the choice that *most logically completes the text*. Read the text and highlight the main ideas. The text describes an experiment in which people *used social media* to engage with accounts belonging to people they knew as well as *users unknown to the participants*. The text contrasts the reduction in appearance satisfaction for known and unknown targets, stating that there was a greater reduction for known targets. Therefore, unknown targets caused a lesser reduction in appearance satisfaction. Eliminate any answer that states a conclusion that isn't supported by the text.

- (A) is wrong because it states the opposite of what the last sentence indicates.

- (B) is wrong because no conclusion can be drawn about the effectiveness of the *scale* that was used.

- (C) is wrong because there is no evidence from the text to say whether the correlation is *significant* or not.

- (D) is correct because it matches the relationship described in the last sentence.

18. **D** In this Rules question, verb forms are changing in the answer choices, so it's testing sentence structure. The phrase after the second dash describes how the two scientists created an *Ebola vaccine*. Eliminate any answer that does not make the phrase clear and correct.

- (A) is wrong because it makes the creation of the vaccine an item in a list, but there is no other *-ing* verb to form the list.

- (B) is wrong because there is no clear subject for the verb *created*.

- (C) is wrong because it's not clear who or what is *creating* the vaccine.

- (D) is correct because it states that the gene was *eliminated...to create a potential Ebola vaccine*, which provides a clear and correct meaning.

19.   **B**   In this Rules question, punctuation is changing in the answer choices. The main meaning of the sentence is *The watering of cultivated crops is sometimes based on a system known as irrigation scheduling, in which farmers use certain factors about the land and weather...to determine when and how much water is needed.* The phrase *specifically, the soil quality and projected rainfall* is a describing phrase that has a dash before it, so it must have a dash after it to show that it is not essential to the sentence's meaning. Eliminate answers that do not have a dash after the describing phrase.

- (A), (C), and (D) are wrong because they don't use a dash.

- (B) is correct because it uses a dash after the non-essential information.

20.   **B**   In this Rules question, punctuation with a transition is changing in the answer choices. Look for independent clauses. The first part of the sentence says *The audience was determined*. The part after *however* doesn't have a subject, so it's not an independent clause. Eliminate any answer that doesn't correctly link the independent clause to the phrase after it.

- (A) and (C) are wrong because a semicolon links two independent clauses, but the second part isn't an independent clause.

- (B) is correct because it puts commas before and after *however*, which is a word that isn't essential to the meaning of the sentence.

- (D) is wrong because the word *however* needs commas before and after to show that it's non-essential.

21.   **C**   In this Rules question, punctuation is changing in the answer choices. Look for independent clauses. The first part of the sentence says *A recent study by a team of researchers at the University of Washington discovered a surprising source of atmosphere- and climate-changing gases*, which is an independent clause. The second part of the sentence is not an independent clause and explains what the source of the gases was. Eliminate any option that doesn't correctly connect the independent clause to the explanation of the source.

- (A) is wrong because the period makes *volcanoes' passive degassing...* its own sentence, which doesn't work because it's not an independent clause.

- (B) is wrong because a semicolon links two independent clauses, but the second part isn't an independent clause.

- (C) is correct because a colon is used when the second part of the sentence elaborates on the first.

- (D) is wrong because some punctuation is needed between the independent clause and the explanation of the source.

22. **D** In this Rules question, punctuation is changing in the answer choices. Look for independent clauses. The first part of the sentence says *A 2006 edition of the book added two more patterns of thinking*, which is an independent clause. The second part of the sentence says *some autistic people may be music and math thinkers, others verbal logic thinkers*, which is an independent clause that states the new *patterns of thinking*. Eliminate any option that doesn't correctly connect the independent clause to new *patterns of thinking*.

- (A) and (B) are wrong because the second part is the *new patterns of* thinking, not a contrast from the first part of the sentence as *though* implies.

- (C) is wrong because a comma alone can't separate two independent clauses.

- (D) is correct because a colon is used when the second part of the sentence elaborates on the first.

23. **B** This is a transition question, so highlight ideas that relate to each other. The preceding sentence says *There were a few time periods when it briefly went out due to power failures and other technological challenges*, and this sentence says *the bulb was connected to an uninterruptible power supply to determine how long it could actually burn*. These ideas agree, so a same-direction transition is needed. Make an annotation that says "agree." Eliminate any answer that doesn't match.

- (A) is wrong because this sentence doesn't provide a different idea that has something in common with the previous sentence.

- (B) is correct because *Consequently* is same-direction, and the *uninterruptible power supply* is a consequence of the *power failures and other technological challenges*.

- (C) is wrong because this sentence isn't an additional point.

- (D) is wrong because it is an opposite-direction transition.

24. **A** This is a Rhetorical Synthesis question, so highlight the goal(s) stated in the question: *explain how the law school of Berytus prepared jurists*. Eliminate any answer that doesn't fulfill this purpose.

- (A) is correct because it shows the techniques used by Berytus (*classes that included lectures and analyses*).

- (B), (C), and (D) are wrong because they don't include any information about the techniques.

25. **D** This is a Rhetorical Synthesis question, so highlight the goal(s) stated in the question: *emphasize how high satellites in geosynchronous orbit are relative to those in low and medium orbits*. Eliminate any answer that doesn't fulfill this purpose.

- (A) is wrong because it doesn't include the altitudes of satellites in *low and medium orbits*.

- (B) is wrong because it doesn't include the altitude of satellites in *geosynchronous orbit*.

- (C) is wrong because it doesn't give any information about the altitudes of satellites in any orbit.

- (D) is correct because it includes the altitude of satellites in *geosynchronous orbit* and compares this altitude to satellites in *low and medium orbits*.

26. **C** This is a Rhetorical Synthesis question, so highlight the goal(s) stated in the question: *emphasize a similarity between the two ways animals use colors*. Eliminate any answer that doesn't fulfill this purpose.

- (A), (B), and (D) are wrong because they describe the *two ways animals use colors* but don't include a *similarity*.

- (C) is correct because it includes a *similarity* between the *two ways animals use colors*—they are both *determined by the time of day the animals' ancestors were active*.

27. **C** This is a Rhetorical Synthesis question, so highlight the goal(s) stated in the question: *present the study and its methodology*. Eliminate any answer that doesn't fulfill this purpose.

- (A) is wrong because it includes the results of the study but does not *present* what the study was actually doing.

- (B) is wrong because it includes information about the goal of the study but not the *methodology*.

- (C) is correct because it introduces the purpose of the study and describes the *methodology* (what the researchers did).

- (D) is wrong because it doesn't *introduce* the study, such as by presenting its purpose.

PRACTICE TEST 2—MATH EXPLANATIONS

Module 1

1. **D**   The question asks for a value given a specific situation. The question states that the equation $p = 45d$ represents the *relationship between the number of posts, p, and the number of days, d*. Since the question asks for the number of posts during a 3-day period, plug in 3 for d to get $p = 45(3)$. Simplify the right side of the equation to get $p = 135$. The correct answer is (D).

2. **B**   The question asks for the equation that represents a line. Translate the information in bite-sized pieces and eliminate after each piece. The answer choices are all in slope-intercept form, $y = mx + b$, in which m is the slope and b is the y-intercept. One piece of information says that the line *has a slope of –3*, so $m = -3$. Eliminate (C) and (D) because they have the wrong slope. The y-intercept is the point where the graph crosses the y-axis, which happens when $x = 0$. Thus, the point $(0, 10)$ is the y-intercept, and b in slope-intercept form is 10. Eliminate (A) because it has the wrong y-intercept. The correct answer is (B).

3. **7**   The question asks for the value of an expression based on an equation. When a Digital SAT question asks for the value of an expression, there is usually a straightforward way to solve for the expression without needing to completely isolate the variable. Since $\dfrac{12}{x}$ is the reciprocal of $\dfrac{x}{12}$, take the reciprocal of both sides of the equation. The reciprocal of $\dfrac{1}{7}$ is $\dfrac{7}{1}$, or 7, so the equation becomes $\dfrac{12}{x} = 7$. The correct answer is 7.

4. **A**   The question asks for the value of the measure of an angle on a geometric figure. Start by drawing two triangles on the scratch paper. Similar triangles have the same angle measures and proportional side lengths, so draw two triangles that look alike but are different sizes. Be sure to match up the corresponding angles that are given in the question. Then label the figure with the given information. Label angles N and Y as 90° or with the right-angle symbol, and label angle X as 23°. The drawing should look something like this:

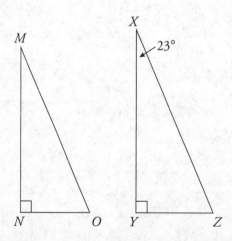

The question asks for the measure of angle M, which corresponds to angle X. Thus, angle M also measures 23°. The correct answer is (A).

5. **C** The question asks for an equivalent form of an expression. Although there are variables in the answer choices, plugging in on this question would be difficult given all the exponents. Instead, use bite-sized pieces and process of elimination to tackle this question. Start with the a terms. When dealing with exponents, remember the exponent rules, which spell MADSPM. The MA part of the acronym indicates that Multiplying matching bases means to Add the exponents. Add the exponents on the a terms to get $(a^2)(a^3) = a^5$. Eliminate (A) and (D) because they have the wrong exponent on a. Compare the remaining answers. One difference is the exponent on the g terms. Add the exponents on the g terms to get $(g^{-4})(g^{-2}) = g^{-6}$. Eliminate (B) because it has the wrong exponent on g. The correct answer is (C).

6. **D** The question asks which statements must be true given data in two box plots. Check each answer and eliminate the ones that are false. A box plot can be used to determine the median, range, and interquartile range of a data set, but it cannot be used to determine the mean. Eliminate (A) and (B) because it is not possible to compare the means. Compare the remaining answer choices, (C) and (D), which compare the medians of the two data sets. In a box plot, the median is the value at the vertical line inside the box. The line representing the median for store A is at 5 feet, and the line representing the median for store B is at approximately 8 feet. Eliminate (C) because the median of store A is less than the median of store B, not greater than. The correct answer is (D).

7. **C** The question asks for the value of the x-coordinate of the solution to a system of equations. One method is to enter both equations into the built-in graphing calculator, then scroll and zoom as needed to find the points of intersection. The graph shows two points of intersection, (−12, 150) and (12, 150), so the x-coordinate is either −12 or 12. Only 12 is an answer choice, so choose (C). To solve the system for the x-coordinate algebraically, substitute 150 for y in the first equation to get $150 = x^2 + 6$. Subtract 6 from both sides of the equation to get $144 = x^2$. Both 12^2 and $(-12)^2$ equal 144, so x can equal 12 or −12. Using either method, the correct answer is (C).

8. **C** The question asks about the most appropriate conclusion based on a survey and a margin of error. A margin of error expresses the amount of random sampling error in a survey's results. The margin of error is 0.07, meaning that results within a range of 0.07 above and 0.07 below the estimate are reasonable. Since the estimated proportion of adults with insomnia is 0.35, subtract the margin of error to get $0.35 - 0.07 = 0.28$, and add the margin of error to get $0.35 + 0.07 = 0.42$. The most appropriate conclusion is that a proportion of adults between 0.28 and 0.42 have insomnia. Eliminate (A) because it only addresses the lower range of plausible results. In addition, it is unlikely that the proportion will be less than the lower end of the range. Eliminate (B) for the same reasons: it only addresses the upper end of the range, and it is unlikely that the proportion will be greater than the upper end of the range. Choice (C) matches the range and says it is plausible that the proportion is within that range, so keep (C). Eliminate (D) because it does not account for the margin of error. The correct answer is (C).

9. **B**   The question asks for the number of points of intersection in a system of equations. One method is to use the built-in graphing calculator. Enter both equations into the calculator, then scroll and zoom to see where, if at all, they intersect. The lines intersect once at (2, 0). To solve algebraically, multiply the entire first equation by 2 to get $2y = 20x - 40$. Now that both equations are equal to $2y$, set them equal to each other to get $20x - 40 = 10x - 20$. Subtract $10x$ from both sides of the equation to get $10x - 40 = -20$, and then add 40 to both sides of the equation to get $10x = 20$. Divide both sides of the equation by 10 to get $x = 2$. Plug $x = 2$ into the first equation to get $y = 10(2) - 20$, which becomes $y = 20 - 20$, and then $y = 0$. There is one point of intersection at (2, 0). Using either method, the correct answer is (B).

10. **A**   The question asks for the equation that defines a function. In function notation, the number inside the parentheses is the x-value that goes into the function, or the input, and the value that comes out of the function is the y-value, or the output. The question provides two pairs of input and output values, so plug those into the answer choices and eliminate answers that don't work with both points. Start by plugging $x = -3$ and $g(x) = 39$ into the answer choices. Choice (A) becomes $39 = -12(-3) + 3$, or $39 = 36 + 3$, and then $39 = 39$. This is true, so try the second pair of values in (A). Plug $x = 0$ and $g(x) = 3$ into the equation in (A) to get $3 = -12(0) + 3$, or $3 = 0 + 3$, and then $3 = 3$. This is also true. Since both points work in the function defined by (A), it is the correct equation. The correct answer is (A).

11. $\dfrac{1}{2}$ **or .5**   The question asks for the value of a constant in a system of equations. Both expressions are equal to 27, so set them equal to each other to get $ab = 2abk$. Divide both sides of the equation by ab to get $1 = 2k$, and then divide both sides of the equation by 2 to get $\dfrac{1}{2} = k$. The answer can also be entered in the fill-in box in decimal form as .5. The correct answer is $\dfrac{1}{2}$ or .5.

12. **B**   The question asks for a value based on a function. The question states that d represents the amount in dollars saved and w represents the number of weeks, and it asks for the amount of money saved every week. Plug in two values for w to see what happens to the amount of money saved. Plug in $w = 1$ to get $d(1) = 150 + 50(1)$, which becomes $d(1) = 150 + 50$, and then $d(1) = 200$. Sarah's amount saved after one week is $200. Next, plug in $w = 2$ to get $d(2) = 150 + 50(2)$, which becomes $d(2) = 150 + 100$, and then $d(2) = 250$. Sarah's amount saved after two weeks is $250. After one additional week, the amount saved increased by $250 - $200 = $50, so the amount increases by $50 every week. The correct answer is (B).

13. **A**   The question asks for a description of a function that models a specific situation. Compare the answer choices. Two choices say the function is increasing, and two say it is decreasing. The question states that *the population of a certain town decreases*, so eliminate (C) and (D) because they describe an increasing function. The difference between (A) and (B) is whether the function is linear or exponential. Determine this by plugging in an initial value for the population, such as 1,000. After 5 years, the population is $1,000 - 150 = 850$. After another 5 years, the population is $850 - 150 = 700$. The population decreased by the same amount each year, so the relationship between population and time is linear. Eliminate (B) because it describes an exponential function. The correct answer is (A).

14. **−39** The question asks for the value of the x-coordinate of the solution to a system of equations. One method is to enter both equations into the built-in graphing calculator, then scroll and zoom as needed to find the point of intersection. The lines intersect at $(−39, −1)$, so the x-coordinate is $−39$. To solve the system for the x-coordinate algebraically, find a way to make the y-coordinates disappear when stacking and adding the equations. Compare the y-terms: one coefficient, $−27$, is 3 times the other one, $−9$. Multiply the entire first equation by $−3$ to get the same coefficient with opposite signs on the y-terms. The first equation becomes $−3x + 27y = 90$. Now stack and add the two equations.

$$\begin{array}{rcr} −3x + 27y &=& 90 \\ +\ \underline{x − 27y} &=& \underline{−12} \\ −2x\quad\ &=& 78 \end{array}$$

Divide both sides of the resulting equation by $−2$ to get $x = −39$. Using either method, the correct answer is $−39$.

15. **−8** The question asks for the value of the x-coordinate when a quadratic function reaches its minimum. A parabola reaches its minimum or maximum value at its vertex, so find the x-coordinate of the vertex. One method is to enter the equation into the built-in graphing calculator, then scroll and zoom as needed to find the vertex. The vertex is at $(−8, −103)$, so the value of the x-coordinate is $−8$. To solve algebraically, find the value of h, which is the x-coordinate of the vertex (h, k). When a quadratic is in standard form, which is $ax^2 + bx + c$, the x-coordinate of the vertex can be found using the formula $h = -\dfrac{b}{2a}$. In this quadratic, $a = 1$ and $b = 16$, so the formula becomes $h = -\dfrac{16}{2(1)}$. Solve to get $h = -\dfrac{16}{2}$, or $h = −8$. Using either method, the correct answer is $−8$.

16. **B** The question asks for the difference between two values based on the graph of a function. One method is to use the built-in graphing calculator. Enter the equation of the line, then scroll and zoom as needed to find the intercepts, which are indicated by gray dots. The x-intercept is at $(6, 0)$, and the y-intercept is at $(0, 12)$. Thus, $m = 6$, $n = 12$, and $m − n = 6 − 12 = −6$, which matches (B). To solve algebraically, plug the given points into the equation of the line. Plug in $x = m$ and $g(x) = 0$ to get $0 = 12 − 2m$. Add $2m$ to both sides of the equation to get $2m = 12$, and then divide both sides of the equation by 2 to get $m = 6$. Next, plug in $x = 0$ and $g(x) = n$ to get $n = 12 − 2(0)$. Simplify to get $n = 12 − 0$, or $n = 12$. Plug $m = 6$ and $n = 12$ into $m − n$ to get $6 − 12 = −6$. Using either method, the correct answer is (B).

17. **64** The question asks for a value given a proportional relationship between two geometric figures. Start by drawing two squares of different sizes, then label the figure with the given information. The question only gives information about a relationship, not specific values, so plug in. Pick a small value for the area of the scale model, such as 4. The question states that the scale model *has an area*

that is $\dfrac{1}{4,096}$ *of the area of the actual park*, so the area of the actual park is 4,096(4) = 16,384. To find the side lengths of both squares, write out the formula for the area of a square, which is $A = s^2$. Plug in the area of the scale model to get $4 = s^2$. Take the square root of both sides of the equation to get $2 = s$. Label this on the smaller square. Plug the area of the actual park into the area formula to get $16,384 = s^2$. Take the square root of both sides of the equation to get $128 = s$. Label this on the larger square. To find the value of x, divide the side length of the actual park by the side length of the scale model to get $\dfrac{128}{2} = 64$. The side length of the actual park is 64 times the side length of the scale model, or $x = 64$. The correct answer is 64.

18. **B** The question asks for a value on a scatterplot. Find 1.25 on the x-axis: it is halfway between the labeled vertical line for 1 and the labeled vertical line for 1.5. Move up from there to the line of best fit, using the mouse pointer or scratch paper as a ruler if necessary. From there, move left to the y-axis to see that the value is between the labeled horizontal line for 1.4 and the labeled horizontal line for 1.6. Eliminate (A), (C), and (D) because those values are not between 1.4 and 1.6. The correct answer is (B).

19. **D** The question asks for the measure of an angle in radians. Start by finding the measure of angle B in degrees. The question states that *angle A measures 150 degrees, and the measure of angle B is* $\dfrac{1}{3}$ *the measure of angle A*, so take one-third of 150 to find that the measure of angle B is $\dfrac{1}{3}(150) = 50$ degrees. The combined measure of both angles is $150 + 50 = 200$ degrees. Either write down a conversion between radians and degrees from memory or open the reference sheet, which states that the number of degrees of arc in a circle is 360 and that the number of radians of arc in a circle is 2π. Thus, 360 degrees = 2π radians. Set up a proportion, being sure to match up units. The proportion is $\dfrac{360 \text{ degrees}}{2\pi \text{ radians}} = \dfrac{200 \text{ degrees}}{x \text{ radians}}$. Cross-multiply to get $(2\pi)(200) = (360)(x)$. Simplify to get $400\pi = 360x$, then divide both sides of the equation by 360 to get $\dfrac{400\pi}{360} = x$. Reduce the fraction by dividing both the numerator and the denominator by 40 to get $\dfrac{10\pi}{9} = x$. The correct answer is (D).

20. **C** The question asks for the value of a constant based on an equation. The question refers to exponential growth, so write down the growth and decay formula. The formula is *final amount =* (*original amount*)(*multiplier*)^(*number of changes*). The question states that *a sample of a certain radioactive element is tested and found to have 16,000 radioactive units*, so the *original amount*, or *S*, is 16,000. The question also states that *it is tested again and found to have 4,000 radioactive units*, so the *final amount*, or *R*, is 4,000. Finally, the question states that *t* is the number of remaining hours after the first test and that the second test was *two hours later*, so *t* = 2. Plug these values into the equation to get $4,000 = 16,000(0.25)^{2p}$. Divide both sides of the equation by 16,000 to get $\frac{1}{4} = (0.25)^{2p}$. Since $\frac{1}{4} = 0.25$, both sides of the equation have the same base, so the exponents must be equal. The value on the left side of the equation does not have an exponent written, so it has an implied exponent of 1. Thus, $1 = 2p$. Divide both sides of the equation by 2 to get $\frac{1}{2} = p$. The correct answer is (C).

21. **8** The question asks for a solution to an equation. One approach is to enter the equation into the built-in graphing calculator, then scroll and zoom as needed to find the solutions. The graph shows solutions at –7 and 8. Since the question asks for the greatest solution, the answer is 8. To solve algebraically, start by multiplying both sides of the equation by the denominator to get rid of the fraction. The equation becomes $\sqrt{(x+3)^2} = \sqrt{7x+65}$. Then, square both sides of the equation to remove the square root signs. The equation becomes $(x+3)^2 = 7x + 65$. Expand the left side of the equation using FOIL to get $x^2 + 6x + 9 = 7x + 65$. Put the quadratic into standard form by setting one side equal to 0. Subtract 7*x* and 65 from both sides of the equation, which becomes $x^2 - x - 56 = 0$. Find two numbers that multiply to –56 and add to –1. These are –8 and 7. Thus, the quadratic factors into $(x - 8)(x + 7) = 0$. To find the values of *x*, set each factor equal to 0 to get two equations: *x* – 8 = 0 and *x* + 7 = 0. Add 8 to both sides of the first equation to get *x* = 8. Subtract 7 from both sides of the second equation to get *x* = –7. The greatest solution is 8. Using either method, the correct answer is 8.

22. **D** The question asks for solutions to an equation. A solution to an equation is a value of *x* that makes the equation true, so test each statement by substituting the value in it for *x*. Half of the answer choices contain statement (III), so start there. Plug *x* = 1 – 3*c* into the equation to get [(1 – 3*c*) + 3*c*] [80 + (1 – 3*c*)] = [80 + (1 – 3*c*)]. Simplify both sides of the equation to get (1)(81 – 3*c*) = (81 – 3*c*), which becomes 81 – 3*c* = 81 – 3*c*. This is true, so 1 – 3*c* is a solution to the equation, and statement (III) is true. Eliminate (A) and (C) because they do not include statement (III).

Compare the remaining answer choices. The difference between (B) and (D) is statement (I), so try it next. Plug *x* = –80 into the equation to get (–80 + 3*c*)[80 + (–80)] = [80 + (–80)]. Simplify both sides of the equation to get (–80 + 3*c*)(0) = 0, which becomes 0 = 0. Thus, –80 is a solution to the equation, and statement (I) is true. Eliminate (B) because it does not contain statement (I). The correct answer is (D).

Module 2 – Easier

1. **C** The question asks for a percentage of a number. Translate the English to math in bite-sized pieces. Translate *what* as a variable, such as x. Translate *is* as equals. *Percent* means out of 100, so translate 60% as $\frac{60}{100}$. Translate *of* as times. The translated equation is $x = \frac{60}{100}(300)$. Solve by hand or with a calculator to get $x = 180$. The correct answer is (C).

2. **C** The question asks for a value on a graph. First, check the units on each axis of the bar graph. Soap brands are on the x-axis, so find Brand Y on the x-axis. Look at the top of the bar for Brand Y, and then look left to the y-axis, using the mouse pointer or the edge of the scratch paper as a ruler. The y-axis shows the number of consumers, and the top of the bar for Brand Y comes almost all the way up to 55. Thus, the number of consumers who chose Brand Y must be a little less than 55. Eliminate (A) and (B) because 43 and 46 are too small. Eliminate (D) because 57 is greater than 55. The correct answer is (C).

3. **78** The question asks for the solution to an equation. To solve for b, isolate the variable. First, add 12 to both sides of the equation to get $2b = 156$. Next, divide both sides of the equation by 2 to get $b = 78$. The correct answer is 78.

4. **7** The question asks for a value given a rate. Begin by reading the question to find information about the rate. The question states that *a street artist takes 5 minutes to draw one portrait*. Set up a proportion to determine how many portraits can be drawn in 35 minutes at this rate. The proportion is $\frac{5 \text{ minutes}}{1 \text{ portrait}} = \frac{35 \text{ minutes}}{x \text{ portraits}}$. Cross-multiply to get $(1)(35) = (5)(x)$, which becomes $35 = 5x$. Divide both sides of the equation by 5 to get $7 = x$. The correct answer is 7.

5. **4** The question asks for a value given a function. In function notation, the number inside the parentheses is the x-value that goes into the function, or the input, and the value that comes out of the function is the y-value, or the output. The question provides an output value of 10, but there are no answers to plug in, so substitute 10 for $h(x)$ and solve for the input value, x. The equation becomes $10 = 3x - 2$. Add 2 both sides of the equation to get $12 = 3x$, and then divide both sides of the equation by 3 to get $4 = x$. The correct answer is 4.

6. **B** The question asks for a value given a function. In function notation, the number inside the parentheses is the x-value that goes into the function, or the input, and the value that comes out of the function is the y-value, or the output. The question provides an output value of 49, and the answers have numbers that could represent the x-value, so use the values in the answers. Start with one of the middle numbers and try (B), 8. Plug 8 into the function for x to get $49 = 8^2 - 15$, which becomes $49 = 64 - 15$, or $49 = 49$. This is true, so stop here. The correct answer is (B).

7. **A** The question asks for the *y*-intercept of a graph. This is the point at which *x* = 0. Eliminate (C) and (D) because they do not have an *x*-value of 0. Find *x* = 0 on the graph and move straight up to see that the graph crosses the *y*-axis at *y* = 5. Points on a graph are represented as ordered pairs in the form (*x*, *y*), with the *x*-value first and the *y*-value second, so the point at the *y*-intercept is (0, 5). The correct answer is (A).

8. **D** The question asks for an equation that models a specific situation. Translate the information into bite-sized pieces and eliminate after each piece. One piece of information says that *Dalisha is given a stipend of $3,600.* Since the stipend is only given once, 3,600 should not be multiplied by another value. Eliminate (B) and (C) because they multiply 3,600 by another value. The question also states that the stipend is used to *pay her student housing rent of $450 per month,* so the monthly rent must be subtracted from the initial stipend. Eliminate (A) because it subtracts the stipend from the monthly rent. The correct answer is (D).

9. **A** The question asks for an equivalent form of an expression. There are variables in the answer choices, so plug in. Make *y* = 5 because it will make the denominator of the second fraction equal 1. The expression becomes $\frac{3}{6-3(5)} + \frac{1}{5-4} = \frac{3}{6-15} + \frac{1}{1} = \frac{3}{-9} + 1$. Use a common denominator of 9 and make $1 = \frac{9}{9}$ to get $-\frac{3}{9} + \frac{9}{9} = \frac{6}{9}$, which reduces to $\frac{2}{3}$. This is the target value; write it down and circle it. Now plug *y* = 5 into the answer choices, and eliminate any that do not match the target value. Choice (A) becomes $-\frac{6}{(5-4)[6-3(5)]} = -\frac{6}{(1)(6-15)} = -\frac{6}{-9} = \frac{2}{3}$. This matches the target value, so keep (A), but check the remaining answers just in case. Choice (B) is the same fraction as (A), but it doesn't have the negative sign, so it will equal $-\frac{2}{3}$. This does not match the target value, so eliminate (B). Choice (C) becomes $\frac{4}{2(5)+2} = \frac{4}{10+2} = \frac{4}{12} = \frac{1}{3}$. Eliminate (C). Choice (D) has the same denominator as (A) with a different numerator, so it cannot equal the same value; eliminate (D). The correct answer is (A).

10. **B** The question asks for correct values on a graph. When given a graph and asked for the table of values, check one point at a time and eliminate answers that contain a point that is not on the graph. Two of the answers contain the point (–3, –3), and two contain the point (–3, 3). On the graph, when *x* = –3, *y* = 3. Eliminate (A) and (C) because they have the wrong *y*-value for this point. Compare the remaining answer choices to see that they have different *y*-values for an *x*-value of –2. On the graph, when *x* = –2, *y* = 1. Eliminate (D) because it has the wrong *y*-value for this point. The correct answer is (B).

11. **125**   The question asks for the value of an angle on a figure. The figure is already drawn and labeled, but redraw it on the scratch paper if that makes it easier to see what's going on. When a line intersects two parallel lines, two kinds of angles are created: big and small. All of the small angles are equal to each other, all of the big angles are equal to each other, and any small angle plus any big angle = 180°. The angle marked $y°$ is a big angle, and the angle marked 55° is a small angle. Thus, $y + 55 = 180$. Subtract 55 from both sides of the equation to get $y = 125$. The correct answer is 125.

12. **C**   The question asks for a measurement of a geometric figure. Start by drawing a circle on the scratch paper. Next, label the figure with information from the question: label the radius as 4. The drawing should look something like this:

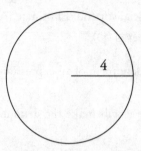

Next, write down the formula for the circumference of a circle, either from memory or after looking it up on the reference sheet. The formula is $C = 2\pi r$. Plug in the value of the radius, 4, to get $C = 2\pi(4)$, which becomes $C = 8\pi$. The correct answer is (C).

13. **A**   The question asks for an equation in terms of a specific variable. The question asks about the relationship among variables and there are variables in the answer choices, so one option is to plug in. However, that might get messy with an equation and three variables. All of the answer choices have a by itself, so the other option is to solve for a. To isolate a, add $2b$ to both sides of the equation to get $9a = 2b + c$. Divide both sides of the equation by 9 to get $a = \dfrac{2b + c}{9}$. The correct answer is (A).

14. **C**   The question asks for the system of inequalities that contains a specific point. Use the point given in the question, and plug $x = 2$ and $y = -5$ into the answer choices to see which one works. Choice (A) becomes $2 \le 0$ and $-5 \le 0$. Only the second inequality is true, so eliminate (A). Since $y \le 0$ is true, the correct answer should include it. Eliminate (B) and (D) because they have $y \ge 0$ instead. Since $2 \ge 0$, the first inequality is also true in (C). The correct answer is (C).

15. **D**   The question asks for an equation that represents a graph. One method is to use the built-in graphing calculator. Enter each of the equations in the answer choices into the graphing calculator and see which line looks most like the line of best fit of the scatterplot given. Another method is to translate the information into bite-sized pieces and eliminate after each piece. The equations in the answer choices are all in slope-intercept form, $y = mx + b$, in which m is the slope and b is the y-intercept. The y-intercept is the point where $x = 0$, which is between 2 and 3 on this graph. Eliminate (A) and (C) because they have

negative *y*-intercepts. Compare the remaining answer choices. The difference between (B) and (D) is the sign of the slope. If the line of best fit were graphed, it would ascend from left to right, so it would have a positive slope. Eliminate (B) because it has a negative slope. Using either method, the correct answer is (D).

16. **B**   The question asks for an equation that represents a specific situation. The population of fish is decreasing by a certain percent over time, so this question is about exponential decay. Write down the growth and decay formula, which is *final amount* = (*original amount*)(1 ± *rate*)^*number of changes*. The question states that the number of fish 5 years from now will be 804,944. Eliminate (A) and (C) because they do not have 804,944 as the final amount on the left side of the equation. Since this situation involves a decrease, the original amount must be multiplied by (1 − *rate*), so the value in parentheses should be less than 1. Eliminate (D), which has a value in parentheses greater than 1. The only remaining answer is (B), and it matches the decay formula because the original amount is multiplied by (1 − 0.04) = (0.96). The correct answer is (B).

17. **−14**   The question asks for a solution to an equation with absolute values. One method is to enter the equation into the built-in graphing calculator, replacing *a* with *x* in order to see a graph of the equation. The values of *x* are shown by vertical lines; scroll and zoom as needed to see that these cross the *x*-axis at −14 and 10. The question asks for the negative solution, which is −14. To solve algebraically, recall that, with an absolute value, the value inside the absolute value bars can be either positive or negative, so this equation has two possible solutions. To start solving for *a*, treat the absolute value as a term and combine the absolute value terms on the left side of the equation to get $-2|a + 2| = -24$. Next, divide both sides of the equation by −2 to get $|a + 2| = 12$. The value in the absolute values bars could equal 12 or −12, so set $a + 2$ equal to each. When $a + 2 = 12$, subtract 2 from both sides of the equation to get $a = 10$. When $a + 2 = -12$, subtract 2 from both sides of the equation to get $a = -14$. The question asks for the negative value, which is −14. Using either method, the correct answer is −14.

18. **7**   The question asks for the value of a constant. To avoid the chance of distributing incorrectly with exponents, plug in for *x* and solve for *a*. Keep the math simple and make $x = 2$. The first expression becomes $a(2)^7[8(2) + 7] = a(128)(16 + 7) = a(128)(23) = 2,944a$. The second expression becomes $56(2)^8 + 49(2)^7 = 56(256) + 49(128) = 14,336 + 6,272 = 20,608$. The two expressions are equivalent, so set them equal to each other: $2,944a = 20,608$. Divide both sides of the equation by 2,944 to get $a = 7$. The correct answer is 7.

19. **C**   The question asks for an expression based on a geometric figure. One method is to recognize that the expression $\pi(3r)(r)^2$ looks like the right side of the formula for the volume of a cylinder, $V = \pi r^2 h$. The question states that *r* is the radius, and π is a constant, so the other term, 3*r*, must be the height, making (C) correct. Another method is to draw a cylinder on the scratch paper, then label the figure with the given information. No specific values are given, so plug in. Make $r = 2$, and plug it into the expression given in the question to get $\pi[(3)(2)](2)^2$, or $\pi(6)(4)$, or 24π. This is the volume of the cylinder. Next, write down the formula for the volume of a cylinder, either from memory or after

looking it up on the reference sheet. The formula is $V = \pi r^2 h$. Substitute the volume of 24π and the radius of 2 to get $24\pi = \pi(2)^2 h$. Simplify to get $24\pi = 4\pi h$, and then divide both sides of the equation by 4π to get $6 = h$. This is the target value; write it down and circle it. Now plug $r = 2$ into each answer choice and eliminate any that do not match the target value of 6. Choice (A) becomes 2. This does not match the target value, so eliminate (A). Choice (B), 3, does not equal 6; eliminate (B). Choice (C) becomes $3(2) = 6$; keep (C). Choice (D) becomes $(2)^2 = 4$; eliminate (D). Using either method, the correct answer is (C).

20.   **A**   The question asks for the inequality that represents the values shown in a table. When given a table of values and asked for an inequality, plug values from the table into the inequalities to see which ones work. Plugging in 1 is likely to make more than one answer work, and negative numbers can be tricky, so start with the third pair of values in the table. Plug $p = 4$ and $q = 20$ into each inequality in the answer choices. Choice (A) becomes $20 < 6(4) + 3$. Simplify to get $20 < 24 + 3$, and then $20 < 27$. This is true, so keep (A), but check the remaining answers. Choice (B) becomes $20 > 6(4) + 3$. Simplify to get $20 > 24 + 3$, and then $20 > 27$. This is not true, so eliminate (B). Choice (C) becomes $20 < 3(4) + 6$. Simplify to get $20 < 12 + 6$, and then $20 < 18$; eliminate (C). Choice (D) becomes $20 > 3(4) + 6$. Simplify to get $20 > 12 + 6$, and then $20 > 18$; keep (D). Since there are two answers left, try another pair of values. Plug $p = -2$ and $q = -10$ into the remaining answer choices. Choice (A) becomes $-10 < 6(-2) + 3$. Simplify to get $-10 < -12 + 3$, and then $-10 < -9$; keep (A). Choice (D) becomes $-10 > 3(-2) + 6$. Simplify to get $-10 > -6 + 6$, and then $-10 > 0$; eliminate (D). The correct answer is (A).

21.   **D**   The question asks for the product of constants given a function. In function notation, $f(x) = y$. The number inside the parentheses is the x-value that goes into the function, or the input, and the value that comes out of the function is the y-value, or the output. One method is to use the built-in graphing calculator. Enter the equations for both functions into the built-in calculator. Either use the color-coding or click on the entry field with the $h(x)$ equation to see that the parabola on the left is the graph of $h(x)$. Scroll and zoom as needed to find the values of the x-intercepts, which are represented by gray dots. The x-intercepts of $h(x)$ are $(-6, 0)$, $(-1, 0)$, and $(1, 0)$. This means that m, n, and p are -6, -1, and 1. It is impossible to know which letter has which value, but that won't matter when they are multiplied together. Therefore, $mnp = (-6)(-1)(1) = 6$.

It is also possible to solve using knowledge of the transformation of graphs. The x-intercepts of a quadratic are the values that give an output of 0. Function g is already factored, so set each factor equal to 0 and solve to find all of the x-intercepts. The x-intercepts of $g(x)$ are $(2, 0)$, $(4, 0)$ and $(-3, 0)$. When graphs are transformed, or translated, adding inside the parenthesis shifts the graph to the left. Thus, $x + 3$ shifts the graph three units to the left, which shifts the x-intercepts to $(-1, 0)$, $(1, 0)$, and $(-6, 0)$. The x-coordinates of the x-intercepts of function h are -1, 1, and -6, and $mnp = (-1)(1)(-6) = 6$. Using either method, the correct answer is (D).

22. **B** The question asks for a value based on a geometric figure. Start by drawing a circle inscribed in a square. *Inscribed* means it takes up as much space as possible without going outside of the boundaries of the outer shape, so the circle touches each side of the square at one point. Draw the diagonal of the square, as well. When two geometric figures overlap, look for something they have in common. In this case, the diameter of the circle is also equal in length to a side of the square. Add this to the drawing, which should look something like this:

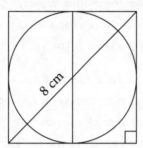

When a square is divided in half by a diagonal, two identical isosceles right triangles, or 45:45:90 triangles, are created. It may help to draw a second figure for one of the 45:45:90 triangles. Write down the ratio of the sides of a 45:45:90 triangle, either from memory or after looking it up on the reference sheet. The ratio is $s:s:s\sqrt{2}$. The diagonal of the square is the hypotenuse of each triangle, so $s\sqrt{2} = 8$. Divide both sides of the equation by $\sqrt{2}$ to get $s = \dfrac{8}{\sqrt{2}}$. Rationalize the denominator by multiplying the fraction by $\dfrac{\sqrt{2}}{\sqrt{2}}$ to get $\left(\dfrac{8}{\sqrt{2}}\right)\left(\dfrac{\sqrt{2}}{\sqrt{2}}\right) = 4\sqrt{2}$. Label the legs of the triangle as $4\sqrt{2}$. The legs of the 45:45:90 triangle are also sides of the square, so each side of the square has length $4\sqrt{2}$.

Since the side of the square has the same length as the diameter of the circle, the diameter of the circle is also $4\sqrt{2}$; label this on the figure. The radius of a circle is half the diameter, so the radius is $\dfrac{4\sqrt{2}}{2} = 2\sqrt{2}$. Write down the formula for the area of a circle, either from memory or after looking it up on the reference sheet. The area of a circle is $A = \pi r^2$, so the area of this circle is $A = \pi\left(2\sqrt{2}\right)^2$, which becomes $A = 8\pi$. The correct answer is (B).

Module 2 – Harder

1. **B** The question asks for the table that contains values that are solutions to an equation. When given an equation and asked for a table of values, plug values from the table into the equation to see which ones work. All of the tables include an x-value of 4, so start there. Plug $x = 4$ into the equation to get $y - 7 = 4$. Add 7 to both sides of the equation to get $y = 11$. Eliminate (A) and (D) because they have different y-values when $x = 4$. Now try another value from the table. Plug $x = 5$ into the equation to get $y - 7 = 5$. Add 7 to both sides of the equation to get $x = 12$. Eliminate (C) because it has a different y-value when $x = 5$. The correct answer is (B).

2. **C** The question asks for the value of an angle on a figure. The figure is already drawn and labeled, but redraw it on the scratch paper if that makes it easier to see what's going on. When a line intersects two parallel lines, two kinds of angles are created: big and small. All of the small angles have measures that are equal to each other, all of the big angles have measures that are equal to each other, and the measure of any small angle plus the measure of any big angle equals 180°. The angle labeled $y°$ is a big angle, and the angle labeled 83° is a small angle. Thus, $y + 83 = 180$. Subtract 83 from both sides of the equation to get $y = 97$. The correct answer is (C).

3. **B** The question asks for a percent based on the information provided. Translate the English to math in bite-sized pieces. Translate *is* as equals. Translate *what* as a variable, such as x. *Percent* means out of 100, so translate *what percentage* as $\frac{x}{100}$. Translate *of* as times. The equation becomes $24 = \frac{x}{100}(80)$. Simplify the right side of the equation to get $24 = \frac{8x}{10}$. Multiply both sides of the equation by 10 to get $240 = 8x$, and then divide both sides of the equation by 8 to get $30 = x$. The correct answer is (B).

4. **5** The question asks for a value given a function. In function notation, the number inside the parentheses is the x-value that goes into the function, or the input, and the value that comes out of the function is the y-value, or the output. The question provides an output value of 27, but there are no answers to plug in, so set $f(x) = 27$ and solve for x. The equation becomes $3x + 12 = 27$. Subtract 12 from both sides of the equation to get $3x = 15$. Divide both sides of the equation by 3 to get $x = 5$. The correct answer is 5.

5. **C** The question asks for the value of a function. In function notation, the number inside the parentheses is the x-value that goes into the function, or the input, and the value that comes out of the function is the y-value, or the output. The question gives an input value of $\frac{1}{3}$, so plug that into the function to get $g\left(\frac{1}{3}\right) = 120\left(\frac{1}{3}\right)^0$. Either solve with a calculator or recall that any value raised to the power of zero is 1 to get $g\left(\frac{1}{3}\right) = 120(1)$, or $g\left(\frac{1}{3}\right) = 120$. The correct answer is (C).

6.   **C**   The question asks for the value of a trigonometric function. Begin by drawing a triangle and labeling the vertices, being certain to put the longest side opposite the right angle N. The drawing should look something like this:

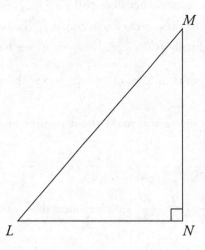

Next, write out SOHCAHTOA to remember the trig functions. The TOA part defines the tangent as $\dfrac{opposite}{adjacent}$, and the question states that $\tan(L) = \dfrac{\sqrt{7}}{3}$. Label the side opposite angle L as $\sqrt{7}$, and label the side adjacent angle L as 3. The drawing now looks like this:

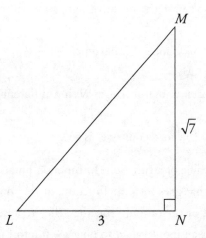

Use the Pythagorean Theorem, $a^2 + b^2 = c^2$, to solve for the length of the hypotenuse. Plug in the known side lengths to get $3^2 + \left(\sqrt{7}\right)^2 = c^2$. Square the terms on the left side of the equation to get $9 + 7 = c^2$, or $16 = c^2$. Take the positive root of both sides of the equation to get $4 = c$. Label the hypotenuse as 4. The SOH part of SOHCAHTOA defines the sine as $\dfrac{opposite}{hypotenuse}$. The side opposite angle M is 3, and the hypotenuse is 4. Therefore, $\sin(M) = \dfrac{3}{4}$. The correct answer is (C).

7. **D** The question asks for the y-intercept of the graph of a function. One method is to enter the equation into the built-in graphing calculator, then scroll and zoom as needed to find the y-intercept. Click on the gray dot to see that the coordinates are $(0, -28)$, which is (D). To solve mathematically, plug $x = 0$ into the function. The function becomes $g(0) = (-11)(5)^0 - 17$. Either use a calculator or remember that any number raised to the power of zero equals 1. The function becomes $g(0) = (-11)(1) - 17$, then $g(0) = (-11) - 17$, and finally $g(0) = -28$. Using either method, the correct answer is (D).

8. **A** The question asks for an equivalent form of an expression. There are variables in the answer choices, so plug in. Make $y = 5$ because it will make the denominator of the second fraction equal 1. The expression becomes $\dfrac{3}{6 - 3(5)} + \dfrac{1}{5 - 4} = \dfrac{3}{6 - 15} + \dfrac{1}{1} = \dfrac{3}{-9} + 1$. Use a common denominator of 9 and make $1 = \dfrac{9}{9}$ to get $-\dfrac{3}{9} + \dfrac{9}{9} = \dfrac{6}{9}$, which reduces to $\dfrac{2}{3}$. This is the target value; write it down and circle it. Now plug $y = 5$ into the answer choices, and eliminate any that do not match the target value. Choice (A) becomes $-\dfrac{6}{(5 - 4)[6 - 3(5)]} = -\dfrac{6}{(1)(6 - 15)} = -\dfrac{6}{-9} = \dfrac{2}{3}$. This matches the target value, so keep (A), but check the remaining answers just in case. Choice (B) is the same fraction as (A), but it doesn't have the negative sign, so it will equal $-\dfrac{2}{3}$. This does not match the target value, so eliminate (B). Choice (C) becomes $\dfrac{4}{2(5) + 2} = \dfrac{4}{10 + 2} = \dfrac{4}{12} = \dfrac{1}{3}$. Eliminate (C). Choice (D) has the same denominator as (A) with a different numerator, so it cannot equal the same value; eliminate (D). The correct answer is (A).

9. **−172** The question asks for the value of a function. In function notation, $f(x) = y$. The number inside the parentheses is the x-value that goes into the function, or the input, and the value that comes out of the function is the y-value, or the output. Together, they represent points on the graph of the function. The question provides an input value, so plug $x = 0$ into function q to get $q(0) = (0 - 9)(0 + 2)(0 + 9)$, which becomes $q(0) = (-9)(2)(9)$, and then $q(0) = -162$. The question states that the graph of function r is the result of translating the graph of function q down 10 units. This means decreasing the value of y by 10. Because $f(x) = y$, this is the same as subtracting 10 from the value of $r(0)$, which becomes $r(0) = -162 - 10$, or $r(0) = -172$. Another method is to enter the equation for function q into the built-in graphing calculator. Scroll and zoom as needed to find the point at $(0, -162)$, then count down ten to the point at $(0, -172)$. Using either method, the correct answer is −172.

10. **2440** The question asks for the surface area of a geometric figure. Draw a rectangular prism as best as possible, and then write down the relevant formulas. Write down the formula for the volume of a rectangular prism, either from memory or after looking it up on the reference sheet. The formula is $V = lwh$. Plug in the values for the volume, height, and length given in the question to get 6,000 = 12(w)(10) or 6,000 = 120w. Divide both sides of the equation by 120 to get w = 50.

The surface area of a geometric figure is the sum of the areas of its sides. A rectangular prism has 2 sides with an area of length × width, 2 sides with an area of length × height, and 2 sides with an area of width × height, so the formula for the surface area of a rectangular prism is $SA = 2(lw + lh + wh)$. Plug the length of 12, width of 50 and height of 10 into the surface area formula to get $SA = 2[(12)(50) + (12)(10) + (50)(10)]$. Simplify to get $SA = 2(600 + 120 + 500)$, which becomes $SA = 2(1,220)$, and then $SA = 2,440$. Leave out the comma when entering the answer in the fill-in box. The correct answer is 2440.

11. **D** The question asks for a function that represents a specific situation. The value of the function is increasing by a certain percent as x increases, so this question is about exponential growth. Knowing the parts of the growth and decay formula can help with this question. That formula is *final amount* = (*original amount*)(1 ± *rate*)$^{number\ of\ changes}$. In this case, $f(x)$ is the final amount. The original amount is the value when $x = 0$, so the original amount is 11. Eliminate (A) and (B) because they do not have 11 as the original amount in front of the parentheses. Since this situation involves an increase, the original amount must be multiplied by (1 + *rate*). The rate is given as 28%, which translates to 0.28, so the value in parentheses should be 1 + 0.28 = 1.28. Eliminate (C) because it does not have this value in the parentheses. The only remaining answer is (D), and it matches the growth formula.

Without this formula, it is still possible to answer this question. Plug in two values of x to see how the function changes over time. When $x = 0$, $f(x) = 11$, so plug these numbers into the answer choices. Any number raised to the power of zero equals 1, so only (C) and (D) work with these values. When x increases by 1, $f(x)$ increases by 28%. Thus, $f(1) = 11 + \left(\dfrac{28}{100}\right)(11)$, which becomes $f(1) = 11 + 3.08$, and then $f(1) = 14.08$. Plug $x = 1$ and $f(1) = 14.08$ into the remaining answers. Choice (C) becomes $14.08 = 11(0.72)^1$, or $14.08 = 7.92$. This is not true, so eliminate (C), Choice (D) becomes $14.08 = 11(1.28)^1$, or $14.08 = 14.08$. Using either method, the correct answer is (D).

12. **B** The question asks for the table that contains values that are solutions to an inequality. When given an inequality and asked for a table of values, plug values from the table into the inequality and eliminate tables with values that don't work. All of the tables include an x-value of 2, so start there. Plug $x = 2$ into the inequality to get $y > 4(2) - 5$, which becomes $y > 8 - 5$, and then $y > 3$. Eliminate (A) and (D) because their y-values when $x = 2$ are not greater than 3. Compare the remaining answer choices. Choices (B) and (C) have different y-values when $x = 6$, so plug $x = 6$ into the inequality to get $y > 4(6) - 5$, which becomes $y > 24 - 5$, and then $y > 19$. Eliminate (C) because 19 is not greater than 19. The correct answer is (B).

13. **C** The question asks which binomials are factors of a quadratic. When given a quadratic in standard form, which is $ax^2 + bx + c$, one approach is to factor it. This quadratic is difficult to factor, but the statements provide possible factors. Start with statement (I). Use the factor $(x - 11)$ to find the other factor. If $(x - 11)$ is a factor, then the first part of the second factor must multiply by x to result in $5x^2$. Divide $5x^2$ by x to get $5x$ as the first term in the second factor. Similarly, the second term in the second factor must multiply by -11 to get 66. Divide 66 by -11 to get -6 as the second term of the second factor. Therefore, the second factor must be $(5x - 6)$. Now use FOIL on the two factors to see if these factors result in $5x^2 - 61x + 66$. The expression becomes $(x - 11)(5x - 6) = 5x^2 - 6x - 55x + 66$. Combine the middle terms to get $5x^2 - 61x + 66$. Both $(x - 11)$ and $(5x - 6)$ are factors of the quadratic, so statements (I) and (II) are both true. The correct answer is (C).

14. **A** The question asks for the value of a constant in a system of equations. When a system of linear equations has infinitely many solutions, the two equations are equivalent. Rewrite the two equations so they have the same terms in the same order. For the first equation, add $5y$ to both sides of the equation to get $4 = 7x + 10y$. Subtract 4 from both sides of the equation to get $0 = 7x + 10y - 4$. For the second equation, subtract ky from both sides of the equation to get $7x - ky - 4 = 0$. Both equations are now equal to 0, so set them equal to each other to get $7x + 10y - 4 = 7x - ky - 4$. Subtract $7x$ from both sides of the equation and add 4 to both sides of the equation to get $10y = -ky$. Divide both sides of the equation by $-y$ to get $-10 = k$. Rearranging the two equations into another familiar form—such as slope-intercept form or standard form—would also result in $k = -10$. The correct answer is (A).

15. **−14** The question asks for a solution to an equation with absolute values. One method is to enter the equation into the built-in graphing calculator, replacing a with x in order to see a graph. The values of x are shown by vertical lines; scroll and zoom as needed to see that these cross the x-axis at -14 and 10. The question asks for the negative solution, which is -14. To solve algebraically, recall that, with an absolute value, the value inside the absolute value bars can be either positive or negative, so this equation has two possible solutions. To start solving for a, treat the absolute value symbols the as a term and combine the absolute value terms on the left side of the equation to get $-2|a + 2| = -24$. Next, divide both sides of the equation by -2 to get $|a + 2| = 12$. The value in the absolute values bars could equal 12 or -12, so set $a + 2$ equal to each. When $a + 2 = 12$, subtract 2 from both sides of the equation to get $a = 10$. When $a + 2 = -12$, subtract 2 from both sides of the equation to get $a = -14$. The question asks for the negative value, which is -14. Using either method, the correct answer is -14.

16. **249** The question asks for a maximum value given a specific situation. Translate the English to math in bite-sized pieces. The number of vases can be represented by v and the number of bowls by b. One piece of information states that *the maximum combined number of vases and bowls she can sell during one weekend is 750*, so the combined total is no more than 750. Represent this with the inequality $v + b \leq 750$. Another piece of information states that *a vendor sells vases for $6.50 and bowls for $12.30*. Multiply the amount earned per vase by the number of vases to get $6.50v$, and multiply the amount earned per bowl by the number of bowls to get $12.30b$. The question states that the *she sells only vases*

and bowls and earns at least $7,780, so the total amount earned is greater than or equal to $7,780. Represent this with the inequality $6.50v + 12.30b \geq 7{,}780$. Now there are two inequalities with two variables:

$$v + b \leq 750$$
$$6.50v + 12.30b \geq 7{,}780$$

The question asks for the number of vases, which is v, so find a way to make the b-terms disappear. Multiply the entire first inequality by –12.30, remembering to flip the inequality sign, to get $-12.30v - 12.30b \geq -9{,}225$. Now the two inequalities have the same b-value with opposite signs, so add the two inequalities.

$$
\begin{aligned}
-12.30v - 12.30b &\geq -9{,}225 \\
+ \; \underline{6.50v + 12.30b} &\geq \underline{\;\;7{,}780} \\
-5.8v \qquad\qquad &\geq -1{,}445
\end{aligned}
$$

Divide both sides of the resulting inequality by –5.8, remembering again to flip the inequality sign, to get $v \leq 249.14$. The number of vases must be an integer less than or equal to 249.14, so round down to 249. The correct answer is 249.

17. **B** The question asks for the value of a percent increase given a function that represents a specific situation. The value of the function is increasing by a certain percent, so this question is about exponential growth. Write down the growth and decay formula, which is *final amount* = (*original amount*)$(1 \pm rate)^{number\ of\ changes}$. The *number of changes* is given in seconds, but the question asks about the increase each <u>minute</u>, so convert seconds to minutes. One minute is equivalent to 60 seconds, so plug 60 into the function to see the amount after 1 minute: $g(60) = 78{,}500(1.52)^{\frac{60}{60}}$, which becomes $g(60) = 78{,}500(1.52)^1$. The value of the number of moles of product is increasing once, so $1.52 = 1 + rate$. Subtract 1 from both sides of the equation to get *rate* = 0.52. The question asks for the rate as a percentage, so multiply 0.52 by 100 to get 52%. The correct answer is (B).

18. **D** The question asks for the equation that defines a function. In function notation, the number inside the parentheses is the x-value that goes into the function, or the input, and the value that comes out of the function is the y-value, or the output. There are variables in the answer choices, so plug in. Make $x = 2$ to keep the math easy. Since $h(x) = g(x + 3)$, $h(2) = g(2 + 3)$, or $h(2) = g(5)$. Plug $x = 5$ into the g function to get $g(5) = -3(5)^5$, which becomes $g(5) = -3(3{,}125)$, and then $g(5) = -9{,}375$. Since $h(2) = g(5)$, $h(2)$ also equals –9,375. This is the target value; write it down and circle it. Now plug $x = 2$ into the answer choices and eliminate any that do not match the target value. Choice (A) becomes $h(2) = -27(125)^2$, or $h(2) = -27(15{,}625)$, and then $h(2) = -421{,}875$. This does not match

the target value, so eliminate (A). Choice (B) becomes $h(2) = -9(15)^2$, or $h(2) = -9(225)$, and then $h(2) = -2,025$; eliminate (B). Choice (C) becomes $h(2) = -9(5)^2$, or $h(2) = -9(25)$, and then $h(2) = -225$; eliminate (C). The remaining answer must be correct, and (D) becomes $h(2) = -375(5)^2$, or $h(2) = -375(25)$, and then $h(2) = -9,375$. This matches the target value. The correct answer is (D).

19.   **A**   The question asks for the value of a constant in the solution to a quadratic. The question asks for a specific value and the answers contain numbers in order, so working with the answers is a good option. First, enter the quadratic into the built-in graphing calculator, then scroll and zoom as needed to find the solutions. Either enter the equation the way it is to see vertical lines at the solutions or leave out "= 0" to see a parabola. Either way, the coordinates of the solutions are $(-6.243, 0)$ and $(2.243, 0)$. Next, plug in each answer choice for c until one of them makes $-2 - \sqrt{c}$ equal one of the solutions. Start with one of the middle answers and try (B), 23. Enter $-2 - \sqrt{23}$ into the calculator to get approximately -6.796. This is approximately 0.5 away from one of the solutions, so eliminate (B). A smaller value for c will make the result larger, so try (A) next. Enter $-2 - \sqrt{18}$ into the calculator to get approximately -6.243. This is one of the solutions, so stop here. the correct answer is (A).

20.   **8**   The question asks for the value of a constant in a quadratic. To determine when a quadratic equation has two real solutions, use the discriminant. The discriminant is the part of the quadratic formula under the square root sign and is written as $D = b^2 - 4ac$. When the discriminant is positive, the quadratic has exactly two real solutions; when the discriminant is 0, the quadratic has exactly one real solution; and when the discriminant is negative, the quadratic has no real solutions. Thus, the discriminant of this quadratic must equal a positive number. First, put the quadratic in standard form, which is $ax^2 + bx + c = 0$, by distributing $7x$ on the left side of the equation to get $49x^2 + 42x = -c$. Then add c to both sides of the equation to get $49x^2 + 42x + c = 0$. Now that the quadratic is in standard form, $a = 49$, $b = 42$, and $c = c$. Plug these into the discriminant formula to get $D = (42)^2 - 4(49)(c)$, or $D = 1,764 - 196c$. Since there are exactly two real solutions, $1,764 - 196c > 0$. Add $196c$ to both sides of the inequality to get $1,764 > 196c$, then divide both sides of the inequality by 196 to get $9 > c$. The greatest integer that is smaller than 9 is 8. The correct answer is 8.

21.   **C**   The question asks for the function that represents a certain situation. In function notation, the number inside the parentheses is the x-value that goes into the function, or the input, and the value that comes out of the function is the y-value, or the output. The question gives an input value of 6 and an output value of \$900. Plug these into the functions in the answer choices, and eliminate any that do not work. Choice (A) becomes $900 = 150(6)$, or $900 = 900$. Keep (A), but check the remaining answers just in case. Choice (B) becomes $900 = 150(6) + 500$, or $900 = 1,400$. This is not true, so eliminate (B). Choice (C) becomes $900 = 200(6) - 300$, or $900 = 900$; keep (C). Choice (D) becomes $900 = 200(6) + 500$, or $900 = 1,700$; eliminate (D).

Two answers worked with the first pair of values, so plug in a different value for x. The question states that the band member earns \$500 for 4 concerts, so plug these input and output values into the remaining answers. Choice (A) becomes $500 = 150(4)$, or $500 = 600$; eliminate (A). Choice (C) becomes $500 = 200(4) - 300$, or $500 = 500$; keep (C). The correct answer is (C).

22. **D**   The question asks for the greatest possible difference in the mean, or average, of two data sets. For averages, use the formula $T = AN$, in which T is the *Total*, A is the *Average*, and N is the *Number of things*. Each of the data sets has 35 integers, so the number of things for each is 35. Because the number of things is equal, a larger total will lead to a larger average. Data set 1 contains integers between 200 and 600, so it is likely to have a smaller total and average, while data set 2 contains integers between 300 and 700, so it is likely to have a larger total and average. Thus, to find the greatest possible difference between the mean of data set 1 and the mean of data set 2, find the smallest possible mean for data set 1 and the largest possible mean for data set 2.

Start with finding the smallest possible mean of data set 1. This means the total should be as small as possible. Since the intervals can include the smallest number in the intervals, data set 1 could contain 12 values of 200, 7 values of 300, 4 values of 400, and 12 values of 500. Multiply and then add these numbers: $(12)(200) + (7)(300) + (4)(400) + (12)(500) = 2{,}400 + 2{,}100 + 1{,}600 + 6{,}000 = 12{,}100$. The average formula for data set 1 becomes $12{,}100 = (A)(35)$. Divide both sides of the equation by 35 to get $\dfrac{12{,}100}{35} = A$. To find the largest possible mean of data set 2, make the total as large as possible. Since the intervals do not include the largest number in the intervals, select the integer that is one less than the upper boundary of the interval. Data set 2 could contain 12 values of 399, 7 values of 499, 4 values of 599, and 12 values of 699. Multiply and then add these numbers to get $12(399) + 7(499) + 4(599) + 12(699) = 4{,}788 + 3{,}493 + 2{,}396 + 8{,}388 = 19{,}065$.

The average formula for data set 2 becomes $19{,}065 = (A)(35)$. Divide both sides of the equation by 35 to get $\dfrac{19{,}065}{35} = A$. Finally, find the difference of the two averages: $\dfrac{19{,}065}{35} - \dfrac{12{,}100}{35} = \dfrac{6{,}965}{35}$, which is 199. The correct answer is (D).

Chapter 5
Practice Test 3

HOW TO EMULATE THE DIGITAL SAT ON PAPER

Practice Test 4 is available in your online student tools in a digital, adaptive environment. The three tests in this physical book are printed on paper, but otherwise emulate the digital test in every way: test style, difficulty, and content. Please use the checklist below to ensure that you are able to emulate the adaptive nature of the test and get the preparation that you need for test day. Feel free to use the versions of Module 2 that you do not take during your test as additional practice.

- ☐ Take Reading and Writing (RW) Module 1, allowing yourself 32 minutes to complete it.

- ☐ Go to the answer key starting on page 312 and determine the number of questions you got correct in RW Module 1.

- ☐ If you get fewer than 15 questions correct, take RW Module 2 – Easier, which starts on page 262. If you get 15 or more questions correct, take RW Module 2 – Harder, which starts on page 273.

- ☐ Whichever RW Module 2 you take, start immediately and allow yourself 32 minutes to complete it.

- ☐ Take a 10-minute break between RW Module 2 and Math Module 1.

- ☐ Take Math Module 1, allowing yourself 35 minutes to complete it.

- ☐ Go to the answer key starting on page 312 and determine the number of questions you got correct in Math Module 1.

- ☐ If you get fewer than 14 questions correct, take Math Module 2 – Easier, which starts on page 294. If you get 14 or more questions correct, take Math Module 2 – Harder, which starts on page 302.

- ☐ Whichever Math Module you take, start it immediately and allow yourself 35 minutes to complete it.

- ☐ After you finish the test, check your answers to RW Module 2 and Math Module 2.

- ☐ Only after you complete the entire test should you read the explanations for the questions, which start on page 313.

SAT Prep Test 3—Reading and Writing
Module 1

Turn to Section 1 of your answer sheet to answer the questions in this section.

---

1 ☐ Mark for Review

The intergenerational Bulgarian female choir group Bistritsa Babi has been working to preserve customary songs and dances from the Shopluk region of the country since 1939. Through these _____ performances, members of Bistritsa Babi hope to keep this centuries-old ritual of expression alive. In 2005, the group was added to the UNESCO List of Intangible Cultural Heritage for Eastern Europe.

Which choice completes the text with the most logical and precise word or phrase?

(A) traditional

(B) obscure

(C) discreet

(D) eccentric

---

2 ☐ Mark for Review

Located in the old city of Marrakesh, Jemaa el-Fnaa, the main square, is a marketplace and vibrant hub for residents and visitors alike. During the day, snake charmers and stalls selling beverages fill the square, while at night the _____ center is filled with throngs of people coming to hear storytellers tell traditional fables, watch the performances of magicians, and browse multiple booths offering herbal medicines. As the night goes on, dozens of food vendors set up their stalls to feed the crowds.

Which choice completes the text with the most logical and precise word or phrase?

(A) formal

(B) bustling

(C) unpredictable

(D) deserted

CONTINUE ➡

3 ☐ Mark for Review

When developing the procedure for LASIK eye surgery, inventor Gholam A. Peyman faced many obstacles in trying to create a way to use lasers on the delicate tissues within the eye without causing pain or scarring. Through many experiments, he was able to gather that using a flap of tissue instead of performing surgery on the surface of the cornea could greatly reduce the incidence of _____ of the procedure. Peyman was able to secure patents in the US for his ideas and furthered his research to help the field of ophthalmology.

Which choice completes the text with the most logical and precise word or phrase?

- (A) characteristics
- (B) prospects
- (C) efficacy
- (D) repercussions

4 ☐ Mark for Review

The process of rainwater harvesting includes gathering and reserving rainwater instead of allowing it to trickle away. When it rains, water is collected from an awning or roof and _____ in a large vessel like a well or reservoir where it can drain back to the ground water source for things like domestic and livestock use.

Which choice completes the text with the most logical and precise word or phrase?

- (A) aggregated
- (B) dissipated
- (C) percolated
- (D) collaborated

5 ☐ Mark for Review

In 2012, thousands of scientists working at the Large Hadron Collider in Switzerland were finally able to _____ the existence of the long-predicted Higgs boson particle, first theorized as necessary in order to explain the mass of a fundamental particle by Peter Higgs and François Englert in 1964. These scientists confirmed a pattern of decay products that could be explained only by the Higgs boson particle.

Which choice completes the text with the most logical and precise word or phrase?

- (A) corroborate
- (B) exonerate
- (C) contextualize
- (D) postulate

6 ☐ Mark for Review

A highly influential leader of the US civil rights movement, Martin Luther King Jr. _____ his commitment to nonviolent resistance by organizing and directing numerous peaceful protests and sit-ins across the United States in the 1960s: his actions revealed his unwavering dedication to advancing the cause of civil rights without resorting to violence.

Which choice completes the text with the most logical and precise word or phrase?

- (A) characterized
- (B) evinced
- (C) elided
- (D) gauged

CONTINUE ➡

7 ☐ Mark for Review

An experiment headed by University of Wisconsin psychologist Sohad Murrar provides compelling evidence that individuals feel more inclusive toward other groups when they are informed that pro-diversity attitudes and behaviors are extremely popular among their peers. <u>Students were presented with either a neutrally messaged poster or a poster that displayed fellow students of diverse ethnic backgrounds, a statement about valuing diversity, and statistics indicating their fellow students' strong support for the statement.</u> The study found that students were more likely to embrace inclusive statements and reject racist statements even weeks after they were exposed to the pro-diversity poster.

Which choice best describes the function of the underlined sentence in the text as a whole?

(A) To analyze the implications of the results of the experiment

(B) To demonstrate the difficulty of assessing individuals' views on inclusivity and racism

(C) To highlight a specific instance in which the findings of the experiment were confirmed

(D) To describe certain aspects of the design and methodology of the experiment

8 ☐ Mark for Review

The following text is adapted from Alphonse Daudet's short story "The Siege of Berlin." The narrator is a doctor, coming to the aid of a grandfather who has fallen unconscious.

He had a fine face, magnificent teeth, a thick head of curly white hair, and though eighty years old did not look more than sixty. Near him his granddaughter knelt weeping. There was a strong family resemblance between them. Seeing them side by side, you thought of two beautiful Greek medals struck from the same matrix, but one old and worn and the other bright and clear-cut with all the brilliancy and smoothness of a first impression. I found the child's grief very touching.

According to the text, what is true about the granddaughter and grandfather?

(A) They look alike.

(B) They are of Greek heritage.

(C) They look younger than their ages.

(D) They are lying side-by-side.

CONTINUE →

Restaurant Distribution and Average
Rock Pigeon Abundance

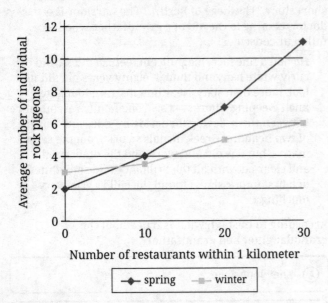

Number of restaurants within 1 kilometer

◆ spring   ■ winter

Urbanization invariably results in a decrease in overall species diversity and abundance, though certain species seem to preternaturally thrive in city environments. *Columba livia,* the rock pigeon, is thought to be well-suited to survival in urbanized environments because of the anthropogenic food sources supplied in the form of refuse from restaurants. Thus, researchers Jeffrey A. Brown, Susannah B. Lerman, and colleagues hypothesized that the number of nearby restaurants might be a predictor of the abundance of rock pigeons in the area. They visited 57 sites during spring and winter for three years and logged the number of restaurants and the number of rock pigeons in the vicinity. Looking at the lines of best fit for the scatterplot of the compiled data, the researchers concluded that there is indeed a relationship between proximity to restaurants and abundance of rock pigeons and that this relationship was especially strong in the spring, noting that _____

9   ☐ Mark for Review

Which choice most effectively uses data from the graph to complete the statement?

(A) around ten rock pigeons were observed at a site with three restaurants within one kilometer, while around thirty rock pigeons were observed at a site with six restaurants within one kilometer.

(B) around three rock pigeons were observed at a site with ten restaurants within one kilometer, while around six rock pigeons were observed at a site with thirty restaurants within one kilometer.

(C) fewer than five rock pigeons were observed at a site with ten restaurants within one kilometer, while more than ten rock pigeons were observed at a site with thirty restaurants within one kilometer.

(D) fewer than ten rock pigeons were observed at a site with five restaurants within one kilometer, while more than thirty rock pigeons were observed at a site with ten restaurants within one kilometer.

CONTINUE ➡

10 Mark for Review

Chandra Wickramasinghe, director of the University of Buckingham's Centre for Astrobiology, is an influential proponent of the controversial theory of panspermia, which suggests that life on Earth originated from microorganisms that were carried to our planet by comets or other celestial bodies. Wickramasinghe has argued for panspermia using several sources of scientific data including the detection of living microorganisms at extremely high altitudes in Earth's atmosphere and the confirmation of complex organic molecules in interstellar dust and comets.

Which choice best describes the main idea of the text?

(A) Wickramasinghe's theory of panspermia is far too controversial to be accepted by other astrobiologists.

(B) Wickramasinghe has presented evidence that life on Earth may in fact come from somewhere beyond Earth.

(C) The preponderance of available scientific data strongly supports Wickramasinghe's theory of panspermia.

(D) If microorganisms can survive at extremely high altitudes in Earth's atmosphere, then they can also survive space travel.

11 Mark for Review

C. difficile is a bacterium that causes an inflammation of the colon that can be life-threatening. The metabolic processes by which *C. difficile* takes advantage of a host's inflammatory process to increase toxin production are not well understood. Previously, higher levels of sorbitol (a sugar alcohol) were found to be released by the immune system during inflammation from toxin production. Thus, a team of researchers decided to investigate sorbitol metabolism in *C. difficile* and its effect on toxin production in mice. In the study, mice with *C. difficile* that ingested sorbitol were found to have lower levels of toxin production than mice that did not ingest sorbitol. One possible explanation is that metabolizing sorbitol prevents *C. difficile* from producing toxins.

Which finding, if true, would most directly strengthen the potential explanation?

(A) *C. difficile* lacks the enzyme that metabolizes sorbitol and thus reduces its production of toxins when sorbitol is ingested.

(B) *C. difficile* metabolizes sorbitol at a faster rate than it does other naturally occurring sugar alcohols.

(C) Low levels of sorbitol reduce inflammation in mice and prevent toxin production.

(D) Mice naturally produce sorbitol in their intestines and do not contract *C. difficile*.

CONTINUE

12 ☐ Mark for Review

Scholars generally agree that amputations were dangerous and deadly prior to 10,000 years ago due to a lack of proper surgical tools and techniques. The earliest evidence of a successful limb-removal surgery was a 7,000-year-old skeleton found in France that had an amputation above the elbow. Recently, archaeologists uncovered a 31,000-year-old skeleton with an amputated leg in Indonesia. Analysis of the early stone age skeleton shows that the amputation occurred when the man was just a child and lacked any evidence of infection. Thus, _____.

Which choice most logically completes the text?

Ⓐ early stone age people must have had doctors who performed these successful amputations.

Ⓑ life as an amputee must have been difficult for early stone age people without access to post-operational care.

Ⓒ there is insufficient evidence to support that most amputations performed prior to 10,000 years ago were deadly.

Ⓓ early stone age people prior to 10,000 years ago may have been more advanced than was previously acknowledged.

13 ☐ Mark for Review

In game theory, the prisoner's dilemma is a thought experiment in which two people who are isolated from each other each have the choice to betray the other. An individual who betrays the other person will experience a personal benefit; however, if both players choose to betray each other then they will both experience a worse punishment than if neither betrays the other. Game theorists generally agree that the choice to cooperate (that is, refusing to betray the other person) is irrational, as it defies one's self-interest; therefore, these game theorists suggest that _____.

Which choice most logically completes the text?

Ⓐ it is more rational for one to betray the other participant.

Ⓑ both individuals should cooperate, as their punishment will be reduced.

Ⓒ people always act in their own self-interest, as it is the rational choice.

Ⓓ the thought experiment likely has limited relevance in everyday life.

14 ☐ Mark for Review

Karni Mata Temple is a Hindu temple located in the town of Deshnoke in India. The temple is dedicated to Karni Mata and is an important pilgrimage site. Numerous rats, known as *kābā* and considered holy, live in Karni Mata Temple, earning the temple _____ nickname, "Temple of Rats."

Which choice completes the text so that it conforms to the conventions of Standard English?

Ⓐ it's

Ⓑ its

Ⓒ their

Ⓓ they're

CONTINUE ➡

15 ⬛ 🔖 Mark for Review

In addition to her research into the effects of hormones, ultraviolet light, and chemotherapy agents on cell _____ Jewel Plummer Cobb served as dean at Connecticut College and Rutgers University and as president of California State University, Fullerton, where she led many projects expanding the school's facilities.

Which choice completes the text so that it conforms to the conventions of Standard English?

(A) division: biologist

(B) division. Biologist

(C) division biologist

(D) division, biologist

16 ⬛ 🔖 Mark for Review

Poetra Asantewa is a performer from Ghana who combines three elements to create her _____ lyrics incorporating social issues, vocalization evoking different emotions, and rhythms using soulful elements.

Which choice completes the text so that it conforms to the conventions of Standard English?

(A) pieces

(B) pieces,

(C) pieces:

(D) pieces;

17 ⬛ 🔖 Mark for Review

Compared to other Ukrainian scientists and mathematicians, _____ she has worked with differential equations, partial differential equations, and integrable systems in Dnipro, Cyprus, and Kyiv.

Which choice completes the text so that it conforms to the conventions of Standard English?

(A) there is a wide range of fields and Ukrainian cities that Olena Vaneeva has worked in:

(B) many Ukrainian cities and fields have been home to Olena Vaneeva:

(C) the range of fields and Ukrainian cities that Olena Vaneeva has worked in is very wide:

(D) Olena Vaneeva has worked in a wide range of fields and Ukrainian cities:

18 ⬛ 🔖 Mark for Review

Astronaut William Anders was a member of the Apollo 8 mission, the first human spaceflight to reach the Moon and orbit it. During the mission, Anders took a photo of Earth rising above the lunar surface, an _____ was later named *Earthrise*.

Which choice completes the text so that it conforms to the conventions of Standard English?

(A) image, that

(B) image

(C) image that

(D) image,

CONTINUE ➡

19 ⬚ Mark for Review

French philosopher Denis Diderot was the chief editor of the *Encyclopédie*, which was completed by 1772. Motivated by the principles of the Enlightenment, the writers of the *Encyclopédie* _____ to compile all of the world's knowledge in a single resource available to the ordinary person.

Which choice completes the text so that it conforms to the conventions of Standard English?

(A) attempted

(B) are attempting

(C) will attempt

(D) attempt

20 ⬚ Mark for Review

As one of the most prominent French astrophysicists, Françoise Combes has contributed to research about how galaxies form and _____ she has studied the composition of galaxies and how they interact with each other.

Which choice completes the text so that it conforms to the conventions of Standard English?

(A) evolve; additionally,

(B) evolve additionally

(C) evolve, additionally,

(D) evolve, additionally;

21 ⬚ Mark for Review

American avant-garde jazz composer and guitarist Mary Halvorson's musical discography includes *Dragon's Head*, an album created with bassist John Hébert and drummer Ches _____ a solo album; and *Away with You*, which featured pedal steel player Susan Alcorn, cellist Tomeka Reid, and saxophonist Ingrid Laubrock.

Which choice completes the text so that it conforms to the conventions of Standard English?

(A) Smith; *Meltframe,*

(B) Smith; *Meltframe*

(C) Smith, *Meltframe,*

(D) Smith, *Meltframe:*

22 ⬚ Mark for Review

Mice were studied in an experiment focused on the relationship between room temperature and cancer growth. Cooler room temperatures were found to stimulate fat cells that eradicate the sugar molecules that sustain cancer cells. _____ the cancer cells started to die off in the mice exposed to cooler room temperatures.

Which choice completes the text with the most logical transition?

(A) Consequently,

(B) For example,

(C) However,

(D) In comparison,

CONTINUE ➔

23 Mark for Review

While researching a topic, a student has taken the following notes:

- Satyajit Ray was an Indian filmmaker.
- He is well-known for *The Apu Trilogy*.
- The first film in the trilogy, *Pather Panchali*, is about the childhood of a small Bengali boy named Apu.
- The second film, *Aparajito*, depicts Apu in his adolescence and his relationship to both his mother and their home.
- In *Apur Sansar*, the third film, adult Apu marries Aparna and has a son, Kajal.

The student wants to emphasize how Apu changed throughout the trilogy. Which choice most effectively uses relevant information from the notes to accomplish this goal?

(A) Apu went from being a child in *Pather Panchali* to an adult with his own family in *Apur Sansar*.

(B) Satyajit Ray, an Indian filmmaker, made *The Apu Trilogy* about a boy named Apu.

(C) The three films of *The Apu Trilogy* are *Pather Panchali*, *Aparajito*, and *Apur Sansar*.

(D) The character Apu grew up in Bengal and eventually marries and has a son.

24 Mark for Review

While researching a topic, a student has taken the following notes:

- Haenyeo are female divers on Jeju Island, a Korean province.
- Haenyeo earn money by harvesting mollusks and shellfish, such as abalone, sea urchins, and oysters.
- They dive without the use of oxygen masks and tanks.
- They can hold their breath for over three minutes.
- They can dive up to 30 meters below the surface of the water.
- Jellyfish, sharks, and poor weather are different dangers they face while diving.

The student wants to emphasize the abilities of haenyeo. Which choice most effectively uses relevant information from the notes to accomplish this goal?

(A) Haenyeo are female divers on Jeju Island who harvest shellfish.

(B) While diving, haenyeo contend with jellyfish, sharks, and poor weather.

(C) Haenyeo earn money by selling abalone, sea urchins, and oysters, which they harvest by diving without oxygen masks and tanks.

(D) Haenyeo can dive 30 meters below the surface and hold their breath for over three minutes.

CONTINUE →

25 ☐ Mark for Review

While researching a topic, a student has taken the following notes:

- Heliconian Hall was built in 1876 as the Olivet Congregational Church.
- Heliconian Hall is in the Yorkville neighborhood of Toronto.
- The Heliconian Club purchased and renamed Heliconian Hall in 1923.
- The Heliconian Club's membership includes women professional artists.
- Heliconian Hall hosts music, art, dance, drama, and literature events.

The student wants to describe the history of Heliconian Hall to an audience familiar with the Heliconian Club. Which choice most effectively uses relevant information from the notes to accomplish this goal?

(A) Heliconian Hall was purchased in 1923 by the Heliconian Club, an organization which includes women professional artists.

(B) Heliconian Hall, located in the Yorkville neighborhood of Toronto, hosts music, art, dance, drama, and literature events.

(C) Heliconian Hall, formerly known as the Olivet Congregational Church, is in the Yorkville neighborhood of Toronto.

(D) Heliconian Hall, built as the Olivet Congregational Church in 1876, was purchased and renamed by the Heliconian Club in 1923.

26 ☐ Mark for Review

While researching a topic, a student has taken the following notes:

- Evan Adams is an Indigenous Canadian actor.
- He is well-known for his role as Thomas in the film *Smoke Signals*.
- The film was released in 1998.
- It is about two friends, Thomas and Victor, and their complicated relationships with Victor's father, Arnold.
- Adams is also known for his role as Seymour in *The Business of Fancydancing* (2002).

The student wants to introduce Evan Adams and his role in *Smoke Signals* to a new audience. Which choice most effectively uses relevant information from the notes to accomplish this goal?

(A) Evan Adams, an Indigenous Canadian actor, has starred as Thomas in *Smoke Signals* and Seymour in *The Business of Fancydancing*.

(B) *Smoke Signals*, released in 1998, explores the complicated relationships of friends Thomas and Victor.

(C) Evan Adams starred in the film *Smoke Signals* before he starred in *The Business of Fancydancing*.

(D) Indigenous Canadian actor Evan Adams starred as Thomas in the 1998 film *Smoke Signals*, which depicts two friends, Thomas and Victor, and their complicated relationships with Victor's father, Arnold.

CONTINUE ➡

27 ☐ Mark for Review

While researching a topic, a student has taken the following notes:

- Marie Byrd Land is an unclaimed region of Antarctica.
- Construction of Byrd Station in Marie Byrd Land was begun in 1956 by the US.
- Byrd Station was abandoned in 1972.
- John Carpenter used Byrd Station as a model for an Antarctic station in crisis for his movie *The Thing*.
- James Rollins used Byrd Station as a model for an Antarctic station in crisis for his novel *The 6th Extinction*.

The student wants to highlight a similarity between fictional depictions of a real-world location. Which choice most effectively uses relevant information from the notes to accomplish this goal?

(A) Both John Carpenter's movie *The Thing* and James Rollins's novel *The 6th Extinction* used Byrd Station as a model for an Antarctic station in crisis.

(B) In 1956, the US began construction of Byrd Station in Marie Byrd Land, an unclaimed region of Antarctica.

(C) Abandoned in 1972, Byrd Station was the model for an Antarctic station in crisis in John Carpenter's *The Thing*.

(D) John Carpenter used byrd station as a model for an Antarctic station in crisis for his movie *The Thing*; however, James Rollins used Byrd Station as a model for an Antarctic station in crisis for his novel *The 6th Extinction*.

YIELD
Once you've finished (or run out of time for) this section, use the answer key to determine how many questions you got right. If you got fewer than 15 questions right, move on to Module 2—Easier, otherwise move on to Module 2—Harder.

SAT Prep Test 3—Reading and Writing
Module 2—Easier

Turn to Section 1 of your answer sheet to answer the questions in this section.

1 ☐ Mark for Review

During World War II, hundreds of scientists, including many prominent physicists such as Robert Oppenheimer, _____ the Manhattan Project, pooling their efforts and expertise in order to develop the first bombs that successfully exploited the tremendous power of nuclear energy.

Which choice completes the text with the most logical and precise word or phrase?

(A) collaborated on

(B) invested with

(C) plotted against

(D) learned from

2 ☐ Mark for Review

Advising farmers on how to prevent the disruption of soil due to plowing, experts in agriculture have recommended the method of no-till farming. This _____ allows for soil to remain settled while seeds are planted, unlike traditional practices in which the soil is disturbed in order for new crops to be grown, thus making sowing easier to manage. Through no-till farming, agriculturalists are able to grow new batches with very little labor or equipment required.

Which choice completes the text with the most logical and precise word or phrase?

(A) intention

(B) agenda

(C) distraction

(D) technique

CONTINUE ➡

3 ☐ Mark for Review

Ethologists and beekeepers use the phrase "waggle dance" to describe the movement a bee makes in order to communicate with other bees in the colony about the location of resources. This silent _____ of information among the bees allows them to pass on knowledge of how close or far away a source is and what direction it is in. The source being broadcasted can be a site for possible nesting or an opportunity for sustenance.

Which choice completes the text with the most logical and precise word or phrase?

Ⓐ transmission

Ⓑ confidence

Ⓒ prolongation

Ⓓ devastation

4 ☐ Mark for Review

Chronic hepatitis B (CHB) can _____ affect Asians Americans and Pacific Islanders (AAPIs), who are not affected by most other major hepatitis strains. While everyone should be screened for hepatitis viruses, AAPIs are strongly encouraged to get tested and treated for chronic hepatitis B.

Which choice completes the text with the most logical or precise word or phrase?

Ⓐ disproportionately

Ⓑ exclusively

Ⓒ essentially

Ⓓ initially

5 ☐ Mark for Review

There are countless stories of people whose hair turns white overnight from fright in a condition called canities subita, also known as Marie Antoinette syndrome. Scientists _____ this as historical fiction and explain that visible hair is dead material that can be changed by undergoing a chemical drying process, but not by experiencing a great shock.

Which choice completes the text with the most logical or precise word or phrase?

Ⓐ trivialize

Ⓑ illustrate

Ⓒ dismiss

Ⓓ promote

CONTINUE ➡

6 ☐ Mark for Review

The following text is adapted from Honoré de Balzac's 1829 novel *The Chouans*. Marie, an aristocrat, is tidying a room and speaking to Francine, her maid.

She began to arrange the silk and muslin curtains which draped the window, making them intercept the light and produce in the room a voluptuous chiaro-scuro.

"Francine," she said, "take away those knick-knacks on the mantelpiece; leave only the clock and the two Dresden vases. I'll fill those vases myself with the flowers Corentin brought me. Take out the chairs, I want only this sofa and a fauteuil. Then sweep the carpet, so as to <u>bring out</u> the colors, and put wax candles in the sconces and on the mantel."

As used in the text, what does the word "bring out" most nearly mean?

Ⓐ Distribute

Ⓑ Transport

Ⓒ Introduce

Ⓓ Emphasize

7 ☐ Mark for Review

The following text is adapted from Jane Austin's 1811 novel *Sense and Sensibility*. Elinor Dashwood is in her cottage speaking with her Uncle Edward and her younger sister Marianne.

"I have frequently detected myself in such kind of mistakes," said Elinor, "in a total misapprehension of character in some point or other: fancying people so much more gay or grave, or ingenious or stupid than they really are, and I can hardly tell why or in what the deception originated. Sometimes one is guided by what they say of themselves, and very frequently by what other people say of them, without giving oneself time to deliberate and judge."

Which choice best describes the overall structure of the text?

Ⓐ The speaker describes how someone can be deceived by the impressions of others and then promises to be more careful in the future.

Ⓑ The speaker relates her misgivings of the character of another individual and then rationalizes her mistaken perception.

Ⓒ The speaker considers the duplicity of human nature and then issues a warning about the misconceptions of personal opinion.

Ⓓ The speaker describes a type of error and then reveals the sources of information that lead to such errors.

CONTINUE ➡

8 ⬚ Mark for Review

In order to combat the effects of human life on the planet's climate, many environmental and governmental establishments lay the foundation for forests in localities that previously did not have woodland areas, also known as afforestation. To begin the operation, potential sites are first surveyed in order to select regions with the best factors in terms of aspects such as vegetation, amount of human activity, weather, and soil quality. Once a site has been selected, the land must then be developed for planting. After the land has been prepared, trees can be planted with different methods of seeding, depending on the site and soil present.

Which choice best describes the overall structure of the text?

(A) It presents a solution to a widespread issue, then elaborates on why the issue should be solved.

(B) It defines a strategy, then lists the reasons why the strategy is useful.

(C) It examines an effective practice, then argues that the practice has negative consequences.

(D) It introduces a process, then explains the steps taken in executing that process.

9 ⬚ Mark for Review

Text 1

A recent series of psychological studies that included subjects from different parts of the world looked at the effects that nostalgia, the feeling and experience of thinking about one's own past, has on psychological well-being. The results of the studies demonstrated a relationship between nostalgia and authenticity, one's sense of being aligned with one's true self. A greater sense of authenticity was found to correlate with greater measurements of all aspects of psychological well-being.

Text 2

While there has been some demonstration that nostalgia is associated with mental health benefits, it is important to remember that there are different types of nostalgia and that some can be highly destructive. A recent study performed by psychologists David B. Newman, Arthur A. Stone, and Norbert Schwarz found that conscious acts of extreme nostalgia have positive effects, while smaller and momentary, more unconscious nostalgic experiences can result in negative mental health effects, such as neuroticism.

Based on the texts, what would Newman, Stone, and Schwarz (Text 2) say about the results of the studies discussed in Text 1?

(A) They are completely consistent with the results of other studies on the subject.

(B) They are from studies that fail to differentiate between different types of nostalgia and so provide an incomplete picture of nostalgia's impact on mental health.

(C) They provide empirical evidence for a hypothesis long untested but assumed to be true.

(D) They suggest a possible new direction for future research but provide no definitive resolutions.

CONTINUE ➜

Impact of Package Label on Consumer Choices

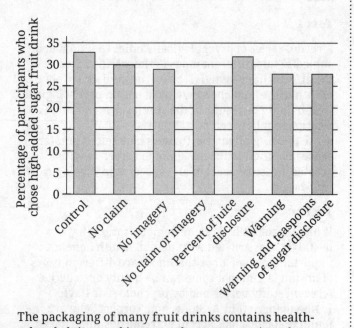

The packaging of many fruit drinks contains health-related claims and imagery that can sometimes be misleading to parents who purchase such drinks for their children. To assess the impact of the front of packaging on consumers' purchasing decisions, nutrition researchers Aviva A. Musicus, Christina A. Roberto, and Alyssa J. Moran conducted a study wherein participants were shown fruit drinks with high amounts of sugar added with seven different conditions of packaging: with claim and imagery (control), no claim, no imagery, no claim or imagery, disclosure of percentage of juice, a warning, and disclosure of amount of added sugar in teaspoons. At the end of the study, the researchers concluded that the presence of warnings and absence of claims and imagery may reduce likelihood of purchase, whereas disclosure of percentage of juice may have very little impact.

10 ⬚ Mark for Review

Which choice most effectively uses data from the graph to support the researchers' conclusion?

(A) The percentage of participants who selected the high-added sugar fruit drink was highest when a warning was placed on the front of the packaging.

(B) The percentage of participants who selected the high-added sugar fruit drink when the percentage of juice was disclosed on the front of the packaging was comparable to the percentage who selected the drink in the control group.

(C) The absence of the claim had the same impact as did the absence of imagery from the front of the packaging.

(D) When the front of packaging disclosed the amount of added sugar in teaspoons, participants were more likely to select a low-added sugar fruit drink than a high-added sugar fruit drink.

CONTINUE ➤

11 ▢ Mark for Review

"The Emerald Eyes" is an 1861 short story by Gustavo Adolfo Bécquer, originally written in Spanish. In the story, the protagonist, Fernando, is continually drawn to a Poplar fountain in an attempt to learn the identity of a mysterious woman with emerald eyes. Fernando's friend Iñigo is worried and tries to warn him to stay away from the fountain when he says, _____

Which quotation from a translation of the "The Emerald Eyes" most effectively illustrates the claim?

Ⓐ "Do you not see that [the stag] is going toward the fountain of the Poplars, and if he lives to reach it we must give him up for lost?"

Ⓑ "I exposed myself to death under his horse's hoofs to hold him back."

Ⓒ "You do not go to the mountains now preceded by the clamorous pack of hounds, nor does the blare of your horns awake the echoes."

Ⓓ "I conjure you by that which you love most on earth not to return to the fountain of the Poplars."

12 ▢ Mark for Review

Anthony Doerr won a Pulitzer Prize, among other literary awards, for his work in fiction novels, and his short stories have been anthologized in collections of American literature. In an essay about Doerr's works, a student claims that Doerr uses children as his protagonists in order to create a story from an unbiased and hopeful perspective of humanity.

Which quotation from a literary critic best supports the student's claim?

Ⓐ "Doerr's novels are influenced by the themes present in fables, thus presenting an ordeal through which the protagonist learns a lesson about life."

Ⓑ "Doerr prefers to have the protagonist's story told through the eyes of a child who seeks to learn more about the world."

Ⓒ "Doerr's novels often contain multiple story arcs or perspectives culminating in a universal truth."

Ⓓ "Doerr's protagonists are often children who see the world with an open mind and contribute towards the betterment of humanity."

CONTINUE ▶

13 ⬚ Mark for Review

Ratings of Mood and Need Satisfaction after Social Inclusion and Exclusion

	Human exclusion	Human inclusion	Computer exclusion	Computer inclusion
Need satisfaction scale, reflexive stage	3.13	5.88	3.29	5.94
Mood, reflexive stage	3.29	5.50	3.43	4.59
Need satisfaction scale, reflective stage	3.38	5.03	3.81	5.38
Mood, reflective stage	3.46	4.71	4.43	4.09

Social exclusion can have a detrimental impact on an individual's mental and emotional state. Psychologists Melissa Jauch, Selma Carolin Rudert, and Rainer Greifendeder hypothesized that individuals would experience equivalent effects of social exclusion regardless of whether the source of exclusion was human or computer. The researchers conducted a study in which subjects played a word riddle game. The subjects were grouped with other players who were computer-generated, though some subjects were told that they were playing with other humans. Throughout the game, the other players would either include the subjects or exclude them from participating. After the game, researchers measured the subjects' need satisfaction (a psychological metric of the degree to which an individual's basic needs are met) and mood on a scale of 1 to 9 immediately after the game (the reflexive stage) as well as after some time had passed (the reflective stage).

Which choice most effectively uses data from the table to support the researchers' hypothesis?

Ⓐ At the reflexive stage, subjects' ratings in both mood and need satisfaction when excluded by a human were comparable to the corresponding ratings when excluded by a computer.

Ⓑ Subjects reported higher mood and need satisfaction ratings when included than they did when excluded.

Ⓒ When included by a human or a computer, subjects exhibited lower need satisfaction at the reflective stage than they did at the reflexive stage.

Ⓓ Subjects experienced the highest mood rating when they believed they were socially included by a human.

CONTINUE ➤

14 ☐ Mark for Review

It is commonly accepted that the Cretaceous–Paleogene extinction event some 66 million years ago was caused by an asteroid impact, believed to correspond to an impact crater in Chicxulub, Mexico, that dates to the same time and is the second-largest impact structure on Earth. Geologist Uisdean Nicholson discovered an undersea impact crater while reviewing seismic survey data and conducted a study that demonstrated that this crater also formed around 66 million years ago. Nicholson claims that the rock whose impact caused the formation of the undersea crater could have broken off from a parent asteroid that also caused the Chicxulub impact.

Which finding, if true, would most directly support Nicholson's claim?

Ⓐ The undersea impact would have caused major earthquakes and tsunamis, leading to significant damage to the planet.

Ⓑ Some evidence points to a gradual Cretaceous–Paleogene extinction rather than a sudden one caused by an asteroid.

Ⓒ Many species of marine animals, in addition to land animals, went extinct during the Cretaceous–Paleogene extinction.

Ⓓ The undersea impact crater contains some of the same minerals not normally found on Earth that were also found at the Chicxulub impact site.

15 ☐ Mark for Review

In a study of neuronal sleeping patterns, researchers tracked the electrical waves (using EEG) and blood flow patterns (using fMRI) in participants while they slept. Researchers hypothesized that a correlation between electrical wave activity and blood flow patterns could indicate which regions of the brain, if any, fell asleep or awoke first. Like with previous studies, the researchers found that the thalamus, a region located near the center of the brain, had decreased blood flow patterns in association with increased electrical sleep waves in the early minutes of sleep activity. This suggests that _____

Which choice most logically completes the text?

Ⓐ the thalamus is one of the first brain regions to fall asleep.

Ⓑ increased blood flow patterns in association with decreased electrical sleep waves indicate a brain region that is asleep.

Ⓒ the thalamus is the last brain region to fall asleep.

Ⓓ humans may use only one hemisphere of the brain while asleep.

CONTINUE ➤

16 ☐ Mark for Review

In order to avoid physical damage, a formula is used to calculate the maximum gross weight for a commercial vehicle traveling over a bridge. The Federal Bridge Gross Weight Formula takes into account not only the weight of the vehicle but also its number of axles (shafts for wheels) and the spacing between axles, given that a shorter vehicle with its weight concentrated in a smaller area could cause more damage than could a longer vehicle of the same weight whose mass is more dispersed. This suggests that, when comparing a two-axle vehicle to a 4-axle vehicle, _____

Which choice most logically completes the text?

Ⓐ the four-axle vehicle likely has a lower weight limit on a given bridge than does the two-axle vehicle.

Ⓑ the vehicles likely have the same weight limit on a given bridge.

Ⓒ the two-axle vehicle is unlikely to surpass the bridge's weight limit, as it is smaller.

Ⓓ the two-axle vehicle likely has a lower weight limit on a given bridge than does the four-axle vehicle.

17 ☐ Mark for Review

A recent study looked at whether students who took photos of PowerPoint slides during lessons remembered the content. When students took a photo of the slides, they were able to better remember the information on those slides compared to slides _____ did not photograph.

Which choice completes the text so that it conforms to the conventions of Standard English?

Ⓐ they

Ⓑ one

Ⓒ it

Ⓓ we

18 ☐ Mark for Review

Soft drinks have become very popular in recent years, but consuming too many is associated with many diseases and intellectual deterioration. Scientists wanted to explore another question related to this topic: _____

Which choice completes the text so that it conforms to the conventions of Standard English?

Ⓐ does the consumption of soft drinks cause changes in mammal behavior?

Ⓑ does the consumption of soft drinks cause changes in mammal behavior.

Ⓒ the consumption of soft drinks causes changes in mammal behavior?

Ⓓ the consumption of soft drinks causes changes in mammal behavior.

19 ☐ Mark for Review

Heat islands are urban areas that, due to a high number of buildings and limited greenery, have a higher temperature compared to outlying areas. There are several strategies and technologies to counteract the higher temperatures of heat islands. For example, green roofs, which are rooftops covered in vegetation, reduce the temperatures of _____ cool pavements, which are made with materials that reflect solar energy, can lower the temperatures above the pavement surface and the surrounding air.

Which choice completes the text so that it conforms to the conventions of Standard English?

Ⓐ roofs, while

Ⓑ roofs; while

Ⓒ roofs. While

Ⓓ roofs: while

CONTINUE ➤

20 ☐ Mark for Review

With a focus on public health, Abla Mehio Sibai is currently working at a university in Lebanon. She primarily focuses on the process of aging, especially in the context of different demographics, and _____ to research on noncontagious illnesses.

Which choice completes the text so that it conforms to the conventions of Standard English?

(A) contribute

(B) contributes

(C) are contributing

(D) have contributed

21 ☐ Mark for Review

Bribery is recognized as a problem in India by local and international organizations. In response to this problem, 5th Pillar, a non-governmental organization, printed a zero-rupee _____ imitation banknote that resembles real money and is covered in anti-corruption slogans.

Which choice completes the text so that it conforms to the conventions of Standard English?

(A) note. An

(B) note, an

(C) note an

(D) note; an

22 ☐ Mark for Review

Scientists wanted to learn how verbal statements can alter someone's visual interpretation of a situation. Participants were shown an image of 100 colored dots alongside a written hint and asked to identify the dominant color. When the hint accurately identified the dominant color, participants self-identified as more confident and _____ quicker response times.

Which choice completes the text so that it conforms to the conventions of Standard English?

(A) exhibit

(B) exhibits

(C) exhibiting

(D) exhibited

23 ☐ Mark for Review

Quantum computers rely on entangled building blocks to perform computational calculations. Scientists are attempting to find a new source for these building _____ photons, or small quanta of light, emitted by an atom.

Which choice completes the text so that it conforms to the conventions of Standard English?

(A) blocks, such as:

(B) blocks

(C) blocks,

(D) blocks:

CONTINUE ➔

---

24 ☐ Mark for Review

Suzan Shown Harjo initially worked to write poems and produce news shows advocating for equal rights for Native Americans. _____ she moved to Washington, D.C., and served as Congressional Liaison for Indian Affairs for President Jimmy Carter while continuing to produce powerful pieces.

Which choice completes the text with the most logical transition?

Ⓐ As a rule,

Ⓑ Despite this,

Ⓒ Conversely,

Ⓓ After some time,

---

25 ☐ Mark for Review

Scientists studied how electrical stimulation to the brain affected honeybees' ability to steer while flying. They were able to determine the parameters for honeybee flight and develop strategies to manipulate it. _____ scientists hope to use a similar technique to control the flight of miniature drones that will perform a variety of tasks for the military and other industries.

Which choice completes the text with the most logical transition?

Ⓐ In contrast,

Ⓑ Eventually,

Ⓒ On one hand,

Ⓓ Specifically,

---

26 ☐ Mark for Review

In order to study an abrupt increase in global mean lower stratosphere temperatures, scientists used a time-specific analysis of wildfires in Australia. They determined that the wildfires are the source of this abrupt increase in temperature. _____ reducing the number of wildfires in Australia may help return the temperature to a normal value.

Which choice completes the text with the most logical transition?

Ⓐ On the other hand,

Ⓑ Meanwhile,

Ⓒ Instead,

Ⓓ Therefore,

---

27 ☐ Mark for Review

Ed Yost designed the first modern hot air balloon with an in-flight heating system after working with General Mills on the company's research balloons. The first piloted hot air balloon was designed in France, but it heated the air on the ground and came with a large risk of explosion. _____ Yost's balloon design involved heating the fuel in the air and was much safer.

Which choice completes the text with the most logical transition?

Ⓐ Ultimately,

Ⓑ On the other hand,

Ⓒ Otherwise,

Ⓓ Despite this fact,

STOP

If you finish before time is called, you may check your work on this section only. Do not turn to any other section.

SAT Prep Test 3—Reading and Writing
Module 2—Harder

Turn to Section 1 of your answer sheet to answer the questions in this section.

---

1 ☐ Mark for Review

As an educator, artistic creator, and supporter of Māori culture, Cliff Whiting spent a significant portion of his career advocating for the inclusion of Māori arts in the schools of New Zealand. While mentoring students and artists within these communities, Whiting was encouraged to broaden his contributions and work on the renovation of historic buildings. By way of this, he became one of the chief officials on the _____ of Māori buildings in New Zealand. Whiting's ability to create a close-knit relationship with local communities aided his success in these preservation projects.

Which choice completes the text with the most logical and precise word or phrase?

(A) repossession

(B) rehabilitation

(C) reciprocation

(D) reindustrialization

---

2 ☐ Mark for Review

Used to test the resistance to corrosion of surface coatings and materials, the salt spray test is a common method employed to aid in quality testing of metallic, ceramic, stone, and polymer products. The _____ process is brief, low-cost, and highly methodized, allowing for producers to easily spot differences in quality and adjust their manufacturing accordingly.

Which choice completes the text with the most logical and precise word or phrase?

(A) rudimentary

(B) pervasive

(C) erroneous

(D) intermittent

CONTINUE

3 ▢ Mark for Review

Dr. Jane Goodall has worked tirelessly to _____ the effects of climate change on chimpanzees in Tanzania: her research has shown that government commitments to reforestation efforts can help lessen the negative impacts of warming temperatures on chimpanzee populations in Tanzania as well as in other African countries.

Which choice completes the text with the most logical and precise word or phrase?

(A) insulate

(B) downplay

(C) tolerate

(D) mitigate

4 ▢ Mark for Review

In 1968, surrealistic artist William Nelson Copley and his friend and fellow artist Dimitri Petrov founded an innovative artists' magazine known as S.M.S., in which contributors enjoyed complete freedom to create artistic works that Copley and Petrov would then reproduce with _____ fidelity, sparing no expense in producing a biweekly folio of painstakingly replicated art facsimiles.

Which choice completes the text with the most logical and precise word or phrase?

(A) evenhanded

(B) prudent

(C) scrupulous

(D) complacent

5 ▢ Mark for Review

The following text is adapted from L. Frank Baum's 1911 novel *The Sea Fairies*. Mayre Griffiths, nicknamed Trot, is a little girl. Cap'n Bill Weedles is a retired sailor with a wooden leg.

Trot liked Cap'n Bill and had a great deal of confidence in his wisdom, and a great admiration for his ability to make tops and whistles and toys with that marvelous jackknife of his. In the village were many boys and girls of her own age, but she never had as much fun playing with them as she had wandering by the sea accompanied by the old sailor and listening to his fascinating stories.

Which choice best describes the function of the underlined sentence in the text as a whole?

(A) It reiterates Trot's fascination with Cap'n Bill's impressive creative talents.

(B) Its comparison conveys the depth of Trot's regard and affection for Cap'n Bill.

(C) It contrasts the carefree pleasures of youth with the weighty responsibilities of adulthood.

(D) It reveals the subtle differences between Trot's assessment of Cap'n Bill and his assessment of her.

CONTINUE ➡

6 ☐ Mark for Review

The following text is adapted from Fyodor Dostoyevsky's 1864 novella *Notes from the Underground*. The narrator is an unnamed Russian man employed as a civil servant.

   I could never stand more than three months of dreaming at a time without feeling an irresistible desire to plunge into society. To plunge into society meant to visit my superior at the office .... I was overcome by a sort of paralysis; but this was pleasant and good for me. On returning home I deferred for a time my desire to embrace all humankind.

Which choice best states the main purpose of the text?

(A) To convey the man's apprehension about his employment and his relationship with his employer

(B) To foreshadow the man's imminent termination from his job for daydreaming

(C) To suggest that the man's social engagement with a colleague prolonged his isolation from society

(D) To advocate the social benefits of working with others in an office environment

7 ☐ Mark for Review

The following text is from Alexander S. Pushkin's 1834 short story "The Queen of Spades." A man named Tomsky is sharing with friends a story about his grandmother.

   "On returning home, my grandmother removed the patches from her face, took off her hoops, informed my grandfather of her loss at the gaming-table, and ordered him to pay the money. My deceased grandfather, as far as I remember, was a sort of house-steward to my grandmother. He dreaded her like fire; but, on hearing of such a heavy loss, he almost went out of his mind; he calculated the various sums she had lost, and pointed out to her that in six months she had spent half a million francs, that neither their Moscow nor Saratov estates were in Paris, and finally refused point blank to pay the debt."

Which choice best states the function of the underlined sentence in the text as a whole?

(A) It explains the previous dynamic between the narrator's grandparents.

(B) It provides background information on the narrator's relationship with his grandfather.

(C) It reveals why the grandmother lost money at the gaming-table.

(D) It establishes the memories of the narrator in his house.

CONTINUE

8 🔖 Mark for Review

Nuclear energy, a power source expected to grow in the coming decades, relies upon an element that is considered a finite resource on land: uranium. However, vast amounts of uranium exist in low concentrations in seawater. The time, effort, and cost needed to extract uranium from seawater has long been prohibitive, but a team of researchers from the Indian Institute of Science Education and Research has created a metal-organic framework that was able to pull 96.3% of uranium from seawater samples in two hours, representing a significant improvement from previous methods. Nevertheless, the new method has not yet been tested in a real-world marine setting, and it's expected that even with the improvements it is not likely to result in a net energy gain.

Which choice best describes the overall structure of the text?

(A) It presents a scientific challenge, then describes a failed attempt to address that challenge.

(B) It evaluates the effectiveness of a method of energy production, then addresses a potential criticism of the method.

(C) It explains the significance of a technological advancement, then qualifies its current usability.

(D) It establishes the problems associated with obtaining a resource, then cautions against reliance on that resource.

9 🔖 Mark for Review

Text 1

There have been many theories put forward to explain the decline of the Ancient Maya societies. One such theory points to various primary sources that indicate an escalation in infighting among rival factions in the society that coincided with increasing droughts. Thus, some anthropologists have proposed that climate change put a strain on the social, political, and economic institutions and played a crucial role in the demise of those institutions.

Text 2

There has been much debate surrounding the role that the changing climate played in the dissolution of Ancient Maya political systems. While it is often correctly pointed out that drought conditions of the time were correlated with the fall of the social order and the rise of civil unrest, it was more specifically the increasing unpredictability of precipitation patterns that had the strongest impact on the health of Maya society.

Based on the texts, how would the author of Text 2 most likely respond to the claims of the author of Text 1?

(A) By disagreeing with the premise that droughts corresponded to social unrest

(B) By asserting that if Maya society leaders were increasingly unable to predict the weather, it would logically follow that the population would increasingly mistrust the political institutions

(C) By conceding that water resources played a vital role in the decline of Maya societies but noting that the relevant factor was the society's inability to predict rainfall rather than strictly the lack of rainfall

(D) By arguing that if weather patterns had remained stable, Maya civilization would not have declined

CONTINUE ➡

10 ☐ Mark for Review

Characteristics of Common pH Indicators

pH indicator	pH range	Acid form color	Base form color
thymol blue	1.2–2.8	red	yellow
p-Nitrophenol	5.0–7.0	colorless	yellow
alizarin yellow	10.0–12.0	yellow	lilac
Nile blue	10.1–11.1	blue	red
nitramine	11.0–13.0	colorless	orange-brown

A student in chemistry class is studying acid-base titrations. For her experiment, she needs to use a pH indicator that has a colorless acid form and a pH range above a pH of 10. Based on the characteristics of common pH indicators, she selected _____

Which choice most effectively uses data from the table to complete the text?

- Ⓐ thymol blue.

- Ⓑ p-Nitrophenol.

- Ⓒ alizarin yellow.

- Ⓓ nitramine.

11 ☐ Mark for Review

"Remembrance" is a 1906 poem by Walter de la Mare. In the poem, the author describes a sense of profound emptiness: _____

Which quotation from "Remembrance" most effectively illustrates the claim?

- Ⓐ "The sky was like a waterdrop / In shadow of a thorn."

- Ⓑ "Lightning along its margin ran; / A rumour of the sea."

- Ⓒ "Lofty and few the elms, the stars / In the vast boughs most bright."

- Ⓓ "Not wonder, worship, not even peace / Seemed in my heart to be."

CONTINUE →

Concentration of Circulating Leukocytes Before and After Administration of Probiotics

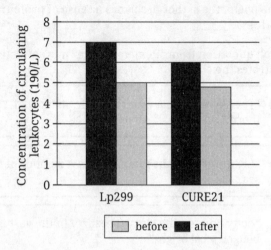

During inflammation, the body's immune system response to infection or tissue damage, leukocytes (also known as white blood cells) are released into the bloodstream. While inflammation can be normal and healthy, it can be harmful when the process lasts too long or occurs in healthy cell tissue, so the development of anti-inflammatory therapies is in demand. One such therapy under consideration is the use of certain bacteria called probiotics. To learn more about the systemic impact of these bacteria, medical researchers Christina Stene, Andrada Röme, and colleagues gave test subjects a daily dose of one of two probiotic strains, *Lactiplantibacillus plantarum* 299 (Lp299) and *Bifidobacterium infantis* CURE21 (CURE21). The researchers compared the concentration of leukocytes in the subjects' bloodstreams at the start and end of a six-week period and concluded that both Lp299 and CURE21 have anti-inflammatory properties, citing that

12 ☐ Mark for Review

Which choice best describes data from the graph to support the researchers' conclusion?

(A) there was a larger number of leukocytes in the test subjects' bloodstreams before the treatment with either Lp299 or CURE21 than there was after the treatment.

(B) subjects treated with Lp299 experienced a larger decrease in leukocytes than did those treated with CURE21.

(C) those who were given the CURE21 treatment had a smaller number of leukocytes in their bloodstream at the start of study than did those who were given Lp299.

(D) at the end of the study, the group of subjects that received Lp299 exhibited a number of leukocytes in their bloodstream comparable to that of the group that received CURE21.

CONTINUE

13 🔖 Mark for Review

Traumatic brain injury (TBI) can have short-term symptoms as well as long-term consequences. Researchers continue to investigate methods that can improve detection and treatment of TBI. GFAP and UCH-L1 are two protein biomarkers that have been associated with severe TBI and subsequent death. In a study, researchers analyzed blood samples from over 1,000 patients on the same day as their injuries. They found that patients with GFAP values greater than the top 20th percentile were at 23 times greater risk of death in the next six months, while patients with UCH-L1 values greater than the top 20th percentile were at 63 times greater risk of death in the next six months. According to the researchers, this suggests that <u>the level of these biomarkers can detect TBI and indicate its severity.</u>

Which finding, if true, would most directly weaken the underlined claim?

(A) Follow-up visits of patients with low GFAP and UCH-L1 showed that over 50% had improved symptoms.

(B) Patients with high UCH-L1 levels but low GFAP levels showed severe TBI symptoms within six months after injury.

(C) GFAP and UCH-L1 occur in high levels immediately following an injury but significantly decrease after a few days, before many people seek treatment for a potential TBI.

(D) Follow-up visits of patients with high GFAP and UCH-L1 levels showed that 70% had died within six months after injury.

14 🔖 Mark for Review

Prometheus Bound is a circa 460 BCE Greek tragedy written by Aeschylus, translated in 1921 by E. D. A. Morshead. The play follows the punishment of Prometheus for defying Zeus and providing humanity with the gift of fire. In the play, Prometheus questions the justice of his punishment and denounces Zeus as a cruel ruler, as when he says, _____

Which quotation from a translation of *Prometheus Bound* most effectively illustrates the claim?

(A) "O Earth, the Mighty Mother, and thou Sun, / Whose orbed light surveyeth all – attest, / What ills I suffer from the gods, a god!"

(B) "Such and so shameful is the chain / Which Heaven's new tyrant doth ordain / To bind me helpless here."

(C) "Ay, stern is Zeus, and Justice stands, / Wrenched to his purpose, in his hands –"

(D) "Such the aid / I gave the lord of heaven – my meed for which / He paid me thus, a penal recompense!"

CONTINUE ➤

15 ☐ Mark for Review

Mindfulness has been found to be useful in minimizing stress or pain as well as improving empathy. A team of researchers in Toronto was interested in testing whether short-term exposure to mindfulness treatment resulted in greater empathy and helpfulness toward a stranger. To do so, the researchers had participants in an experimental group undergo two sessions of mindfulness therapy while participants in a control group listened to a lecture on empathy and helping strangers. Then the participants watched an interview detailing a stranger's story and were evaluated on their levels of empathy and commitment to helping the stranger. Participants in the experimental group were found to have increased levels of empathy toward the stranger, while participants in the control group did not. However, both groups had similar levels of commitment to help the stranger, which suggests that _____

Which choice most logically completes the text?

- Ⓐ though mindfulness improved levels of empathy in the experimental group, there remained a greater lack of willingness to help the stranger than there was in the control group.

- Ⓑ participants in both experimental and control groups were willing to volunteer help to the stranger.

- Ⓒ short-term mindfulness can improve empathy, but more mindfulness therapy sessions are needed to change behavior.

- Ⓓ an increase in empathy does not necessarily result in an increased willingness to volunteer help.

16 ☐ Mark for Review

A large silicified sandstone block in Kent, England, dubbed the Coffin Stone, was long believed to be part of a now-destroyed chambered long barrow, a style of monument consisting of a long mound with linear ditches on each side. It was believed that the chambered long barrow would have been constructed in the fourth millennium BCE by a pastoralist community, given that such barrows are associated with agricultural traditions and were constructed during the Early Neolithic period. In the 2000s, however, archaeologists found no evidence of a chambered long barrow at the location of the Coffin Stone and determined that the stone had been placed at its current location in the 15th or 16th century. Therefore, the archaeologists concluded that _____

Which choice most logically completes the text?

- Ⓐ pastoral communities from the Early Neolithic period did not construct chambered long barrows.

- Ⓑ the Coffin Stone is not associated with a chambered long barrow.

- Ⓒ the Coffin Stone must have been part of a chambered long barrow elsewhere before it was moved.

- Ⓓ the chambered long barrow that included the Coffin Stone was destroyed in the 15th or 16th century.

CONTINUE ➡

17 🔖 Mark for Review

Most individuals in America don't walk as much as is
_____ when a group of individuals was given step-
trackers, researchers found that these individuals took
more steps.

Which choice completes the text so that it conforms to
the conventions of Standard English?

- Ⓐ recommended
- Ⓑ recommended,
- Ⓒ recommended, but
- Ⓓ recommended but

18 🔖 Mark for Review

Learning and practicing new skills over a long period
of time can cause the brain to _____ for individuals
who become blind, areas of the brain that are normally
responsible for vision may change and become involved
in other important processes, such as touch.

Which choice completes the text so that it conforms to
the conventions of Standard English?

- Ⓐ change
- Ⓑ change,
- Ⓒ change;
- Ⓓ change and

19 🔖 Mark for Review

Swedish inventor Ninni Kronberg is known for her
work on creating powdered milk. She developed
processes for milk serum and longer-lasting powdered
milk. Sweden used powdered milk produced using
Kronberg's methods as part of _____ emergency food
supply during World War II.

Which choice completes the text so that it conforms to
the conventions of Standard English?

- Ⓐ its
- Ⓑ her
- Ⓒ their
- Ⓓ one's

20 🔖 Mark for Review

Chemical engineer Kristi Anseth works with a
number of multidisciplinary teams on projects such as
developing hydrogel materials to help promote tissue
_____ a particularly important area of research
because some tissues such as cartilage cannot regrow,
unlike other tissues such as bone or muscle.

Which choice completes the text so that it conforms to
the conventions of Standard English?

- Ⓐ regeneration; and
- Ⓑ regeneration,
- Ⓒ regeneration
- Ⓓ regeneration and

CONTINUE ➜

21 🔖 Mark for Review

The jet streams are fast flowing air currents in the upper atmosphere which occur due to the Earth's rotation and can shift location over time. The movements of the northern polar jet stream _____ important for airlines looking to save time and fuel on eastbound flights.

Which choice completes the text so that it conforms to the conventions of Standard English?

- (A) has been
- (B) was
- (C) are
- (D) is

22 🔖 Mark for Review

Meiro Koizumi creates videos that explore the relationship between an individual and his or her role in a situation of _____ his videos might portray a commonplace situation converted into a site of tension or conflict and allow the viewer to process how he or she would respond in the situation.

Which choice completes the text so that it conforms to the conventions of Standard English?

- (A) conflict, for example;
- (B) conflict; for example,
- (C) conflict, for example,
- (D) conflict for example

23 🔖 Mark for Review

Quantum physicist Jacquiline Romero is working to develop a new quantum alphabet, in which a single photon can encode more information than the two binary options used in classical computing. Romero is not solely focused on _____ emphasizing that it is possible to be a parent and have a successful science career.

Which choice completes the text so that it conforms to the conventions of Standard English?

- (A) research; however,
- (B) research, however,
- (C) research, however
- (D) research, however;

24 🔖 Mark for Review

Barefoot running decreases the risk of ankle sprains, plantar fasciitis, and chronic leg injuries. _____ running in shoes decreases the risk of puncture wounds, thermal injuries, and bruising.

Which choice completes the text with the most logical transition?

- (A) Therefore,
- (B) In contrast,
- (C) Similarly,
- (D) Additionally,

CONTINUE ➡

25 ☐ Mark for Review

During the War of 1812, dispatch runners traveling between Montreal and present-day Mackinaw City, Michigan, faced difficulties with their long greatcoats in deep snow drifts. _____ a shorter jacket, the Mackinaw jacket, was developed.

Which choice completes the text with the most logical transition?

(A) Hence,

(B) Similarly,

(C) However,

(D) Furthermore,

26 ☐ Mark for Review

While researching a topic, a student has taken the following notes:

- Cargo bikes are bikes that feature built-in boxes to carry goods or people.
- Boxes can be as large as 6 square feet and carry up to 450 pounds.
- A large grocery load typically weighs around 100 pounds.
- Some cargo bikes use electric motors to assist in pedaling.
- Other cargo bikes rely solely on the rider for propulsion.

The student wants to explain the usefulness of cargo bikes for grocery shopping to an audience unfamiliar with cargo bikes. Which choice most effectively uses relevant information from the notes to accomplish this goal?

(A) Some cargo bikes use electric motors to assist in pedaling, yet other cargo bikes lack electric motors and rely on the rider's pedaling alone.

(B) A cargo bike can carry the 100-pound weight of a typical large grocery load.

(C) The built-in box of a cargo bike, intended for goods or people, can be as large as 6 square feet and carry up to 450 pounds.

(D) A cargo bike, which is a bike that features a built-in box to carry goods or people, can have a carrying capacity of up to 400 pounds, which is more than sufficient to handle the typical large grocery load of 100 pounds.

CONTINUE →

27 ☐ Mark for Review

While researching a topic, a student has taken the following notes:

- *Te lapa* is a Polynesian term for flashing light on or under the surface of the ocean.

- Polynesian sailors use te lapa to navigate by following the light towards an island.

- It is unknown what causes te lapa.

- Many phenomena have been ruled out as the causes of te lapa.

- Kent State professor Richard Feinberg has expressed skepticism about the usefulness of te lapa for navigation.

The student wants to highlight a dispute about te lapa to an audience familiar with the phenomenon. Which choice most effectively uses relevant information from the notes to accomplish this goal?

Ⓐ While it is unknown what causes te lapa, many phenomena have been ruled out as the causes of te lapa.

Ⓑ Te lapa, flashing light on or under the surface of the ocean, is used by Polynesian sailors to navigate by following the light towards an island.

Ⓒ Polynesian sailors use te lapa to navigate by following the light towards an island, but Kent State professor Richard Feinberg has expressed skepticism about the usefulness of te lapa for that purpose.

Ⓓ Kent State professor Richard Feinberg has expressed skepticism about the usefulness of te lapa—flashing lights on or under the surface of the ocean—for navigation.

STOP
**If you finish before time is called, you may check your work on this section only.
Do not turn to any other section in the test.**

THIS PAGE LEFT INTENTIONALLY BLANK.

SAT Prep Test 3—Math
Module 1

The questions in this section address a number of important math skills.
Use of a calculator is permitted for all questions.

Unless otherwise indicated:

- All variables and expressions represent real numbers.
- Figures provided are drawn to scale.
- All figures lie in a plane.
- The domain of a given function f is the set of all real numbers x for which $f(x)$ is a real number.

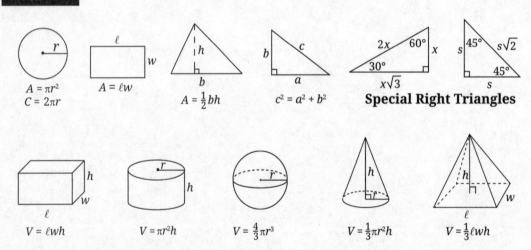

$A = \pi r^2$
$C = 2\pi r$

$A = \ell w$

$A = \frac{1}{2}bh$

$c^2 = a^2 + b^2$

Special Right Triangles

$V = \ell wh$

$V = \pi r^2 h$

$V = \frac{4}{3}\pi r^3$

$V = \frac{1}{3}\pi r^2 h$

$V = \frac{1}{3}\ell wh$

The number of degrees of arc in a circle is 360.
The number of radians of arc in a circle is 2π.
The sum of the measures in degrees of the angles of a triangle is 180.

CONTINUE

For multiple-choice questions, solve each problem, choose the correct answer from the choices provided, and then fill in the circle with the answer letter. Enter only one answer for each question. You will not get credit for questions with more than one answer entered, or for questions with no answers entered.

For student-produced response questions, solve each problem and write your answer in the test book as described below.

- Enter your answer into the box provided.
- If you find **more than one correct answer**, enter only one answer.
- Your answer can be up to 5 characters for a **positive** answer and up to 6 characters (including the negative sign) for a **negative** answer.
- If your answer is a **fraction** that is too long (over 5 characters for positive, 6 characters for negative), write the decimal equivalent.
- If your answer is a **decimal** that is too long (over 5 characters for positive, 6 characters for negative), truncate it or round at the fourth digit.
- If your answer is a **mixed number** (such as $3\frac{1}{2}$), write it as an improper fraction (7/2) or its decimal equivalent (3.5).
- Don't enter **symbols** such as a percent sign, comma, or dollar sign in your answer.

CONTINUE ➡

1 Mark for Review

If $4s = 28$, what is the value of $8s + 13$?

Ⓐ 7

Ⓑ 56

Ⓒ 69

Ⓓ 84

2 Mark for Review

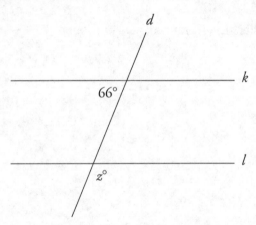

Note: Figure not drawn to scale.

In the figure, line k is parallel to line l. What is the value of z?

Ⓐ 24

Ⓑ 66

Ⓒ 106

Ⓓ 114

3 Mark for Review

Infant	Height	Infant	Height
A	25	G	22
B	22	H	26
C	23	I	30
D	27	J	21
E	24	K	27
F	30	L	25

The table shows the heights, in inches, of 12 infants at a daycare. According to the table, what is the mean height, in inches, of these infants?

4 Mark for Review

During a certain week, Jan worked j hours each day for 3 days, and Noah worked n hours each day for 5 days. Which of the following represents the total combined number of hours worked that week by Jan and Noah?

Ⓐ $3j + 5n$

Ⓑ $5j + 3n$

Ⓒ $8jn$

Ⓓ $15jn$

CONTINUE

5 ☐ Mark for Review

Which of the following is equivalent to $b^{\frac{3}{4}}$ for all values of b?

Ⓐ $\sqrt[4]{b^{\frac{1}{3}}}$

Ⓑ $\sqrt[4]{3b}$

Ⓒ $\sqrt[4]{b^3}$

Ⓓ $\sqrt[3]{b^4}$

6 ☐ Mark for Review

Species	Eye color		Total
	Yellow	Brown	
Grey wolf	16	2	18
Coyote	7	5	12
Total	23	7	30

The table shows the distribution by species and eye color for the 30 canids living in a nature conservancy. If one canid is selected at random, what is the probability that it will be either a grey wolf with yellow eyes or a coyote with brown eyes?

Ⓐ $\frac{11}{30}$

Ⓑ $\frac{17}{30}$

Ⓒ $\frac{21}{30}$

Ⓓ $\frac{23}{30}$

7 ☐ Mark for Review

A random sample of 75 students in a first-year medical school class of 265 students was surveyed to determine the distribution of blood types among the students. Based on the survey, it is estimated that 39% of the students have O-positive blood type, with an associated margin of error of 6%. Based on these results, what is a plausible number of students out of the entire first-year class who have O-positive blood type?

Ⓐ 16

Ⓑ 39

Ⓒ 74

Ⓓ 100

8 ☐ Mark for Review

$$w = 3{,}150 + 450l$$

A marine biologist uses the given equation to estimate the weight, w, of a mature great white shark, in pounds, in terms of the shark's fork length, l, in feet. Based on the equation, what is the estimated weight increase, in pounds, for each foot of growth in fork length in a great white shark?

Ⓐ 450

Ⓑ 1,350

Ⓒ 2,700

Ⓓ 3,150

CONTINUE

9 ☐ Mark for Review

$$|2x - 6| + 6 = 74$$

For the given equation, which of the following is a possible value of x?

(A) −37

(B) −31

(C) 31

(D) 34

10 ☐ Mark for Review

At the end of each year, an item loses 6% of the value that it had at the beginning of the year. What type of function best represents this scenario?

(A) Decreasing exponential

(B) Decreasing linear

(C) Increasing exponential

(D) Increasing linear

11 ☐ Mark for Review

The function f is defined by $f(x) = \frac{5}{3}x + k$, where k is a constant. If $f(90) = 120$, what is the value of $f(-30)$?

(A) −120

(B) −80

(C) −30

(D) −20

12 ☐ Mark for Review

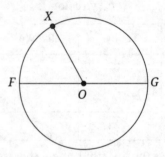

The circle shown has center O, and $\overline{FG}$ is a diameter. If the length of arc FXG is 14π, what is the length of line segment $\overline{XO}$?

(A) 7

(B) 14

(C) 28

(D) 56

CONTINUE ➤

13 ☐ Mark for Review

$$x + y = -10$$
$$2x + y = -33$$

What is the value of y in the system of equations shown?

```
┌─────────┐
│         │
│ ─────── │
└─────────┘
```

14 ☐ Mark for Review

A bank account contains $5,400 today. The account earns interest annually at a rate of 7%. The bank uses the equation $A = 5,400(r)^y$ to determine the amount of money in the account, A, after y years if no other deposits or withdrawals are made. To the nearest whole dollar, how much money will be in the account four years from now?

Ⓐ $4,039

Ⓑ $5,778

Ⓒ $6,912

Ⓓ $7,078

15 ☐ Mark for Review

$$G = \frac{ab}{d^2}$$

The given equation relates a, b, d, and G, which are distinct constants. Which of the following equations correctly expresses d^2 in terms of a, b, and G?

Ⓐ $d^2 = \frac{Gb}{a}$

Ⓑ $d^2 = \frac{Ga}{b}$

Ⓒ $d^2 = \frac{ab}{G}$

Ⓓ $d^2 = \frac{G}{ab}$

16 ☐ Mark for Review

In the xy-plane, the line determined by the points $(c, 3)$ and $(27, c)$ intersects the origin. Which of the following could be the value of c?

Ⓐ 0

Ⓑ 3

Ⓒ 6

Ⓓ 9

CONTINUE

17 🔖 Mark for Review

A certain cone has a height of 15 centimeters (cm) and a volume of 80π cm^3. What is the diameter, in cm, of this cone?

Ⓐ 4

Ⓑ 8

Ⓒ 16

Ⓓ 32

18 🔖 Mark for Review

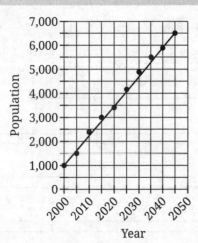

The scatterplot shows the population of town T starting in 2000 and projected through 2045. According to the line of best fit, which of the following best approximates the year in which the population of town T is projected to reach 5,000?

Ⓐ 2027

Ⓑ 2032

Ⓒ 2038

Ⓓ 2043

19 🔖 Mark for Review

In triangle DEF, angle D is a right angle. If $\sin(E) = \frac{21}{29}$, what is the value of $\sin(F)$?

20 🔖 Mark for Review

If $x = 3\sqrt{5}$ and $5x = \sqrt{5y}$, what is the value of y?

CONTINUE

21 ☐ Mark for Review

At 9:00 A.M. on Monday, a trash can with a capacity of 20 cubic feet contains 8 cubic feet of garbage. Each day after Monday, 3 cubic feet of garbage are added to the trash can. If no garbage is removed and d represents the number of days after Monday, which of the following inequalities describes the set of days for which the trash can is full or overflowing?

(A) $8 + 3d \geq 20$

(B) $12 \geq 3d$

(C) $20 - 3 \leq d$

(D) $20 \leq 3d$

22 ☐ Mark for Review

The equation of a parabola is written in the standard form $y = ax^2 + bx + c$, where a, b, and c are constants. When graphed in the xy-plane, the parabola reaches its maximum at $(-3, 8)$. Which of the following could be equivalent to $a + b + c$?

(A) -8

(B) 8

(C) 16

(D) 24

YIELD

Once you've finished (or run out of time for) this section, use the answer key to determine how many questions you got right. If you got fewer than 14 questions right, move on to Module 2—Easier, otherwise move on to Module 2—Harder.

SAT Prep Test 3—Math
Module 2—Easier

The questions in this section address a number of important math skills.
Use of a calculator is permitted for all questions.

NOTES

Unless otherwise indicated:

- All variables and expressions represent real numbers.
- Figures provided are drawn to scale.
- All figures lie in a plane.
- The domain of a given function f is the set of all real numbers x for which $f(x)$ is a real number.

REFERENCE

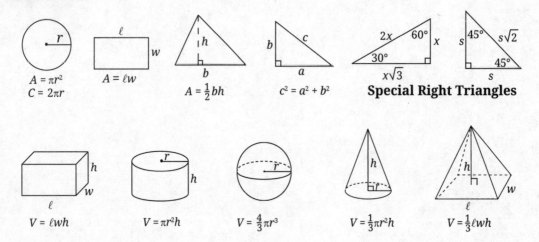

$A = \pi r^2$
$C = 2\pi r$

$A = \ell w$

$A = \frac{1}{2}bh$

$c^2 = a^2 + b^2$

Special Right Triangles

$V = \ell wh$

$V = \pi r^2 h$

$V = \frac{4}{3}\pi r^3$

$V = \frac{1}{3}\pi r^2 h$

$V = \frac{1}{3}\ell wh$

The number of degrees of arc in a circle is 360.
The number of radians of arc in a circle is 2π.
The sum of the measures in degrees of the angles of a triangle is 180.

CONTINUE

For multiple-choice questions, solve each problem, choose the correct answer from the choices provided, and then fill in the circle with the answer letter. Enter only one answer for each question. You will not get credit for questions with more than one answer entered, or for questions with no answers entered.

For student-produced response questions, solve each problem and write your answer in the test book as described below.

- Enter your answer into the box provided.
- If you find **more than one correct answer**, enter only one answer.
- Your answer can be up to 5 characters for a **positive** answer and up to 6 characters (including the negative sign) for a **negative** answer.
- If your answer is a **fraction** that is too long (over 5 characters for positive, 6 characters for negative), write the decimal equivalent.
- If your answer is a **decimal** that is too long (over 5 characters for positive, 6 characters for negative), truncate it or round at the fourth digit.
- If your answer is a **mixed number** (such as $3\frac{1}{2}$), write it as an improper fraction (7/2) or its decimal equivalent (3.5).
- Don't enter **symbols** such as a percent sign, comma, or dollar sign in your answer.

CONTINUE ➤

1 ⬚ Mark for Review

What is 90% of 1,000?

Ⓐ 90

Ⓑ 100

Ⓒ 900

Ⓓ 910

2 ⬚ Mark for Review

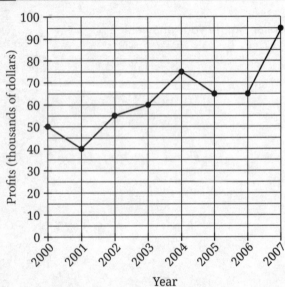

The line graph shows the annual profits of a particular clothing store from 2000 to 2007. According to the graph, in which year was the store's profit the least?

Ⓐ 2000

Ⓑ 2001

Ⓒ 2004

Ⓓ 2007

3 ⬚ Mark for Review

If $y^2 = 36$ and $y < 0$, what is the value of y?

⬚⬚⬚

4 ⬚ Mark for Review

A contractor creates a mosaic floor pattern in which there are 9 blue tiles for every 80 tiles in total. At this rate, how many blue tiles will there be in a floor pattern of 4,800 tiles?

⬚⬚⬚

5 ⬚ Mark for Review

When 6 times a number a is subtracted from 15, the result is the number b. Which of the following equations represents the relationship between a and b?

Ⓐ $\frac{15}{6a} = b$

Ⓑ $6a - 15 = b$

Ⓒ $15 - 6a = b$

Ⓓ $90a = b$

CONTINUE ➤

6 ☐ Mark for Review

The function g is defined by the equation $g(x) = 4x - 7$. What is the value of $g(x)$ when $x = -3$?

(A) -19

(B) -1

(C) 1

(D) 5

7 ☐ Mark for Review

The circumference of a circle is 56π. What is the radius of the circle?

☐

8 ☐ Mark for Review

The number of members of a club in April was three times the number of members of the club in February. If the club had 27 members in April and m members in February, which of the following equations is true?

(A) $\dfrac{m}{3} = 27$

(B) $m + 27 = 3$

(C) $3m = 27$

(D) $27m = 3$

9 ☐ Mark for Review

If $4x = 20$, what is the value of $12x - 4$?

☐

10 ☐ Mark for Review

$$g(x) = 2x^2 - 16$$

The function g is defined by the given equation. What is the value of $g(2)$?

(A) -12

(B) -8

(C) 0

(D) 3

11 ☐ Mark for Review

A ride-sharing service uses the function $g(x) = 2.40 + 0.30x$ to calculate the total charge, in dollars, for a ride that is x miles long. How long, in miles, was a ride that had a total charge of $3.60?

(A) 2

(B) 3

(C) 4

(D) 12

CONTINUE

12 ☐ Mark for Review

Which expression is equivalent to $(4x^2 + 3x - 2) - (3x^2 - 8x + 9)$?

(A) $x^2 - 5x - 11$

(B) $x^2 + 11x - 11$

(C) $x^2 + 11x + 7$

(D) $7x^2 + 11x - 11$

13 ☐ Mark for Review

x	1	2	3	4	5
$g(x)$	–3	1	5	9	13

The table shows selected values of the linear function g. Which of the following best defines g?

(A) $g(x) = x - 1$

(B) $g(x) = 2x - 4$

(C) $g(x) = 3x - 5$

(D) $g(x) = 4x - 7$

14 ☐ Mark for Review

$$4x - 1 \leq y$$
$$2 > x + y$$

Which of the following ordered pairs (x, y) satisfies the given system of inequalities?

(A) $(-3, -1)$

(B) $(2, -5)$

(C) $(3, 1)$

(D) $(4, -1)$

15 ☐ Mark for Review

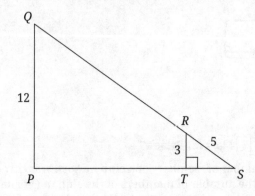

In the figure, $\overline{PQ}$ is parallel to $\overline{RT}$. What is the length of $\overline{PS}$?

CONTINUE →

16 ☐ Mark for Review

The population of a small town is currently 800. It is estimated that the population of the town will decrease by 14% per year for the next five years. This estimate is modeled by the equation $P = 800(k)^x$, where P is the population of the town after x years. What value should be used for k in this model?

17 ☐ Mark for Review

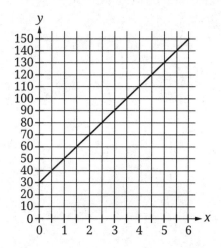

The graph shows the relationship between x and y. Which of the following could be the equation of the graph?

Ⓐ $y = 25x$

Ⓑ $y = x + 30$

Ⓒ $y = 10x + 30$

Ⓓ $y = 20x + 30$

18 ☐ Mark for Review

$$g(x) = \sqrt{4x^2 + 28}$$

The function g is defined by the given equation. For what value of x does $g(x) = 8$?

Ⓐ 3

Ⓑ 4

Ⓒ 5

Ⓓ 6

19 ☐ Mark for Review

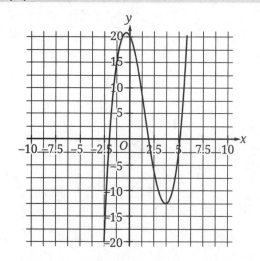

The function f is graphed in the xy-plane, where $y = f(x)$. Which of the following could be the equation of $f(x)$?

Ⓐ $f(x) = (x - 5)(x - 2)^2$

Ⓑ $f(x) = (x - 5)(x - 2)(x + 2)$

Ⓒ $f(x) = (x - 2)(x + 2)(x + 5)$

Ⓓ $f(x) = (x + 5)(x + 2)^2$

CONTINUE ▶

20 ☐ Mark for Review

When three numbers are added together, the result is 665. The largest number is four-thirds the sum of the other two numbers. What is the value of the largest number?

(A) 95

(B) 245

(C) 350

(D) 380

21 ☐ Mark for Review

$$y = x^2 + 2x + k$$
$$y = 2x$$

If the given system of equations has exactly one real solution, which of the following is the value of k?

(A) −4

(B) 0

(C) 2

(D) 4

CONTINUE

22 Mark for Review

$$LM = 180$$
$$MN = 385$$
$$NL = 425$$

Triangles LMN and PQR are similar right triangles, where L corresponds to P and M corresponds to Q. The side lengths of triangle LMN are shown. What is the value of $\cos R$?

(A) $\frac{36}{85}$

(B) $\frac{36}{77}$

(C) $\frac{77}{85}$

(D) $\frac{85}{36}$

STOP
**If you finish before time is called, you may check your work on this section only.
Do not turn to any other section.**

SAT Prep Test 3—Math
Module 2—Harder

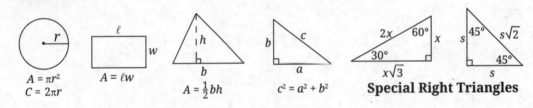

$A = \pi r^2$
$C = 2\pi r$

$A = \ell w$

$A = \frac{1}{2}bh$

$c^2 = a^2 + b^2$

Special Right Triangles

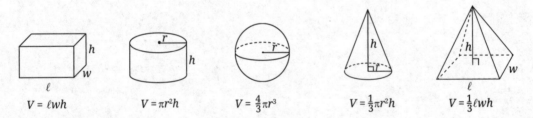

$V = \ell wh$

$V = \pi r^2 h$

$V = \frac{4}{3}\pi r^3$

$V = \frac{1}{3}\pi r^2 h$

$V = \frac{1}{3}\ell wh$

The number of degrees of arc in a circle is 360.
The number of radians of arc in a circle is 2π.
The sum of the measures in degrees of the angles of a triangle is 180.

CONTINUE

For multiple-choice questions, solve each problem, choose the correct answer from the choices provided, and then fill in the circle with the answer letter. Enter only one answer for each question. You will not get credit for questions with more than one answer entered, or for questions with no answers entered.

For student-produced response questions, solve each problem and write your answer in the test book as described below.

- Enter your answer into the box provided.
- If you find **more than one correct answer**, enter only one answer.
- Your answer can be up to 5 characters for a **positive** answer and up to 6 characters (including the negative sign) for a **negative** answer.
- If your answer is a **fraction** that is too long (over 5 characters for positive, 6 characters for negative), write the decimal equivalent.
- If your answer is a **decimal** that is too long (over 5 characters for positive, 6 characters for negative), truncate it or round at the fourth digit.
- If your answer is a **mixed number** (such as $3\frac{1}{2}$), write it as an improper fraction (7/2) or its decimal equivalent (3.5).
- Don't enter **symbols** such as a percent sign, comma, or dollar sign in your answer.

CONTINUE ➤

---

1 ☐ Mark for Review

The expression $5a^3 - 3a^3 + 6a^2$ is equivalent to which of the following expressions?

(A) $2a^3 + 6a^2$

(B) $5a^3 + 3a^2$

(C) $6a^2 - 15a^6$

(D) $8a^2$

2 ☐ Mark for Review

x	$g(x)$
2	−4
3	−2
4	0
5	2

The table shows four values of x and their corresponding values of $g(x)$ for function g. Which equation defines function g?

(A) $g(x) = x - 6$

(B) $g(x) = 2x - 8$

(C) $g(x) = 3x - 12$

(D) $g(x) = 4x - 12$

3 ☐ Mark for Review

Yesterday, Tiki cycled 13 fewer miles than Irina. If the two of them cycled a total of 51 miles yesterday, how many miles did Irina cycle?

(A) 19

(B) 32

(C) 38

(D) 64

4 ☐ Mark for Review

$$8x - 5y = 27$$
$$5x + 10y = 30$$

The solution set of the given system of equations is (x, y). What is the value of y?

5 ☐ Mark for Review

$$g(x) = 2x^2 - kx + 14$$

Function g is defined by the given equation. If the graph of function g in the xy-plane contains the point $(4, -2)$, what is the value of k?

CONTINUE →

6 ☐ Mark for Review

The total rainfall, in inches, for a certain county from 2010 to 2020 can be modeled by the equation $y = -0.14x + 7.8$, where x is the number of years since 2010 and y is the total annual rainfall. Which of the following is the best interpretation of the number -0.14 in this context?

(A) The total annual rainfall in 2010

(B) The total annual rainfall in 2020

(C) The difference between the total rainfall in 2010 and the total rainfall in 2020

(D) The decrease in average rainfall per year from 2010 to 2020

7 ☐ Mark for Review

$$3y < 7$$
$$x < 3y + 4$$

If the point (x, y) is a solution to the given system of inequalities, what is the greatest possible integer value of x?

☐

8 ☐ Mark for Review

$$-3x + 4y = 5$$

In the xy-plane, the graph of which of the following equations is perpendicular to the graph of the given equation?

(A) $3x + 6y = 5$

(B) $3x + 8y = 2$

(C) $4x + 3y = 5$

(D) $4x + 6y = 5$

9 ☐ Mark for Review

Banerji currently owns 6,500 baseball cards. He is gradually selling his collection and estimates that the number of cards he owns will decrease by 20 percent every 6 months. Which of the following functions best models Banerji's estimate of the number of baseball cards, B, he will own m months from now?

(A) $B(m) = 6,500(0.2)^{\frac{m}{6}}$

(B) $B(m) = 6,500(0.2)^{6m}$

(C) $B(m) = 6,500(0.8)^{\frac{m}{6}}$

(D) $B(m) = 6,500(0.8)^{6m}$

CONTINUE

10 ▢ Mark for Review

The volume of a cube is $v = \frac{1}{8}c^3$, where c is a positive constant. Which of the following gives the surface area of the cube?

(A) $6\left(\frac{c}{2}\right)^2$

(B) $6\left(\frac{c^2}{2}\right)$

(C) $6c^2$

(D) $12c^2$

11 ▢ Mark for Review

$$y = (x - 7)(3x + 4)$$
$$x = 3y - 1$$

At how many points do the graphs of the given equations intersect in the xy-plane?

(A) Exactly one

(B) Exactly two

(C) Infinitely many

(D) Zero

12 ▢ Mark for Review

Jessica owns a store that sells only laptops and tablets. Last week, her store sold 90 laptops and 210 tablets. This week, the sales, in number of units, of laptops increased by 50 percent, and the sales, in number of units, of tablets increased by 30 percent. By what percentage did total sales, in units, in Jessica's store increase?

(A) 20 percent

(B) 25 percent

(C) 36 percent

(D) 80 percent

13 ▢ Mark for Review

$$-2(5 - 9x) = 6(3x + 4)$$

The given equation has how many solutions?

(A) Exactly one

(B) Exactly two

(C) Infinitely many

(D) Zero

CONTINUE

14 ◻ Mark for Review

The mean weight of 6 people in an elevator is 160.5 pounds. If the person with the lowest weight gets off, the mean weight of the remaining 5 people becomes 168 pounds. What is the weight, in pounds, of the person with the lowest weight?

15 ◻ Mark for Review

$$4x^2 - 5x = k$$

In the given equation, k is a constant. If the equation has two real solutions, which of the following could be the value of k?

Ⓐ −4

Ⓑ −3

Ⓒ −2

Ⓓ −1

16 ◻ Mark for Review

$$x^2 = y$$
$$6x + 9 = -3(2y - 3)$$

If (x, y) is a solution to the given system of equations and $x < 0$, what is the value of xy?

Ⓐ −3

Ⓑ −2

Ⓒ −1

Ⓓ 1

17 ◻ Mark for Review

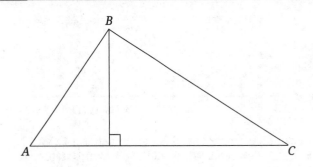

In triangle ABC, $\sin(A) = \cos(C)$. If angle A measures $6m - 9$ degrees and angle C measures $8m - 6$ degrees, what is the value of m?

Ⓐ 5.4

Ⓑ 7.5

Ⓒ 10.5

Ⓓ 13.5

CONTINUE

18 ⬚ Mark for Review

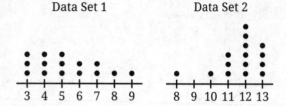

Data Set 1   Data Set 2

The dot plots represent 15 values in data set 1 and 15 values in data set 2. Which of the following statements about the standard deviations and ranges of the two data sets is true?

(A) The standard deviation of data set 1 is less than the standard deviation of data set 2, and the range of data set 1 is greater than the range of data set 2.

(B) The standard deviation of data set 1 is less than the standard deviation of data set 2, and the range of data set 1 is equal to the range of data set 2.

(C) The standard deviation of data set 1 is greater than the standard deviation of data set 2, and the range of data set 1 is equal to the range of data set 2.

(D) The standard deviation of data set 1 is greater than the standard deviation of data set 2, and the range of data set 1 is greater than the range of data set 2.

19 ⬚ Mark for Review

$$\frac{1}{2}x + ay = 16$$
$$4y = 48 - bx$$

In the given system of equations, a and b are constants. If there are infinitely many solutions to this system, what is the value of $a + b$?

⬚

20 ⬚ Mark for Review

In the equation $43x^2 + (43d + e)x + de = 0$, d and e are positive constants. If the sum of the solutions to the given equation is $k(43d + e)$, where k is a constant, what is the value of k?

(A) $-\frac{1}{45}$

(B) $-\frac{1}{43}$

(C) 43

(D) 45

CONTINUE ➡

21 ☐ Mark for Review

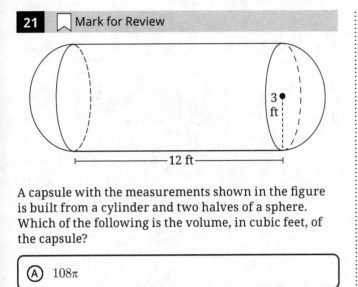

12 ft

3 ft

A capsule with the measurements shown in the figure is built from a cylinder and two halves of a sphere. Which of the following is the volume, in cubic feet, of the capsule?

(A) 108π

(B) 126π

(C) 144π

(D) 180π

22 ☐ Mark for Review

In the xy-plane, the graph of $4x^2 + 20x + 4y^2 - 12y = 110$ is a circle. What is the radius of the circle?

[answer box]

STOP
If you finish before time is called, you may check your work on this section only.
Do not turn to any other section.

Chapter 6
Practice Test 3:
Answers and
Explanations

PRACTICE TEST 3: MULTIPLE-CHOICE ANSWER KEY

Reading and Writing		
Module 1	Module 2 (Easier)	Module 2 (Harder)
1. A	1. A	1. B
2. B	2. D	2. B
3. D	3. A	3. D
4. A	4. A	4. C
5. A	5. C	5. B
6. B	6. D	6. C
7. D	7. D	7. A
8. A	8. D	8. C
9. C	9. B	9. C
10. B	10. B	10. D
11. A	11. D	11. D
12. D	12. D	12. A
13. A	13. A	13. C
14. B	14. D	14. B
15. D	15. A	15. D
16. C	16. D	16. B
17. D	17. A	17. C
18. C	18. A	18. C
19. A	19. A	19. A
20. A	20. B	20. B
21. A	21. B	21. C
22. A	22. D	22. B
23. A	23. D	23. B
24. D	24. D	24. B
25. D	25. B	25. A
26. D	26. D	26. D
27. A	27. B	27. C

Math		
Module 1	Module 2 (Easier)	Module 2 (Harder)
1. C	1. D	1. A
2. D	2. B	2. B
3. 25.16 or 25.17	3. −6	3. B
4. A	4. 540	4. 1
5. C	5. C	5. 12
6. C	6. A	6. D
7. D	7. 28	7. 10
8. A	8. C	8. C
9. B	9. 56	9. C
10. A	10. B	10. A
11. B	11. C	11. B
12. B	12. B	12. C
13. 13	13. D	13. D
14. D	14. A	14. 123
15. C	15. 16	15. D
16. D	16. 0.86 or .86	16. C
17. B	17. D	17. B
18. B	18. A	18. D
19. $\frac{20}{29}$	19. B	19. $\frac{17}{6}$ or 2.833
20. 225	20. D	20. B
21. A	21. B	21. C
22. A	22. C	22. 6

PRACTICE TEST 3—READING AND WRITING EXPLANATIONS

Module 1

1. **A** This is a Vocabulary question, as it asks for *the most logical and precise word or phrase*. Read the text and highlight what can help to fill in the blank, which describes the *performances*. The text describes the group as *working to preserve customary songs and dances* and mentions the *centuries-old ritual*. Write "customary" in the annotation box and use Process of Elimination.

    •   (A) is correct because it matches with "customary."

    •   (B) is wrong because *obscure* means "little-known."

    •   (C) is wrong because *discreet* means "not publicly shown."

    •   (D) is wrong because *eccentric* means "unusual."

2. **B** This is a Vocabulary question, as it asks for *the most logical and precise word or phrase*. Read the text and highlight what can help to fill in the blank, which describes the *center*. The text says that it is *filled with throngs of people* and later mentions *crowds*, so write "crowded" in the annotation box and use Process of Elimination.

    •   (A) is wrong because *formal* means "done ceremoniously."

    •   (B) is correct because *bustling* matches with "crowded."

    •   (C) is wrong because *unpredictable* doesn't match with "crowded."

    •   (D) is wrong because *deserted* is the opposite of "crowded."

3. **D** This is a Vocabulary question, as it asks for *the most logical and precise word or phrase*. Read the text and highlight what can help to fill in the blank, which refers to something that can happen during *the procedure*. The text states that Peyman's research allowed him to *reduce the incidence* of something, and considering the positive tone of the text, he accomplished something good. Therefore, he must have reduced the incidence of "bad things happening." Write that in the annotation box and use Process of Elimination.

    •   (A) is wrong because *characteristics* doesn't match with "bad things happening."

    •   (B) and (C) are wrong because they are positive words.

    •   (D) is correct because *repercussions* matches with "bad things happening."

4. **A**   This is a Vocabulary question, as it asks for *the most logical and precise word or phrase*. Read the text and highlight what can help to fill in the blank, which refers to what rainwater does *in a large vessel*. The text describes *gathering and reserving water*, so the vessel must "gather" the water. Write "gathered" in the annotation box and use Process of Elimination.

    •   (A) is correct because *aggregated* means "collected together."

    •   (B) is wrong because *dissipated* means "went away," which is the opposite.

    •   (C) is wrong because *percolated* means "filtered through."

    •   (D) is wrong because *collaborated* means "worked as a team."

5. **A**   This is a Vocabulary question, as it asks for the most logical and precise word or phrase. Read the text and highlight what can help to fill in the blank, which refers to what *scientists* were *finally able to* do with respect to *the existence of the long-predicted Higgs boson particle*. The final sentence says *These scientists confirmed* something that *could be explained only by the Higgs boson particle*, so write "confirm" in the annotation box and use Process of Elimination.

    •   (A) is correct because it matches with "confirm."

    •   (B) is wrong because *exonerate* means "free from blame."

    •   (C) is wrong because *contextualize* means "give background information."

    •   (D) is wrong because *postulate* means "theorize."

6. **B**   This is a Vocabulary question, as it asks for *the most logical and precise word or phrase*. Read the text and highlight what can help to fill in the blank, which refers to what King did to *his commitment to nonviolent resistance*. The first part of the sentence is followed by a colon, which suggests that the second part will expand on the first. It states that *his actions revealed his unwavering dedication to advancing the cause…without resorting to violence*, which suggests that he was committed to nonviolent resistance and showed it through his actions. Write "showed" in the annotation box and use Process of Elimination.

    •   (A) is wrong because he didn't *characterize* his commitment through his actions.

    •   (B) is correct because *evinced* means "showed clearly."

    •   (C) is wrong because *elided* means "passed over."

    •   (D) is wrong because *gauged* means "assessed."

7. **D** This is a Purpose question, as it asks for the *function* of a sentence. Read the text and highlight what can help to understand the function of the underlined sentence. The text introduces an *experiment* and states the *evidence* provided by the experiment. Then, in the underlined sentence, the text explains what was done in the experiment. Write "describe the experiment" in the annotation box and use Process of Elimination.

- (A) is wrong because the *results* are given in other sentences, not the underlined one.

- (B) is wrong because this sentence doesn't mention any *difficulty*.

- (C) is wrong because the sentence gives an overall explanation of the study, not *a specific instance*.

- (D) is correct because it matches the annotation.

8. **A** This is a Retrieval question, as it says *According to the text*. Read the text and highlight what it says about the *granddaughter and grandfather*. The third sentence says *There was a strong family resemblance between them*, and the text goes on to describe how they were *struck from the same matrix* but differ because of their ages. Eliminate any answer that isn't supported by the text.

- (A) is correct because it matches with *strong family resemblance between them*.

- (B) is wrong because the text says that they would make one think of *beautiful Greek medals struck from the same matrix*, not that they are *of Greek heritage*.

- (C) is wrong because neither is described as looking *younger*.

- (D) is wrong because the text states that the granddaughter *knelt* near the grandfather.

9. **C** This is a Charts question, as it asks for *data from the graph*. The graph charts the number of pigeons in both spring and winter, based on the number of restaurants nearby. Highlight the conclusion in the text, which is that *there is indeed a relationship between proximity to restaurants and abundance of rock pigeons* and *this relationship was especially strong in the spring*. Look at the line for spring and eliminate any answers that are inconsistent with the graph or don't support the conclusion.

- (A) is wrong because *three restaurants* doesn't correspond with *ten rock pigeons*.

- (B) is wrong because these numbers are consistent with the winter line, but the conclusion is about *spring*.

- (C) is correct because the information is consistent with the graph and the conclusion.

- (D) is wrong because *more than thirty rock pigeons* weren't observed anywhere.

10. **B** This is a Main Idea question, as it asks for the *main idea*. Read and highlight the main phrases or lines that the other sentences seem to support. The text introduces Wickramasinghe's viewpoint, that *life on Earth originated from microorganisms that were carried to our planet by comets or other celestial bodies*. Then, it mentions the *sources of scientific data* that Wickramasinghe uses to support this view. Write "CW thinks life came from space" in the annotation box and use Process of Elimination.

- (A) is wrong because the text describes the theory as *controversial* but doesn't go so far as to say that it can't be *accepted by other astrobiologists*.

- (B) is correct because it matches the annotation.

- (C) is wrong because the text describes the theory as *controversial* and does not state that the *preponderance* (majority) of data *strongly supports* the theory.

- (D) is wrong because the main idea is about Wickramasinghe's theory, not specifics about *microorganisms*.

11. **A** This is a Claims question, as it asks for an answer that would *strengthen the potential explanation*. Read the text and highlight the *potential explanation*, which is that *metabolizing sorbitol prevents C. difficile from producing toxins*. Read more of the text to understand what this is explaining. The third sentence says that *higher levels of sorbitol…were found to be released* as a result of *C. difficile* inflammation. Then the text describes a study in which *mice that ingested sorbitol were found to have lower levels of toxin production than mice that did not ingest sorbitol*. Eliminate answers that don't *strengthen* the given explanation for this outcome.

- (A) is correct because it provides a reason that ingesting sorbitol would reduce the production of toxins.

- (B) and (D) are wrong because they don't mention *toxins*.

- (C) is wrong because giving sorbitol to the mice caused *lower levels of toxins*, so *Low levels of sorbitol* preventing toxin production contradicts the explanation.

12. **D** This is a Conclusions question, as it asks for the choice that *most logically completes the text*. Read the text and highlight the main ideas. The text states that *Scholars generally agree that amputations were dangerous and deadly prior to 10,000 years ago* and then states that the first known *successful limb-removal surgery* was 7,000 years ago. Then, the text describes a recent discovery of a *31,000-year-old skeleton* that had a successful amputation. Eliminate any answer that states a conclusion that isn't supported by the text.

- (A) is wrong because the text doesn't provide evidence suggesting that it must have been a *doctor* who did the amputation.

- (B) is wrong because there is no information on *life as an amputee* or *post-operational care*.

- (C) is wrong because the text offers no information about *most amputations*.

- (D) is correct because the text contrasts the viewpoint that *a lack of proper surgical tools and techniques* prevented successful amputations prior to 10,000 years ago with the fact that a successful one did occur long before that.

13. **A** This is a Conclusions question, as it asks for the choice that *most logically completes the text*. Read the text and highlight the main ideas. The text introduces *the prisoner's dilemma* and then describes possible outcomes. Then it explains that *Game theorists generally agree that the choice to cooperate…is irrational, as it defies one's self-interest*, suggesting that the choice to not cooperate (betray the other person) is rational. Eliminate any answer that states a conclusion that isn't supported by the text.

- (A) is correct because it logically follows from the information in the last sentence.

- (B) is wrong because, while this might provide a benefit to both people, the *game theorists* are focused on what is *rational*, which the text says refers to acting in *one's self-interest*.

- (C) is wrong because it's too strong; there is no evidence that people *always* act in their self-interest, even if the text says that this is *rational*.

- (D) is wrong because there is no information in the text regarding the *relevance* of the thought experiment to *everyday life*.

14. **B** In this Rules question, pronouns and apostrophes are changing in the answer choices, so it's testing consistency with pronouns. Find and highlight the phrase that the pronoun refers back to: *Karni Mata Temple*. This phrase is singular, so in order to be consistent, a singular pronoun is needed. Eliminate any answer that isn't consistent with *Karni Mata Temple* or is incorrectly punctuated.

- (A) is wrong because it means "it is."

- (B) is correct because it is singular and possessive.

- (C) and (D) are wrong because they are plural.

15. **D** In this Rules question, punctuation is changing in the answer choices. The first part of the sentence says *In addition to her research into the effects of hormones, ultraviolet light, and chemotherapy agents on cell division*, which is an introductory phrase that is not essential to the meaning of the sentence. It should therefore be followed by a comma to separate it from the rest of the sentence. Eliminate answers that do not have a comma.

- (A), (B), and (C) are wrong because they don't use a comma.

- (D) is correct because it uses a comma after the non-essential information.

16.   **C**   In this Rules question, punctuation is changing in the answer choices. Look for independent clauses. The first part of the sentence says *Poetra Asantewa is a performer from Ghana who combines three elements to create her pieces*, which is an independent clause. The second part of the sentence says *lyrics incorporating social issues, vocalization evoking different emotions, and rhythms using soulful elements*, which is a list of what she combines. Eliminate any option that doesn't correctly connect the independent clause to the list.

- (A) is wrong because some punctuation is needed to separate the independent clause from the list.

- (B) is wrong because the comma makes it look like *create her pieces* is part of the list, but it's not.

- (C) is correct because a colon is used when the second part explains the first, such as by providing a list of things.

- (D) is wrong because a semicolon can only connect two independent clauses, and the list isn't an independent clause.

17.   **D**   In this Rules question, the subjects of the answers are changing, which suggests it may be testing modifiers. Look for and highlight a modifying phrase: *Compared to other Ukrainian scientists and mathematicians*. Whoever is *Compared to* other scientists and mathematicians needs to come immediately after the comma. Eliminate any answer that doesn't start with someone who can be compared to scientists and mathematicians.

- (A) is wrong because *there is* can't be compared with scientists and mathematicians.

- (B) is wrong because *many Ukrainian cities* can't be compared with scientists and mathematicians.

- (C) is wrong because *the range of fields* can't be compared with scientists and mathematicians.

- (D) is correct because *Olena Vaneeva* can be compared with other scientists and mathematicians.

18.   **C**   In this Rules question, commas and the word *that* are changing in the answers, which suggests that the question is testing the construction of describing phrases. The first part of the sentence says *During the mission, Anders took a photo of Earth rising above the lunar surface*, which is an independent clause followed by a comma. Eliminate any answer that isn't consistent with the first part of the sentence.

- (A) is wrong because a phrase starting with *that* is essential to the meaning of the sentence and never follows a comma.

- (B) is wrong because it creates two independent clauses separated by a comma, which is never allowed.

- (C) is correct because it correctly forms a phrase to describe the *image*.

- (D) is wrong because it leaves the verb *was* with no subject.

19. **A**   In this Rules question, verbs are changing in the answer choices, so it's testing consistency with verbs. Find and highlight the subject, *writers*, which is plural, so a plural verb is needed. All of the answers work with a plural subject, so look for a clue regarding tense. The previous sentence uses past tense verbs: *was* and *was completed*. Highlight those verbs, which are past tense, and write an annotation that says "past." Eliminate any answer not in past tense.

- (A) is correct because it's in past tense.

- (B) and (D) are wrong because they're in present tense.

- (C) is wrong because it's in future tense.

20. **A**   In this Rules question, punctuation with a transition is changing in the answer choices. Look for independent clauses. The first part of the sentence says *Françoise Combes has contributed to research about how galaxies form and evolve*. There is an option to add *additionally* to this independent clause, but it's not adding on to a previous idea as nothing came before it. Eliminate options with *additionally* in the first part.

- (A) is correct because it puts *additionally* with the second independent clause and puts a semi-colon between the independent clauses.

- (B) and (C) are wrong because the sentence contains two independent clauses, which need some punctuation other than commas to properly connect them.

- (D) is wrong because it puts *additionally* with the first independent clause.

21. **A**   In this Rules question, commas and semicolons are changing in the answer choices. The sentence already contains a semicolon near the end, and the part after it is not an independent clause, which suggests that the sentence contains a list separated by semicolons. Use the third example to determine the structure of each item: Title, Comma, Description. Make an annotation of this pattern and eliminate any answer that doesn't follow it.

- (A) is correct because it follows the pattern of the third item.

- (B) is wrong because it doesn't have a comma after the title of the second album.

- (C) and (D) are wrong because they don't have a semicolon after the first item.

22. **A**   This is a transition question, so highlight ideas that relate to each other. The preceding sentence says *Cooler room temperatures were found to stimulate fat cells that eradicate the sugar molecules that sustain cancer cells*, and this sentence says *the cancer cells started to die off in the mice exposed to cooler room temperatures*. These ideas agree, so a same-direction transition is needed. Make an annotation that says "agree." Eliminate any answer that doesn't match.

- (A) is correct because *Consequently* is same-direction and conveys that the events of the third sentence happened as a result of what was said in the second sentence.

- (B) is wrong because this sentence is not an example of the previous idea.

- (C) and (D) are wrong because they are opposite-direction transitions.

23. **A** This is a Rhetorical Synthesis question, so highlight the goal(s) stated in the question: *emphasize how Apu changed throughout the trilogy*. Eliminate any answer that doesn't fulfill this purpose.

- (A) is correct because it includes *how Apu changed* and specifies when those changes occurred within the *trilogy*.

- (B) and (C) are wrong because they don't mention a change.

- (D) is wrong because it doesn't explain how the changes occurred in relation to the *trilogy*.

24. **D** This is a Rhetorical Synthesis question, so highlight the goal(s) stated in the question: *emphasize the abilities of haenyeo*. Eliminate any answer that doesn't fulfill this purpose.

- (A) and (B) are wrong because they don't mention any specific abilities.

- (C) is wrong because it doesn't include specific details about the *abilities*.

- (D) is correct because it includes specific details about the *abilities*.

25. **D** This is a Rhetorical Synthesis question, so highlight the goal(s) stated in the question: *describe the history of Heliconian Hall to an audience familiar with the Heliconian Club*. Eliminate any answer that doesn't *describe the history* in a way that assumes the audience is *familiar with the Heliconian Club*.

- (A) is wrong because it explains the *Heliconian Club*, but the audience is already familiar with it.

- (B) and (C) are wrong because they don't *describe the history of Heliconian Hall*.

- (D) is correct because describes the *history of Heliconian Hall* and doesn't explain the *Heliconian Club* since the audience is familiar with it.

26. **D** This is a Rhetorical Synthesis question, so highlight the goal(s) stated in the question: *introduce Evan Adams and his role in Smoke Signals to a new audience*. Eliminate any answer that doesn't *introduce Evan Adams* in a way that assumes the audience is not familiar with him.

- (A) is wrong because it doesn't focus on Adams's *role in Smoke Signals*.

- (B) is wrong because it doesn't *introduce Evan Adams*.

- (C) is wrong because it doesn't mention Adams's specific *role in Smoke Signals*.

- (D) is correct because it introduces *Evan Adams* and describes *his role in Smoke Signals*.

27.   **A**   This is a Rhetorical Synthesis question, so highlight the goal(s) stated in the question: *highlight a simi-larity between fictional depictions of a real-world location*. Eliminate any answer that doesn't fulfill this purpose.

- (A) is correct because it includes a *similarity*.

- (B) and (C) are wrong because they don't include a *similarity*.

- (D) is wrong because the similarity is set up as a contrast with the word *however*.

Module 2 – Easier

1.   **A**   This is a Vocabulary question, as it asks for *the most logical and precise word or phrase*. Read the text and highlight what can help to fill in the blank, which refers to what *hundreds of scientists* did with regards to *the Manhattan Project*. Right after this, the text says that they were *pooling their efforts and expertise*, so write "worked together on" in the annotation box and use Process of Elimination.

- (A) is correct because it matches with "worked together on."

- (B), (C), and (D) are wrong because they don't match with "worked together on."

2.   **D**   This is a Vocabulary question, as it asks for *the most logical and precise word or phrase*. Read the text and highlight what can help to fill in the blank, which refers to something previously mentioned (given the word *This*) that *allows for soil to remain settled while seeds are planted, unlike traditional practices*. Thus, the blank must be another *practice*, and specifically it's *the method of no-till farming*, mentioned in the first sentence. Write "method" in the annotation box and use Process of Elimination.

- (A) is wrong because *intention* means "goal."

- (B) is wrong because *agenda* means "plan."

- (C) is wrong because *distraction* doesn't match with "method."

- (D) is correct because *technique* matches with "method."

3.   **A**   This is a Vocabulary question, as it asks for *the most logical and precise word or phrase*. Read the text and highlight what can help to fill in the blank, which comes after the words *This silent*, so it refers to something that was previously mentioned. The first sentence refers to the *"waggle dance"* that allows bees to *communicate with other bees*. Given that the blank is followed by *of information*, the blank must be something like "communication." Write that in the annotation box and use Process of Elimination.

- (A) is correct because it matches with "communication."

- (B) is wrong because *confidence* doesn't match with "communication."

- (C) is wrong because *prolongation* means "lasting longer than planned."

- (D) is wrong because *devastation* means "destruction."

4. **A**   This is a Vocabulary question, as it asks for *the most logical and precise word or phrase*. Read the text and highlight what can help to fill in the blank, which refers to how chronic hepatitis B *affects Asian Americans and Pacific Islanders*. The second sentence draws a contrast between *everyone* needing to be screened for the disease and AAPIs being particularly encouraged to do so. This suggests that this group of people is overly affected by the disease compared to the general population. Write "overly" in the annotation box and use Process of Elimination.

  •   (A) is correct because *disproportionately* means "more or less than the general population."

  •   (B) is wrong because *exclusively* is too strong; the second sentence states that *everyone should be screened*, so it's not true that the disease only affects AAPIs.

  •   (C) is wrong because *essentially* means "at its essence."

  •   (D) is wrong because *initially* means "at the beginning."

5. **C**   This is a Vocabulary question, as it asks for *the most logical and precise word or phrase*. Read the text and highlight what can help to fill in the blank, which refers to how *Scientists* view *canities subita*. The second sentence indicates that scientists have an explanation that contradicts the *stories* from the first sentence, and the part after the blank says *as historical fiction*, which suggests that they think the stories are historical fiction. It is unclear whether the blank suggests a word like "describe" or a word like "reject," so use Process of Elimination to eliminate any answer that doesn't clearly indicate that the scientists don't believe the stories.

  •   (A) is wrong because *trivialize* means "portray as unimportant," which doesn't convey the scientists' skepticism.

  •   (B) is wrong because there is no evidence from the text that scientists are illustrating the condition.

  •   (C) is correct because *Scientists dismiss this as historical fiction* accurately conveys their viewpoint.

  •   (D) is wrong because there isn't evidence that scientists are promoting their point of view, just that they disagree with the *stories*.

6. **D**   This is a Vocabulary question, as it asks what a word *most nearly means*. Read the text and highlight what can help to understand the underlined word. Marie instructs Francine to *sweep the carpet* in order to *bring out the colors*, which is one of several instructions given to make the room look nicer. Write "make it look better" in the annotation box and use Process of Elimination.

  •   (A) and (B) are wrong because these words wouldn't suggest improving the look of the room.

  •   (C) is wrong because it would suggest that the carpet doesn't have any color prior to being swept, which isn't implied by the text.

  •   (D) is correct because emphasizing the colors would help the look of the room.

7. **D** This is a Purpose question, as it asks for the *overall structure*. Read the text and highlight what can help to understand the overall structure. In the text, Elinor mentions *mistakes* she has *frequently* made, thinking someone is a certain way but the person isn't that way. Then, in the last sentence, she says that this is caused by not *giving oneself time to deliberate and judge*, so write "Elinor's mistake and why people make it" in the annotation box and use Process of Elimination.

    •   (A) is wrong because Elinor never *promises to be more careful in the future*.

    •   (B) is wrong because the text isn't about a specific *individual*, and Elinor doesn't rationalize her *mistaken perception*.

    •   (C) is wrong because it's too strong; *duplicity* (deceitfulness) *of human nature* is much broader than the mistake Elinor mentions, and her assessment of the cause isn't a *warning*.

    •   (D) is correct because it matches the annotation.

8. **D** This is a Purpose question, as it asks for the *overall structure*. Read the text and highlight what can help to understand the overall structure. The text introduces *afforestation* and then describes the steps that go into that process, so write "how afforestation is done" in the annotation box and use Process of Elimination.

    •   (A) is wrong because it only relates to the first sentence, not the *overall structure*.

    •   (B) is wrong because the text lists the steps for the *strategy*, not the *reasons why the strategy is useful*.

    •   (C) is wrong because no *negative consequences* are mentioned.

    •   (D) is correct because it matches the annotation.

9. **B** This is a Dual Texts question, as it has two texts. The question asks what *Newman, Stone, and Schwarz (Text 2)* would *say about the results of the studies discussed in Text 1*. Start by understanding the *results of the studies* in Text 1. Text 1 states that *The results of the studies demonstrated a relationship between nostalgia and authenticity*, and then says that this *was found to correlate with greater measurements of all aspects of psychological well-being*. Next, look for a similar idea in Text 2 to see how its author feels about this view. Text 2 begins by acknowledging that *nostalgia is associated with mental health benefits* but then draws a contrast by saying that *there are different types of nostalgia* and *some can be highly destructive*. Then, it describes a study that found that some *more unconscious nostalgic experiences can result in negative mental health effects*. Therefore, the psychologists in Text 2 would "say some kinds of nostalgia are bad." Write that in the annotation box and use Process of Elimination.

    •   (A) and (C) are wrong because they are only positive, but the texts express disagreement.

    •   (B) is correct because it matches the annotation.

    •   (D) is wrong because Text 2 never mentions *future research*.

10. **B** This is a Charts question, as it asks for *data from the graph*. The graph charts the percentage of participants who chose the sugary drink for a control package and for packaging with various changes. Highlight the conclusion in the text, which is that *the presence of warnings and absence of claims and imagery may reduce the likelihood of purchase, whereas disclosure of percentage of juice may have very little impact*. Eliminate any answers that are inconsistent with the graph or don't support the conclusion.

- (A) is wrong because the claim says that warnings *may reduce likelihood of purchase*, so this statement contradicts the claim.

- (B) is correct because comparing the percent disclosure to the control demonstrates the *little impact* that disclosure had.

- (C) is wrong because it doesn't state what the *impact* of these absences was, so it doesn't support the claim.

- (D) is wrong because the option to select a *low-added sugar fruit drink* isn't in the graph or text.

11. **D** This is a Claims question, as it asks for a *quotation* that *illustrates the claim*. Read the text and highlight the *claim*, which is that *Fernando's friend…is worried and tries to warn him to stay away from the fountain*. Eliminate answers that don't *illustrate* this idea.

- (A) is wrong because it doesn't relate to Fernando going to or staying away from the fountain.

- (B) and (C) are wrong because they don't mention the *fountain*.

- (D) is correct because it provides a warning *not to return to the fountain of the Poplars*.

12. **D** This is a Claims question, as it asks for a *quotation* that *supports the student's claim*. Read the text and highlight the *claim*, which is that *Doerr uses children as his protagonists in order to create a story from an unbiased and hopeful perspective of humanity*. Eliminate answers that don't *support* this idea.

- (A) and (C) are wrong because they don't mention *children*.

- (B) is wrong because *seeks to learn more about the world* doesn't match with *unbiased and hopeful perspective of humanity*.

- (D) is correct because it mentions *children*, the phrase *see the world with an open mind* matches with *unbiased*, and *betterment of humanity* matches with *hopeful perspective of humanity*.

13. **A** This is a Charts question, as it asks for *data from the table*. The graph charts the need satisfaction scale and mood in two stages with respect to human and computer inclusion and exclusion. Highlight the *hypothesis* in the text, which is that *individuals would experience equivalent effects of social exclusion regardless of whether the source of exclusion was human or computer*. Eliminate any answers that are inconsistent with the table or don't support the conclusion.

- (A) is correct because *comparable to* matches with *equivalent effects*, and like the hypothesis it compares something between humans and computers.

- (B) and (D) are wrong because they don't draw a comparison between human and computer inclusion/exclusion.

- (C) is wrong because it contrasts the *reflective* and *reflexive* stages instead of comparing human and computer inclusion/exclusion.

14. **D** This is a Claims question, as it asks for an answer that would *support Nicholson's claim*. Read the text and highlight the *claim*, which is that *the rock whose impact caused the formation of the undersea crater could have broken off from a parent asteroid that also caused the Chicxulub impact*. Eliminate answers that don't *support* this claim.

- (A), (B), and (C) are wrong because they don't mention the *Chicxulub impact*.

- (D) is correct because if the two sites contain *some of the same minerals not normally found on Earth*, this would suggest that the asteroids that created those craters could have come from the same source.

15. **A** This is a Conclusions question, as it asks for the choice that *most logically completes the text*. Read the text and highlight the main ideas. The text states that *a correlation between* certain things *could indicate which regions of the brain…fell asleep or awoke first*. Then it states that in the experiment *the thalamus* had such a correlation, so it may have fallen asleep or awoken first. Eliminate any answer that states a conclusion that isn't supported by the text.

- (A) is correct because it matches with the correlation stated.

- (B) and (D) are wrong because the text is focused on which regions of the brain fall asleep or awaken first, not what happens during sleep.

- (C) is wrong because it's the opposite of what the text suggests.

16. **D** This is a Conclusions question, as it asks for the choice that *most logically completes the text*. Read the text and highlight the main ideas. The text states that the formula *takes into account not only the weight of the vehicle but also its number of axles*. Then it explains that *a shorter vehicle with its weight concentrated in a smaller area could cause more damage than could a longer vehicle of the same weight whose mass is dispersed*. The text then compares *a two-axle vehicle to a four-axle vehicle*. Eliminate any answer that states a conclusion that isn't supported by the text.

- (A) is wrong because it's the opposite of what the text indicates; a four-axle vehicle would likely be longer and have its weight more dispersed, so it could be heavier.

- (B) is wrong because the text draws a contrast between vehicles of different lengths, not a comparison.

- (C) is wrong because it doesn't relate to the four-axle vehicle.

- (D) is correct because it is consistent with the text, as the two-axle vehicle would likely be shorter and therefore need to have a lower weight, given what the text stated about shorter vehicles.

17.   **A**   In this Rules question, pronouns are changing in the answer choices, so it's testing consistency with pronouns. Find and highlight the word the pronoun refers back to, *students*, which is plural, so a plural pronoun is needed. Write an annotation saying "plural." Eliminate any answer that isn't plural or doesn't clearly refer back to *students*.

- (A) is correct because *they* is plural and is consistent with *students*.

- (B) and (C) are wrong because they are singular.

- (D) is wrong because *we* doesn't refer back to *students*.

18.   **A**   In this Rules question, periods and question marks are changing in the answer choices, so it's testing questions versus statements. The beginning of the sentence states that *Scientists wanted to explore another question related to this topic*, so the second part of the sentence should be a question. Eliminate answers that aren't correctly written as questions.

- (A) is correct because it's correctly written as a question.

- (B) and (D) are wrong because they are statements.

- (C) is wrong because it has a question mark but is written as a statement.

19.   **A**   In this Rules question, punctuation is changing in the answer choices. Look for independent clauses. The first part of the sentence says *For example, green roofs, which are rooftops covered in vegetation, reduce the temperatures of roofs*, which is an independent clause. The second part of the sentence says *while cool pavements, which are made with materials that reflect solar energy, can lower the temperatures above the pavement surface and the surrounding air*, which is a dependent clause. Eliminate any option that doesn't correctly connect an independent + a dependent clause.

- (A) is correct because independent + dependent can be connected with a comma.

- (B), (C), and (D) are wrong because independent + dependent cannot be connected with punctuation other than a comma.

20.   **B**   In this Rules question, verb forms are changing in the answer choices, so it's testing sentence structure. The subject of the sentence is *She*, and the main verb is *focuses*. The second part of the sentence follows *and* and describes a second thing that Sibai does, so the answer must be consistent with *focuses*. Eliminate any answer that isn't consistent with *focuses*.

- (A), (C), and (D) are wrong because they aren't consistent with *focuses*.

- (B) is correct because it's consistent with *focuses*.

21. **B** In this Rules question, punctuation is changing in the answer choices. The last part of the sentence says *an imitation banknote that resembles real money and is covered in anti-corruption slogans*, which is a describing phrase. Noun phrases beginning with "a" or "an" are always non-essential to the meaning of the sentence and should be set off with commas. Eliminate answers that do not have a comma.

- (A) and (D) are wrong because the second part isn't an independent clause, and a semicolon or period can only be used when both clauses are independent.

- (B) is correct because it uses a comma after the non-essential information.

- (C) is wrong because a comma is needed for non-essential information.

22. **D** In this Rules question, verb forms are changing in the answer choices, so it's testing sentence structure. The subject of the sentence is *participants*, and the main verb is *self-identified*. The second part of the sentence follows *and* and describes a second thing that the participants did, so the answer must be consistent with *self-identified*. Eliminate any answer that isn't consistent with *self-identified*.

- (A), (B), and (C) are wrong because they aren't consistent with *self-identified*.

- (D) is correct because it's consistent with *self-identified*.

23. **D** In this Rules question, punctuation is changing in the answer choices. The first part of the sentence says *Scientists are attempting to find a new source for these building blocks*, which is an independent clause. The second part of the sentence is not an independent clause and tells what the *new source* is. Eliminate any answer that doesn't correctly connect the independent clause to the source.

- (A) is wrong because adding *such as* to the first part makes it no longer independent, in which case it can't be followed by a colon.

- (B) is wrong because some punctuation is needed to link the independent clause to the explanation of the source that follows.

- (C) is wrong because it makes it sound like *building blocks*, *photons*, and *small quanta of light* are part of a list, which isn't the intended meaning.

- (D) is correct because a colon is used when the second part of the sentence elaborates on the first.

24. **D** This is a transition question, so highlight ideas that relate to each other. The preceding sentence describes what Harjo *initially* did, and this sentence describes some other things she did. These ideas agree, so a same-direction transition is needed. Make an annotation that says "agree." Eliminate any answer that doesn't match.

- (A) is wrong because this sentence doesn't indicate a rule.

- (B) and (C) are wrong because they are opposite-direction transitions.

- (D) is correct because *After some time* matches with *initially* in the preceding sentence.

25. **B**   This is a transition question, so highlight ideas that relate to each other. The preceding sentence says *They were able to determine the parameters for honeybee flight and develop strategies to manipulate it*, and this sentence says *scientists hope to use a similar technique to control the flight of miniature drones*. These ideas agree, so a same-direction transition is needed. Make an annotation that says "agree." Eliminate any answer that doesn't match.

   - (A) and (C) are wrong because they are opposite-direction transitions.

   - (B) is correct because *Eventually* is same-direction and matches the link between what scientists did do and what they *hope* to do.

   - (D) is wrong because this sentence is not a more specific version of the preceding sentence.

26. **D**   This is a transition question, so highlight ideas that relate to each other. The preceding sentence says *They determined that the wildfires are the source of this abrupt increase in temperature*, and this sentence says *reducing the number of wildfires in Australia may help return the temperature to a normal value*. These ideas agree, so a same-direction transition is needed. Make an annotation that says "agree." Eliminate any answer that doesn't match.

   - (A) and (C) are wrong because they are opposite-direction transitions.

   - (B) is wrong because this sentence doesn't indicate something that happened while the preceding sentence was occurring.

   - (D) is correct because *Therefore* is same-direction and suggests a conclusion that can be drawn from the information in the previous sentence.

27. **B**   This is a transition question, so highlight ideas that relate to each other. The preceding sentence says *The first piloted hot air balloon…heated the air on the ground and came with a large risk of explosion*, and this sentence says *Yost's balloon design involved heating the fuel in the air and was much safer*. These ideas disagree, so an opposite-direction transition is needed. Make an annotation that says "opposite." Eliminate any answer that doesn't match.

   - (A) is wrong because it is a same-direction transition.

   - (B) is correct because *On the other hand* is opposite-direction.

   - (C) and (D) are wrong because they do not convey the comparison between *Yost's balloon* and the *first piloted hot air balloon*.

Module 2 – Harder

1. **B** This is a Vocabulary question, as it asks for *the most logical and precise word or phrase*. Read the text and highlight what can help to fill in the blank, which refers to what was to be done with the *buildings*. The previous sentence mentions *the renovation of historic buildings*, and the last sentence says *these preservation projects*, so write "renovation" in the annotation box and use Process of Elimination.

   - (A) is wrong because *repossession* means "taking back ownership."

   - (B) is correct because *rehabilitation* matches with "renovation."

   - (C) is wrong because *reciprocation* means "giving in return."

   - (D) is wrong because *reindustrialization* means "revitalizing industry," and there is no evidence that the buildings will be used for industrial purposes.

2. **B** This is a Vocabulary question, as it asks for *the most logical and precise word or phrase*. Read the text and highlight what can help to fill in the blank, which describes the *process* of *the salt spray test*. The text describes the test as *a common method*, so write "common" in the annotation box and use Process of Elimination.

   - (A) is wrong because *rudimentary* means "at a low level."

   - (B) is correct because *pervasive* matches with "common."

   - (C) is wrong because *erroneous* means "incorrect."

   - (D) is wrong because *intermittent* means "happening at intervals."

3. **D** This is a Vocabulary question, as it asks for *the most logical and precise word or phrase*. Read the text and highlight what can help to fill in the blank, which refers to what Goodall has tried to do to *the effects of climate change on chimpanzees*. The part after the colon describes a way to *help lessen the negative impacts of warming temperatures*, which is another way of saying *climate change*, so write "lessen" in the annotation box and use Process of Elimination.

   - (A) is wrong because *insulate* means "prevent outside exposure."

   - (B) is wrong because *downplay* means "act like something is not as bad as it is," which isn't what she is doing; the text suggests that the effects of climate change are *negative*, and she wants to do something about it.

   - (C) is wrong because it's the opposite of the clue in the sentence.

   - (D) is correct because *mitigate* means "make better."

4. **C**   This is a Vocabulary question, as it asks for *the most logical and precise word or phrase*. Read the text and highlight what can help to fill in the blank, which refers to the *fidelity* (accuracy) with which the artists would *reproduce* the *artistic works*. The last part of the sentence states that their magazine included *painstakingly replicated art facsimiles*, which means "exact copies." Therefore, the artists used "painstaking" fidelity when reproducing the works. Write "painstaking" in the annotation box and use Process of Elimination.

    - (A) is wrong because *evenhanded* means "fair."

    - (B) is wrong because *prudent* means "wise."

    - (C) is correct because *scrupulous* means "exact and precise."

    - (D) is wrong because *complacent* means "satisfied."

5. **B**   This is a Purpose question, as it asks for the *function* of a sentence. Read the text and highlight what can help to understand the function of the underlined sentence. The first sentence explains what Trot *liked* about Cap'n Bill, and the second sentence elaborates on this by comparing the fun she had with Cap'n Bill to the lesser enjoyment she experienced among the children. Write "she has more fun with Bill than with kids" in the annotation box and use Process of Elimination.

    - (A) is wrong because his *creative talents* aren't mentioned in this sentence.

    - (B) is correct because it matches the annotation.

    - (C) is wrong because it's too broad; the sentence is about Trot's feelings, not about *youth* and *adulthood* in general.

    - (D) is wrong because *his assessment of her* is not mentioned.

6. **C**   This is a Purpose question, as it asks for the *main purpose*. Read the text and highlight what can help to understand the overall purpose. The text begins by introducing the narrator's *desire to plunge into society* after some time and then states that he visited his *superior at the office*. Then it states that although the visit was *pleasant and good* for him, he *deferred* (put off) *for a time* his *desire to embrace all humankind*, so write "he goes to office and then doesn't want to see people for a while" in the annotation box and use Process of Elimination.

    - (A) is wrong because no *apprehension* (anxiety) *about his employment* is conveyed.

    - (B) is wrong because the text doesn't say that the man is about to be terminated.

    - (C) is correct because it matches the annotation.

    - (D) is wrong because the text is describing one man's experience and thoughts, not *social benefits* in general.

7. **A** This is a Purpose question, as it asks for the *function* of a sentence. Read the text and highlight what can help to understand the function of the underlined sentence. In the text, the speaker describes his grandmother ordering his grandfather to *pay the money*. Then, the underlined sentence describes the relationship between the grandparents, suggesting that the grandfather is somewhat subservient to the grandmother. The following sentences contrast this by explaining how he stood up to her and *refused...to pay the debt*. Write "relationship between grandparents" in the annotation box and use Process of Elimination.

- (A) is correct because it matches the annotation; this is how the grandparents interacted before the grandfather's apparently unusual response.

- (B) is wrong because the narrator himself isn't described in relation to the grandparents.

- (C) is wrong because this sentence doesn't mention the loss of money.

- (D) is wrong because nothing about *his house* is mentioned here.

8. **C** This is a Purpose question, as it asks for the *overall structure*. Read the text and highlight what can help to understand the overall structure of the text. The text states that nuclear energy *relies upon* uranium, a *finite resource on land* that exists in large quantities *in seawater*. Then it describes a technology that is a *significant improvement* in its ability to extra uranium from seawater. The last sentence begins with a contrast and explains some downsides to the new method. Write "new method to get uranium from seawater but has some downsides" in the annotation box and use Process of Elimination.

- (A) is wrong because the technology isn't a *failed attempt*; it just isn't perfect yet.

- (B) is wrong because while the last sentence could be called a *potential criticism*, the author does not *address this*; the author is the one stating it.

- (C) is correct because it matches the annotation: *qualifies* means that it explains an exception, as the text describes some ways that the technology isn't perfect.

- (D) is wrong because the text never *cautions against reliance* on uranium.

9. **C** This is a Dual Texts question, as it has two texts. The question asks how *the author of Text 2* would respond to *the claims of the author of Text 1*. Start by understanding the *claims of the author* in Text 1. Text 1 describes a theory that *an escalation in infighting* that *coincided with increasing droughts* caused *the decline of the Ancient Maya societies*. It goes on to say that *climate change* was behind *the demise* of the societies. Next, look for a similar idea in Text 2 to see how its author feels about this view. Text 2 acknowledges that the *drought conditions...were correlated with the fall of the social order and the rise of civil unrest* but contrasts this by stating that *it was more specifically the increasing unpredictability of precipitation patterns*. Therefore, the author of Text 2 would "say it's unpredictable precipitation patterns rather than drought." Write that in the annotation box and use Process of Elimination.

- (A) is wrong because Text 2 states that *it is often correctly pointed out that drought conditions... were correlated* with the social unrest, so Text 2 doesn't disagree with this view.

- (B) is wrong because this statement isn't related to anything from Text 1.

- (C) is correct because it matches the annotation.

- (D) is wrong because Text 2 never says what *would have* happened.

10. **D** This is a Charts question, as it asks for *data from the table*. The table charts pH range, acid form color, and base form color for several pH indicators. The text provides two criteria: *colorless acid form and a pH range above a pH of 10*. The first criterion narrows it down to p-Nitrophenol and nitramine, and the second one leaves only nitramine.

- (A), (B), and (C) are wrong because they don't meet both criteria.

- (D) is correct because it meets both criteria.

11. **D** This is a Claims question, as it asks for a *quotation* that *illustrates the claim*. Read the text and highlight the *claim*, which is that *the author describes a sense of profound emptiness*. Eliminate answers that don't *illustrate* this idea.

- (A), (B), and (C) are wrong because they focus on nature and don't say anything related to *profound emptiness*.

- (D) is correct because it describes the author's feeling of nothing being in his heart, which matches with *profound emptiness*.

12. **A** This is a Charts question, as it asks for *data from the graph*. The graph charts the concentration of circulating leukocytes before and after people were given two probiotic strains. Highlight the conclusion in the text, which is that *both Lp299 and CURE21 have anti-inflammatory properties*. Read more of the text to understand the link between the conclusion and the graph: *leukocytes* are released during *inflammation*, so if these probiotics are *anti-inflammatory*, they should cause a reduction in leukocytes. Eliminate any answers that are inconsistent with the graph or don't support the conclusion.

- (A) is correct because it demonstrates a reduction in leukocytes and thus a reduction in inflammation.

- (B), (C), and (D) are wrong because the conclusion doesn't relate to a comparison between the two probiotics; the conclusion states that they're both effective.

13. **C** This is a Claims question, as it asks for an answer that would *weaken the underlined claim*. Read the text and highlight the *claim*, which is that *the level of these biomarkers can detect TBI and indicate its severity*. Read more of the text to understand the terms used here. The text introduces two biomarkers that have been associated with severe traumatic brain injury and then describes a study that showed a link between higher levels of these biomarkers and people's risk of death. Eliminate answers that don't *weaken* the claim.

- (A) is wrong because it strengthens the claim, as low levels of the biomarkers would correspond to people who were at less risk of dying.

- (B) is wrong because the claim doesn't relate to a difference between the two biomarkers.

- (C) is correct because the claim states that the level of the biomarkers *can detect TBI*, but this answer suggests that people might have a TBI but have low levels of the biomarkers.

- (D) is wrong because it strengthens the claim, as the claim indicates that high levels of the biomarkers would correlate with greater likelihood of death.

14. **B**   This is a Claims question, as it asks for a *quotation* that *illustrates the claim*. Read the text and highlight the *claim*, which is that *Prometheus questions the justice of his punishment and denounces Zeus as a cruel ruler*. Eliminate answers that don't *illustrate* this idea.

- (A) is wrong because it says *What ills I suffer from the gods* but doesn't question whether this punishment is just.

- (B) is correct because *tyrant* matches with *cruel ruler*, *bind me helpless here* matches with *punishment*, and stating that the punishment is *shameful* supports the idea of questioning the punishment.

- (C) is wrong because it doesn't say anything about *punishment*.

- (D) is wrong because it doesn't describe a *cruel ruler*.

15. **D**   This is a Conclusions question, as it asks for the choice that *most logically completes the text*. Read the text and highlight the main ideas. The text describes a study testing the link between *short-term exposure to mindfulness treatment* and *empathy and helpfulness to a stranger*. The result was that those who had mindfulness therapy had *increased levels of empathy*, while those who didn't have the treatment *did not*; however, *both groups had similar levels of commitment to help the stranger*. Eliminate any answer that states a conclusion that isn't supported by the text.

- (A) is wrong because it contradicts the last sentence.

- (B) is wrong because the text never says whether people were *willing to volunteer help*; the groups had *similar levels of commitment*, but that level could be unwillingness.

- (C) is wrong because it's too strong; the results can't provide information on what is *needed to change behavior*.

- (D) is correct because the treatment group had greater empathy but not greater willingness to help compared to the control group.

16. **B** This is a Conclusions question, as it asks for the choice that *most logically completes the text*. Read the text and highlight the main ideas. The text states that the Coffin Stone *was long believed to be part of a now-destroyed chambered long barrow* and states that this structure would have been *constructed in the fourth millennium BCE by a pastoralist community*. Then it contrasts this by describing a finding that there was *no evidence of a chambered long barrow* and that *the stone had been placed at its current location in the 15th or 16th century*. Eliminate any answer that states a conclusion that isn't supported by the text.

- (A) is wrong because it contradicts the text, which says that these communities are associated with creating chambered long barrows.

- (B) is correct because the newer research suggests that the chambered long barrow theory isn't supported.

- (C) is wrong because there is no information in the text suggesting what the stone might have been *part of* before it was moved.

- (D) is wrong because the text doesn't indicate when the barrow would have been *destroyed*, if it ever existed.

17. **C** In this Rules question, punctuation is changing in the answer choices. Look for independent clauses. The first part of the sentence says *Most individuals in America don't walk as much as is recommended*, which is an independent clause. The second part says *when a group of individuals was given step-trackers, researchers found that these individuals took more steps*, which is also an independent clause. Eliminate any answer that can't correctly connect two independent clauses.

- (A) is wrong because some type of punctuation is needed in order to connect two independent clauses.

- (B) is wrong because a comma without a coordinating conjunction can't connect two independent clauses.

- (C) is correct because it connects the independent clauses with a comma + a coordinating conjunction (*but*), which is acceptable.

- (D) is wrong because a coordinating conjunction (*but*) without a comma can't connect two independent clauses.

18. **C** In this Rules question, punctuation is changing in the answer choices. Look for independent clauses. The first part of the sentence says *Learning and practicing new skills over a long period of time can cause the brain to change*, which is an independent clause. The second part says *for individuals who become blind, areas of the brain that are normally responsible for vision may change and become involved in other important processes, such as touch*, which is also an independent clause. Eliminate any answer that can't correctly connect two independent clauses.

- (A) is wrong because some type of punctuation is needed in order to connect two independent clauses.

- (B) are wrong because a comma without a coordinating conjunction can't connect two independent clauses.

- (C) is correct because a semicolon can connect two independent clauses.

- (D) is wrong because a coordinating conjunction (*and*) without a comma can't connect two independent clauses.

19. **A** In this Rules question, pronouns are changing in the answer choices, so it's testing consistency with pronouns. Find and highlight the word the pronoun refers back to, *Sweden*, which is singular, so a singular pronoun is needed. Write an annotation saying "singular." Eliminate any answer that isn't singular or doesn't clearly refer back to *Sweden*.

- (A) is correct because *its* is singular and is consistent with *Sweden*.

- (B) is wrong because *her* refers to a person, not a country.

- (C) is wrong because it's plural.

- (D) is wrong because *one's* doesn't refer back to a specific thing.

20. **B** In this Rules question, punctuation is changing in the answer choices. Look for independent clauses. The first part of the sentence says *Chemical engineer Kristi Anseth works with a number of multidisciplinary teams on projects such as developing hydrogel materials to help promote tissue regeneration*, which is an independent clause. The second part of the sentence says *a particularly important area of research because some tissues such as cartilage cannot regrow, unlike other tissues such as bone or muscle*, which is not an independent clause. Eliminate any option that doesn't correctly connect the independent clause to the describing phrase that follows.

- (A) is wrong because a semicolon connects two independent clauses, but the second part of the sentence isn't an independent clause.

- (B) is correct because a comma can be used to connect the independent clause to the describing phrase.

- (C) is wrong because a comma is needed to separate the independent clause and the describing phrase.

- (D) is wrong because the second part is meant to describe the first, but the word *and* makes this unclear.

21. **C** In this Rules question, verbs are changing in the answer choices, so it's testing consistency with verbs. Find and highlight the subject, *movements*, which is plural, so a plural verb is needed. Write an annotation saying "plural." Eliminate any answer that is not plural.

- (A), (B), and (D) are wrong because they are singular.

- (C) is correct because it's plural.

22. **B** In this Rules question, punctuation with a transition is changing in the answer choices. Look for independent clauses. The first part of the sentence says *Meiro Koizumi creates videos that explore the relationship between an individual and his or her role in a situation of conflict.* There is an option to add *for example* to this independent clause, but it's not giving an example of a previous idea as nothing came before it. Eliminate options with *for example* in the first part.

- (A) is wrong because it puts *for example* with the first independent clause.

- (B) is correct because it puts *for example* with the second independent clause and puts a semi-colon between the independent clauses.

- (C) and (D) are wrong because the sentence contains two independent clauses, which must be connected with some type of punctuation other than commas.

23. **B** In this Rules question, punctuation is changing in the answer choices. Look for independent clauses. The first part of the sentence says *Romero is not solely focused on research*, which is an independent clause. The second part of the sentence says *emphasizing that it is possible to be a parent and have a successful science career*, which is not an independent clause. Eliminate any option that doesn't correctly connect the independent clause to the describing phrase that follows.

- (A) and (D) are wrong because a semicolon connects two independent clauses, but the second part is not an independent clause.

- (B) is correct because a comma should be used to connect the independent clause to the describing phrase.

- (C) is wrong because *however* is a non-essential word that needs to be surrounded by commas.

24. **B** This is a transition question, so highlight ideas that relate to each other. The first sentence says *Barefoot running decreases the risk of* several things, and this sentence says *running in shoes decreases the risk of* several other things. These ideas disagree, so an opposite-direction transition is needed. Make an annotation that says "disagree." Eliminate any answer that doesn't match.

- (A), (C), and (D) are wrong because they are all same-direction transitions.

- (B) is correct because it's an opposite-direction transition.

25. **A** This is a transition question, so highlight ideas that relate to each other. The first sentence says *dispatch runners…faced difficulties with their long greatcoats*, and this sentence says *a shorter jacket… was developed*. These ideas agree, so a same-direction transition is needed. Make an annotation that says "agree." Eliminate any answer that doesn't match.

- (A) is correct because *Hence* is same-direction and conveys that the shorter jacket was developed as a result of the difficulties with the longer jacket.

- (B) is wrong because the second sentence is not a second point that shares a similarity with the previous point.

- (C) is wrong because it is opposite-direction.

- (D) is wrong because this sentence doesn't provide an additional point.

26.   **D**   This is a Rhetorical Synthesis question, so highlight the goal(s) stated in the question: *explain the usefulness of cargo bikes for grocery shopping to an audience unfamiliar with cargo bikes.* Eliminate any answer that doesn't *explain the usefulness of cargo bikes for grocery shopping* in a way that assumes the audience is *unfamiliar with cargo bikes.*

- (A) is wrong because it doesn't *explain the usefulness of cargo bikes.*

- (B) and (C) are wrong because they don't explain what a cargo bike is, and the audience is *unfamiliar* with it.

- (D) is correct because it *explains the usefulness* of cargo bikes (*handle the typical large grocery load*) and describes what a cargo bike is.

27.   **C**   This is a Rhetorical Synthesis question, so highlight the goal(s) stated in the question: *highlight a dispute about te lapa to an audience familiar with the phenomenon.* Eliminate any answer that doesn't *highlight a dispute* in a way that assumes the audience is *familiar with* te lapa.

- (A) and (B) are wrong because they don't provide a *dispute.*

- (C) is correct because it highlights *a dispute* (Feinberg's skepticism) and doesn't explain te lapa since the audience is familiar with it.

- (D) is wrong because it explains te lapa, but the audience is already familiar with it.

PRACTICE TEST 3—MATH EXPLANATIONS

Module 1

1. **C** The question asks for the value of an expression. The question states that $4s = 28$. Divide both sides of this equation by 4 to get $s = 7$. Plug $s = 7$ into the expression to get $8(7) + 13$, which becomes $56 + 13$, and then 69. The correct answer is (C).

2. **D** The question asks for the value of an angle on a figure. The figure is already drawn and labeled, but redraw it on the scratch paper if that makes it easier to see what's going on. When a line intersects two parallel lines, two kinds of angles are created: big and small. All of the small angles are equal to each other, all of the big angles are equal to each other, and any small angle plus any big angle = 180°. The angle marked 66° is a small angle, and the angle marked $z°$ is a big angle. Thus, $66 + z = 180$. Subtract 66 from both sides of the equation to get $z = 114$. The correct answer is (D).

3. **25.16 or 25.17** The question asks for the mean, or average, of data shown in a table. For averages, use the formula $T = AN$, in which T is the *total*, A is the *average*, and N is the *number of things*. There are 12 infants at the daycare, so that is the *number of things*. Add up all of the heights in the table to get a *total* of 302. The formula becomes $302 = A(12)$. Divide both sides of the equation by 12 to get $25.1\overline{6}$. When the answer is positive on a fill-in question, there is room in the fill-in box for five characters, including the decimal point. Either stop when there's no more room and enter 25.16, or round the last digit and enter 25.17. The correct answer is 25.16 or 25.17.

4. **A** The question asks for an expression that represents a specific situation. Translate the information into bite-sized pieces and eliminate after each piece. One piece of information says that Jan worked j hours a day for 3 days, so translate her total number of hours worked as $3j$. Eliminate (B), (C), and (D) because they do not include the term. Choice (A) also correctly translates the number of hours Noah worked as $5n$ and adds the two values to represent the total combined hours worked. The correct answer is (A).

5. **C** The question asks for an equivalent expression. The expression includes a fractional exponent. With fractional exponents, the numerator is the power and the denominator is the root. To rewrite $b^{\frac{3}{4}}$, make 3 the power, or the exponent, and make 4 the root. The expression becomes $\sqrt[4]{b^3}$. It is possible to get the question right without knowing how to work with fractional exponents. Plug in a value for b, use the calculator to find the result, and then plug in the same value for b into the answer choices and eliminate any that do not equal the same result. Using either method, the correct answer is (C).

6.   **C**   The question asks for a probability based on data in a table. Probability is defined as $\dfrac{\text{\# of outcomes that fit requirements}}{\text{total \# of outcomes}}$. Read the table carefully to find the numbers to make the probability. There are 30 total canids in the nature conservancy, so that is the *total # of outcomes*. The question asks for the probability of selecting either a grey wolf with yellow eyes or a coyote with brown eyes, so look up both values. Find where the column for Yellow eyes and the row for Grey wolf meet: the value is 16. Find where the column for Brown eyes and the row for Coyote meet: the value is 5. The *# of outcomes that fit requirements* is 16 + 5 = 21. Therefore, the probability that a canid chosen at random is either a grey wolf with yellow eyes or a coyote with brown eyes is $\dfrac{21}{30}$. The correct answer is (C).

7.   **D**   The question asks for a plausible value based on survey results and a margin of error. A margin of error expresses the amount of random sampling error in a survey's results. The question states that 39% of students in the survey have O-positive blood type, so apply this percent to the number of students in the entire first-year class: $\dfrac{39}{100}$ (265) = 103.35. Eliminate (A) and (B) because they are not close to this value and do not represent a plausible number of students in the first-year class who have O-positive blood type. Only (D) is close to 103.35, so it is likely correct. To check, calculate the range based on the margin of error. The margin of error is 6%, meaning that results within a range of 6% above and 6% below the estimate are reasonable. Since 100 is less than 103.35, start with the lower limit of the range. To find the lower limit, subtract 6% from the actual percent of 39% to get 33%. Take 33% of the number of students to get $\dfrac{33}{100}$ (265) = 87.45. Since 100 is between 87.45 and 103.35, it is a plausible number of students in the first-year class with an O-positive blood type. The correct answer is (D).

8.   **A**   The question asks for a change in value based on a function. Plug in two values for the fork length to see what happens to the weight. Start with a fork length of 2. Fork length is represented by l, so plug $l = 2$ into the function to get $w = 3{,}150 + 450(2)$, or $w = 3{,}150 + 900$, and then $w = 4{,}050$. The question asks about the weight increase for each foot of growth of the fork length, so increase the fork length to 2 + 1 = 3. Plug $l = 3$ into the function to get $w = 3{,}150 + 450(3)$, or $w = 3{,}150 + 1{,}350$, and then $w = 4{,}500$. The weight increases by 4,500 − 4,050 = 450. The correct answer is (A).

9. **B** The question asks for a solution to an equation with an absolute value. One method is to enter the equation into the built-in graphing calculator. The values of x are shown by vertical lines; scroll and zoom as needed to see that these cross the x-axis at –31 and 37. Only –31 is an answer choice, so it must be correct. To solve algebraically, recall that, with an absolute value, the value inside the absolute value bars can be either positive or negative, so this equation has two possible solutions. To start solving for x, subtract 6 from both sides of the equation to get $|2x - 6| = 68$. The value in the absolute values bars could equal 68 or –68, so set $2x - 6$ equal to each. When $2x - 6 = 68$, add 6 to both sides of the equation to get $2x = 74$, and then divide both sides of the equation by 2 to get $x = 37$. When $2x - 6 = -68$, add 6 to both sides of the equation to get $2x = -62$, and then divide both sides of the equation by 2 to get $x = -31$. Using either method, the correct answer is (B).

10. **A** The question asks for a description of a function that models a specific situation. Compare the answer choices. Two choices say the function is increasing, and two say it is decreasing. The question states that *an item loses 6% of the value*. Eliminate (C) and (D) because they describe an increasing function. The difference between (A) and (B) is whether the function is exponential or linear. Determine this by plugging in an initial value of the item. Plug in \$100 to make it easy to work with percents. *Percent* means out of 100, so translate 6% as $\frac{6}{100}$. The value of the item decreases the first year by $\frac{6}{100}$ (\$100) = \$6. Subtract this from the original value to get \$100 – \$6 = \$94. Now decrease the new value by 6% to get \$94 – $\frac{6}{100}$ (\$94) = \$94 – \$5.64 = \$88.36. The value decreased by \$6 the first year and by \$5.64 the second year. A linear function would change by the same amount every year, so eliminate (B). The relationship between the value of the item and time is exponential. The correct answer is (A).

11. **B** The question asks for the value of a function. In function notation, $f(x) = y$. The number inside the parentheses is the x-value that goes into the function, or the input, and the value that comes out of the function is the y-value, or the output. The question provides an input value and an output value, so plug $x = 90$ and $f(x) = 120$ into the function, and solve for k. The function becomes $120 = \frac{5}{3}(90) + k$. Simplify to get $120 = 150 + k$, and then subtract 150 from both sides of the equation to get $-30 = k$. The question gives a second input value of –30, so plug $x = -30$ and $k = -30$ into the function to get $f(-30) = \frac{5}{3}(-30) + (-30)$. Simplify to get $f(-30) = -50 - 30$, and then $f(-30) = -80$. The correct answer is (B).

12. **B** The question asks for the value of a length on a geometric figure. Redraw the figure on the scratch paper, then label it with the information given. Label arc *FXG* as 14π. Since the line segment that defines arc *FXG* is a diameter of the circle, the arc is a semicircle, which makes its length half of the circumference. The circumference is thus 14π(2) = 28π. Write down the formula for the circumference of a circle, either from memory or after looking it up on the reference sheet. The formula is $C = 2\pi r$. Plug in the length of the circumference to get 28π = 2πr. Divide both sides of the equation by 2π to get 14 = r. Since $\overline{XO}$ is a radius, its length is 14. The correct answer is (B).

13. **13** The question asks for the value of the *y*-coordinate of the solution to a system of equations. One method is to enter both equations into the built-in graphing calculator, then scroll and zoom as needed to find the point of intersection. The graph shows one point of intersection at (−23, 13). The question asks for the *y*-coordinate, which is 13. To solve the system for the *y*-coordinate algebraically, find a way to make the *x*-coordinates disappear when stacking and adding the equations. Compare the *x*-terms: the larger coefficient, 2, is 2 times the smaller one, 1. Multiply the entire first equation by −2 to get the same coefficient with opposite signs on the *x*-terms. The first equation becomes −2x − 2y = 20. Now stack and add the two equations.

$$-2x - 2y = 20$$
$$+\ \underline{2x\ +\ y = -33}$$
$$-y = -13$$

Divide both sides of the resulting equation by −1 to get y = 13. Using either method, the correct answer is 13.

14. **D** The question asks for a value based on an equation that describes a specific situation. The value of the account is increasing by a certain percent over time, so this question is about exponential growth. Write down the growth and decay formula, which is *final amount* = (*original amount*)(1 ± *rate*)^*number of changes*. The question states that the *original amount* is $5,400. The amount increases by 7%, so the *rate* is 0.07, and the value in parentheses is 1 + 0.07, or 1.07. The account earns annual interest, so the *number of changes* is the number of years, which is *y*. The question asks for the amount four years from now, so plug in 4 for *y*. The equation becomes *final amount* = $5,400(1.07)^4$. Solve with a calculator to get *final amount* ≈ $7,078.30. The correct answer is (D).

15. **C** The question asks for an equation in terms of a specific variable. The question asks about the relationship among variables and there are variables in the answer choices, so one option is to plug in. However, that might get messy with an equation and three variables. All of the answer choices have d^2 by itself, so the other option is to solve for d^2. To isolate d^2, multiply both sides of the equation by d^2 to get $d^2G = ab$. Divide both sides of the equation by G to get $d^2 = \dfrac{ab}{G}$. The correct answer is (C).

16. **D** The question asks for a constant in two points on a line. The question states that the line intersects the origin, which is (0, 0), as well as the points $(c, 3)$ and $(27, c)$. Any two points are sufficient to determine the slope of a line, so find the slope using two pairs of points. Find the slope by using the formula $slope = \dfrac{y_2 - y_1}{x_2 - x_1}$. Start with the points $(c, 3)$ and $(0, 0)$. The slope formula becomes $slope = \dfrac{3 - 0}{c - 0}$, or $\dfrac{3}{c}$. Use the points $(27, c)$ and $(0, 0)$ to get $slope = \dfrac{c - 0}{27 - 0}$, or $\dfrac{c}{27}$. Set the two slopes equal to get $\dfrac{3}{c} = \dfrac{c}{27}$. Cross-multiply to get $(c)(c) = (3)(27)$, or $c^2 = 81$. Take the square root of both sides of the equation to get $c = 9$. The correct answer is (D).

17. **B** The question asks for the value of a length on a geometric figure. Draw a cone as best as possible, and then write down the formula for the volume of a cone, either from memory or after looking it up on the reference sheet. The formula is $V = \dfrac{1}{3}\pi r^2 h$. Plug in the given values to get $80\pi = \dfrac{1}{3}\pi r^2 (15)$. Simplify the right side of the equation to get $80\pi = 5\pi r^2$. Divide both sides of the equation by 5π to get $16 = r^2$, then take the square root of both sides of the equation to get $4 = r$. Read carefully: the question asks for the diameter, which is twice the length of the radius. The diameter is $2(4) = 8$. The correct answer is (B).

18. **B** The question asks for a value on a scatterplot. First, check the units on each axis of the line graph. Population is on the y-axis, so find 5,000 on that axis. Move right from there to the line of best fit, using the mouse pointer or edge of the scratch paper if necessary. From there, move down to the x-axis to see that the value is between the labeled vertical line for 2030 and the unlabeled vertical line for 2035. Eliminate (A), (C), and (D) because those values are not between 2030 and 2035. The correct answer is (B).

19. $\dfrac{20}{29}$ The question asks for the value of a trigonometric function. Begin by drawing a right triangle and labeling the vertices, being certain to put the longest side opposite right angle D. The drawing should look something like this:

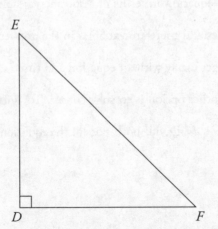

Next, write out SOHCAHTOA to remember the trig functions. The SOH part defines the sine as $\frac{opposite}{hypotenuse}$, and the question states that $\sin(E) = \frac{21}{29}$. Label the side opposite angle E as 21, and label the hypotenuse as 29. The drawing now looks like this:

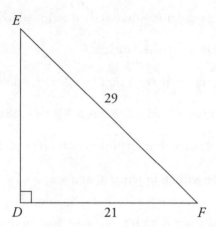

Use the Pythagorean Theorem, $a^2 + b^2 = c^2$, to solve for the length of the remaining side. Plug in the known side lengths to get $a^2 + 21^2 = 29^2$, which becomes $a^2 + 441 = 841$. Subtract 441 from both sides of the equation to get $a^2 = 400$, then take the square root of both sides of the equation to get $a = 20$. Label this on the figure. Use SOHCAHTOA again: the side opposite F is 20, and the hypotenuse is 29, so $\sin(F) = \frac{opposite}{hypotenuse} = \frac{20}{29}$. The correct answer is $\frac{20}{29}$.

20. **225** The question asks for a value given two equations with square roots. Substitute $3\sqrt{5}$ for x in the second equation to get $5(3\sqrt{5}) = \sqrt{5y}$. Distribute the 5 on the left side of the equation to get $15\sqrt{5} = \sqrt{5y}$. Square both sides of the equation to get $(225)(5) = 5y$, or $1,125 = 5y$. Divide both sides of the equation by 5 to get $225 = y$. The correct answer is 225.

21. **A** The question asks for an inequality that represents a specific situation. Translate the information in bite-sized pieces and eliminate after each piece. One piece of information says that *each day after Monday, 3 cubic feet of garbage are added*. Therefore, after d days, $3d$ cubic feet have been added. Eliminate (C) because it does not include the term $3d$. Another piece of information says that, on Monday, the trash can *contains 8 cubic feet of garage*. The 3 cubic feet per day are added to this, so the amount of garbage in the trash can after d days is $8 + 3d$. Eliminate (B) and (D) because they do not include the initial 8 cubic feet. Choice (A) also includes ≥ 20, which correctly represents when the amount of trash in the trash can is at or above the maximum capacity of 20 cubic feet. The correct answer is (A).

22. **A** The question asks for the sum of three constants in a quadratic equation. Plug the point given in the question into the equation to get $8 = a(-3)^2 + b(-3) + c$. Simplify to get $8 = 9a - 3b + c$. The point $(-3, 8)$ is the maximum of the parabola, and a parabola reaches its minimum or maximum value at its vertex. When a quadratic is in standard form, which is $ax^2 + bx + c$, the x-coordinate of the vertex can be found using the formula $h = -\dfrac{b}{2a}$. Since $h = -3$, this formula becomes $-3 = -\dfrac{b}{2a}$. Multiply both sides of the equation by $-2a$ to get $6a = b$. Substitute $6a$ for b in the first equation to get $8 = 9a - 3(6a) + c$, which becomes $8 = 9a - 18a + c$. Combine the a-terms to get $8 = -9a + c$, and then add $9a$ to both sides of the equation to get $9a + 8 = c$.

    Now all three terms can be written in terms of a: $a = a$, $b = 6a$, and $c = 9a + 8$. Thus, $a + b + c = a + 6a + 9a + 8$, which becomes $a + b + c = 16a + 8$. Since the parabola has a maximum, it opens downward, which means that a is negative. Set $16a + 8$ equal to each answer choice, and eliminate any that do not result in a negative value of a. Choice (A) becomes $16a + 8 = -8$. Subtract 8 from both sides of the equation to get $16a = -16$, and then divide both sides of the equation by 16 to get $a = -1$. This is negative, so keep (A). Choice (B) becomes $16a + 8 = 8$. Subtract 8 from both sides of the equation to get $16a = 0$, and then divide both sides of the equation by 16 to get $a = 0$. A larger value will make a positive, so stop here. The correct answer is (A).

Module 2 – Easier

1. **C** The question asks for a percentage of a number. Translate the English to math in bite-sized pieces. Translate *what* as a variable, such as x. Translate *is* as equals. *Percent* means out of 100, so translate 90% as $\dfrac{90}{100}$. Translate *of* as times. The translated equation is $x = \dfrac{90}{100}(1,000)$. Solve by hand or with a calculator to get $x = 900$. The correct answer is (C).

2. **B** The question asks for a value on a graph. First, check the units on each axis of the line graph. Profits are on the y-axis, so find the point at which the line is lowest, which indicates the least profit. Year is on the x-axis, so move down from the lowest point on the line to the x-axis, using the mouse pointer or edge of the scratch paper if necessary. The year is 2001, so that is when the store's profit was the least. The correct answer is (B).

3. **−6** The question asks for the solution to an equation. To solve for y, take the square root of both sides of the equation to get $y = \pm 6$. The question states that $y < 0$, so it is −6. The correct answer is −6.

4. **540** The question asks for a value given a rate. Begin by reading the question to find information about the rate. The question states that the mosaic floor pattern has *9 blue tiles for every 80 tiles in total*. Set up a proportion to determine how many blue tiles will be in a floor with 4,800 tiles at this rate. The proportion is $\frac{9 \text{ blue tiles}}{80 \text{ total tiles}} = \frac{x \text{ blue tiles}}{4,800 \text{ total tiles}}$. Cross-multiply to get $(80)(x) = (9)(4,800)$, which becomes $80x = 43,200$. Divide both sides of the equation by 80 to get $x = 540$. The correct answer is 540.

5. **C** The question asks for an equation that represents a relationship among values. Translate the English to math in bite-sized pieces and eliminate after each piece. Translate *6 times a number a* as $6a$. Eliminate (D) because it does not have this piece. Translate *is subtracted from 15* as $15 -$. Eliminate (A) and (B) because they do not have this piece. The correct answer is (C).

6. **A** The question asks for the value of a function. In function notation, the number inside the parentheses is the *x*-value that goes into the function, or the input, and the value that comes out of the function is the *y*-value, or the output. The question gives an input value of –3, so plug that into the function to get $g(-3) = 4(-3) - 7$, which becomes $g(-3) = -12 - 7$, and then $g(-3) = -19$. The correct answer is (A).

7. **28** The question asks for a measurement of a geometric figure. Write down the formula for the circumference of a circle, either from memory or after looking it up on the reference sheet. The formula is $C = 2\pi r$. Plug in the value given for the circumference to get $56\pi = 2\pi r$. Divide both sides of the equation by 2π to get $28 = r$. The correct answer is 28.

8. **C** The question asks for an equation that represents a specific situation. Translate the English to math in bite-sized pieces and eliminate after each piece. The question states that *m* is the number of members of the club in February, so translate *three times the number of members of the club in February* as $3m$. Eliminate (A), (B), and (D) because they do not have this term. Choice (C) also correctly translates *was* as = and sets $3m$ equal to the number of members of the club in April, which is 27. The correct answer is (C).

9. **56** The question asks for the value of an expression based on an equation. When a Digital SAT question asks for the value of an expression, there is usually a straightforward way to solve for the expression without needing to completely isolate the variable. Multiply both sides of the equation by 3 to get $12x = 60$. Subtract 4 from both sides of the equation to get $12x - 4 = 56$. The correct answer is 56.

10. **B** The question asks for the value of a function. In function notation, the number inside the parentheses is the *x*-value that goes into the function, or the input, and the value that comes out of the function is the *y*-value, or the output. The question provides an input value, so plug $x = 2$ into function *g* to get $g(2) = 2(2)^2 - 16$, which becomes $g(2) = 2(4) - 16$. Continue solving to get $g(2) = 8 - 16$, and then $g(2) = -8$. The correct answer is (B).

11.   **C**   The question asks for a value given a specific situation. Since the question asks for a specific value and the answers contain numbers in increasing order, use the values in the answers. Rewrite the answers on the scratch paper and label them "miles." Next, start with one of the middle numbers and try (B), 3. The question states that the base fee is $2.40, and that *there is an additional charge of $0.30 per mile.* The additional charge for a 3-mile trip is ($0.30)(3) = $0.90. Add this to the base fee to get $2.40 + $0.90 = $3.30. This is not $3.60, so eliminate (B). The result was too small, so also eliminate (A), and try (C), 4, next. The additional charge for a 4-mile trip is ($0.30)(4) = $1.20. Add this to the base fee to get $2.40 + $1.20 = $3.60. This matches the information in the question, so stop here. The correct answer is (C).

12.   **B**   The question asks for an equivalent form of an expression. Use Bite-Sized Pieces and Process of Elimination to tackle this question. Start by combining the terms that have x^2 to get $4x^2 - 3x^2 = x^2$. Eliminate (D) because it does not include this term. Next, combine the terms that have x to get $3x - (-8x) = 3x + 8x = 11x$. Eliminate (A) because it does not include this term. Finally, combine the integer terms to get $-2 - 9 = -11$. Eliminate (C) because it does not include this term. The correct answer is (B).

13.   **D**   The question asks for the equation that defines a function. In function notation, the number inside the parentheses is the x-value that goes into the function, or the input, and the value that comes out of the function is the y-value, or the output. The table provides several pairs of input and output values, so plug those into the answer choices and eliminate answers that don't work. Plugging in 1 often makes more than one answer work, so start with the third point, and plug $x = 3$ and $g(x) = 5$ into each answer choice. Choice (A) becomes $5 = 3 - 1$, or $5 = 2$. This is not true, so eliminate (A). Choice (B) becomes $5 = 2(3) - 4$, or $5 = 2$; eliminate (B). Choice (C) becomes $5 = 3(3) - 5$, or $5 = 4$; eliminate (C). Choice (D) becomes $5 = 4(3) - 7$, or $5 = 5$; keep (D). The correct answer is (D).

14.   **A**   The question asks for a point that satisfies a system of inequalities. One method is to enter both inequalities into the built-in graphing calculator, then see which point in the answer choices is in the shaded area that represents the solution to the system. Only $(-3, -1)$ is in that shaded area, so (A) is correct. Another approach is to use the values in the answers. Rewrite the answer choices on the scratch paper and label them "(x, y)." Start with one of the answers in the middle and try (C). Plug $x = 3$ and $y = 1$ into the first inequality to get $4(3) - 1 \leq 1$, which becomes $12 - 1 \leq 1$, and then $11 \leq 1$. This is not true, so eliminate (C). The left side of the first inequality should be smaller, so try (A). Plug $x = -3$ and $y = -1$ into the first inequality to get $4(-3) - 1 \leq -1$, which becomes $-12 - 1 \leq -1$, and then $-13 \leq -1$. This is true, so plug the same values into the second inequality to get $2 > -3 + (-1)$, which becomes $2 > -4$. This is also true, so the point $(-3, -1)$ satisfies the system of inequalities. Using either method, the correct answer is (A).

15.   **16**   The question asks for a measurement on a geometric figure. Start by redrawing the figure on the scratch paper. Since $\overline{PQ}$ is parallel to $\overline{RT}$, angle P is also a right angle; label this on the figure. The two triangles share angle S, so they are similar triangles. This means the sides are proportional. Sides $\overline{RT}$ and $\overline{PQ}$ are opposite the same angle, so they are proportional. Sides $\overline{PS}$ and $\overline{TS}$ are

proportional for the same reason, so find the length of side $\overline{TS}$. Either recognize one of the Pythagorean Triples or use the Pythagorean Theorem to get $TS = 4$; label this on the figure, which now looks like this.

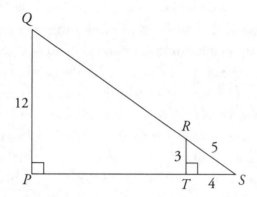

Now set up a proportion: $\dfrac{RT}{PQ} = \dfrac{TS}{PS}$. Plug in the known values to get $\dfrac{3}{12} = \dfrac{4}{PS}$. Cross-multiply to get $(12)(4) = 3(PS)$, which becomes $48 = 3(PS)$. Divide both sides of the equation by 3 to get $16 = PS$. The correct answer is 16.

16. **0.86** The question asks for the value of a constant given a function that represents a specific situation. The value of the function is decreasing by a certain percent, so this question is about exponential decay. Write down the growth and decay formula, which is *final amount = (original amount)*$(1 \pm rate)^{number\ of\ changes}$. The constant k is in parentheses, so it represents $1 \pm rate$. The question states that the population *will decline by 14 percent per year*, so the *rate* is 14%. Convert this to a decimal to get 0.14. The population is declining, so the value in parentheses, or k, is $1 - 0.14 = 0.86$. The correct answer is 0.86.

17. **D** The question asks for the equation that represents a graph. Every point on the graph must make the equation true, so plug in points from the graph. Since 0 and 1 are likely to make more than one answer work, start with the point at $(2, 70)$. Plug in $x = 2$ and $y = 70$, and eliminate answers that don't work. Choice (A) becomes $70 = 25(2)$, or $70 = 50$. This is not true, so eliminate (A). Choice (B) becomes $70 = 2 + 30$, or $70 = 32$; eliminate (B). Choice (C) becomes $70 = 10(2) + 30$, or $70 = 50$; eliminate (C). Choice (D) becomes $70 = 20(2) + 30$, or $70 = 70$; keep (D). The correct answer is (D).

18. **A** The question asks for a value given a function. In function notation, the number inside the parentheses is the x-value that goes into the function, or the input, and the value that comes out of the function is the y-value, or the output. The question provides an output value of 8, and the answers have numbers that could represent the x-value, so use the values in the answers. Start with one of the middle numbers and try (B), 4. Plug $x = 4$ into the function to get $g(4) = \sqrt{4(4)^2 + 28}$, which becomes $g(4) = \sqrt{4(16) + 28}$. Continue solving to get $g(4) = \sqrt{64 + 28}$, and then $g(4) = \sqrt{92}$. Use a calculator to get $g(4) \approx 9.59$. This does not match the output value of 8, so eliminate (B). The result was too large, so also eliminate (C) and (D). The correct answer is (A).

19. **B**   The question asks for an equation that represents a graph. In function notation, $f(x) = y$. The number inside the parentheses is the x-value that goes into the function, or the input, and the value that comes out of the function is the y-value, or the output. Together, they represent points on the graph of the function. One method is to use the built-in graphing calculator. Enter each of the equations in the answer choices into the graphing calculator and see which one looks most like the graph. Another option is to use knowledge of the graphs of higher-degree polynomials. There are three x-intercepts on the graph, at $(-2, 0)$, $(2, 0)$, and $(5, 0)$. These are three distinct values, so there should be three distinct factors. Eliminate (A) and (D) because they square one of the factors, which would result in a double root where the graph touches $y = 0$ and then curves away. To check (B) and (C), plug in a point from the graph. Starting with the point $(5, 0)$, plug $x = 5$ and $f(x) = 0$ into the remaining answers. Choice (B) becomes $0 = (5 - 5)(5 - 2)(5 + 2)$, or $0 = (0)(3)(7)$, and then $0 = 0$. This is true, so keep (B). Choice (C) becomes $0 = (5 - 2)(5 + 2)(5 + 5)$, or $0 = (3)(7)(10)$, and then $0 = 210$. This is not true, so eliminate (C). It is also possible to plug in points from the graph and eliminate answers without knowing about double roots. Using any method, the correct answer is (B).

20. **D**   The question asks for an equation that represents a relationship among values. Since the question asks for a specific value and the answers contain numbers in increasing order, try using values from the answers. Rewrite the answer choices on the scratch paper and label them as "largest #." Next, start with a number in the middle and try (B), 245. The question states that when *three numbers are added together, the result is 665*. If the largest number is 245, the sum of the other two numbers is $665 - 245 = 420$. The question also states that the *largest number is four-thirds the sum of the other two numbers*. If the sum of the other two numbers is 420, the largest number is $\frac{4}{3}(420) = 560$. There are two different values for the largest number, 245 and 560, so eliminate (B). The two values were not close to each other, and (A) is too small to be the largest number, so try (D), 380, next. If the largest number is 380, the sum of the other two numbers is $665 - 380 = 285$. If the sum of the other two numbers is 285, the largest number is $\frac{4}{3}(285) = 380$. The two results for the largest number match, so 380 is the correct value. The answer is (D).

21. **B**   The question asks for the value of a constant in a quadratic with exactly one real solution. One method is to enter both equations into the built-in graphing calculator and plug in each answer choice for k. Only when $k = 0$ does the graph of the system have exactly one real solution, so $k = 0$, and the answer is (B). To solve algebraically, use the discriminant. The discriminant is the part of the quadratic formula under the square root sign and is written as $D = b^2 - 4ac$. When the discriminant is positive, the quadratic has exactly two real solutions; when the discriminant is 0, the quadratic has exactly one real solution; and when the discriminant is negative, the quadratic has no real solutions. Thus,

the discriminant of this quadratic must equal 0. First, substitute $2x$ for y in the first equation to get $2x = x^2 + 2x + k$. Next, put the quadratic in standard form, which is $ax^2 + bx + c = 0$, by subtracting $2x$ from both sides of the equation to get $0 = x^2 + k$. Now that the quadratic is in standard form, $a = 1$, $b = 0$, and $c = k$. Plug these into the discriminant formula to get $D = (0)^2 - 4(1)(k)$, or $D = -4k$. Since there is exactly one real solution, $-4k = 0$. Divide both sides of the equation by -4 to get $0 = k$. Using either method, the correct answer is (B).

22. **C** The question asks for the value of a trigonometric function. Start by drawing two right triangles that are similar to each other, meaning they have the same proportions but are different sizes. Be certain to match up the corresponding angles that are given in the question, and put the longest side opposite the right angle. Next, label the figures with the information given, and label the side lengths of triangle *LMN*. The drawing should look something like this:

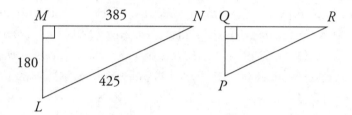

Trig functions are proportional, and angle R corresponds to angle N, so $\cos(R) = \cos(N)$. Use SOHCAHTOA to remember the trig functions. The CAH part of the acronym defines the cosine as $\dfrac{adjacent}{hypotenuse}$. The side adjacent to angle N is 385, and the hypotenuse is 425, so $\cos(N) = \dfrac{385}{425}$. Thus, $\cos(R)$ is also $\dfrac{385}{425}$. Reduce the fraction by dividing the numerator and denominator by 5 to get $\cos(R) = \dfrac{77}{85}$. It is also possible to use a calculator to find the decimal form of $\dfrac{385}{425}$ and the decimal form of each answer choice, and see which answer matches. The correct answer is (C).

Module 2 – Harder

1. **A** The question asks for an equivalent form of an expression. Use bite-sized pieces and process of elimination to tackle this question. Start by combining the terms that have a^3. Subtract the coefficients to get $5a^3 - 3a^3 = 2a^3$. Eliminate (B), (C), and (D) because they do not include this term. Choice (A) also correctly leaves $6a^2$ by itself because no other terms have an exponent of 2. The correct answer is (A).

2. **B**   The question asks for the equation that defines a function. In function notation, the number inside the parentheses is the *x*-value that goes into the function, or the input, and the value that comes out of the function is the *y*-value, or the output. The table provides several pairs of input and output values, so plug those into the answer choices and eliminate answers that don't work. Pairs of values that include 0 often make more than one answer work, and negative numbers can be tricky to work with, so start with the fourth pair of values. Plug *x* = 5 and *g*(*x*) = 2 into each answer choice. Choice (A) becomes 2 = 5 – 6, or 2 = –1. This is not true, so eliminate (A). Choice (B) becomes 2 = 2(5) – 8, or 2 = 2. This is true, so keep (B), but check the remaining answers. Choice (C) becomes 2 = 3(5) – 12, or 2 = 3; eliminate (C). Choice (D) becomes 2 = 4(5) – 12, or 2 = 8; eliminate (D). The correct answer is (B).

3. **B**   The question asks for a value given a specific situation. Since the question asks for a specific value and the answers contain numbers in increasing order, use the values in the answers. Rewrite the answer choices on the scratch paper and label them "miles Irina cycled." Start with one of the values in the middle and try (B), 32. The question states that *Tiki cycled 13 fewer miles than Irina*. If Irina cycled 32 miles, Tiki cycled 32 – 13 = 19 miles. The question also states that *the two of them cycled a total of 51 miles*. If Irina cycled 32 miles and Tiki cycled 19 miles, they cycled a combined 32 + 19 = 51 miles. This matches the information in the question, so stop here. The correct answer is (B).

4. **1**   The question asks for the value of the *y*-coordinate of the solution to a system of equations. One method is to enter both equations into the built-in graphing calculator, then scroll and zoom as needed to find the point of intersection. The lines intersect at (4, 1), so the *y*-coordinate is 1. To solve the system for the *y*-coordinate algebraically, find a way to make the *x*-coordinates disappear when stacking and adding the equations. Compare the *x*-terms: a common multiple of 8 and 5 is 40. Multiply the entire first equation by 5 to get $40x - 25y = 135$. Multiply the entire second equation by –8 to get the same coefficient with opposite signs on the *x*-terms. The second equation becomes $-40x - 80y = -240$. Now stack and add the two equations.

$$40x - 25y = 135$$
$$+ \underline{-40x - 80y = -240}$$
$$-105y = -105$$

Divide both sides of the resulting equation by –105 to get *y* = 1. Using either method, the correct answer is 1.

5. **12**   The question asks for the value of a constant in a function. In function notation, the number inside the parentheses is the *x*-value that goes into the function, or the input, and the value that comes out of the function is the *y*-value, or the output. The question provides a point on the graph, which means that an input value of 4 has an output value of –2. Plug *x* = 4 and *g*(*x*) = –2 into the function to get $-2 = 2(4)^2 - 4k + 14$. Simplify the right side of the equation to get $-2 = 2(16) - 4k + 14$, then $-2 = 32 - 4k + 14$, and then $-2 = 46 - 4k$. Subtract 46 from both sides of the equation to get $-48 = -4k$, and then divide both sides of the equation by –4 to get 12 = *k*. The correct answer is 12.

6. **D** The question asks for the interpretation of a term in context. Start by reading the final question, which asks for the meaning of −0.14. Rewrite the equation on the scratch paper. Then label the parts of the equation with the information given, and eliminate answers that do not match the labels. The question states that *x represents the number of years since 2010*, and that *y is the total annual rainfall*. Thus, −0.14 has something to do with each year. Eliminate (A) and (B) because the total annual rainfall in one year is represented by *y*, not by *x*. Eliminate (C) because it is the difference between the *y*-value for 2010 and the *y*-value for 2020. Choice (D) describes something that occurs every year, and −0.14 is multiplied by the number of years, so this fits the information in the question. The correct answer is (D).

7. **10** The question asks for the greatest possible *x*-value of the solution to a system of inequalities. According to the first inequality, $3y$ cannot be greater than 7. Plug in 7 for $3y$ in the second inequality to get $x < 7 + 4$, which becomes $x < 11$. The question asks for the greatest integer value of *x*, and the greatest integer less than 11 is 10. The correct answer is 10.

8. **C** The question asks for the equation of a line that is perpendicular to the given line. Perpendicular lines have slopes that are negative reciprocals. The given equation and the equations in the answer choices are all in standard form, $Ax + By = C$. When a linear equation is in standard form, the slope is $-\dfrac{A}{B}$. The slope of the first equation is $-\dfrac{-3}{4}$, or $\dfrac{3}{4}$. The slope of a line perpendicular to this line will be $-\dfrac{4}{3}$. Determine the slope of each answer choice to see which one matches this value. For (A), the slope is $-\dfrac{3}{6}$, or $-\dfrac{1}{2}$. This is not equal to the target slope of $-\dfrac{4}{3}$, so eliminate (A). For (B), the slope is $-\dfrac{3}{8}$; eliminate (B). For (C), the slope is $-\dfrac{4}{3}$, which matches the target slope, so stop here. The correct answer is (C).

9. **C** The question asks for an equation that represents a specific situation. The number of baseball cards in the collection is decreasing by a certain percent over time, so this question is about exponential decay. Write down the growth and decay formula, which is *final amount* = (*original amount*)(1 ± *rate*)^*number of changes*. The question states that the *original amount* is 6,500, and all of the answers include this piece. The question also states that the number *will decrease by 20 percent*. This is the *rate*, and 20% in decimal form is 0.2. Because the number of cards is decreasing, the value inside the parentheses is (1 − *rate*), which is (1 − 0.2) = 0.8. Eliminate (A) and (B) because they have the wrong value inside the parentheses. The number of cards decreases once every 6 months, and the exponents in the answer choices are in terms of *m* months. Plug in a value for *m*. After 12 months, the number of cards in the collection will decrease twice, so when *m* = 12, the *number of changes* is 2.

Plug $m = 12$ into the exponent in (C) to get $\frac{12}{6} = 2$; keep (C). Plug $m = 12$ into the exponent in (D) to get $6(12) = 72$; eliminate (D). The correct answer is (C).

10.   **A**   The question asks for the surface area of a geometric figure. Draw a cube as best as possible, and then write down the relevant formulas. Write down the formula for the volume of a cube, either from memory or after looking it up on the reference sheet. The reference sheet doesn't give the formula for the volume of a cube, but it does give the volume of a rectangular solid: $V = lwh$. All three sides of a cube are the same length, so the formula becomes $V = s^3$. There is a variable in the question and the answers, so plug a value for c into the equation given in the question to find the volume of the cube. Plug in $c = 4$ to get $V = \frac{1}{8}(4)^3$, then $V = \frac{1}{8}(64)$, and finally $V = 8$. Plug this volume into the volume formula for a cube to solve for the side length: $8 = s^3$. Take the positive cube root of both sides of the equation to get $2 = s$. Label this on the figure.

The surface area of a geometric figure is the sum of the areas of its sides. Since a cube has 6 sides that are identical squares, and the formula for the area of a square is $A = s^2$, the formula for the surface area of a cube is $SA = 6s^2$. Plug the side length of 2 into the surface area formula to get $SA = 6(2)^2 = 6(4) = 24$. This is the target value; write it down and circle it. Now plug $c = 4$ into the answer choices and eliminate any that do not match the target value. Choice (A) becomes $6\left(\frac{4}{2}\right)^2 = 6(2)^2 = 6(4) = 24$. This matches the target value, so keep (A), but check the remaining answers just in case. Choice (B) becomes $6\left(\frac{4^2}{2}\right) = 6\left(\frac{16}{2}\right) = 6(8) = 48$. This does not match the target value, so eliminate (B). Choice (C) becomes $6(4)^2 = 6(16) = 96$; eliminate (C). Choice (D) will have an even larger result than (C), so eliminate (D). The correct answer is (A).

11.   **B**   The question asks for the number of solutions to a system of equations. The most efficient method is to enter both equations into the built-in graphing calculator, then scroll and zoom as needed to see how many times, if at all, the two graphs intersect. There are two points of intersection, at $(-1.329, -0.11)$ and $(7.107, 2.702)$, so the equation has two real solutions. The correct answer is (B).

12.   **C**   The question asks for a change in value expressed as a percentage. One method is to ballpark. The number of units sold of both products increased, one by 50% and the other by 30%, so the total increase must be between 30% and 50%. Only (C) is within this range, so it must be correct.

Another method is to translate the English to math in bite-sized pieces. One piece of information says that the sales of laptops *increased by 50%* this week. Since *percent* means out of 100, translate 50% as $\frac{50}{100}$, and find 50% of the 90 laptops sold: $\frac{50}{100}(90) = 45$. Add this to the number of laptops sold last week to get $90 + 45 = 135$. Another piece of information says that the store sold 210 tablets last week, and that the sales of tablets *increased by 30%*. Follow the same steps to get $210 + \frac{30}{100}(210) = 210 + 63 = 273$. The total number of units sold this week is $135 + 273 = 408$. Add the number of laptops and tablets sold last week to get a total number of units sold last week of $90 + 210 = 300$. Now, plug in the answer choices to see which percent increases the sales from 300 to 408. Start with (B), 25%. A 25% increase from 300 is $300 + \frac{25}{100}(300) = 300 + 75 = 375$. This is not 408, so eliminate (B). The result was too small, so also eliminate (A) and try (C) next. A 36% increase from 300 is $300 + \frac{36}{100}(300) = 300 + 108 = 408$. This matches the information in the question, so stop here. Using either method, the correct answer is (C).

13. **D** The question asks for the number of solutions to an equation. Distribute on both sides of the equation to get $-10 + 18x = 18x + 24$. Subtract $18x$ from both sides of the equation to get $-10 = 24$. This is not true, so the equation has no solutions. Another approach is to enter each expression in a separate entry field in the built-in graphing calculator to see that the lines are parallel and never intersect. Using either method, the correct answer is (D).

14. **123** The question asks for a value based on means, or averages. For averages, use the formula $T = AN$, in which T is the *Total*, A is the *Average*, and N is the *Number of things*. When there are 6 people on the elevator, the *average* is 160.5 and the *number of things* is 6, so the equation becomes $T = (160.5)(6)$, or $T = 963$. When the person with the lowest weight gets off the elevator, the *average* is 168 and the *number of things* is 5. The average equation becomes $T = (168)(5)$, or $T = 840$. To find the weight of the person with the lowest weight, subtract the two totals to get $963 - 840 = 123$. The correct answer is 123.

15. **D** The question asks for the value of a constant in a quadratic. One method is to enter the equation into the built-in graphing calculator, then plug in each answer choice for k until one of them shows a graph with two solutions. Only -1 does this, so (D) is correct. To determine when a quadratic equation has two real solutions algebraically, use the discriminant. The discriminant is the part of the quadratic formula under the square root sign and is written as $D = b^2 - 4ac$. When the discriminant is positive, the quadratic has exactly two real solutions; when the discriminant is 0, the quadratic has exactly one real solution; and when the discriminant is negative, the quadratic has no real solutions. Thus, the discriminant of this quadratic must equal a positive number. First, put the quadratic in standard form, which is $ax^2 + bx + c = 0$, by subtracting k from both sides of the

equation to get $4x^2 - 5x - k = 0$. Now that the quadratic is in standard form, $a = 4$, $b = -5$, and $c = -k$. Plug these into the discriminant formula to get $D = (-5)^2 - 4(4)(-k)$, or $D = 25 + 16k$. Since there are two real solutions, $25 + 16k > 0$. Subtract 25 from both sides of the inequality to get $16k > -25$, then divide both sides of the inequality by 16 to get $k > -1.5625$. The only answer choice greater than -1.5625 is -1. Using either method, the correct answer is (D).

16. **C** The question asks for the product of the two coordinates of the solution to a system of equations. One method is to enter both equations into the built-in graphing calculator, then scroll and zoom as needed to find the points of intersection. The graph shows one point of intersection at $(0, 0)$, but the question states that $x < 0$. The other point of intersection is at $(-1, 1)$. Thus, $x = -1$, $y = 1$, and $xy = -1$.

To solve algebraically, by substituting x^2 for y in the second equation to get $6x + 9 = -3(2x^2 - 3)$. Simplify the right side of the equation to get $6x + 9 = -6x^2 + 9$. Subtract 9 from both sides of the equation to get $6x = -6x^2$. Divide both sides of the equation by $-6x$ to get $-1 = x$. Plug $x = -1$ into the first equation to solve for y: $(-1)^2 = y$, so $y = 1$. Finally, solve for xy: $(-1)(1) = -1$. Using either method, the correct answer is (C).

17. **B** The question asks for a value given information about trigonometric functions. Redraw the figure, and then label it with information from the question. The question asks for a specific value and the answers contain numbers in increasing order, so use the values in the answers. Rewrite the answer choices and label them "m." Start with one of the middle numbers and try (B), 7.5. If $m = 7.5$, the measure of angle A is $6(7.5) - 9 = 45 - 9 = 36$; label this on the figure. The measure of angle C is $8(7.5) - 6 = 60 - 6 = 54$; label this on the figure. Use a calculator in degree mode to get $\sin(36) \approx 0.588$ and $\cos(54) \approx 0.588$. The values are equal, which matches the information in the question, so stop here. The correct answer is (B).

18. **D** The question asks for a true statement based on the data. Use bite-sized pieces and process of elimination to tackle this question. The answer choices compare the ranges of the two data sets, and range is the difference between the greatest value and the least value, so start there. The range of the values in data set 1 is $9 - 3 = 6$, and the range of the values in data set 2 is $13 - 8 = 5$. Eliminate (B) and (C) because they say the ranges are equal when the range of data set 1 is greater than the range of data set 2. Standard deviation is a measure of the spread of a group of numbers. A group of numbers close together has a small standard deviation, whereas a group of numbers spread out has a large standard deviation. The values in data set 1 are spread out almost equally among the numbers, whereas the values in data set 2 are clustered around 12. Thus, the standard deviation of data set 1 is greater than the standard deviation of data set 2. Eliminate (A) because it says that the standard deviation of data set 1 is less than that of data set 2. The correct answer is (D).

19. $\dfrac{17}{6}$ **or** The question asks for the sum of two constants in a system of linear equations. When two linear

2.833 equations have infinitely many solutions, the two equations are the same line. Therefore, make the two equations look the same. First, put the equations in the same order by adding bx to both sides of the second equation to get $bx + 4y = 48$. Next, multiply the entire first equation by 3 to make both equations equal 48. The first equation becomes $\dfrac{3}{2}x + 3ay = 48$. Set the x-terms equal to each other to get $\dfrac{3}{2}x = bx$. Divide both sides of this equation by x to get $\dfrac{3}{2} = b$. Set the y-terms equal to each other to get $3ay = 4y$. Divide both sides of this equation by $3y$ to get $a = \dfrac{4}{3}$. Finally, add a and b: $\dfrac{3}{2} + \dfrac{4}{3}$. Either use a calculator or a common denominator of 6 to get $a + b = \dfrac{17}{6}$. The answer can also be entered in the fill-in box in decimal form, entering digits until there is no more room, as 2.833. The correct answer is $\dfrac{17}{6}$ or 2.833.

20. **B** The question asks for the value of a constant in an equation. When a quadratic is in standard form, which is $ax^2 + bx + c$, the shortcut to find the sum of the solutions is $-\dfrac{b}{a}$. In this quadratic, $a = 43$ and $b = (43d + e)$, so the sum of the solutions is $-\dfrac{(43d + e)}{43}$. The question states that the sum of the solutions can also be written as $k(43d + e)$, so set these values equal to each other: $-\dfrac{(43d + e)}{43} = k(43d + e)$. Multiply both sides of the equation by 43 to get $-(43d + e) = 43k(43d + e)$. Divide both sides of the equation by $(43d + e)$ to get $-1 = 43k$. Finally, divide both sides of the equation by 43 to get $-\dfrac{1}{43} = k$. The correct answer is (B).

21. **C** The question asks for the volume of a geometric figure. Find the volume of each piece of the capsule separately, and then add the volumes together. The figure is already drawn and labeled, but redraw it on the scratch paper if that makes it easier to see what's going on. Write down the relevant formulas, either from memory or after looking them up on the reference sheet. The formula for the volume of a cylinder is $V = \pi r^2 h$, and the formula for the volume of a sphere is $V = \dfrac{4}{3}\pi r^3$. The radius of the cylinder is given on the figure as 3, and the height is given as 12, so the volume of the cylinder is $V = \pi(3)^2(12)$, which becomes $V = \pi(9)(12)$, and then $V = 108\pi$. The two ends of the capsule make up one complete sphere, and the radius of the sphere is given on the figure as 3. The volume of the complete sphere is $V = \dfrac{4}{3}\pi(3)^3$, which becomes $V = \dfrac{4}{3}\pi(27)$, and then $V = 36\pi$. The volume of the entire capsule is $108\pi + 36\pi = 144\pi$. The correct answer is (C).

22. **6** The question asks for radius of a circle given an equation for its graph. The most efficient approach is to enter the equation into the built-in graphing calculator. Click on the gray dots at the maximum and minimum y-values to find the two ends of the diameter. The maximum y-value is at $(-2.5, 7.5)$, and the minimum y-value is at $(2.5, -4.5)$. Since the two points have the same x-coordinate, the distance between them is the diameter of the circle. Find the difference to get a diameter of $7.5 - (-4.5) = 12$. The radius of a circle is half the diameter, so the radius is 6. The correct answer is 6.

Chapter 7
Extra Practice

SAT Prep—Reading and Writing
Extra Practice: Harder

Turn to Section 1 of your answer sheet to answer the questions in this section.

---

1 Mark for Review

Initially a dedicated civil rights lawyer, Thurgood Marshall had countless victories in cases disputed before the Supreme Court, which brought immense changes in racial disparities in education. He was particularly notable for his role in arguing the landmark case *Brown v. Board of Education*, where segregation in public schools was declared unconstitutional. Marshall was nominated by President Lyndon B. Johnson to become the first African American Supreme Court justice, where the _____ jurist continued to serve the American justice system until retirement.

Which choice completes the text with the most logical and precise word or phrase?

(A) despondent

(B) apathetic

(C) ardent

(D) animated

---

2 Mark for Review

In an effort to facilitate a compromise regarding the expansion of slavery in newly admitted Western states and garner electoral support in slaveholding border states in his 1860 presidential campaign, Abraham Lincoln _____ any suggestion that he would interfere with slavery where it already existed, but he also made it clear that he would not allow it to spread into new territories.

Which choice completes the text with the most logical and precise word or phrase?

(A) advocated

(B) reconciled

(C) alienated

(D) repudiated

CONTINUE

3 ⬚ Mark for Review

Marie Tharp was an American geologist and oceanographic cartographer who _____ Alfred Wegener's long-dismissed theory of continental drift with her discovery of the 10,000-mile-long Mid-Atlantic Ridge—a finding that showed that the sea floor was actively spreading and proved that continental plates are indeed moving.

Which choice completes the text with the most logical or precise word or phrase?

(A) usurped

(B) vindicated

(C) obliterated

(D) accommodated

4 ⬚ Mark for Review

As early as the 5th century BCE, palm-leaf manuscripts were used in South Asia. The use of dehydrated leaves from palm trees as stationery allowed individuals to make inscriptions on the leaves and then apply colored substances to them. Once this was done, the creators would wipe away the excess, and the color would be left in the indentations, making the lettering visible. While this was a widely used technique, it had its drawbacks. Preservation of the organic material was difficult, as the leaves were prone to decompose due to exposure to humidity and moisture. To avoid the threat of _____, inscriptions on decaying leaves would need to be copied onto new, dried leaves in order to preserve and keep records of the texts carved into them.

Which choice completes the text with the most logical and precise word or phrase?

(A) emancipation

(B) desiccation

(C) putrefaction

(D) promulgation

5 ⬚ Mark for Review

During the 1930s, thousands of people across Europe experienced a _____ fear of a looming second world war: the German government's aggressive expansionist policies caused intense alarm and concern among those who all too viscerally remembered the devastation of the First World War.

Which choice completes the text with the most logical or precise word or phrase?

(A) reprehensible

(B) subdued

(C) palpable

(D) minimal

6 ⬚ Mark for Review

The following text is from Archibald Lampman's 1895 poem "Forest Moods."

> There is singing of birds in the deep wet woods,
> In the heart of the listening solitudes,
> Pewees, and thrushes, and sparrows, not few,
> And all the notes of their throats are true.
> The thrush from the innermost ash takes on
> A tender dream of the treasured and gone;
> But the sparrow singeth with pride and cheer
> Of the might and light of the present and here.

Which choice best states the main purpose of the text?

(A) To describe the smells of the wet woods

(B) To reveal the treasures of the forest

(C) To explain the technique sparrows use to sing

(D) To illustrate the atmosphere of the forest

CONTINUE ▶

7 ☐ Mark for Review

The Carnival of Barranquilla is known as one of the most significant cultural celebrations in Colombia. This annual, four-day festival attracts locals and visitors to the city that puts its daily life completely on pause for the four days prior to Lent, the period of fasting leading up to Easter. <u>During the carnival, the streets are full of musical performances, parades, and individuals dressed in disguises.</u> Each of the four days is marked by specific events, concerts, and processions.

Which choice best describes the function of the underlined portion in the text as a whole?

- Ⓐ It elaborates on the customs associated with an event introduced in the previous sentences.

- Ⓑ It states the purpose of the carnival and how the carnival is carried out each year.

- Ⓒ It informs readers of what to beware during the festival.

- Ⓓ It describes the fundraising events that take place during each day of the carnival.

8 ☐ Mark for Review

The following text is from Pedro Antonio de Alarcón's circa 1860 short story "Captain Veneno's Proposal of Marriage." The captain is speaking to Augustias, the woman he has just proposed to.

"Shall I tell you? We love each other. Do not tell me I am mistaken! That would be lying. And here is the proof: if you did not love me, I, too, should not love you! Let us try to meet one another halfway. I ask for a delay of ten years. When I shall have completed my half century, and when, a feeble old man, I shall have become familiar with the idea of slavery, then we will marry without anyone knowing about it. We will leave Madrid, and go to the country, where we shall have no spectators, where there will be nobody to make fun of me. But until this happens, please take half of my income secretly, and without any human soul ever knowing anything about it. You continue to live here, and I remain in my house. We will see each other, but only in the presence of witnesses—for instance, in society. We will write to each other every day."

Which choice best describes the overall structure of the text?

- Ⓐ The captain corrects a mistake, then tries to persuade Augustias to continue living the same way.

- Ⓑ The captain decides that he and Augustias will marry right away, then wonders whether they should leave Madrid shortly after.

- Ⓒ The captain asserts that there are mutual feelings between himself and Augustias, then relays his plan for their future married life.

- Ⓓ The captain lies to Augustias about his love, then offers her his wages.

CONTINUE →

9   Mark for Review

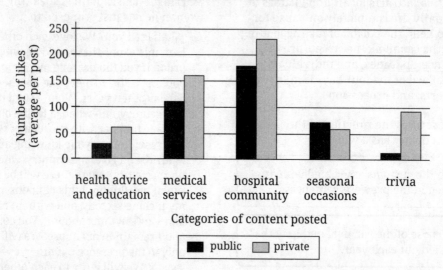

A Comparison of Public and Private Hospital Social Media Accounts

Social media has become a powerful outlet for community engagement and communication. A team of researchers was interested in analyzing the impact of public and private hospital social media accounts on the viewing public. To do so, posted content was divided into five categories and the average number of likes was measured per post. The team claimed that account followers preferred content involving information about the hospital community rather than hospital education and advice.

Which choice most effectively uses data from the graph to illustrate the research team's claim?

Ⓐ Private hospitals had a greater number of likes than did public hospitals on heath advice and education posts.

Ⓑ Public hospitals had a lower number of likes than did private hospitals on trivia posts.

Ⓒ Public and private hospitals had the greatest number of likes on hospital community posts compared with every other post category.

Ⓓ Public and private hospitals had a similar number of likes on seasonal occasions posts.

CONTINUE

10 ☐ Mark for Review

Text 1

Conventional wisdom says that the results of a study must be reproducible in order for its insights to be reliable. Psychologist Brian Nosek and colleagues undertook a project to reproduce 100 psychological studies, 97% of which had exhibited statistically significant results when originally published. However, when reproduced, only 36% of the studies met that criterion. Some researchers have consequently declared that there is a <u>crisis</u> in the methodology of psychological studies and thus the results of these studies cannot be trusted.

Text 2

While the failure to reproduce the majority of psychological studies does admittedly sound alarming, this does not indicate that there is anything wrong with the field of psychology itself. The importance of reproducibility of studies is well-established and agreed upon by professionals, but there are economic incentives that encourage researchers to consistently publish novel studies with seemingly revolutionary results that challenge previously held beliefs. These incentives discourage researchers from repeating old studies.

Based on the texts, how would the author of Text 2 most likely respond to the "crisis" discussed by the researchers in Text 1?

- (A) By agreeing that it sounds worrisome while criticizing the selection of studies that were chosen for reproduction

- (B) By praising the decision to reproduce studies as a worthwhile practice and agreeing that there is reason to mistrust the results of most studies

- (C) By discounting the premise that studies must be reproducible in order for them to be trustworthy

- (D) By asserting that it is overstated and that the problem is that most researchers are not appropriately incentivized to reproduce studies

11 ☐ Mark for Review

Effect of Difference in Wing Tip of Zebra Finches in Captive-Bred and Wild-Bred Populations

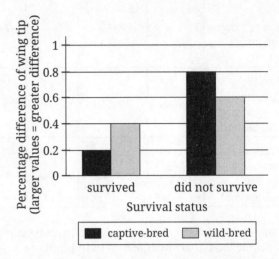

A bird's wing tip shape is formed by its longest primary feather and the two feathers adjacent to the longest primary feather above (distal) and below (proximal). A research conservation team theorized that variations in the length of a captive-bred bird's wing tip shape can have a negative consequence on migration flight survival rates. To test this theory, the team compared the wing tip measurements of zebra finches, both captive-bred and wild-bred, and tracked whether they survived their first migration flight. They found that zebra finches with _____

Which choice most effectively uses data from the graph to complete the statement?

- (A) greater wing tip differences were more likely to survive if captive-bred than wild-bred.

- (B) lower wing tip differences were less likely to survive if wild-bred than captive-bred.

- (C) greater wing tip differences were less likely to survive in both captive- and wild-bred populations.

- (D) lower wing tip differences were less likely to survive in both captive- and wild-bred populations.

CONTINUE ➡

Different Eye Movement Measures by Painting Type

Eye movement	Abstract	Landscape	Portrait	People
Number of fixations (average range per painting type)	4–5	8–10	3–4	7–9
Saccade amplitude (average range in milliseconds)	45–65	80–100	35–55	70–90
Number of blinks (average range per painting type)	6–7	1–2	8–10	3–5

A team of researchers was interested in investigating how people look at art by tracking individual eye movements across different types of paintings including abstract paintings, portraits, landscapes, and paintings of people. The team analyzed the eye movements according to the number of fixations (locations at which eye movement stopped), the amplitude of saccades (eye movement across a visual field), and the number of blinks (which occur less during increased eye movement). Following analysis of the data, the team concluded that participants had greater eye movement when viewing landscapes or people than when viewing portraits, given that _____

---

12 ☐ Mark for Review

Which choice most effectively uses data from the table to support the research team's conclusion?

Ⓐ the number of fixations was higher for landscapes and paintings of people than for portraits, while the saccade amplitude was highest for portraits.

Ⓑ the saccade amplitude was highest for landscapes and paintings of people, while the number of blinks was lower for landscapes and paintings of people than for portraits.

Ⓒ the number of fixations was lower for portraits than for landscapes or paintings of people, while the number of blinks was highest for landscapes.

Ⓓ the saccade amplitude was lower for abstract paintings than for landscapes, while the number of blinks was higher for portraits than for abstract paintings.

CONTINUE

13 ☐ Mark for Review

Louisa is a 1784 verse-novel by Anna Seward. In the poem, the speaker expresses doubt regarding how to alleviate the pain brought on by memories of the past: _____

Which quotation from *Louisa* most effectively illustrates the claim?

Ⓐ "Cruel Remembrance! how shall I assuage / The yearning pangs of thy incessant rage?"

Ⓑ "What balmy comfort can the Heart pervade, / When bitter tears his broken faith upbraid."

Ⓒ "Detested impotence of flatter'd charms, / That could not bind my Wanderer to my arms!"

Ⓓ "Yet, tho' from Pain, and Grief for ever free, / Throw back soft Pity's tender glance on thee!"

14 ☐ Mark for Review

Previously, it was believed that the Bantu Expansion, a series of migrations through sub-Saharan Africa of the Proto-Bantu-speaking people, occurred around 2,500 years ago through the Sangha River Interval along the rainforest. Since the early Bantu people were agriculturists, it seemed improbable that they could have successfully migrated through the rainforest. However, recent linguistic models trace the migration patterns of over 400 Bantu languages through the rainforest over 4,000 years ago. Therefore, _____

Which choice most logically completes the text?

Ⓐ the Bantu Expansion occurred many years earlier than was previously thought.

Ⓑ early Bantu people were unsuccessful in migrating through the rainforest 4,000 years ago.

Ⓒ linguistic models are unique methods of tracing evolutionary patterns.

Ⓓ this evidence supports previously held beliefs regarding the Bantu Expansion.

15 ☐ Mark for Review

C-type, or carbonaceous, asteroids are remnants of the solar nebula that created the early solar system. The Ryugu asteroid, found orbiting the sun between Earth and Mars, is thought to be a C-type asteroid that contains primitive materials dating from the start of the solar system, based on prior research. Recently, an analysis of samples collected from Ryugu by a team of researchers found the sample composition to be the closest match to the solar nebula ever found to date. This suggests that _____

Which choice most logically completes the text?

Ⓐ Ryugu used to be part of the planetary bodies that formed the solar nebula.

Ⓑ C-type asteroids are usually found orbiting the sun between Earth and Mars.

Ⓒ Ryugu contains the same primitive materials that composed the solar nebula.

Ⓓ the recent composition samples contradict previous findings regarding C-type asteroids.

16 ☐ Mark for Review

Indian economist Amartya Sen argues that many famines throughout history _____ from unjust food distribution policies by unelected governments rather than simply from natural downturns in food production.

Which choice completes the text so that it conforms to the conventions of Standard English?

Ⓐ is resulting

Ⓑ results

Ⓒ have resulted

Ⓓ has resulted

CONTINUE ➡

17 ☐ Mark for Review

Senegalese novelist Boubacar Boris Diop is known for his novels, including his best-known work, *Murambi: The Book of Bones*, and *Doomi Golo*, one of the few novels written in the Wolof language. His literary career goes beyond writing _____ he is also the founder of an independent newspaper in Senegal called *Sol*.

Which choice completes the text so that it conforms to the conventions of Standard English?

Ⓐ novels, though,

Ⓑ novels, though:

Ⓒ novels though

Ⓓ novels. Though,

18 ☐ Mark for Review

Chinese Zhusuan is a traditional method of performing mathematical calculations using an _____ it involves manipulating beads on a specially designed frame to represent numbers and perform arithmetic operations.

Which choice completes the text so that it conforms to the conventions of Standard English?

Ⓐ abacus while

Ⓑ abacus:

Ⓒ abacus

Ⓓ abacus, while

19 ☐ Mark for Review

As a renowned photographer and artist, _____ such as sexism, personal identity, racism, and political disputes.

Which choice completes the text so that it conforms to the conventions of Standard English?

Ⓐ Carrie Mae Weems' works on different media displayed issues facing African Americans in their daily lives,

Ⓑ Carrie Mae Weems used a wide variety of media to display issues facing African Americans in their daily lives,

Ⓒ African Americans' many issues were displayed by Carrie Mae Weems through a variety of media,

Ⓓ African Americans were represented by Carrie Mae Weems in a variety of media,

20 ☐ Mark for Review

English poet Rupert Brooke is known for his idealistic war sonnets written at the beginning of World War I as well as his charm and good looks. Literary critic George Edward Woodberry, at the beginning of his introduction to *The Collected Poems of Rupert Brooke* (1915), noted that "Brooke was both fair to see and winning in his _____ a fitting description of how those who knew Brooke remembered him shortly after his death.

Which choice completes the text so that it conforms to the conventions of Standard English?

Ⓐ ways,"

Ⓑ ways";

Ⓒ ways"

Ⓓ ways" and

CONTINUE ➡

21 ☐ Mark for Review

Una Winifred Atwell was a celebrated Trinidadian pianist and the first Black woman to reach number one on the UK Singles _____ she began headlining national tours, Atwell had humble beginnings, playing piano for American servicemen at the Air Force base in Trinidad and Tobago.

Which choice completes the text so that it conforms to the conventions of Standard English?

(A) Chart before

(B) Chart. Before

(C) Chart, before

(D) Chart and before

22 ☐ Mark for Review

The hammered dulcimer, a percussion instrument, consists of strings stretched over a sound board, usually trapezoidal in shape. The instrument is played by striking the strings with a small mallet hammer. The dulcimer is related to the psaltery, an _____ is played by plucking the strings.

Which choice completes the text so that it conforms to the conventions of Standard English?

(A) instrument,

(B) instrument, that

(C) instrument

(D) instrument that

23 ☐ Mark for Review

Lonnie Johnson invented the Super Soaker, a top-selling water gun, in 1989. Johnson came up with the idea for the design while working on nuclear weapons and stealth bombers with the US Air Force. _____ he partnered with Hasbro to sell his design, but he eventually had to sue the company after being underpaid royalties.

Which choice completes the text with the most logical transition?

(A) Similarly,

(B) Not surprisingly,

(C) Then,

(D) Therefore,

24 ☐ Mark for Review

Researchers at the National University of Singapore have determined that the light in a primate's environment may help determine that primate's eye color. _____ these scientists hypothesize that lighter eyes may help tune primates' circadian clocks by allowing more blue light to reach the retinas.

Which choice completes the text with the most logical transition?

(A) Therefore,

(B) In conclusion,

(C) Nevertheless,

(D) Indeed,

CONTINUE →

25 ☐ Mark for Review

University of Michigan scientists Robert Bradley, Charlotte Mistretta, and Carrie Ferrario discovered that, in rats, the responsiveness of the nerves that transmit sweetness signals to the brain was reduced by almost 50% in rats fed a high-sugar diet when compared to those rats fed a normal diet. _____ it may be the case that humans who consume a high-sugar diet also have a reduced responsiveness of the nerves that transmit sweetness signals to the brain.

Which choice completes the text with the most logical transition?

(A) Therefore,

(B) On the other hand,

(C) Nevertheless,

(D) For example,

26 ☐ Mark for Review

While researching a topic, a student has taken the following notes:

- High-elevation alpine ecosystems are home to life forms that are adapted to live and thrive in extreme environmental conditions.
- Monitoring biodiversity in high-elevation alpine areas can be useful when it comes to observing the impact of climate changes.
- Researchers were interested in the high-elevation alpine ecosystem on Mt. Everest, Earth's highest mountain.
- Environmental DNA sequencing was used to assess biodiversity.
- Environmental DNA was collected from ponds and streams that were between 4,500 and 5,500 meters above sea level.
- The study detected that about 16% of global taxonomic orders were present in the samples from Mt. Everest.

The student wants to emphasize the aim of the research study. Which choice most effectively uses relevant information from the notes to accomplish this goal?

(A) Researchers wanted to assess the biodiversity in the high-elevation alpine ecosystem on Mt. Everest.

(B) Researchers used environmental DNA sequencing on samples taken from ponds and streams that were between 4,500 and 5,500 meters above sea level.

(C) High-elevation alpine ecosystems, like the one on Mt. Everest, are home to life forms adapted to extreme environmental conditions.

(D) The high-elevation alpine ecosystem on Mt. Everest contains about 16% of global taxonomic orders.

CONTINUE

27 ⬗ Mark for Review

While researching a topic, a student has taken the following notes:

- Dairy cows spend much of their time in barns.
- Feed is typically outside of each cow's stall.
- One chore on a dairy farm is to move feed towards the cows' stalls.
- This chore is known as feed pushing.
- When feed is pushed more frequently, cows produce more milk.
- Robots can push feed 24 hours a day.

The student wants to explain the benefits of robots on a dairy farm to an audience familiar with feed pushing. Which choice most effectively uses relevant information from the notes to accomplish this goal?

Ⓐ Feed pushing, which involves moving feed toward cow stalls, is a chore on a dairy farm.

Ⓑ In the barns in which dairy cows spend much of their time, feed is typically located outside each cow's stall.

Ⓒ Robots can push feed 24 hours a day, which helps cows produce more milk.

Ⓓ Feed pushing—moving feed towards cows' stalls—can be accomplished by robots that can work 24 hours a day, helping cows produce more milk.

STOP
If you finish before time is called, you may check your work on this section only.
Do not turn to any other section in the test.

SAT Prep—Math
Extra Practice: Harder

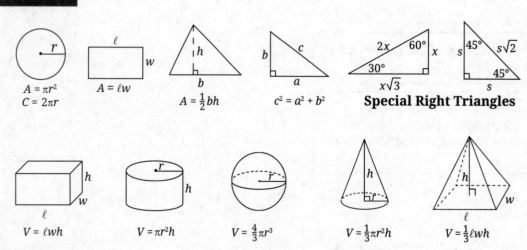
CONTINUE

For **multiple-choice questions,** solve each problem, choose the correct answer from the choices provided, and then fill in the circle with the answer letter. Enter only one answer for each question. You will not get credit for questions with more than one answer entered, or for questions with no answers entered.

For **student-produced response questions,** solve each problem and write your answer in the test book as described below.

- Enter your answer into the box provided.
- If you find **more than one correct answer**, enter only one answer.
- Your answer can be up to 5 characters for a **positive** answer and up to 6 characters (including the negative sign) for a **negative** answer.
- If your answer is a **fraction** that is too long (over 5 characters for positive, 6 characters for negative), write the decimal equivalent.
- If your answer is a **decimal** that is too long (over 5 characters for positive, 6 characters for negative), truncate it or round at the fourth digit.
- If your answer is a **mixed number** (such as $3\frac{1}{2}$), write it as an improper fraction (7/2) or its decimal equivalent (3.5).
- Don't enter **symbols** such as a percent sign, comma, or dollar sign in your answer.

CONTINUE

1 ☐ Mark for Review

A randomly selected sample from the 250 apple trees in an orchard is analyzed to determine whether the trees' apples are ripe. Among the trees in the sample, 64% have ripe apples. Which of the following is the best estimate of the total number of apple trees with ripe apples in the orchard based on this analysis?

Ⓐ 64

Ⓑ 90

Ⓒ 160

Ⓓ 250

2 ☐ Mark for Review

A carpenter works for a total of 35 hours each week making chairs and tables one at a time. The carpenter spends 3 hours making each chair and 7 hours making each table. Which of the following equations could represent the relationship between the number of chairs, c, and tables, t, the carpenter makes in a week?

Ⓐ $3c + 7t = 35$

Ⓑ $7c + 3t = 35$

Ⓒ $(c + t)(3 + 7) = 35$

Ⓓ $(3 + c)(7 + t) = 35$

3 ☐ Mark for Review

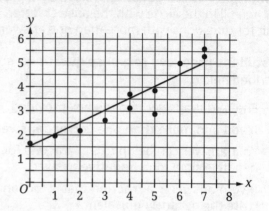

Which of the following linear equations most nearly represents the line of best fit as shown in the scatterplot?

Ⓐ $y = -0.5x - 1.5$

Ⓑ $y = -0.5x + 1.5$

Ⓒ $y = 0.5x - 1.5$

Ⓓ $y = 0.5x + 1.5$

CONTINUE

4 ☐ Mark for Review

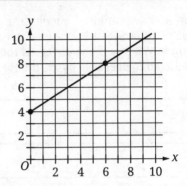

A line graphed in the xy-plane is shown. The point $(5, a)$ is on the line. What is the value of a?

(A) $\frac{3}{2}$

(B) $\frac{19}{3}$

(C) $\frac{43}{6}$

(D) $\frac{22}{3}$

5 ☐ Mark for Review

x	$h(x)$
0	19
1	27
2	37

For the quadratic function h, the table shows three values of x and their corresponding values of $h(x)$. Which of the following equations defines h?

(A) $h(x) = x^2 + 7x + 19$

(B) $h(x) = 2x^2 + 6x + 19$

(C) $h(x) = 3x^2 + 5x + 19$

(D) $h(x) = 6x^2 + 2x + 19$

6 ☐ Mark for Review

$$g(x) = \frac{3}{4}x + 6$$

The function g is defined by the given equation. If m is a constant and $g(m) = 12$, what is the value of m?

(A) 8

(B) 9

(C) 12

(D) 15

7 ☐ Mark for Review

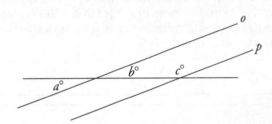

Note: Figure not drawn to scale.

The figure shows parallel lines o and p. What is the value of c if $a = 3x + 10$ and $b = 9x - 8$?

(A) 3

(B) 19

(C) 38

(D) 161

CONTINUE

8 ▢ Mark for Review

Line m is parallel to line l in the xy-plane, and line l is defined by $21y + \frac{7}{2} = -3x$. What is the slope of line m?

(A) -7

(B) $-\frac{1}{7}$

(C) $\frac{1}{7}$

(D) 7

9 ▢ Mark for Review

A solid brick in the shape of a rectangular prism has a length of 24 centimeters (cm), a width of 11.2 cm, and a height of 7 cm. The mass of the brick is 3,100 grams. To the nearest tenth, what is the density of the brick in grams per cubic centimeter?

(A) 0.3

(B) 0.6

(C) 1.6

(D) 3.9

10 ▢ Mark for Review

The function $R(v) = 120(0.98)^{\frac{1}{2}v}$ models the value, in thousands of dollars, of a house on a street with v vacant lots on it. What is the value of r if the value of the house is predicted to decrease by $r\%$ for every 2 vacant lots?

(A) 0.5

(B) 0.98

(C) 1

(D) 2

11 ▢ Mark for Review

The equation $\frac{81}{23}x - \frac{27}{7} = 3(ax + b)$ has infinitely many solutions. If a and b are constants, what is the value of b?

▭

12 ▢ Mark for Review

The seniors of school A are planning to invite the seniors from school B and school C to an event, and they need to estimate the numbers of seniors. There are 168 seniors at school A, which is 40% fewer than at school B. If school B has 160% of the number of seniors that school C has, how many seniors are at school C?

CONTINUE ▶

13 ☐ Mark for Review

The equation $-x^2 + 10x = k$, where k is a constant, has exactly two real solutions. If $s < k$, what is the greatest possible integer value of s?

(A) 4

(B) 10

(C) 24

(D) 25

14 ☐ Mark for Review

In trivia competitions, the 4 players on team X score a mean of 815 points each. The 6 players on team Y score a mean of 740 points each. If the two teams combine to form team Z, what will be the mean number of points likely to be scored by each player on Team Z?

[____]

15 ☐ Mark for Review

$$9x^2 - bx - 28 = (fx - g)(x + h)$$

In the given equation, f, g, and h are all integer constants, and b is a constant. Which of the following must be an integer?

(A) $\frac{28}{f}$

(B) $\frac{28}{g}$

(C) $\frac{b}{f}$

(D) $\frac{b}{g}$

16 ☐ Mark for Review

$$y = 3$$
$$y = -2x^2 + 4x + k$$

In the given system of equations, k is a constant. What is the value of k if the system of equations has exactly one real solution?

[____]

17 ☐ Mark for Review

$$ay = -\frac{6}{5}x + 2$$
$$x + 5 = 4x + y$$

The given system of equations has infinitely many solutions. What is the value of the constant a?

(A) $-\frac{6}{5}$

(B) $-\frac{2}{5}$

(C) $\frac{2}{5}$

(D) $\frac{6}{5}$

CONTINUE

18 ☐ Mark for Review

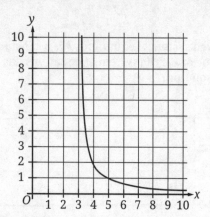

A partial graph of the rational function g is shown.

The equation of $y = g(x)$ can be written in the form $g(x) = \dfrac{a}{x+b}$, where a and b are constants. If $h(x) = g(x - 3)$, which equation could define function h?

Ⓐ $h(x) = \dfrac{2(x-3)}{(x-3)}$

Ⓑ $h(x) = \dfrac{2}{x-6}$

Ⓒ $h(x) = \dfrac{2}{(x-3)}$

Ⓓ $h(x) = \dfrac{2}{x}$

19 ☐ Mark for Review

$$21, 24, 25, 19, 24, 18, 23$$

The given list shows 7 of the 8 positive integers greater than 10 that make up a data set. The mean of these integers is 22, and the mean of the full data set is an integer less than 22. What is the value of the smallest integer in the full data set?

Ⓐ 6

Ⓑ 14

Ⓒ 19

Ⓓ 21

CONTINUE

20 ☐ Mark for Review

$$x^2 + y^2 - 2x - 4y - 11 = 0$$

The equation of a circle is shown. What is the circle's radius when it is graphed in the xy-plane?

21 ☐ Mark for Review

The equation $4 = x(ax + 12)$, in which a is an integer constant, has at least one real solution. What is the least possible value of a?

22 ☐ Mark for Review

Two identical right cylinders each have a height of 120 inches (in) and a surface area of A in^2. If the cylinders are combined along the circular bases, the resulting cylinder has a surface area of $\frac{41}{21}A$ in^2. What is the radius, in inches, of each cylinder?

(A) 2

(B) 3

(C) 6

(D) 36

CONTINUE

Chapter 8
Extra Practice:
Answers and
Explanations

EXTRA PRACTICE: MULTIPLE-CHOICE ANSWER KEY

Reading and Writing
Module (Harder)
1. C
2. D
3. B
4. C
5. C
6. D
7. A
8. C
9. C
10. D
11. C
12. B
13. A
14. A
15. C
16. C
17. B
18. B
19. B
20. A
21. B
22. D
23. C
24. D
25. A
26. A
27. C

Math
Module (Harder)
1. C
2. A
3. D
4. D
5. A
6. A
7. D
8. B
9. C
10. D
11. $-\dfrac{9}{7}$
12. 175
13. C
14. 770
15. B
16. 1
17. C
18. B
19. B
20. 4
21. −9
22. C

EXTRA PRACTICE—READING AND WRITING EXPLANATIONS

1. **C** This is a Vocabulary question, as it asks for *the most logical and precise word or phrase*. Read the text and highlight what can help to fill in the blank, which describes the *jurist* (Marshall). The text describes Marshall as being *a dedicated civil rights lawyer* before joining the Supreme Court and says that he *continued to serve the American justice system until retirement*. Write "dedicated" in the annotation box and use Process of Elimination.

    - (A) is wrong because *despondent* means "hopeless."

    - (B) is wrong because *apathetic* means "not caring."

    - (C) is correct because *ardent* means "passionate and dedicated."

    - (D) is wrong because *animated* means "lively and energetic," which isn't stated in the text.

2. **D** This is a Vocabulary question, as it asks for *the most logical and precise word or phrase*. Read the text and highlight what can help to fill in the blank, which refers to what Lincoln did to *any suggestion that he would interfere with slavery where it already existed*. The first part of the sentence states that Lincoln was trying to *facilitate a compromise* and *garner electoral support in slaveholding border states*. The last part of the sentence begins with a contrast (*but*) and states that he *made it clear that he would not allow it to spread into new territories*. This contrast suggests that he wouldn't let it spread, but he would let it exist where it was. Therefore, the blank should be something like "denied." Write "denied" in the annotation box and use Process of Elimination.

    - (A) and (B) are wrong because they are positive words, and the answer should be negative.

    - (C) is wrong because *alienated* means "caused to turn away," and it's not as precise as (D) in terms of going against the suggestion.

    - (D) is correct because *repudiated* means "rejected."

3. **B** This is a Vocabulary question, as it asks for *the most logical and precise word or phrase*. Read the text and highlight what can help to fill in the blank, which refers to what Tharp did to *Wegener's long-dismissed theory*. His theory was about *continental drift*, and she discovered *that the sea floor was actively spreading* and *continental plates are indeed moving*. Thus, she "found support for" his theory. Write "found support for" in the annotation box and use Process of Elimination.

    - (A) is wrong because *usurped* means "stole," and the text doesn't indicate that Tharp unfairly took over the theory.

    - (B) is correct because *vindicated* means "justify," and she found support for his claim that had been *long-dismissed*.

- (C) is wrong because *obliterated* means "destroyed," which is the opposite of what she did.

- (D) is wrong because *accommodated* means "allowed," which isn't strong enough to match with "found support for."

4. **C** This is a Vocabulary question, as it asks for *the most logical and precise word or phrase*. Read the text and highlight what can help to fill in the blank, which described the *threat* that needed to be avoided. The text explains *palm-leaf manuscripts* and then describes their *drawbacks*, including that *Preservation…was difficult* because the leaves would *decompose due to exposure to humidity and moisture*. Therefore, the threat is of decomposing. Write "decomposing" in the annotation box and use Process of Elimination.

    - (A) is wrong because *emancipation* means "becoming free."

    - (B) is wrong because *desiccation* means "drying out," but the end of the text suggests that drying the leaves would be a good thing.

    - (C) is correct because *putrefaction* means "decomposition."

    - (D) is wrong because *promulgation* means "putting forth."

5. **C** This is a Vocabulary question, as it asks for *the most logical and precise word or phrase*. Read the text and highlight what can help to fill in the blank, which describes the *fear*. The first part of the sentence is followed by a colon, which suggests that the second part will explain the first. The second part says the policies *caused intense alarm and concern* among people who *viscerally* (deeply felt) *remembered* World War I. Therefore, their fear was intense and deeply felt. Write "intense" in the annotation box and use Process of Elimination.

    - (A) is wrong because *reprehensible* means "worthy of condemnation," which isn't true about the people's *fear*.

    - (B) and (D) are wrong because they are the opposite of what is needed.

    - (C) is correct because *palpable* means "easily perceptible."

6. **D** This is a Purpose question, as it asks for the *main purpose*. Read the text and highlight what can help to understand the overall purpose. The text describes sounds in *the deep wet woods*, so write "describe sounds of the woods" in the annotation box and use Process of Elimination.

    - (A) is wrong because the text is focused on sounds, not *smells*.

    - (B) is wrong because the text mentions *the treasured* but doesn't state that these are *treasures of the forest*, nor does it *reveal* who or what these are.

    - (C) is wrong because the *technique* the sparrows use isn't mentioned.

    - (D) is correct because the sounds and the description *deep wet woods* convey the *atmosphere*.

7. **A**   This is a Purpose question, as it asks for the *function* of a sentence. Read the text and highlight what can help to understand the function of the underlined sentence. The text introduces the *Carnival of Barranquilla* and explains its significance. Then the underlined sentence describes some things that happen throughout the carnival, and the last sentence gives further details. Write "details about the carnival" in the annotation box and use Process of Elimination.

    - (A) is correct because it matches the annotation.

    - (B) is wrong because the *purpose* of the carnival doesn't appear in this sentence.

    - (C) is wrong because this sentence doesn't contain any information on what to *beware*.

    - (D) is wrong because *fundraising* isn't mentioned in this sentence.

8. **C**   This is a Purpose question, as it asks for the *overall structure*. Read the text and highlight what can help to understand the overall structure of the text. In the text, the captain says that he and Augustias *love each other* and asks for a compromise. After *ten years*, he will marry her *without anyone knowing about it* and they will leave and go to *the country*. In the meantime, he will secretly give her half of his income, and they will live separately, see each other only in public, and *write to each other every day*. Write "captain's plan for their future" in the annotation box and use Process of Elimination.

    - (A) is wrong because no *mistake* is corrected; the captain says he is not *mistaken* in asserting their feelings for each other.

    - (B) is wrong because the text says they will marry in *ten years*, not *right away*.

    - (C) is correct because it matches the annotation.

    - (D) is wrong because there is no evidence that the captain is lying about his feelings.

9. **C**   This is a Charts question, as it asks for *data from the graph*. The graph charts the number of likes on social media posts in different categories for public and private hospitals. Highlight the *claim* in the text, which is that *account followers preferred content involving information about the hospital community rather than hospital education and advice*. Eliminate any answers that are inconsistent with the graph or don't support the claim.

    - (A) and (B) are wrong because the claim isn't about a difference between public and private hospitals.

    - (C) is correct because it matches the claim and is consistent with the chart.

    - (D) is wrong because *seasonal occasions* aren't related to the claim, which is about *hospital community*.

10.   **D**   This is a Dual Texts question, as it has two texts. The question asks how *the author of Text 2* would respond to *the "crisis" discussed by the researchers in Text 1*. Start by understanding the *crisis* in Text 1. Text 1 explains the importance of study results being *reproducible* (shown again) and then describes a study showing that many psychological study results weren't reproduced. This is described as a potential *crisis*. Next, look for a similar idea in Text 2 to see how its author feels about this view. Text 2 acknowledges that the *failure to reproduce…does admittedly sound alarming* but then contrasts this idea by stating that it doesn't mean that *there is anything wrong with the field of psychology*. Then, the author states that *there are economic incentives* that encourage people to *publish novel studies* instead of *repeating old studies*. Therefore, the author of Text 2 would "say it's not a big deal and there's a reason—incentives." Write that in the annotation box and use Process of Elimination.

- (A) is wrong because the first part is supported but nothing in Text 2 suggests *criticizing the selection of studies*.

- (B) is wrong because Text 2 doesn't agree that *there is a reason to mistrust the results of most studies*.

- (C) is wrong because the author states that *The importance of reproducibility of studies is well-established and agreed upon by professionals*, so the author doesn't disagree with this idea.

- (D) is correct because it matches the annotation.

11.   **C**   This is a Charts question, as it asks for *data from the graph*. The graph charts the survival status for captive-bred and wild-bred birds based on their wing tip measurements. The blank needs to provide what the study *found*. Eliminate any answers that are inconsistent with the graph.

- (A) and (B) are wrong because they aren't supported by the graph.

- (C) is correct because the higher wing tip difference correlates with not surviving in both groups.

- (D) is wrong because it's the opposite of what the graph shows.

12.   **B**   This is a Charts question, as it asks for *data from the table*. The table charts several types of eye movements people had for different types of paintings. Highlight the *conclusion* in the text, which is that *participants had greater eye movement when viewing landscapes or people than when viewing portraits*. Eliminate any answers that are inconsistent with the graph or don't support the conclusion.

- (A) is wrong because the saccade amplitude wasn't *highest for portraits*.

- (B) is correct because the information is consistent with the table and the conclusion.

- (C) is wrong because the number of blinks was lowest for landscapes, not highest.

- (D) is wrong because the claim isn't about *abstract* paintings.

13. **A**   This is a Claims question, as it asks for a *quotation* that *illustrates the claim*. Read the text and highlight the *claim*, which is that *the speaker expresses doubt regarding how to alleviate the pain brought on by memories of the past*. Eliminate answers that don't *illustrate* this idea.

- (A) is correct because *Cruel Remembrance* matches with *memories of the past, how shall I assuage* (make better) matches with *doubt regarding how to alleviate*, and *yearning pangs of thy incessant rage* matches with *pain*.

- (B) is wrong because it mentions pain and a lack of *comfort* but has nothing about *memories of the past*.

- (C) is wrong because it doesn't mention anything related to the claim.

- (D) is wrong because it mentions pain but nothing from the rest of the claim.

14. **A**   This is a Conclusions question, as it asks for the choice that *most logically completes the text*. Read the text and highlight the main ideas. The text describes a previous view that the Bantu Expansion *occurred around 2,500 years ago through the Sangha River Interval* and then explains why it was *improbable* that they migrated *through the rainforest*. Then there is a contrast, which states that *recent linguistic models* show the migration happening *through the rainforest over 4,000 years ago*. Eliminate any answer that states a conclusion that isn't supported by the text.

- (A) is correct because the recent model suggests that the expansion happened 4,000 years ago rather than 2,500 years ago.

- (B) is wrong because there is no evidence that the migration was *unsuccessful*.

- (C) is wrong because *linguistic models* aren't described as being *unique*.

- (D) is wrong because the new evidence goes against, not *supports*, previous beliefs.

15. **C**   This is a Conclusions question, as it asks for the choice that *most logically completes the text*. Read the text and highlight the main ideas. The text introduces *C-type asteroids* as *remnants of the solar nebula that created the early solar system* and describes a specific asteroid, *Ryugu*, that is thought to be one *based on prior research*. Then, it describes recent research that *found the sample composition to be the closest match to the solar nebula ever found to date*. Eliminate any answer that states a conclusion that isn't supported by the text.

- (A) is wrong because there isn't evidence that Ryugu was *part of the planetary bodies*; it could have been from something else in the solar nebula.

- (B) is wrong because this is true about Ryugu, but the text doesn't say that this is *usually* the case.

- (C) is correct because if the samples were similar to the composition of the solar nebula, then they must contain the same materials.

- (D) is wrong because Ryugu was already thought to be C-type, so this is a confirmation, not a contradiction, of *previous findings*.

16. **C**   In this Rules question, verbs are changing in the answer choices, so it's testing consistency with verbs. Find and highlight the subject, *famines*, which is plural, so a plural verb is needed. Write an annotation saying "plural." Eliminate any answer that is not plural.

- (A), (B), and (D) are wrong because they are singular.

- (C) is correct because it's plural.

17. **B**   In this Rules question, punctuation with a transition is changing in the answer choices. Look for independent clauses. The first part of the sentence says *His literary career goes beyond writing novels.* There is an option to add *though* to this independent clause. This statement does contrast with the previous sentence, which states that Diop *is known for his novels*, so *though* belongs in the first part of the sentence. Eliminate options with *though* in the second part.

- (A) and (C) are wrong because the sentence contains two independent clauses, which cannot be connected with commas alone or with no punctuation.

- (B) is correct because it puts *though* with the first independent clause and puts a colon between the two independent clauses.

- (D) is wrong because it puts *though* with the second independent clause.

18. **B**   In this Rules question, punctuation is changing in the answer choices. Look for independent clauses. The first part of the sentence says *Chinese Zhusuan is a traditional method of performing mathematical calculations using an abacus*, which is an independent clause. The second part says *it involves manipulating beads on a specially designed frame to represent numbers and perform arithmetic operations*, which is also an independent clause. Eliminate any answer that can't correctly connect two independent clauses.

- (A) and (D) are wrong because these ideas agree, so the contrasting transition *while* isn't appropriate.

- (B) is correct because a colon can connect two independent clauses if the second one elaborates on the first, as it does here.

- (C) is wrong because some type of punctuation is needed in order to connect two independent clauses.

19. **B**   In this Rules question, the subjects of the answers are changing, which suggests it may be testing modifiers. Look for and highlight a modifying phrase: *As a renowned photographer and artist.* Whoever is *a renowned photographer and artist* needs to come immediately after the comma. Eliminate any answer that doesn't start with someone who could be an artist.

- (A) is wrong because her *works* aren't an artist.

- (B) is correct because *Weems* is the artist.

- (C) is wrong because *issues* aren't an artist.

- (D) is wrong because *African Americans* as a group aren't an artist.

20. **A**   In this Rules question, punctuation is changing in the answer choices. The last part of the sentence says *a fitting description of how those who knew Brooke remembered him shortly after his death*, which is a describing phrase. Noun phrases beginning with "a" or "an" are always non-essential to the meaning of the sentence and should be set off with commas. Eliminate answers that do not have a comma.

- (A) is correct because it uses a comma before the non-essential information.

- (B) is wrong because a semicolon connects two independent clauses, but the last part isn't an independent clause.

- (C) is wrong because a comma is needed before the describing phrase.

- (D) is wrong because it makes the last part of the sentence into an item in a list, which isn't correct; it's a description of the quotation.

21. **B**   In this Rules question, punctuation is changing in the answer choices. Look for independent clauses. The first part of the sentence says *Una Winifred Atwell was a celebrated Trinidadian pianist and the first Black woman to reach number one on the UK Singles Chart*, which is an independent clause. The second part says *before she began headlining national tours, Atwell had humble beginnings*, which is also an independent clause. Eliminate any answer that can't correctly connect two independent clauses.

- (A) is wrong because some type of punctuation is needed in order to connect two independent clauses.

- (B) is correct because the period makes each independent clause its own sentence, which is fine.

- (C) is wrong because a comma without a coordinating conjunction can't connect two independent clauses.

- (D) is wrong because a coordinating conjunction (*and*) without a comma can't connect two independent clauses.

22. **D**   In this Rules question, commas and the word *that* are changing in the answers, which suggests that the question is testing the construction of describing phrases. The first part of the sentence says *The dulcimer is related to the psaltery*, which is an independent clause followed by a comma. Eliminate any answer that isn't consistent with the first part of the sentence.

- (A) is wrong because it leaves the verb *is played* with no subject.

- (B) is wrong because a phrase starting with "that" is essential to the meaning of the sentence and never follows a comma.

- (C) is wrong because it creates two independent clauses separated by a comma, which is not allowed.

- (D) is correct because it creates an essential phrase with *that* and no punctuation.

23. **C** This is a transition question, so highlight ideas that relate to each other. The preceding sentences introduce Johnson and his invention, and this sentence describes events that happened later. Eliminate any answer that doesn't match this relationship.

- (A) is wrong because the third sentence isn't something similar to what came before.

- (B) is wrong because there is no evidence regarding whether these events were surprising or not.

- (C) is correct because *Then* supports the sequence of events.

- (D) is wrong because this sentence isn't a conclusion based on what came before.

24. **D** This is a transition question, so highlight ideas that relate to each other. The first sentence states that *the light in a primate's environment may help determine that primate's eye color*, and this sentence describes a hypothesis that *lighter eyes may help tune primates' circadian clocks*. These ideas agree, so a same-direction transition is needed. Make an annotation that says "agree." Eliminate any answer that doesn't match.

- (A) and (B) are wrong because this sentence isn't a conclusion based on the previous sentence.

- (C) is wrong because *Nevertheless* is opposite-direction.

- (D) is correct because *Indeed* supports and reinforces the previous idea.

25. **A** This is a transition question, so highlight ideas that relate to each other. The first sentence says that *the responsiveness of the nerves that transmit sweetness signals to the brain was reduced…in rats fed a high-sugar diet*, and this sentence suggests that this may occur in humans as well. These ideas agree, so a same-direction transition is needed. Make an annotation that says "agree." Eliminate any answer that doesn't match.

- (A) is correct because it's a logical conclusion that if this is the case for mice, it could be for humans as well.

- (B) and (C) are wrong because they are opposite-direction transitions.

- (D) is wrong because this sentence isn't an example of the preceding one.

26. **A** This is a Rhetorical Synthesis question, so highlight the goal(s) stated in the question: *emphasize the aim of the research study*. Eliminate any answer that doesn't fulfill this purpose.

- (A) is correct because it tells what researchers *wanted* to do, so their *aim*.

- (B) is wrong because it tells what the researchers did but not their *aim*.

- (C) and (D) are wrong because they don't mention the *research study* at all.

27. **C** This is a Rhetorical Synthesis question, so follow the basic approach. Highlight the goal(s) stated in the question: *explain the benefits of robots on a dairy farm to an audience familiar with feed pushing.* Eliminate any answer that doesn't *explain the benefits* in a way that assumes the audience is *familiar with feed pushing.*

- (A) and (D) are wrong because they explain feed pushing, but the audience is already familiar with it.

- (B) is wrong because it doesn't mention *robots* or their *benefits*.

- (C) is correct because it mentions robots and their benefits, and it doesn't explain what feed pushing is.

EXTRA PRACTICE—MATH EXPLANATIONS

1. **C**   The question asks for a value based on a percentage. Translate the English to math in bite-sized pieces. *Percent* means out of 100, so translate 64% as $\frac{64}{100}$. Since 64% of the trees in the random sample have ripe apples, apply that percent to the entire 250 trees in the orchard. Taking the percent *of* a number translates to multiplication, so 64% of 250 becomes $\frac{64}{100}(250)$. Use a calculator to get 160 trees with ripe apples. The correct answer is (C).

2. **A**   The question asks for an expression that represents a specific situation. Translate the information into bite-sized pieces and eliminate after each piece. One piece of information says that the *carpenter spends 3 hours making each chair*, and another piece says that *c* is the number of chairs, so translate the total time spent making chairs as 3*c*. Eliminate (B) and (D) because they do not include this term. Choice (C) includes 3*c* after expanding the left side of the equation using FOIL, but it also includes 7*c*, which does not match the information in the question; eliminate (C). The correct answer is (A).

3. **D**   The question asks for an equation that represents a graph. One method is to use the built-in graphing calculator. Enter each of the equations in the answer choices into the graphing calculator and see which line looks most like the line of best fit of the scatterplot given. Another method is to translate the information into bite-sized pieces and eliminate after each piece. The answer choices are all in slope-intercept form, $y = mx + b$, in which *m* is the slope and *b* is the *y*-intercept. The *y*-intercept is the point where $x = 0$, which is close to 1.5 on this graph. Eliminate (A) and (C) because they have negative *y*-intercepts. Compare the remaining answer choices. The difference between (B) and (D) is the sign of the slope. The line of best fit ascends from left to right, so it has a positive slope. Eliminate (B) because it has a negative slope. Using either method, the correct answer is (D).

4. **D**   The question asks for a value on a graph. Find 5 on the *x*-axis: it is halfway between the labeled vertical line for 4 and the labeled vertical line for 6. Move up from there to the line of best fit, using the mouse pointer or scratch paper as a ruler if necessary. From there, move left to the *y*-axis to see that the value is between the unlabeled horizontal line for 7 and the labeled horizontal line for 8. Eliminate (A) and (B) because those values are not between 7 and 8. The find the exact *y*-coordinate of the point (5, *y*), find the slope by using the formula $slope = \frac{y_2 - y_1}{x_2 - x_1}$. The graph has points at (0, 4) and (6, 8), so plug those values into the slope formula to get $slope = \frac{8 - 4}{6 - 0}$, which becomes $slope = \frac{4}{6}$, or $slope = \frac{2}{3}$. Now plug in the points at (0, 4) and (5, *y*) to get $slope = \frac{y - 4}{5 - 0}$, which becomes $slope = \frac{y - 4}{5}$. The line has a slope of $\frac{2}{3}$, so $\frac{y - 4}{5} = \frac{2}{3}$. Cross-multiply to get (5)(2) =

$(y - 4)(3)$. Multiply and distribute to get $10 = 3y - 12$, then add 12 to both sides of the equation to get $22 = 3y$. Divide both sides of the equation by 3 to get $\frac{22}{3} = y$. The correct answer is (D).

5. **A** The question asks for the function that represents values given in a table. In function notation, the number inside the parentheses is the x-value that goes into the function, or the input, and the value that comes out of the function is the y-value, or the output. The table includes three input and output values, and the correct equation must work for every pair of values. Plug in values from the table and eliminate functions that don't work. Because 0 and 1 are likely to make more than one answer work, try the third row of the table and plug $x = 2$ and $h(x) = 37$ into the answer choices. Choice (A) becomes $37 = 2^2 + 7(2) + 19$, or $37 = 4 + 14 + 19$, and then $37 = 37$. This is true, so keep (A), but check the remaining answers just in case. Choice (B) becomes $37 = 2(2)^2 + 6(2) + 19$, or $37 = 8 + 12 + 19$, and then $37 = 39$. This is not true, so eliminate (B). Choice (C) becomes $37 = 3(2)^2 + 5(2) + 19$, or $37 = 12 + 10 + 19$, and then $37 = 41$; eliminate (C). Choice (D) becomes $37 = 6(2)^2 + 2(2) + 19$, or $37 = 24 + 4 + 19$, and then $37 = 47$; eliminate (D). The correct answer is (A).

6. **A** The question asks for a value given a function. In function notation, the number inside the parentheses is the x-value that goes into the function, or the input, and the value that comes out of the function is the y-value, or the output. The question provides an output value of 12, and the answers have numbers that could represent the x-value, m, so use the values in the answers. Start with one of the middle numbers and try (B), 9. Plug 9 into the function for x to get $g(9) = \frac{3}{4}(9) + 6$, which becomes $g(9) = \frac{27}{4} + 6$. This will not result in an integer, so it cannot equal the output value of 12; eliminate (B). The input value must be a multiple of 4 to result in an integer, so also eliminate (D). Try (C) next, and plug 12 into the function for x to get $g(12) = \frac{3}{4}(12) + 6$, which becomes $g(12) = 9 + 6$, or $g(12) = 15$. This is not 12, so eliminate (C). The correct answer is (A).

7. **D** The question asks for the value of an angle on a figure. Redraw the figure and labels on the scratch paper. When a line intersects two parallel lines, two kinds of angles are created: big and small. All of the small angles are equal to each other, all of the big angles are equal to each other, and any small angle plus any big angle = 180°. The angle marked $a°$ is a small angle, and the angle marked $b°$ is also a small angle. Thus, $a = b$, so set the expression equal to a and the expression equal to b equal to each other: $3x + 10 = 9x - 8$. Subtract $3x$ from both sides of the equation to get $10 = 6x - 8$, and then add 8 to both sides of the equation to get $18 = 6x$. Divide both sides of the equation by 6 to get $3 = x$. Plug $x = 3$ into the equation for angle a to get $a = 3(3) + 10$, which becomes $a = 9 + 10$, and then $a = 19$. Label both small angles, a and b, as 19. Since angle c is a large angle, its measure is $180 - 19 = 161$. The correct answer is (D).

8. **B**   The question asks for the slope of a line that is parallel to another line. Parallel lines have the same slope, so calculate the slope of line l. The equation is in neither slope-intercept form nor standard form, so convert to one of those forms. To convert the equation of line l into slope-intercept form, $y = mx + b$, in which m is the slope, subtract $\frac{7}{2}$ from both sides of the equation to get $21y = -3x - \frac{7}{2}$. Divide both sides of the equation by 21 to get $y = -\frac{3}{21}x - \frac{7}{2(21)}$. Reduce the fractions to get $y = -\frac{1}{7}x - \frac{1}{6}$. The slope of line l is $-\frac{1}{7}$. Because line m is parallel to line l, its slope is also $-\frac{1}{7}$. The correct answer is (B).

9. **C**   The question asks for the density of a geometric figure. Start by calculating the volume of the brick. Write down the formula for the volume of a rectangular prism, either from memory or after looking it up on the Reference Sheet. The formula is $V = lwh$. Plug in the information from the question to get $V = (24)(11.2)(7)$, which becomes $V = 1{,}881.6$ cubic centimeters. Next, use the units to figure out how to relate volume, mass, and density. Since density is in grams per cubic centimeter, mass is in grams, and volume is in cubic centimeters, density must be mass divided by volume. This happens to be the formula for density, which can be written as $D = \frac{m}{V}$. Plug in the values for mass and volume to get $D = \frac{3{,}100}{1{,}881.6}$, which becomes $D \approx 1.648$. Round to the nearest tenth to get $D = 1.6$. The correct answer is (C).

10. **D**   The question asks for the value of a rate of decrease given a function that represents a specific situation. The value of the function is decreasing by a certain percent, so this question is about exponential decay. Write down the growth and decay formula, which is *final amount* = (*original amount*)$(1 \pm rate)^{number\ of\ changes}$. The *number of changes* is given in terms of v, the number of vacant lots, and the question states that *the value of the house is predicted to decrease by r% for every 2 vacant lots*, so plug in 2 for v. The function becomes $R(2) = 120(0.98)^{\frac{1}{2}(2)}$, and then $R(2) = 120(0.98)^1$. Thus, the value changes once for every 2 vacant lots. The value of the house is decreasing, so the value in parentheses is $(1 - rate)$. The question gives a value of 0.98, so $0.98 = 1 - rate$. Add *rate* to both sides of the equation, and subtract 0.98 from both sides of the equation to get $rate = 0.02$. The question asks for the rate as a percentage, so multiply 0.02 by 100 to get 2%. The correct answer is (D).

11. $-\dfrac{9}{7}$ The question asks for a constant in a system of linear equations. When a linear equation has infinitely many solutions, the two sides of the equation are identical, and any value of x will make the equation true. Distribute on the right side of the equation to get $\dfrac{81}{23}x - \dfrac{27}{7} = 3ax + 3b$. The two terms with x must be equal, and the two terms without x must be equal. The question asks for the value of b, so focus on the terms without x. Set them equal to each other to get $-\dfrac{27}{7} = 3b$. Divide both sides of this equation by 3 to get $-\dfrac{27}{7(3)} = b$. Reduce the fraction to get $-\dfrac{9}{7} = b$. The correct answer is $-\dfrac{9}{7}$.

12. **175** The question asks for a value based on percentages and a specific situation. Translate the English to math in bite-sized pieces. Start with the sentence relating the number of seniors at school A and school B. Translate *is* as equals. *Percent* means out of 100, so translate 40% as $\dfrac{40}{100}$. Translate *fewer* as subtraction. Thus, 40% fewer is $1 - \dfrac{40}{100}$, or $\dfrac{60}{100}$. Use a variable for the number of seniors at school B, such as b. The equation becomes $168 = \dfrac{60}{100}b$. Multiply both sides of the equation by 100 and divide both sides of the equation by 60 to get $280 = b$. Next, translate the sentence relating the number of seniors at school B and school C. Translate *has* as equals, and translate 160% as $\dfrac{160}{100}$. Use the variable c to represent the number of seniors at school C. The equation becomes $280 = \dfrac{160}{100}c$. Multiply both sides of the equation by 100 and divide both sides of the equation by 160 to get $175 = c$. The correct answer is 175.

13. **C** The question asks for the value of a constant in a quadratic. To determine when a quadratic equation has exactly two real solutions, use the discriminant. The discriminant is the part of the quadratic formula under the square root sign and is written as $D = b^2 - 4ac$. When the discriminant is positive, the quadratic has exactly two real solutions; when the discriminant is 0, the quadratic has exactly one real solution; and when the discriminant is negative, the quadratic has no real solutions. Thus, the discriminant of this quadratic must equal a positive number. First, put the quadratic in standard form, which is $ax^2 + bx + c = 0$, by adding x^2 to both sides of the equation and subtracting $10x$ from both sides of the equation to get $x^2 - 10x + k = 0$. Now that the quadratic is in standard form, $a = 1$, $b = -10$, and $c = k$. Plug these into the discriminant formula to get $D = (-10)^2 - 4(1)(k)$, or $D = 100 - 4k$. Since there are exactly two real solutions, $100 - 4k > 0$. Add $4k$ to both sides of the inequality to get $100 > 4k$, then divide both sides of the inequality by 4 to get $25 > k$. The greatest integer that is less than 25 is 24. The correct answer is (C).

14. **770** The question asks for a mean, or average, based on two other means. For averages, use the formula $T = AN$, in which T is the *Total*, A is the *Average*, and N is the *Number of things*. For team X, the *number of things* is 4 and the *average* is 815, so the formula becomes $T = (815)(4)$, or $T = 3,260$. For team Y, the *number of things* is 6 and the *average* is 740, so the formula becomes $T = (740)(6)$, or $T = 4,440$. Add the *totals* for the two teams to get $3,260 + 4,440 = 7,700$; this is the *total* for team Z. Add the *numbers of things* for the two teams to get $4 + 6 = 10$; this is the *number of things* for team Z. The average formula for team Z becomes $7,700 = (A)(10)$. Divide both sides of the equation by 10 to get $770 = A$, which is the average, or mean, for team Z. The correct answer is 770.

15. **B** The question asks for an expression that must be an integer. Make the two sides of the equation look similar by using FOIL to expand the right side of the equation. The equation becomes $9x^2 - bx - 28 = fx^2 + fhx - gx - gh$. The two terms with x^2 are equivalent, so $9x^2 = fx^2$. Divide both sides of this equation by x^2 to get $9 = f$. Choice (A) is $\dfrac{28}{f}$, so plug in 9 for f to get $\dfrac{28}{9}$. This is not an integer, so eliminate (A). Next, work with the terms that do not have x^2 or x, and set -28 equal to $-gh$. Multiply both sides of this equation by -1 to get $28 = gh$. Choice (B) is $\dfrac{28}{g}$, so rewrite $28 = gh$ by dividing both sides of the equation by g to get $\dfrac{28}{g} = h$. The question states that h is an integer, so $\dfrac{28}{g}$ must also be an integer. The correct answer is (B).

16. **1** The question asks for the value of a constant in a quadratic. To determine when a quadratic equation has exactly one solution, use the discriminant. The discriminant is the part of the quadratic formula under the square root sign and is written as $D = b^2 - 4ac$. When the discriminant is positive, the quadratic has exactly two real solutions; when the discriminant is 0, the quadratic has exactly one real solution; and when the discriminant is negative, the quadratic has no real solutions. Thus, the discriminant of this quadratic must equal 0. First, substitute 3 for y in the second equation to get $3 = -2x^2 + 4x + k$, Next, put the quadratic in standard form, which is $ax^2 + bx + c = 0$, by subtracting 3 from both sides of the equation to get $0 = -2x^2 + 4x + k - 3$. Now that the quadratic is in standard form, $a = -2$, $b = 4$, and $c = k - 3$. Plug these into the discriminant formula to get $D = (4)^2 - 4(-2)(k - 3)$, or $D = 16 + 8(k - 3)$. Distribute the 8 to get $D = 16 + 8k - 24$, and then combine like terms to get $D = -8 + 8k$. Since there is exactly one real solution, $-8 + 8k = 0$. Add 8 to both sides of the equation to get $8k = 8$, and then divide both sides of the equation by 8 to get $k = 1$. The correct answer is 1.

17. **C** The question asks for the value of a constant in a system of linear equations. When two linear equations have infinitely many solutions, the two equations are the same line, and the equations are equivalent. Therefore, make the two equations look the same. First, put the equations in the same order by adding $\frac{6}{5}x$ to both sides of the first equation to get $\frac{6}{5}x + ay = 2$. Do the same with the second equation by subtracting x from both sides to get $5 = 3x + y$, and then switching the two sides of the equation to get $3x + y = 5$. The two equations now look like this:

$$\frac{6}{5}x + ay = 2$$

$$3x + y = 5$$

The two equations must equal each other, so make them both equal 10. Multiply the entire first equation by 5 to get $6x + 5ay = 10$. Multiply the entire second equation by 2 to get $6x + 2y = 10$. Set the y-terms equal to each other to get $5ay = 2y$, and then divide both sides of the equation by $5y$ to get $a = \frac{2}{5}$. The correct answer is (C).

18. **B** The question asks for the equation that defines a function that is graphed in the xy-plane. Since function h is related to function g, use knowledge of the transformation of graphs to tackle this question. When graphs are transformed, or translated, subtracting inside the parentheses shifts the graph to the right. Thus, $x - 3$ shifts the graph three units to the right. Find a point on the graph of $g(x)$, such as $(5, 1)$. When the graph is shifted three units to the right, this point becomes $(8, 1)$. Thus, the equation that defines function h must work for the point $(8, 1)$. Plug $x = 8$ and $h(x) = 1$ into the answer choices, and eliminate any that don't work. Choice (A) becomes $1 = \frac{2(8-3)}{(8-3)}$, or $1 = 2$. This is not true, so eliminate (A). Choice (B) becomes $1 = \frac{2}{8-6}$, or $1 = \frac{2}{2}$, and then $1 = 1$. This is true, so keep (B), but check the remaining answers just in case. Choice (C) becomes $1 = \frac{2}{(8-3)}$, or $1 = \frac{2}{5}$; eliminate (C). Choice (D) becomes $1 = \frac{2}{8}$, or $1 = \frac{1}{4}$; eliminate (D). The correct answer is (B).

19. **B** The question asks for a value given information about the mean, or average, of a data set. For averages, use the formula $T = AN$, in which T is the *Total*, A is the *Average*, and N is the *Number of things*. Start by finding the total of the seven integers given in the question. There are 7 values, so the *number of things* is 7, and the *average* is given as 22. The average formula becomes $T = (22)(7)$, or $T = 154$. The question asks for the smallest integer greater than 10 that results in the full data set having an integer mean that is less than 22. The answers contain numbers that could be the value of the 8th integer, so use the values in the answers. The question states that all 8 integers are greater than 10, so eliminate (A) because 6 is less than 10. Try the next smallest answer and plug in 14 for the 8th integer. The *total* of the full data set becomes $154 + 14 = 168$. The *number of things* is 8, so the average formula becomes $168 = (A)(8)$. Divide both sides of the equation by 8 to get 21. This is an integer less than 22, so it could be the mean of the full data set. Choice (B), 14, is the smallest integer that results in a mean that is an integer less than 22, so stop here. The correct answer is (B).

20. **4** The question asks for radius of a circle given an equation for its graph. The most efficient approach is to enter the equation into the built-in graphing calculator. Click on the gray dots at the maximum and minimum y-values to find the two ends of the diameter. The maximum y-value is at $(1, 6)$, and the minimum y-value is at $(1, -2)$. Since the two points have the same x-coordinate, the distance between them is the diameter of the circle. Find the difference to get a diameter of $6 - (-2) = 8$. The radius of a circle is half the diameter, so the radius is 4. The correct answer is 4.

21. **-9** The question asks for the least possible value of a constant in a quadratic. To determine when a quadratic equation has at least one real solution, use the discriminant. The discriminant is the part of the quadratic formula under the square root sign and is written as $D = b^2 - 4ac$. When the discriminant is positive, the quadratic has exactly two real solutions; when the discriminant is 0, the quadratic has exactly one real solution; and when the discriminant is negative, the quadratic has no real solutions. Thus, the discriminant of this quadratic must be equal to or greater than 0. First, distribute the x on the right side of the equation to get $4 = ax^2 + 12x$, then subtract 4 from both sides of the equation to get $0 = ax^2 + 12x - 4$. Now that the quadratic is in standard form, which is $ax^2 + bx + c = 0$, $a = a$, $b = 12$, and $c = -4$. Plug these into the discriminant formula to get $D = (12)^2 - 4(a)(-4)$, or $D = 144 + 16a$. Since there is at least one real solution, $144 + 16a \geq 0$. Subtract 144 from both sides of the inequality to get $16a \geq -144$. Divide both sides of the inequality by 16 to get $a \geq -9$. The least possible value of a is -9. The correct answer is -9.

22. **C** The question asks for a measurement on a geometric figure. Start by drawing two identical cylinders on the scratch paper, then label the figure with the given information. Label the height of each cylinder as 120. The answer choices contain numbers in increasing order, so use the values in the answers. Rewrite the answers on the scratch paper and label them "radius." Start with one of the answers in the middle and try (C), 6. Label the radius of each cylinder as 6, and then write down the formula for surface area. The surface area of a geometric figure is the sum of the areas of its faces. In the case of a cylinder, two faces are circles. The area of a circle is πr^2, so write this part of the surface area as $2(\pi r^2)$. The other part of the surface of a cylinder is the curved surface that connects the two circles. Think of this as the circumference of the circle at the base stacked as tall as the height, or circumference times height. The circumference of a circle is $2\pi r$, so write this part of the surface area as $2\pi rh$. Add these parts together to get the full formula for the surface area of a cylinder: $SA = 2\pi r^2 + 2\pi rh$.

Next, find the surface area of one of the cylinders using the given height of 120 and the plugged-in radius of 6. The formula becomes $SA = 2\pi(6)^2 + 2\pi(6)(120)$. Solve to get $SA = 72\pi + 1{,}440\pi$, and then $SA = 1{,}512\pi$. The question states that the surface area of one cylinder is A, so $A = 1{,}512\pi$. The question also states that the surface area of the combined cylinder is $\dfrac{41}{21}A$, so the surface area of the combined cylinder is $\dfrac{41}{21}(1{,}512\pi) = 2{,}952\pi$. Find the surface area of the combined cylinder and see if it matches this result. The radius is still 6, and the height becomes $120 + 120 = 240$. The surface area formula becomes $SA = 2\pi(6)^2 + 2\pi(6)(240)$. Solve to get $SA = 72\pi + 2{,}880\pi$, and then $SA = 2{,}952\pi$. This matches the information in the question, so stop here. The correct answer is (C).

645+ Practice Questions for the SAT, 2024 Edition
Diagnostic Drills

YOUR NAME: _____
(Print)   Last   First   M.I.

SIGNATURE: _____ DATE: __/__/__

HOME ADDRESS: _____
(Print)   Number and Street

_____
City   State   Zip Code

PHONE NO.: _____
(Print)

DATE OF BIRTH: ___/___/_____
(Print)   Month / Day / Year

Section 1:
Reading and Writing

1. Ⓐ Ⓑ Ⓒ Ⓓ
2. Ⓐ Ⓑ Ⓒ Ⓓ
3. Ⓐ Ⓑ Ⓒ Ⓓ
4. Ⓐ Ⓑ Ⓒ Ⓓ
5. Ⓐ Ⓑ Ⓒ Ⓓ
6. Ⓐ Ⓑ Ⓒ Ⓓ
7. Ⓐ Ⓑ Ⓒ Ⓓ
8. Ⓐ Ⓑ Ⓒ Ⓓ
9. Ⓐ Ⓑ Ⓒ Ⓓ
10. Ⓐ Ⓑ Ⓒ Ⓓ
11. Ⓐ Ⓑ Ⓒ Ⓓ
12. Ⓐ Ⓑ Ⓒ Ⓓ

Section 2:
Math

1. _____
2. Ⓐ Ⓑ Ⓒ Ⓓ
3. Ⓐ Ⓑ Ⓒ Ⓓ
4. Ⓐ Ⓑ Ⓒ Ⓓ
5. Ⓐ Ⓑ Ⓒ Ⓓ
6. Ⓐ Ⓑ Ⓒ Ⓓ
7. Ⓐ Ⓑ Ⓒ Ⓓ
8. Ⓐ Ⓑ Ⓒ Ⓓ
9. Ⓐ Ⓑ Ⓒ Ⓓ
10. Ⓐ Ⓑ Ⓒ Ⓓ
11. _____
12. Ⓐ Ⓑ Ⓒ Ⓓ

645+ Practice Questions for the SAT, 2024 Edition
Practice Test 1–3

© 2023 by TPR Education IP Holdings, LLC.

YOUR NAME: _____
(Print) Last   First   M.I.

SIGNATURE: _____ DATE: __/__/__

HOME ADDRESS: _____
(Print)   Number and Street

_____
City   State   Zip Code

PHONE NO.: _____
(Print)

DATE OF BIRTH: __/__/____
(Print)   Month / Day / Year

For both the Reading and Writing and the Math, be sure to only fill in the bubbles for the version of Module 2 that you took. If you took the Easier Module 2, only fill in the answer in the Easier column. If you took the Harder Module 2, only fill in the answers in the Harder column.

Section 1: Module 1
Reading and Writing

1. Ⓐ Ⓑ Ⓒ Ⓓ
2. Ⓐ Ⓑ Ⓒ Ⓓ
3. Ⓐ Ⓑ Ⓒ Ⓓ
4. Ⓐ Ⓑ Ⓒ Ⓓ
5. Ⓐ Ⓑ Ⓒ Ⓓ
6. Ⓐ Ⓑ Ⓒ Ⓓ
7. Ⓐ Ⓑ Ⓒ Ⓓ
8. Ⓐ Ⓑ Ⓒ Ⓓ
9. Ⓐ Ⓑ Ⓒ Ⓓ
10. Ⓐ Ⓑ Ⓒ Ⓓ
11. Ⓐ Ⓑ Ⓒ Ⓓ
12. Ⓐ Ⓑ Ⓒ Ⓓ
13. Ⓐ Ⓑ Ⓒ Ⓓ
14. Ⓐ Ⓑ Ⓒ Ⓓ
15. Ⓐ Ⓑ Ⓒ Ⓓ
16. Ⓐ Ⓑ Ⓒ Ⓓ
17. Ⓐ Ⓑ Ⓒ Ⓓ
18. Ⓐ Ⓑ Ⓒ Ⓓ
19. Ⓐ Ⓑ Ⓒ Ⓓ
20. Ⓐ Ⓑ Ⓒ Ⓓ
21. Ⓐ Ⓑ Ⓒ Ⓓ
22. Ⓐ Ⓑ Ⓒ Ⓓ
23. Ⓐ Ⓑ Ⓒ Ⓓ
24. Ⓐ Ⓑ Ⓒ Ⓓ
25. Ⓐ Ⓑ Ⓒ Ⓓ
26. Ⓐ Ⓑ Ⓒ Ⓓ
27. Ⓐ Ⓑ Ⓒ Ⓓ

Section 1: Module 2 (Easier)
Reading and Writing

1. Ⓐ Ⓑ Ⓒ Ⓓ
2. Ⓐ Ⓑ Ⓒ Ⓓ
3. Ⓐ Ⓑ Ⓒ Ⓓ
4. Ⓐ Ⓑ Ⓒ Ⓓ
5. Ⓐ Ⓑ Ⓒ Ⓓ
6. Ⓐ Ⓑ Ⓒ Ⓓ
7. Ⓐ Ⓑ Ⓒ Ⓓ
8. Ⓐ Ⓑ Ⓒ Ⓓ
9. Ⓐ Ⓑ Ⓒ Ⓓ
10. Ⓐ Ⓑ Ⓒ Ⓓ
11. Ⓐ Ⓑ Ⓒ Ⓓ
12. Ⓐ Ⓑ Ⓒ Ⓓ
13. Ⓐ Ⓑ Ⓒ Ⓓ
14. Ⓐ Ⓑ Ⓒ Ⓓ
15. Ⓐ Ⓑ Ⓒ Ⓓ
16. Ⓐ Ⓑ Ⓒ Ⓓ
17. Ⓐ Ⓑ Ⓒ Ⓓ
18. Ⓐ Ⓑ Ⓒ Ⓓ
19. Ⓐ Ⓑ Ⓒ Ⓓ
20. Ⓐ Ⓑ Ⓒ Ⓓ
21. Ⓐ Ⓑ Ⓒ Ⓓ
22. Ⓐ Ⓑ Ⓒ Ⓓ
23. Ⓐ Ⓑ Ⓒ Ⓓ
24. Ⓐ Ⓑ Ⓒ Ⓓ
25. Ⓐ Ⓑ Ⓒ Ⓓ
26. Ⓐ Ⓑ Ⓒ Ⓓ
27. Ⓐ Ⓑ Ⓒ Ⓓ

Section 1: Module 2 (Harder)
Reading and Writing

1. Ⓐ Ⓑ Ⓒ Ⓓ
2. Ⓐ Ⓑ Ⓒ Ⓓ
3. Ⓐ Ⓑ Ⓒ Ⓓ
4. Ⓐ Ⓑ Ⓒ Ⓓ
5. Ⓐ Ⓑ Ⓒ Ⓓ
6. Ⓐ Ⓑ Ⓒ Ⓓ
7. Ⓐ Ⓑ Ⓒ Ⓓ
8. Ⓐ Ⓑ Ⓒ Ⓓ
9. Ⓐ Ⓑ Ⓒ Ⓓ
10. Ⓐ Ⓑ Ⓒ Ⓓ
11. Ⓐ Ⓑ Ⓒ Ⓓ
12. Ⓐ Ⓑ Ⓒ Ⓓ
13. Ⓐ Ⓑ Ⓒ Ⓓ
14. Ⓐ Ⓑ Ⓒ Ⓓ
15. Ⓐ Ⓑ Ⓒ Ⓓ
16. Ⓐ Ⓑ Ⓒ Ⓓ
17. Ⓐ Ⓑ Ⓒ Ⓓ
18. Ⓐ Ⓑ Ⓒ Ⓓ
19. Ⓐ Ⓑ Ⓒ Ⓓ
20. Ⓐ Ⓑ Ⓒ Ⓓ
21. Ⓐ Ⓑ Ⓒ Ⓓ
22. Ⓐ Ⓑ Ⓒ Ⓓ
23. Ⓐ Ⓑ Ⓒ Ⓓ
24. Ⓐ Ⓑ Ⓒ Ⓓ
25. Ⓐ Ⓑ Ⓒ Ⓓ
26. Ⓐ Ⓑ Ⓒ Ⓓ
27. Ⓐ Ⓑ Ⓒ Ⓓ

645+ Practice Questions for the SAT, 2024 Edition
Practice Test 1

YOUR NAME: _____
(Print)   Last   First   M.I.

SIGNATURE: _____ DATE: ___/___/___

HOME ADDRESS: _____
(Print)   Number and Street

_____
City   State   Zip Code

PHONE NO.: _____
(Print)

DATE OF BIRTH: ___/___/___
(Print)   Month / Day / Year

For both the Reading and Writing and the Math, be sure to only fill in the bubbles for the version of Module 2 that you took. If you took the Easier Module 2, only fill in the answer in the Easier column. If you took the Harder Module 2, only fill in the answers in the Harder column.

Section 2: Module 1 Math

1. Ⓐ Ⓑ Ⓒ Ⓓ
2. _____
3. Ⓐ Ⓑ Ⓒ Ⓓ
4. Ⓐ Ⓑ Ⓒ Ⓓ
5. _____
6. Ⓐ Ⓑ Ⓒ Ⓓ
7. Ⓐ Ⓑ Ⓒ Ⓓ
8. Ⓐ Ⓑ Ⓒ Ⓓ
9. Ⓐ Ⓑ Ⓒ Ⓓ
10. _____
11. Ⓐ Ⓑ Ⓒ Ⓓ
12. Ⓐ Ⓑ Ⓒ Ⓓ
13. _____
14. Ⓐ Ⓑ Ⓒ Ⓓ
15. _____
16. _____
17. Ⓐ Ⓑ Ⓒ Ⓓ
18. Ⓐ Ⓑ Ⓒ Ⓓ
19. Ⓐ Ⓑ Ⓒ Ⓓ
20. Ⓐ Ⓑ Ⓒ Ⓓ
21. Ⓐ Ⓑ Ⓒ Ⓓ
22. Ⓐ Ⓑ Ⓒ Ⓓ

Section 2: Module 2 (Easier) Math

1. Ⓐ Ⓑ Ⓒ Ⓓ
2. Ⓐ Ⓑ Ⓒ Ⓓ
3. Ⓐ Ⓑ Ⓒ Ⓓ
4. _____
5. Ⓐ Ⓑ Ⓒ Ⓓ
6. Ⓐ Ⓑ Ⓒ Ⓓ
7. _____
8. _____
9. Ⓐ Ⓑ Ⓒ Ⓓ
10. _____
11. Ⓐ Ⓑ Ⓒ Ⓓ
12. Ⓐ Ⓑ Ⓒ Ⓓ
13. Ⓐ Ⓑ Ⓒ Ⓓ
14. Ⓐ Ⓑ Ⓒ Ⓓ
15. Ⓐ Ⓑ Ⓒ Ⓓ
16. Ⓐ Ⓑ Ⓒ Ⓓ
17. Ⓐ Ⓑ Ⓒ Ⓓ
18. _____
19. Ⓐ Ⓑ Ⓒ Ⓓ
20. Ⓐ Ⓑ Ⓒ Ⓓ
21. Ⓐ Ⓑ Ⓒ Ⓓ
22. Ⓐ Ⓑ Ⓒ Ⓓ

Section 2: Module 2 (Harder) Math

1. Ⓐ Ⓑ Ⓒ Ⓓ
2. Ⓐ Ⓑ Ⓒ Ⓓ
3. Ⓐ Ⓑ Ⓒ Ⓓ
4. Ⓐ Ⓑ Ⓒ Ⓓ
5. Ⓐ Ⓑ Ⓒ Ⓓ
6. Ⓐ Ⓑ Ⓒ Ⓓ
7. _____
8. _____
9. Ⓐ Ⓑ Ⓒ Ⓓ
10. Ⓐ Ⓑ Ⓒ Ⓓ
11. _____
12. Ⓐ Ⓑ Ⓒ Ⓓ
13. _____
14. Ⓐ Ⓑ Ⓒ Ⓓ
15. Ⓐ Ⓑ Ⓒ Ⓓ
16. Ⓐ Ⓑ Ⓒ Ⓓ
17. Ⓐ Ⓑ Ⓒ Ⓓ
18. _____
19. _____
20. Ⓐ Ⓑ Ⓒ Ⓓ
21. Ⓐ Ⓑ Ⓒ Ⓓ
22. Ⓐ Ⓑ Ⓒ Ⓓ

645+ Practice Questions for the SAT, 2024 Edition
Practice Test 2

YOUR NAME: _____
(Print)   Last   First   M.I.

SIGNATURE: _____ DATE: ___/___/___

HOME ADDRESS: _____
(Print)   Number and Street

_____
City   State   Zip Code

PHONE NO.: _____
(Print)

DATE OF BIRTH: ___/___/___
(Print)   Month / Day / Year

For both the Reading and Writing and the Math, be sure to only fill in the bubbles for the version of Module 2 that you took. If you took the Easier Module 2, only fill in the answer in the Easier column. If you took the Harder Module 2, only fill in the answers in the Harder column.

Section 2: Module 1 Math

1. Ⓐ Ⓑ Ⓒ Ⓓ
2. Ⓐ Ⓑ Ⓒ Ⓓ
3. Ⓐ Ⓑ Ⓒ Ⓓ
4. _____
5. Ⓐ Ⓑ Ⓒ Ⓓ
6. Ⓐ Ⓑ Ⓒ Ⓓ
7. Ⓐ Ⓑ Ⓒ Ⓓ
8. Ⓐ Ⓑ Ⓒ Ⓓ
9. Ⓐ Ⓑ Ⓒ Ⓓ
10. Ⓐ Ⓑ Ⓒ Ⓓ
11. _____
12. Ⓐ Ⓑ Ⓒ Ⓓ
13. Ⓐ Ⓑ Ⓒ Ⓓ
14. _____
15. _____
16. Ⓐ Ⓑ Ⓒ Ⓓ
17. _____
18. Ⓐ Ⓑ Ⓒ Ⓓ
19. Ⓐ Ⓑ Ⓒ Ⓓ
20. Ⓐ Ⓑ Ⓒ Ⓓ
21. _____
22. Ⓐ Ⓑ Ⓒ Ⓓ

Section 2: Module 2 (Easier) Math

1. Ⓐ Ⓑ Ⓒ Ⓓ
2. Ⓐ Ⓑ Ⓒ Ⓓ
3. _____
4. _____
5. _____
6. Ⓐ Ⓑ Ⓒ Ⓓ
7. Ⓐ Ⓑ Ⓒ Ⓓ
8. Ⓐ Ⓑ Ⓒ Ⓓ
9. Ⓐ Ⓑ Ⓒ Ⓓ
10. Ⓐ Ⓑ Ⓒ Ⓓ
11. _____
12. Ⓐ Ⓑ Ⓒ Ⓓ
13. Ⓐ Ⓑ Ⓒ Ⓓ
14. Ⓐ Ⓑ Ⓒ Ⓓ
15. Ⓐ Ⓑ Ⓒ Ⓓ
16. Ⓐ Ⓑ Ⓒ Ⓓ
17. _____
18. _____
19. Ⓐ Ⓑ Ⓒ Ⓓ
20. Ⓐ Ⓑ Ⓒ Ⓓ
21. Ⓐ Ⓑ Ⓒ Ⓓ
22. Ⓐ Ⓑ Ⓒ Ⓓ

Section 2: Module 2 (Harder) Math

1. Ⓐ Ⓑ Ⓒ Ⓓ
2. Ⓐ Ⓑ Ⓒ Ⓓ
3. Ⓐ Ⓑ Ⓒ Ⓓ
4. Ⓐ Ⓑ Ⓒ Ⓓ
5. Ⓐ Ⓑ Ⓒ Ⓓ
6. Ⓐ Ⓑ Ⓒ Ⓓ
7. Ⓐ Ⓑ Ⓒ Ⓓ
8. Ⓐ Ⓑ Ⓒ Ⓓ
9. _____
10. _____
11. Ⓐ Ⓑ Ⓒ Ⓓ
12. Ⓐ Ⓑ Ⓒ Ⓓ
13. Ⓐ Ⓑ Ⓒ Ⓓ
14. Ⓐ Ⓑ Ⓒ Ⓓ
15. _____
16. _____
17. Ⓐ Ⓑ Ⓒ Ⓓ
18. Ⓐ Ⓑ Ⓒ Ⓓ
19. Ⓐ Ⓑ Ⓒ Ⓓ
20. _____
21. Ⓐ Ⓑ Ⓒ Ⓓ
22. Ⓐ Ⓑ Ⓒ Ⓓ

645+ Practice Questions for the SAT, 2024 Edition
Practice Test 3

YOUR NAME: _____
(Print)   Last   First   M.I.

SIGNATURE: _____ DATE: ___ / ___ / ___

HOME ADDRESS: _____
(Print)   Number and Street

_____
City   State   Zip Code

PHONE NO.: _____
(Print)

DATE OF BIRTH: ___ / ___ / ___
(Print)   Month / Day / Year

For both the Reading and Writing and the Math, be sure to only fill in the bubbles for the version of Module 2 that you took. If you took the Easier Module 2, only fill in the answer in the Easier column. If you took the Harder Module 2, only fill in the answers in the Harder column.

Section 2: Module 1 Math

1. Ⓐ Ⓑ Ⓒ Ⓓ
2. Ⓐ Ⓑ Ⓒ Ⓓ
3. _____
4. Ⓐ Ⓑ Ⓒ Ⓓ
5. Ⓐ Ⓑ Ⓒ Ⓓ
6. Ⓐ Ⓑ Ⓒ Ⓓ
7. Ⓐ Ⓑ Ⓒ Ⓓ
8. Ⓐ Ⓑ Ⓒ Ⓓ
9. Ⓐ Ⓑ Ⓒ Ⓓ
10. Ⓐ Ⓑ Ⓒ Ⓓ
11. Ⓐ Ⓑ Ⓒ Ⓓ
12. Ⓐ Ⓑ Ⓒ Ⓓ
13. _____
14. Ⓐ Ⓑ Ⓒ Ⓓ
15. Ⓐ Ⓑ Ⓒ Ⓓ
16. Ⓐ Ⓑ Ⓒ Ⓓ
17. Ⓐ Ⓑ Ⓒ Ⓓ
18. Ⓐ Ⓑ Ⓒ Ⓓ
19. _____
20. _____
21. Ⓐ Ⓑ Ⓒ Ⓓ
22. Ⓐ Ⓑ Ⓒ Ⓓ

Section 2: Module 2 (Easier) Math

1. Ⓐ Ⓑ Ⓒ Ⓓ
2. Ⓐ Ⓑ Ⓒ Ⓓ
3. _____
4. _____
5. Ⓐ Ⓑ Ⓒ Ⓓ
6. Ⓐ Ⓑ Ⓒ Ⓓ
7. _____
8. Ⓐ Ⓑ Ⓒ Ⓓ
9. _____
10. Ⓐ Ⓑ Ⓒ Ⓓ
11. Ⓐ Ⓑ Ⓒ Ⓓ
12. Ⓐ Ⓑ Ⓒ Ⓓ
13. Ⓐ Ⓑ Ⓒ Ⓓ
14. Ⓐ Ⓑ Ⓒ Ⓓ
15. _____
16. _____
17. Ⓐ Ⓑ Ⓒ Ⓓ
18. Ⓐ Ⓑ Ⓒ Ⓓ
19. Ⓐ Ⓑ Ⓒ Ⓓ
20. Ⓐ Ⓑ Ⓒ Ⓓ
21. Ⓐ Ⓑ Ⓒ Ⓓ
22. Ⓐ Ⓑ Ⓒ Ⓓ

Section 2: Module 2 (Harder) Math

1. Ⓐ Ⓑ Ⓒ Ⓓ
2. Ⓐ Ⓑ Ⓒ Ⓓ
3. Ⓐ Ⓑ Ⓒ Ⓓ
4. _____
5. _____
6. Ⓐ Ⓑ Ⓒ Ⓓ
7. _____
8. Ⓐ Ⓑ Ⓒ Ⓓ
9. Ⓐ Ⓑ Ⓒ Ⓓ
10. Ⓐ Ⓑ Ⓒ Ⓓ
11. Ⓐ Ⓑ Ⓒ Ⓓ
12. Ⓐ Ⓑ Ⓒ Ⓓ
13. Ⓐ Ⓑ Ⓒ Ⓓ
14. _____
15. Ⓐ Ⓑ Ⓒ Ⓓ
16. Ⓐ Ⓑ Ⓒ Ⓓ
17. Ⓐ Ⓑ Ⓒ Ⓓ
18. Ⓐ Ⓑ Ⓒ Ⓓ
19. _____
20. Ⓐ Ⓑ Ⓒ Ⓓ
21. Ⓐ Ⓑ Ⓒ Ⓓ
22. _____